History of Social Law in Germany

Michael Stolleis

History of Social Law in Germany

Translated from the German by Thomas Dunlap

Springer

Michael Stolleis
Max-Planck-Institut
für europäische Rechtsgeschichte
Frankfurt am Main, Germany

Chapters 1-6 of this book previously published in English in the following publication: Stolleis: Origins of the German Welfare State (German Social Policy, Vol. 2), Springer Berlin Heidelberg, 2013, ISBN 978-3-642-22521-5

ISBN 978-3-662-51367-5 ISBN 978-3-642-38454-7 (eBook)
DOI 10.1007/978-3-642-38454-7
Springer Heidelberg New York Dordrecht London

Printed on acid-free paper

Springer is part of Springer Science+Business Media (www.springer.com)

Contents

I. Introduction

1. The Cultural Conditioning and Changeability of Social Protection

The present chapter provides a historical survey of the development of social protection in Germany up to 1945.[1] It is based on the realization that the modern, complex "system" of social protection is an "evolved" one and can be best understood by knowing how it came into being. It has layers of historical growth and is a far cry from the kind of rigor one expects of "systems" in the scientific or philosophical sense. But in the professional discourse of social theory and social law it may well be referred to as a "system," and this can be useful to the historian if he is asked to specify the past phenomena he is searching for and in which he expects to find a bridge to the present.

Of course, a look back at history can be useful also in that can provide today's actors clues to how much of the past is preserved in the various structures that exist today. If something should or must be changed, it pays to examine the long-term developmental trends. Many declarations of political intent and reform projects have failed simply because they underestimated the inertia of historically evolved material. Long-term trends can be reversed only if one has detailed knowledge about the forces driving them. In this limited sense, historical information—in conjunction with sociological, economic, and legal frameworks—can also serve to lay the groundwork for innovations. Especially in the transition to one of the most difficult periods of social policy in the first decades of the new millennium, it could prove an urgent necessity to regard also the older legacies and institutions as "historically evolved." This entails two things: one, like everything that has grown

Previously published in English in the following publication: Stolleis: Origins of the German Welfare State (German Social Policy, Vol. 2), Springer, Berlin/Heidelberg, 2013.

[1] The best overview is by Scherner (1996).

DOI 10.1007/978-3-642-38454-7_1,

slowly, they are fairly stable; second, as history demonstrates, they are never immovable, but can be changed and adjusted to changing needs.

2. Chronological Parameters

This historical survey does not begin with a striking turning point, but it concludes within the present time in the reunificated Germany. The breakdown of the wall in the extraordinary time of 1989/1990 signified a total change of the political system in the former German Democratic Republic (DDR), but continuity in the western part. Like in the so called "zero hour" of 8 May 1945 there was a "new beginning" in the East—with all financial consequences for the systems of social security. Since 1990 German politics seemed to be arrived in a state of "normality" like other nation-states on the continent and otherwise. The political system[2] and the "Social policy in Germany"[3] are keeping their historical profile, engraved in the collective memory since the medieval times and especially in the nineteenth century with the revolutionary invention of the still existing social insurance, traditionally combined with the name of Otto von Bismarck.

Beyond this somewhat trite justification of the need for a prehistory, there are, however, connections between the past and the present that go back much further and make it advisable to probe the past as deeply as possible. Our modern sense of time is an accelerated one. We experience the world as dynamic and in movement. Changes follow in rapid succession and also seem to overtax us. The social protection of the next generation, especially the future of traditional social insurance, is threatened. While a look at the past cannot allay these anxieties, it does show, first of all, that our current system constitutes a mixture of historically evolved forms of security. All forms of provisioning against risk and its consequences that we know and practice simultaneously can be assigned to specific chronological stages: from family and neighborly help to co-operative self-help, the formation of foundations as the bearers of charitable institutions, the emergence of funds that are meant to ensure against conventional risks—all the way to the modern protection systems that encompass nearly the entire population.[4] Some of these institutions go back to the early Middle Ages (Schilling 1997). Others can be assigned to the period of the emerging cities, to the beginnings of trade, and the formation of the first large fortunes in the fifteen and sixteenth centuries, such as urban hospitals, charitable foundations, or social housing projects like the

---

[2] Schmidt (2007).

[3] Schmidt (2005).

[4] According to Axel von Campenhausen (1997, p. 12) "the oldest member of the Association of German Foundations [*Bundesverband Deutscher Stiftungen*] is the hospital foundation in Wemding in the Ries, which has been operating an a old-age and nursing home for indigent residents with funds donated back in 917."

"Fuggerei" in Augsburg. Others are the products of the society-shaping powers of the churches in the early modern period and especially of the early-modern territorial state, which implemented a new notion of "work," combated "idleness," and created penitentiaries and workhouses. This development has been much discussed in recent years under the heading of "social disciplining" (Schilling 1997). Scholars now realize that this was a highly complex phenomenon, involving the participation in equal measure of the slowly emerging state, the churches that depended on the disciplining of their members, but also the faithful and subjects themselves in rural and urban communities, in guild or church, who acquiesced or resisted. In modern historical scholarship, the hard-working and adjusted individual who eventually emerged from this process is seen as the necessary precondition for the launch of the industrial age.

The modern-day institutions of social protection arose only in the Industrial Revolution, after the high point of Liberalism had already passed (Stolleis 1989). The main pillars of our system of insurance are no more than a 130 years old, counting from Bismarck's new departures in domestic politics between 1878 and 1881. But older forms of safety merged into this new system, and not only as relics, but possibly also as the potential for future social policy.

Of course, what functioned before the Industrial Revolution under very different conditions cannot and should not be revived. But it is at least conceivable that the post-modern world will draw upon the pre-modern world. In recent years, a good deal has been said and written about shifting responsibility back to the individual, the family, and the neighborhood. Even the legislature has made a small attempt in that direction (§ 3a BSHG), and it will have to make further attempts. The more difficult it becomes to finance the large-scale safety systems, the stronger the trend toward a reprivatization of risks could become, and there is no way one can predict how such a process will affect a society that has not been geared toward "self-provisioning" for generations. To be sure, the revitalization of idealistic, voluntary commitments is conceivable, as is the revitalization of ascetic, meditative, and charitable ways of life. Even today, not all forms of social security are monetarized and open to economic analysis. But it is revealing that all previous attempts at an "exit" from the evolved ensemble of social security more or less explicitly expected that the state and society would provide a guarantee against failure. A return to past forms of security would be conceivable only if the social context also changes accordingly, a literal "Renaissance," in other words, which is not very likely.

The future is open, however, and it holds no guarantees about the survival of "tried-and-true systems," as for example the concurrence of social security, provision, and social welfare in the modern form. The framework conditions are constantly changing, as are the safety systems themselves. If industrial society, which once began with the life-long factory work of the male employee, is rebuilt someday into a globally interconnected, mobile information and service society, the preconditions especially of social insurance are no longer in place (Stolleis 1998). In that sense there exists, alongside the purely historical motivation, also a vital interest in those phenomena that lie outside the narrow purview of our current times. Anyone who, under the pressure of day-to-day business, stares transfixed upon today's background data or is guided only by the horizon of the current legislative session, cannot see social protection as a structural problem shared by pre-industrial societies, industrial society, and future ways of life. Such a perspective will be necessary, however, if, as indications suggest, we are entering into an age that will differ in crucial ways from the classic industrial period of the nineteenth and twentieth centuries.

This raises the question about the historical moment from which we can speak, using anachronistic terminology, of "social security," the "social state," and "social law." The transition to the industrial world was undoubtedly a decisive turning point. The suggestion that we "see the origins of the modern social state in those regulations by which the mobility of the productive factors was restricted again during the course of industrialization" (Hockerts 1996, p. 28) has the advantage of clarity. It places the emphasis on the "modern" social state and presupposes the existence of a "state." Moreover, it creates a close connection with the "socio-economic transition to the industrial world" (Hockerts 1996, p. 31), which we can date with a fair degree of precision: in Central Europe, it was the century between 1750 and 1850.

However, if one understands the protection against the typical risks of life as the ongoing, basic challenge in human society, everything that humans have ever thought of and practiced to ward off the dangers of poverty, illness and disability, old age and death can be seen as "social protection." This view has the great disadvantage that its historical dimension is essentially unlimited, and that it blurs the turning point of the transition into the world of industrial society—for the fact is that the political and economic dynamic to create the forms of safety so typical of today was generated only by the population growth and productivity gains of modernity. Whether that entailed a quantum leap, such as that the transition to the compulsory state insurance of industrial workers launched an entirely new era, which is the perception, for example, of the German tradition of social law, should be at least open to discussion. In other industrialized states of the western world, this era began later or never really got off the ground, which makes it doubtful that these countries will now—in the twilight of the system of social insurance—pursue this path at all.

Opening up the historical perspective has other advantages, as well: as I have already indicated, it is clear that we today are practicing forms of safety of varied provenance side by side, among them some from the period before industrialization. Those include not only the care for people who have no income or are unable to earn one, that is, the old communal or "state" poor relief and the charitable activities of the churches, but also the old-age care for state employees and discharged soldiers along with their widows and orphaned children. To understand these forms of safety, we must go back to the time before 1800. This is a practical argument, though one in which the contemporary state of affairs shapes the historical perspective.

Of greater importance is probably another aspect, one that transcends Europe: the modern intertwining of the western industrialized states with regions of the world in which industrialization is just beginning or yet to arrive, confronts western companies and developmental aid programs with forms of social protection that have already vanished in our own world. Precisely the absence of the kind of social protection that is customary in the West is one of the strongest economic incentives for shifting industrial production to these regions. Companies that do so enter—"historically" speaking—into regions that are comparable to the early nineteenth century in Central Europe when it comes to social protection. For example, the fact that it is customary to take de-commissioned tankers to Bangladesh, the poorhouse of the world, to have them scrapped by workers that include children and youths working under the most abysmal conditions, attest to the coexistence of different layers of time, and to the impossibility of isolating the development in Central Europe during the last two centuries also historiographically.

3. The Formation of Society and Social Protection

It is in this sense that a broader, comparative cultural history of "social protection" can be conceived and perhaps even written, a protection, namely that rested on solidarity with others. Understood in these general terms, we are dealing with a phenomenon of human history. Provisions to protect against risks are so old that their traces get lost in the mist of history. The dangers of hunger and disease, injury and death are the companions of all living beings. Already the formation into groups, which demands a minimum of organization, constitutes a certain protection. And the specialization of warriors, priests, healers, farmers, and traders serves, in a wider sense, to safeguard human groups against risks, because specialists are more effective in their respective areas. Experience-based provisions against the risks that are normal for any cycle of life or help after the fact through collectively maintained institutions are thus cultural phenomena—just like human society, as such, and the subsystems of religion, law, culture, and economy that emerge from it.

Embedded within the developmental stages of social formations, the dominant ideas about the risks that should be born by the individual and those that should be born by the collective thus also change. Hunters and gatherers, nomads, farmers, city dwellers, blue and white-collar workers in industrialized societies are confronted by very different life problems and have varying degrees of "sensitivity" to suffering—for suffering, beyond concrete physical pain and needs, is also socially mediated. Especially the physical strain from work has changed through the industrial revolution. Extremely hard and extended labor, daily hikes on foot to the workplace, activities that are highly deleterious to health and child labor have been largely eliminated in the western industrialized states. An entire palette of technical aids and devices ease our burden. Today, most would already regard the workload and privations that were imposed upon the individual as "normal" two or three generations ago as intolerable. In addition, food and its preparation have undergone a profound transformation. The rhythm of our lives during an average work day is no longer comparable to that of our ancestors. We cover vast distances in a few short hours, live in continuously heated and lit rooms, and have global possibilities of entertainment and communication of which even the previous generation would not have dared to dream. The standards of public health and medical care in western industrialized societies are extraordinarily high at the beginning of the twenty-first century. The same is true for the consumption of energy and natural resources, and of the absolute and relative level of social protection. This is where comparative yardsticks fail: on the historical time scale, the situation today is without precedent; in terms of a contemporary comparison across societies, the cultural expectations, the varying ways in which state and society interact and—not least—the objective possibilities are so divergent that comparisons must always begin by noting the fundamental differences.

To that extent it would be wrong to assume that the category "social protection" allows us to grasp a phenomenon that is eternally unchanging across various social formations throughout the centuries. To be sure, all of these manifestations of social protection contain mechanisms to protect people against typical risks. Mutuality of aid is always presupposed, and there is a universal experience that the community can provide better protection than the isolated individual. But beyond these basic notions unfolds a multifarious and changeable history that is always hastening toward an open-ended future.

The forms of social protection are as changeable as human needs and risks. As soon as differences between poverty and wealth become apparent, "strata-specific" forms of safety also emerge. Property, inheritance law, and family law take on correspondingly divergent forms. Family units change their structures parallel to the material and social conditions of their environment. The elaboration of the transfer of material values to the next generation, whether through special forms of the dowry or the bride price, gift and inheritance law, fiduciary use for the clan, or forms of the *Fideikommiss* [entailed property], can also be understood as social mechanisms to compensate for the capacity to work that is lost or gained, and in the broader sense as material protection against risk. And rules about monogamy or polygamy, the remarriage of widows, and the actual number of children are also important indicators of the extent to which progeny were regarded as a "savings bank" and a protection against the dangers of old age.

In addition to all these factors, the social "place" that the individual inhabits exerts an influence. There are group-specific forms of social protection, as for example mutual support in the neighborhoods or alleys of a city, networks of solidarity among ethnic, linguistic, or religious minorities, support groups against particular occupational hazards such as those faced by sailors and miners, and, finally, the traditional help that women offered each other in childbed and much more.

Of great importance is also the geographical "place." Settlement density, alone, is a crucial factor: if the population is sparse with large distances between farms or nomadic groups, the de facto possibilities of receiving help from the outside are already small. Extreme climates demand either unconditional solidarity, or they teach a toughness that would be unacceptable in milder climes. The situation has been different—since antiquity, already—in large cities: quick and specialized help is possible here and many individuals usually face the same problems, which means, on the one hand, that external constraints ease, while, on the other hand, the conditions for artfully organized solutions based on solidarity become more favorable.

The latter become possible primarily if a society has an intensive exchange of goods, but above all a money economy and literacy. As the factors time, labor, and the value of goods become convertible into money, individuals in need of protection could set up funds to which they make equal "contributions." From these funds, the individual was to receive support in the uncertain—but statistically not unlikely—case of a stroke of misfortune or some condition that requires help. The return for the contribution lies in the availability of real support, if needed, but also in relief from anxiety and worry.

The discovery of the mechanism of "insurance through contributions" gave rise to both property insurance, for example of a ship against the loss from shipwreck or capture by pirates, and personal insurance, initially in the form of relief funds for members of particularly dangerous professions. Property insurance is the assumption of a specific external threat for a fee, combined with the promise of payment if the risk materializes. The personal solidarity fund, by contrast, is the common property of all participants and is utilized if misfortune strikes any one of them. Both forms of protection are based on a common idea: the risk that is seen as typical and beyond the powers of the individual is placed on an economic footing and is outsourced, either to the insurer or to the fund. The insured party exchanges a contribution that is economically sustainable over the long term for security against the consequences of a misfortune he would be unable to cope with on his own.

Beginning in the Middle Ages, there thus arose the countless fraternities, orders, gilds, corporations, and brotherhoods, which had not only religious, ritual, economic, and political meaning for their members, but also provided social protection.[5] Some were compulsory organizations (corporations), others were voluntary (associations)—if this kind of distinction is meaningful at all (Oexle 1982, pp. 1–44). The hospitals and poor houses they ran, and especially their member funds for the sick, widows, and orphans were largely still in existence in the nineteenth century and were incorporated into the process that gave rise to social insurance.

If our perspective thus includes the time before the Industrial Revolution, semantics also change. "Social law" and "social protection" are modern terms. In the nineteenth century, two meanings of "social law" run alongside each other. One sees social law as the law of organizations, leagues, and associations—the kind of law, in other words, that establishes itself in the view of its champions (G. v. Beseler, O. Bähr, O. v. Gierke) between the state and the individual and organizes the formation of human society below the level of the state into free, "cooperatives" forms (see Hardtwig 1997). The other meaning of social law, as the "law of social protection," established itself more slowly and really only in the

[5] An overview can be found in Hardtwig (1997); a more specialized essay is that of Fröhlich (1976), Schewe (2000).

twentieth century (Schmid 1981; Stolleis 1990). In this sense, social law is therefore a neologism, which cannot serve as a point of reference prior to the late nineteenth century. Before that we are dealing with different semantic fields, for example help for the poor and the old, for widows, orphans, victims of accident, the sick, and the great mass of people on the move (scholars, craftsmen, entertainers, market visitors, gypsies, discharged soldiers, beggars, and vagrants). To be sure, these fields were aimed not only at premodern "social" help, but also at combating crime and warding off dangers by regulating certain professions. But precisely this phenomenon, the blending of supposedly purely social goals with other goals related to the labor market, the policing of foreigners, warding off danger, or simply reducing costs, is typical for the early modern period and for the "modern state" that arose during it. To that extent the semantic considerations, in particular, and the blending of motives suggest that the older policy of poor relief differed from modern social policy not in principle, but only in means, intensity, and extent. On the other hand, it could be argued on good grounds that the Industrial Revolution, with its migrations, new risks, and enormous acceleration, brought social policy qualitatively into a "new" situation. But like all historical periodicizations, this is a construct driven by specific premises. It bears examining whether this construct does not adopt too much of the view that the "new" nineteenth century had of itself.

References

Fröhlich S (1976) Die soziale Sicherung bei Zünften und Gesellenverbänden. Darstellung, Analyse, Vergleich. Sozialpolitische Schriften 38. Berlin

Hardtwig W (1997) Genossenschaft, Sekte, Verein in Deutschland. Vom Spätmittelalter bis zur französischen Revolution, vol 1. Munich

Hockerts HG (1996) Die historische Perspektive – Entwicklung und Gestalt des modernen Sozialstaats in Europa. In: Walter-Raymond-Stiftung (ed) Sozialstaat- Idee und Entwicklung, Reformzwänge und Reformziele, vol 35. Cologne, pp 27–48

Oexle OG (1982) Die mittelalterliche Zunft als Forschungsproblem. Blätter für Deutsche Landesgeschichte 118:1–44

Scherner K-O (1996) Sozialrechtsgeschichte der Neuzeit. Stand der Forschung und offene Fragen. Zeitschrift für Neuere Rechtsgeschichte 18:102–148

Schewe D (2000) Geschichte der sozialen und privaten Versicherung im Mittelalter in den Gilden Europas. Berlin

Schilling H (1997) Disziplinierung oder Selbstregulierung der Untertanen? Ein Plädoyer für die Doppelperspektive von Makro- und Mikrohistorie bei der Erforschung der frühmodernen Kirchenzucht. Historische Zeitschrift 264:675–691

Schmid F (1981) Sozialrecht und Recht der sozialen Sicherheit. Die Begriffsbildung in Deutschland, Frankreich und der Schweiz. Berlin

Schmidt MG (2005) Sozialpolitik in Deutschland. Historische Entwicklung und internationaler Vergleich, 3rd edn. Wiesbaden

Schmidt MG (2007) Das Politische System Deutschlands. Munich

Stolleis M (1989) Die Entstehung des Interventionsstaates und das öffentliche Recht. Zeitschrift für Neuere Rechtsgeschichte 129ff

Stolleis M (1990) Sozialrecht. In: Erler A, Kaufmann E (eds) Handwörterbuch zur Deutschen Rechtsgeschichte, vol 4. Berlin, columns 1730–1733

Stolleis M (1998) Industrielle Revolution und Sozialversicherung. In: Ruland F (ed) Verfassung, Theorie und Praxis des Sozialstaats, Festschrift für Hans Friedrich Zacher zum 70. Geburtstag, Heidelberg, pp 1081–1099

von Campenhausen A (1997) Der Stiftungsgedanke in heutiger Zeit. In: Institut der Wirtschaftsprüfer (ed) Stiftungen. Rechnungslegung, Kapitalerhaltung, Prüfung und Besteuerung. Düsseldorf

II. Social Protection in the Middle Ages and in the Early Modern State: Alms, Poor Relief [*Armenpolizei*], Care, Social Help

1. Christian Poor Relief

Providing material and immaterial care to the poor, the elderly, widows, and orphans, out of pity or a sense of moral-religious obligation, has become the socio-ethical norm and praxis in nearly all cultures. However, Christianity placed a special emphasis on this obligation from the outset,[1] and it shaped the picture of both individual and corporate practical altruism through multifarious and venerable institutions and activities (Liese 1922; Isensee 1995, §59). For the churches, to use the words of the Federal Constitutional Court, "the fulfillment of the works of altruism through the gift of the individual member of the church is an essential part of the practice of the Christian religion," that is to say, it is a "fundamental function of the church."[2]

The dominant place of religion and the church in the public and private life until well into the nineteenth century was thus mirrored by the important role that Christian poor relief and care for the sick played vis-à-vis efforts to relieve suffering that were driven by secular motives (Uhlhorn 1895; Ratzinger 1868; Neukamm 1987, pp. 610–618). However, that role changed gradually in the wake of the slow rise of secular powers since the thirteenth century. Just as military conquest and religious mission had been constantly interconnected since antiquity and the Early Middle Ages, with the former sometimes leading the way and

Previously published in English in the following publication: Stolleis: Origins of the German Welfare State (German Social Policy, Vol. 2), Springer, Berlin/Heidelberg, 2013.

[1] For example: Mt. 5.43ff; 7.12; 10.40ff.; 22.37ff.; 25.40.—Mk. 12.29ff.—Rom. 13.9f.; 1 Cor. 13.—1 Jn. 4.11.

[2] BVerfGE 24, 236 (248). This line of court decisions has not changed since. See Hollerbach (1981, pp. 218–283, esp. 225–227). However, in recent years emphasis has been placed on the obligation to "the law that applies to all" (Art. 137 III WRV) and on the need for stronger state control over a multitude of faith-based activities.

M. Stolleis, *History of Social Law in Germany*,
DOI 10.1007/978-3-642-38454-7_2, © Springer-Verlag Berlin Heidelberg 2014

sometimes following, secular powers during the European Middle Ages pushed increasingly into spheres that had previously been a matter of the church (Padoa-Schioppa 1997). As population density increased, poverty became a problem also for urban and territorial authorities. The latter not only recognized the socio-revolutionary potential of poverty, they were also interested in a settled and prosperous population for reasons having to do with the ability to control their territories and exact a steady levy of taxes and dues. Beginning in the sixteenth century, these authorities began to take initiatives legitimatized by the claims that it was their duty to ensure "good order" (Maier 1980; Palme 1991; Gömmel 1991; Stolleis 1996; Jütte 1995). While this order was grounded in Christianity, it also contained from the outset admixtures of secular purposes. The emerging early modern state increasingly emphasized these worldly purposes, eventually using Christian terminology merely as a rhetorical garb for its directives. The more the state succeeded in disciplining the poor and itinerant strata through the intensified use of its "good governance" [*Policey*] (Schlumbohm 1997), the more the state itself gained orderliness and the power to exert control. These worldly goals gradually marginalized the religious approaches. At the end of the eighteenth century, the church's work of charity was left with only an auxiliary function. The emphases did not shift again until the nineteenth century, which, under the banner of liberalism, pursued the withdrawal of the state from "welfare work."

In the countryside, the itinerant and the local poor could—since the early Middle Ages—turn to the monasteries for help. The latter were not only centers of education and culture, but also constituted the economic strongholds of entire—still thinly settled—regions. In the cities, with their internal social and legal differentiation that had been slowly evolving since the eleventh century, the problem of supporting the poor was distributed among various institutions. First, monasteries were also found in cities, sometimes within the walls, sometimes outside (plague and leper houses). Second, possibilities of distributing alms developed through the urban churches and the donations they received from the laity with the stipulation that the funds from the donations be used not only to read masses, but also to help the poor. The more "citizens and councils" emancipated themselves from their overlords and regulated the affairs of the community autonomously as the city's authority, the more the social institutions also became a matter for the secular government.

2. The Early Modern State and the Church

The crisis of the church in the fifteenth century and the emergence of a pre-Reformation, secular church governance were interrelated. The rule of the princes that was slowly taking shape moved into the vacuum of political order created by a church that was quarreling and marked by secularization trends. This trend, already visible before 1517, erupted fully when confessional fragmentation gave rise to sub-churches that had to lean on secular powers to ensure their survival.

In the course of the Reformation and the religious wars of the sixteenth century, territorial lords and cities, in a "first secularization," confiscated church property on a massive scale and redirected it into the school system and poor relief (Kreiker 1997). With this, the responsibility for social problems also shifted. It was now the city authorities and the territorial ruler who were admonished by theory and urged by praxis to take the initiative against poverty, and to make sure that the burden of poverty was diminished and transformed into productive labor. This shift of the point of reference from the medieval church to the early modern state demonstrates that this "state" did not appear one day ready-made and took on certain tasks. Rather, we are dealing with a process—nearly imperceptible to contemporaries—by which responsibilities, competencies, and material means were transferred. What is called the "state" from about the middle of the seventeenth century (Weinacht 1968) is a political entity that took shape gradually in response to the shortcomings of competing powers (church, nobility, estates), and which created its ways of acting by doing. Especially after the exhaustion from the religious wars in France and Germany, all relevant political forces pushed for a concentration at the monarchical head of the state, as a way of overcoming the economic and social misery of the states through more intensive legislative activity. In other words: henceforth, fighting poverty became a task of the state, whose apparatus and capabilities, however, were still in the formative process (Scherner 1979, pp. 55–99).

These shifts from the religious to the secular side were based on changes in collective consciousness that had been in the works since the thirteenth century. At the same time, they brought about these transformations only after the fact, which means that the awareness registered late what had already happened. One of the great changes in European consciousness is the gradual emergence of the person as an autonomous entity. Beginning at this time, the individual was recognized as such because he spoke with his or her own voice, and he was able to speak more and more because his intellectual and material realms of action were expanding. Slowly, he became responsible for the conduct of his life before God and his fellow humans.

By leaving the anonymity of the collective, the individual also become the object of intervention for all efforts of improvement undertaken by the church and the wordly authorities. If the individual is in principle the master of his own fate in both this life and the next, he must exert himself in every way. Should he fail to walk the straight and narrow path, he must bear the consequences, and should he fail, all he can hope for is "mercy." With this, the notions about the role of work underwent a fundamental change (Schuck 1995). "Labor and pain" were now interpreted increasingly as punishment imposed by God after the Fall. At the same time, however, they also appeared as the most important worldly means to combat vice.[3] *Müßiggang ist aller Laster Anfang* ["Idleness is the beginning of all vice"]

[3] Especially pronounced in Wenzel Linck, *Von der Arbeit und vom Betteln. Wie man der Faulheit zuvorkommt und jedermann zur Arbeit anhalten sollte* (Zwickau, 1523). Quoted in Sachße and Tennstedt (1980, pp. 59ff.).

is a common proverb in Germany. As a result, there now began a systematic poor policy on the part of the authorities, who were deeply convinced that a person could be brought onto the right path through a combination of solicitude and strictness. This meant that a moral differentiation had to be drawn between native and foreign poor, between those who had caused their own misery and those who had not, between those able and those unable to work. The *police orders* (Stolleis 1996; Härter and Stolleis 1996, vol. 1) that were enacted in all German towns and territories, indeed, throughout Europe, contained a considerable—and until the late seventeenth century steadily growing—number of decrees regulating poverty, alms-giving, and the expulsion and punishment of foreign beggars. The general accepted goal of a state, "*gute Policey*" [good public order], also encompassed care for the poor. However, the emphasis shifted increasingly from the religious motivation behind alms to regulation by the secular authorities, to the suppression of private alms-giving in favor of a disbursement of aid concentrated in the hands of the now emerging "state." In cities and town, this was done through the creation of a "General Fund for the Poor and Alms" [*Allgemeiner Armen- und Almosenkasten*] (Jütte 1984). Alms became an instrument of the state; they were subjected to wordly purposes and used to discipline the recipients. Henceforth we also find a poor administration with an *Armenvogt* [an official charged with ensuring good order], and *Armenbuch* [Poor Book], which took hold of this area of individual charity and subjected it to bureaucratic rules. The subjective gift of alms, prompted by compassion and piety, no longer seemed reliable enough. It is a private decision dependent on the mood of the giver, and can no longer be counted on from an institutional perspective. What emerged alongside the charitable gift was the state that was neither compassionate nor pious, what Hobbes called "the artificial man," for whom poverty was a source of undesired migration, social disorder, and criminality.

The more the state's administrative apparatus developed and solidified, the more it also took on repressive traits in the period from the sixteenth to the eighteenth century (Wright 1977). Beggars turned into a marginal group that deserved to be combatted. The lines demarcating criminality remained blurry. And the authorities were not interested in makes those lines any clearer, lest they unnecessarily constrain their possibilities of intervention. The impetus for precise lines of demarcation emanating from the modern state governed by the rule of law, which the bourgeoisie had to wrest from Absolutism in the eighteenth and nineteenth centuries, was still entirely absent at this time. At any rate, two large groups took shape, which were in turn subdivided: first, the honorable own citizens, the non-excluded *Hausarme* ["house poor"], and the honorable outsiders (travelers who have fallen on hard times, journeymen on the road, whose care was the duty of the guilds). Second, the itinerant, ragged class of former soldiers, gypsies, vagrants of every kind, down to the clearly "harmful folk," that is criminal individuals or gangs. The second group was unwelcome in every regard: not only because of the threat to material possessions, social peace, and the uncontrolled outflow of monetary funds, which would then unavailable for the *Hausarme*, but also because of health policy, since it was well understood that diseases could be "introduced." To that extent, the drawing of a line to the outside world was clear.

The state, which was not able to make poverty disappear, now pursued increasingly a dual strategy: external defense and discipline through work internally. Inclusion of one group and exclusion of the other complemented each other. Who was part of which group was determined by criteria of utility and by characteristics that defined the "outsiders" in authoritative terms. "Borders" emerged against the outside world and "border officers" were needed; signs warned vagrants of every kind not to enter the territory. The "border policy" toward the "itinerant folk" provides a window onto the great historical process of the early modern period, the emergence of the territorial states that ruled a swath of land with subjects and therefore intensified its border demarcations. Governing this land, warding off all outside influences, was now one right of (external) "sovereignty" (Quaritsch 1986; Stolleis 1997). That the insistence on non-intervention from outside was combined with the practice of deporting undesirable across the borders was, of course, inconsistent behavior, but it was dictated by the selfish self-interest of freeing at least one's own territory of these burdensome people (Schott 1978; Schubert 1983; Schulze 1988).

By contrast, internal sovereignty was directed toward the subjects. According to the general belief, it was the duty of the authorities to encourage people to be diligent, thrifty, and lead a well-ordered Christian life. "Work" took on a new dimension. It became a demonstration of earthly fitness and the precondition for salvation from guilt. A person who did not work even though he was able-bodied was wasting his gifts and committing a sing against his fellow citizens. As a result there was now a duty to work, at least for those individuals who were subject to the reach of the administration.

This long arm of the administration was ambivalent. The markers that had originally been used to identify the deserving poor were slowly transformed into a stigma (Roeck 1993, p. 68f.). Every act of registration became a preliminary step toward exclusion and marginalization. The desire to transform "useless" persons into useful one led to public work projects, the establishment of "useful institutions," or to expulsion. The emerging cameralistic and mercantilist economic theory emphasized a high level of omestic productivity, the processing of native raw materials, and independence from imports. Subjects were supposed to be hardworking, pious, and moderate, and after wars they should also contribute to "peopling" the land. Preaching was done in this spirit, and beggar and vagrant codes were enacted. In the seventeenth and eighteenth centuries, houses of correction and work were added, drawn from British and especially Dutch models (Howard 1780, 1784, 1791; Kleinschrod 1789; Wagnitz 1791–1794; Saam 1936; Peitzsch 1968). They took in all those subjects the authorities deemed problematic and "in need of correction," but economically usable. That included convicted criminals, and this soon led to a stigmatization of houses of correction and work as a feared penal institution. The place of strict pedagogy was now taken by the exploitation of labor and the idea of deterrence. The construction of fortresses and castles also absorbed entire armies of such forced laborers.

All these measures were essentially born by the early modern princely state. As the political and economic power shifted from the Empire and the cities to the territories in the second half of the sixteenth century, the competencies and practical efforts to contain the socially harmful consequences of pauperism also migrated there. The place of urban beggar codes and Imperial Statutes (1530, 1548, 1551, 1577) was taken by territorial "police codes," which codified the regulatory intentions of the estates and the respective territorial churches, and of the territorial lord. Territorial *policey* now evolved into the most important motor of social engineering through commandments and prohibitions. Its goal was the elimination of abuses and the establishment of "good order" in the city and the countryside, in the market and the home. The early modern doctrine of the purpose of the state, here applied to social reality, included almost without saying measures of social protection in the form of goals, concrete recommendations, directives, and prohibitions pertaining to doctors and apothecaries, public cleanliness and health, the regulation of begging and alms, the duty to work for "strong" beggars, the expulsion or turning away of foreigners at the borders, conscription into public works, and the use of a variety of means of punishment and deterrence (Härter and Stolleis 1996; Simon 1998; Schilling and Schuck 1999).

Of course, the hospitals and other institutions to support the poor in the cities continued, as did the monasteries and ecclesiastical foundations (Reicke 1932; von Moeller 1906, reprint 1972; Jütte 1996). But the sphere within which the towns and the church were active was shrinking and fell completely under state control. As it was, in Lutheran and reformed territories, the territorial rulers' sovereignty over the church had led to a close alignment of the tasks of the state and those of the church. The Protestant consistories or ecclesiastical councils were state bodies with religious tasks. The visitations they carried out extended not only to the state of pastoral care, but also to "moral discipline," drinking and gaming, dress codes, work ethic, and much more.

The reach of "enlightened Absolutism" in the eighteenth century reduced the church's sphere of action also within Catholic territories. In the name of reason, feast days and church customs were now abolished, in Austria during "Josephinism," in Bavaria during the era of reform between 1799 and 1817. Everywhere one could discern pressure from the state to boost the productivity of the land, bind the largest possible number of the vagrant population to work, and discipline them toward a behavior model of the lower middle class with a combination of punishments and pedagogical measures. Especially the manufactures, the proto-industrial precursors to the nineteenth-century factories, seemed well suited for this purpose: not only did they contribute to the national wealth, but the functioning of the division of labor they practiced required the virtues of hard work, moderation, and punctualness (e.g. de Mandeville 1968, p. 286; Macfarlan 1785; Marperger 1733). There is thus much to be said for the above-mentioned thesis, namely that the social disciplining of the Early Modern Period (the paradigm associated with the names of Norbert Elias and Gerhard Oestreich [Schulze 1987]) contributed to preparing the workers for the industrial age. This is particularly evident, for example, where the religious energies of Pietism and the Enlightenment combined with the techniques of the manufacture system, as in the orphanage that August Hermann Francke (1663–1727) founded in Halle (von Willard 1997). There, the Christian-motivated blend of poor relief, schooling, and mission within the context of the Enlightenment took on traits of the large industrial enterprise. Still, such endeavors revealed the general lack of a "poor policy" that subsumed the state and the church more so than they were able to remedy it.

3. The Transition to the Nineteenth Century

As the image of the state became de-mythologized, a process encapsulated in the sober notion of the social contract that was freely entered into and could be dissolved *in extremis* (Badura and Hofmann 1965; Röhrich 1972), there also grew within the social sphere the optimistic belief that social conditions could be engineered and altered. Under the specific conditions of the Enlightenment in Germany, impulses for social activism came from the educated middle class, for example the reform of poor relief in Hamburg in 1788 (Lindemann 1990; Duda 1982), and from within the sphere of enlightened Absolutism from the top echelons of the state administration. The *Allgemeine Landrecht* [General Law Code] for the Prussian states, which, to be sure, was overtaken and nearly undone by a policy of restoration by the time it took effect (1794) [Schwennicke 1993], for the first time recognized a general obligation to care for the poor in the sense of a "state task," and derived from this the right and duty of the state "to take measures by which the destitution of its citizens could be preempted and excessive waste regulated" (ALR, II, 19, §6). Where special poor funds did not exist, the communities were obligated to support their citizens through the "local poor associations" [*Ortsarmenverbände*]. Where no local citizenship relationship existed, as in the case of the "land poor" [*Landarme*], the state assumed the burden of care through *Landarmenverbände*, their institutions for *Landarme,* and through other installations. Anyone who did not belong to the local poor or the land poor was—as during the previous two centuries—deported across the borders.

Count Montgelas, the minister in charge of these matters in Bavaria, reorganized the poor system in that state along similar lines shortly before this political downfall (1817). He imposed upon local communities "the duty of public care for the poor," though he simultaneously declared that "all subjects resident in and native to a care district [*Pflegebezirk*], without exception" were obligated "to participate proportionately and contribute to regulating the need of the poor."[4] Of course, the "voluntary charity of individuals" was permitted in addition, "although it must not detract from the general obligations of everyone toward the care of the poor by

[4] Decree concerning the system of poor relief, dated November 17, 1816, *Kgl. Baierisches RegBl.* 1816, p. 780, Article 1.7.

communities and district, or run counter to the decrees regarding begging."[5] The sovereign state of the early modern period thus retained the overarching competence, and from this position it was also able to guarantee that the institutions of charitable welfare remained untouched and could develop. In Bavaria, this happened shortly thereafter in the Constitution of 1818 (Titel IV, §9).

The initial moves toward elevating all of social policy into the duty of the state, which was evident also in other German states and represented the late political fruits of the Enlightenment and the legislation of the French Revolution regarding the obligatory care of the poor by the state, were lost again at the beginning of the nineteenth century in the battle of the bourgeoisie for participation in political power. With freedom of the soil and liberation from feudal dues (Hedemann 1930; Stolleis 1976), freedom of trade (Steindl 1984; Ziekow 1997, pp. 140ff.), public legal proceedings (Fögen 1974; Alber 1974), and freedom of the press, freedom of association, and freedom of assembly absorbing the mental energy, and the industrial proletariat—later so threatening to the bourgeoisie—not yet representing an organized force, there was little room left for reforms of the system of poor relief. And the contemptuous dismissal of the Enlightenment and its pedagogical efforts to "improve humankind" did the rest.

The waning of Enlightenment optimism, the absorption of domestic politics by the constitutional question, and the beginning of the industrial revolution resulted not only in a reduction of the overall extent of poor relief, but also in a narrowing to the purely material questions of need. Enlightenment's central idea, to remedy unfortunate circumstances long term through the application of pedagogical reason, was now looked upon with the distrust of those who either opted for individual self-help or trusted in the inner dynamic of the historical "development." Similarly, the early liberal state did not accept health care as a social task of the state. At most, it chose to take freedom-restricting measures where conditions were contrary to the entrepreneurial ethic and produced lasting health effects that were eventually noticed by the army's recruiting boards. The beginning of occupational health and safety legislation through the prohibition against child labor in Prussia (1839) was driven by these premises, though it was also intended to lend a hand to the older and now intensified efforts to implement obligatory school attendance.[6]

The poor laws enacted by the various German states before and after 1848 made only minor changes to the basic framework taken over from Absolutism. There were improvements on the local level, for example, by activating voluntary *Armenpfleger* [visitors to the poor], as in the so-called "Elberfeld System" after 1817 (Münsterberg 1903; Sachße and Tennstedt 1980, vol. 1, p. 214, 1988, vol. 2, pp. 23ff.). Other than that, the effort was made to keep pace with social change by adapting the competency regulations: while the problem of "vagrants" had been paramount in the sixteenth and seventeenth centuries, the poor laws of the late

[5] Ibid., Article 24.

[6] "Regulativ über die Beschäftigung jugendlicher Arbeiter in Fabriken v. 9. März 1839," *PrGS* 1839, 156. On this see Gladen (1974, pp. 12ff.), Mors (1986, pp. 217–229).

eighteenth century could posit a fairly immobile subject against a backdrop of better material conditions. This was still an essentially agrarian and small-town world with little fluctuation. The residents of towns and the countryside, to the extent that they belonged to the third estate, were bound to their localities—that is, they were assigned to a given community—through guild regulations, serfdom, and manorial and feudal structures. In many cases they needed a special permit to become mobile at all. Under these conditions it made sense to link the right and duty of support to the criterion of *Heimatrecht* [right of residence].

However, the perspective changed again with the reforms of the Confederation of the Rhine and Prussia's defeat in 1806. The estate-based society was broken open and was gradually levelled out into a national community formed by the third estate; although differences of estates still existed within this community, they were now under pressure to justify and legitimate themselves. After 1789, the ideas of universal equality and freedom were here to stay. Anyone who wished to restrict them needed special legal titles to do so, and these lay increasingly in the laws passed by the new parliaments. In the *Vormärz* period, these parliaments saw themselves less as legislative organs and more as guardians over the "rights of the people." The freedoms of religion and confession, opinion and the press, assembly and association, were joined by demands for commercial freedom, freedom of the land, freedom of movement, tax equity, and the abolition of the privileges of the nobility and the church. This was the transition to the civic society, which sought to retire Absolutism with its patronizing "law and order policy," primarily in questions relating to the economy and private life, and secondarily also with respect to political participation. The emerging industrial society wanted mobility of capital, a market for land, and people who migrated into the industrial regions or commuted across the borders as seasonal workers. With the acceptance of commercial freedom and freedom of movement, and the abolition of serfdom and manorial dues, the local residency principle as the underpinning of aid to the poor became increasingly questionable. Shifting responsible to the place of origin, which a person had left precisely because of the poor conditions there, created unsolvable problems. Poverty had to be borne where it emerged. A compulsory repatriation of the poor was now out of the question. In 1851/1853, the members of the German Confederation agreed to remedy the difficulties in expelling the homeless poor through reciprocal pledges and to regulate medical care for sick and burials for deceased *Landfremde* [outsiders].[7] The place of the *Heimatprinzip* was increasingly taken by the *Unterstützungswohnsitz* [residential right of relief]. It was recognized in Prussia in 1842, in the North German Confederation in 1870, and extended to Württemberg and Baden after the founding of the *Reich*. Alsace-Lorraine was added in 1910, Bavaria in 1913.[8] The more the internal German

[7] The Gotha Agreement of July 15, 1851, in von Meyer (1859), pp. 582ff.; additional references in Zacher (1993, p. 433).

[8] Prussia: *PrGS* 1843, 8; North German Confederation: *BGBl. des Norddeutschen Bundes* 1870, 360, extended to Württemberg and Baden through the law of April 16, 1871: *RGBl.*, p. 391. Final version in the law of July 7, 1908. See also Hesse (1971).

borders dissolved in the unification process and a uniform legal sphere with legally guaranteed freedom of movement emerged,[9] the more the previous deportation of the foreign poor across territorial borders ceased. Not only the feeling of nationhood argued against deportations within Germany, statistics and the cost-benefit analysis also showed that it was more cost-effective to treat all Germans in all federal states as locals. As a result, the time a person would have to spend in any given location before becoming eligible for support also grew shorter during the nineteenth century: originally it was set at 7, then 5 years; in 1869 it was reduced to 2 years, in 1908, finally, to 1 year. Such obstacles were no longer compatible with a mobile industrial society.

As before, the states, not the *Reich*, were responsible for setting up the system of poor relief. However, the social conditions of the Ancien Régime were still reflected in the old distinction between *Ortsarme* [local poor] and *Landarme* [poor of the land], a distinction that was rooted in the separation of the medieval city with its own law from the countryside with its law, though now it referred to those who had a residential right of relief and those who did not. Thus, there was a local Charitable Union [*Armenverband*] which combined the competencies for one or more communities or manorial estates [*Gutsherrschaften*], and the territorial Charitable Unions [*Landarmenverbände*], whose expenses, as in Prussia, for example, were borne by the province. This old distinction is still evident today in the jurisdiction of the *Landkreise* and in the distribution of competency between local and supra-local tasks of social aid.

Again following tradition, a binding stipulation about the nature and level of aid was avoided. That the poor had no subjective-legal right to poor relief that was actionable in court went without saying. As a Prussian law stated: “A poor person can never assert a claim to support against a Charitable Union through legal avenues, but only with the administrative authorities, whose task it is not to grant claims that exceed the necessities.”[10] However, the same law spoke very clearly about “public support that must be granted in cases of need.” It recognized that the state had an objective duty to act.

Characteristic for the state of poor laws before the founding of the *Reich* is the Bavarian law of 1869 that dealt with public poor and sick relief.[11] Public poor relief was supposed to support the needy and counter pauperization; it was a communal task. What was granted, only in cases of “demonstrated need,” was the subsistence minimum, sick relief, a pauper’s grave, and the “necessary educating and training” of poor children. These services were subsidiary and secondary to aid from family members and from charitable poor relief. Recipients of this aid were also obligated to work; conversely, communities were obligated “to create the institutions that are

[9] “Gesetz über die Freizügigkeit vom 1. November 1867,” *BGBl. des Norddeutschen Bundes 1876*, 55–58.

[10] “Preußisches Gesetz über die Verpflichtung zur Armenpflege vom 31 Dezember 1842,” *PrGS 1843*, 8, §33.

[11] Bayerisches Gesetzblatt 1868/1869, pp. 1093ff.

indispensable to local poor relief," or to enter into appropriate agreements with charitable welfare organizations. For the sick, there were to be sickness funds either within larger enterprises or on the community level. Likewise, there is evidence of the first steps toward state job placement and "assignment of work" to "able-bodied persons who, in spite of serious efforts, were unable to find gainful employment."

Although the nineteenth century had to wrestle with the problems of population growth, pauperism, internal migration, and industrial poverty on an unprecedented scale, it did not succeed in reforming the system of poor relief in any profound way (Münsterberg 1887; von Reitzenstein 1887; Roscher 1894). There are a variety of reasons for this. In the first half of the century, the emerging bourgeois society was largely preoccupied with removing the impediments to individual freedom. The political, religious, economic, and social rights of liberty for human beings and citizens were the central political goals, which activists were hoping to enshrine in inviolable constitutional guarantees and political norms (Stolleis 1992, pp. 56ff.). The comprehensive law-and-order policies of Absolutism were now denounced almost unanimously as representing patronizing and excessive government—of course, more in theory than in administrative praxis, which continued to have an interventionist bent. "Law and order" was now to serve essentially only defense against danger (Preu 1983). However, this early-liberal goal soon saw the return of welfare state elements, the more observers recognized that the withdrawal of the state to a night watchman role could imperil its own existence. The constraints on manorial estates, landownership, and in guilds were to be eliminated—and they did disappear, though the trades, at any rate, recaptured a protective position backed by public law in the course of the nineteenth century (Chamber of Trades, master exam, register of qualified craftsmen). A uniform law of property and contracts was sought but only partially achieved, for example, in the case of landed property through the redemption of the *Grundlasten* [basic impositions on the land] over two generations (Habermann 1976).

Because the administrative and mental structures of the eighteenth century thus radiated well into the nineteenth century, specifically in the reform bureaucracies of Prussia and Austria, as a result of which we can certainly speak of a welfare state undercurrent within the dominant liberalism, the system of poor relief did not change in principle. The political pressure to abandon the existing structures was not strong enough. The system of poor relief in its traditional form was not able to deal effectively with "pauperism," but since an organized workers' movement did not yet exist, the problem could be pushed to the margins for the time being. As it was, increasing the mobility of the population toward the industrial centers, which was welcome, was not to be slowed by local measures of support. The rapidly growing rural population could not be supported; rural workers flocked to the cities, where the trades were already suffering from overcrowding. It was only after the middle of the century that the bourgeoisie can be described as prosperous, while the situation of the proletariat continued to deteriorate before 1848. The slow improvement in material conditions in the course of the nineteenth century had not only a quantifiable economic side to it, but also one of subjective feelings. The two sides did not necessarily change in lockstep, and it would appear that the sense of being excluded persisted longer. The poor, as the lowest stratum of the proletariat, continued to be discriminated against throughout the century politically and in term of social ethics; it manifested itself also in the loss of active and passive suffrage by the recipients of poor relief,[12] a perfectly natural step for theoreticians of early liberalism, who argued that only the person who contributed something to the state could participate in shaping it.

The latent domestic political pressure of the social question led at most to local improvements in the state system of poor relief. Of course, one of the reasons behind this relative stagnation was also that the poverty of the early nineteenth century for the most part manifested itself in the countryside, that is, it was geographically spread out, did not become a revolutionary threat, and could also be hidden more effectively. Moreover, observers noted that the excess population that had fallen onto hard times could be reduced through emigration (Conze 1962; Koselleck 1967). All this was in line with contemporary theory: Robert Malthus's *Essay on the Principle of Population* (1798) had been first translated into German in 1807 and was making quite an impression.[13]

Even if the state did not change the system of poor relief in any real sense before 1848, what did change was the increasingly self-aware society. The more it constituted itself as a civic society separate from the state, the better were the chances for the growth of voluntary social activities. The tradition of civic, mostly urban philanthropy had medieval roots, but beginning in the eighteenth century it grew into a new dimension of sometimes religiously, sometimes more pragmatically motivated concern with the lower classes, whose condition aroused compassion, but increasingly also political fears. Now there emerged aid association during wars and epidemics, as well as in misery-stricken regions of mining and industry. They distributed food, set up soup kitchens, orphanages, and warming rooms, supported women in childbed, looked after neglected youths and released prisoners, fought against alcoholism (Pauli 1838), or organized saving. The most diverse "Associations," "Aid" and "Relief Organizations"[14] came into being and formed a "social structure" (Nipperdey 1976, pp. 174–205). The system of Associations and Cooperatives, with its enormous importance to the self-organization of civic society, provided the legal framework also for the private initiatives in poor relief (Hardtwig 1997). It is no coincidence that in this climate, "self-government" (local

[12] See §35 Constitution of Baden of August 22, 1818, in the version of August 24, 1904; §142 of the Constitution of Württemberg of September 25, 1819, in the version of march 26, 1868; §2, Section 3 of the Reich Suffrage Law of April 12, 1849; Article 67 of the Prussian Constitution of December 5, 1848; §3 of the Electoral Law of the Reichstag for the North German Confederation of May 31, 1869. All of these can be found in Huber (1978/1986). An overview in Aeppli (1988).

[13] Malthus (1798). First German translation: *Versuch ueber (not über) die Beendigung und die Folgen der Volksvermehrung* (1807).

[14] For example: "Centralverein für das Wohl der arbeitenden Klasse" (since 1844), "Verein gegen Verarmung und Bettelei" in Gablonz (Bohemia), which shaped the so-called Gablonz System of poor relief, and the "Deutsche Verein für öffentliche und private Fürsorge" (1880 ss.) in Frankfurt am Main.

communities, universities, trades, churches, social insurance) becomes one of the dominant words of the nineteenth century (Heffter 1969; Stolleis 1990). Since the majorities were middle class associations, the secondary political goal was more or less to keep workers away from the "temptations of Communist or Socialist agitation." This dual motivation was readily apparent: "A part of the bourgeoisie is desirous of redressing social grievances, in order to secure the continued existence of bourgeois society. To this section belong economists, philanthropists, humanitarians, improvers of the condition of the working classes, organizers of charity, members of societies for the prevention of cruelty to animals, temperance fanatics, hole-and-corner reformers of every imaginable kind" (Marx and Engels 1969, *Manifesto of the Communist Party*, part 2). The competition of the early socialist self-help organizations with their bourgeois counterparts was thus also driven by the political struggle for the allegiance of the working class.

Alongside "private charity" stood that of the churches, especially in the second half of the nineteenth century (Sachße and Tennstedt 1980, pp. 227ff.; Becker 1991) Supported by Romanticism and political restoration, the Catholic Church survived the shock of the secularization of 1803 through a respiritualization and a reinvigoration of charitable work through the combined commitment of priests and laity to organize the care of the sick and needy and provide help to women and children, the homeless, and migrant workers. The most important areas of activity for the Caritas associations, the St. Vincent de Paul organizations [*Vinzenzvereine*], Catholic journeymen associations [*Gesellenvereine*], ecclesiastical orders and foundations were care of the sick, education, and the running of homes (W.E. v. Ketteler, A. Kolping; Iserloh 1975). The "*Volksverein für das katholische Deutschland*" [National Association for German Catholics] was set up in 1890. The "*Caritasverband für das katholische Deutschland*" [Caritas Association for German Catholics], established in 1897 by Lorenz Werthmann, for the first time combined the social welfare activities of the nineteenth century on the Reich level (Buchheim 1972). This organization continued to grow slowly until the World War (Wollasch 1978, pp. 1ff.). In addition, the Catholic workers' movement had taken shape in the second half of the nineteenth century. Its crucial manifesto was Pope Leo XIII's encyclical "Rerum novarum" of 1891 (Huber and Huber 1983, vol. 3, no. 126).

Developments on the Protestant side paralleled those on the Catholic side. Here, too, older foundations and charitable organizations from the eighteenth century were carried on. The Halle Orphanage (1695) continued to exist. Other initiatives were added in the early nineteenth century through the so-called Revival Movement: the Kindergarten appeared (J.F. Oberlin), along with youth aid, support for education, prisoners, and migrant workers (Th. Fliedner, J.H. Wichern), homes for epileptics and the mentally ill (F.v. Bodelschwingh), and much more. Leaders in the professionalization of socio-pedagogical and care-taking professions were Johann Heinrich Wichern (1808–1881) with the "Rauhes Haus" in Hamburg-Horn (1833) and the "Johannesstift" in Berlin (1858), which were devoted to care of young people, and Theodor Fliedner with the founding of the "*Mutterhausdiakonie*" [charitable organization of maternity houses] in 1836 (Beyreuther 1962, p. 88; Heidenreich and Kohlmann 1983; Becker 1983). It was also Wichern who, in

1848, founded the "*Centralausschuss für die Innere Mission der deutschen evangelischen Kirche*" [Central Committee for the Inner Mission of the German Protestant Church], at that time still outside of the official churches of the states, which did not yet have an umbrella organization (Wichern 1849; Röper 1998). The Protestant workers' movement developed along similar lines, culminating in 1890 in the formation of a "*Gesamtverband der Evangelischen Arbeitervereine Deutschland*" [Umbrella Organization of the Protestant Workers' Associations in Germany] (Huber and Huber 1983, pp. 314ff.). Finally, 1917 saw the founding of a "*Zentralwohlfahrtsstelle der deutschen Juden e.V*" [Central Welfare Bureau of German Jews] (Scheller 1987).

To this day, strong impulses for state social legislation have come from the two large confessions. The Kindergartens, children's and old-age homes, care and nursing homes, schools, hospitals, and many other institutions set up by the Catholic and Protestant sides have provided models for both the official churches and the state. The same is true of the welfare and educational organizations that emerged out of the workers' movement, though it was not until December 1919 that they combined to form the Social Democratic "*Arbeiterwohlfahrt*" [Workers' Welfare], on the initiative of Marie Juchacz (1879–1956) (Miller 1974).

To the extent that this work was pioneering, it was later in part equalled and overtaken by the state (for example in the area of hospitals), and in part in took on a permanent function of providing relief and acted as a supplement to state activities. In many areas, initiatives from voluntary charities, the churches, and the state stand side by side. To this day there are mixed forms in which the work on the ground is done by personnel from the churches and other social groups, while the state exercises a certain coordinating and security function.

References

Aeppli S (1988) Das beschränkte Wahlrecht im Übergang von der Stände- zur Staatsbürgergesellschaft: Zielsetzungen des Zensuswahlrechts. Zürich

Alber P-P (1974) Die Geschichte der Öffentlichkeit im deutschen Strafverfahren. Berlin

Badura P, Hofmann H (1965) Der Herrschaftsvertrag. Neuwied

Becker H (1983) Das Evangelische Johannesstift in Berlin-Spandau, seine Geschichte von 1858 bis 1983. Berlin

Becker W (1991) Sozialpolitische Vorstellungen der Kirchen und ihre Realisierung im 19. Jahrhundert (bis zu Rerum novarum). In: Pohl H (ed) Staatliche, städtische, betriebliche und kirchliche Sozialpolitik vom Mittelalter bis zur Gegenwart. Stuttgart, pp 177ff

Beyreuther E (1962) Geschichte der Diakonie und Inneren Mission in der Neuzeit. Berlin

Buchheim K (1972) Zeitgeschichtliche Hintergründe zur Geschichte des Deutschen Caritasverbandes. In: Fischer A (ed) 75 Jahre Deutscher Caritasverband. Freiburg im Breisgau

Conze W (1962) Das Spannungsfeld von Staat und Gesellschaft im Vormärz. In: Conze W (ed) Staat und Gesellschaft im deutschen Vormärz 1815–1848. Stuttgart

de Mandeville B (1968) Eine Abhandlung über Barmherzigkeit, Armenpflege und Armenschule. In: de Mandeville B (ed) Die Bienenfabel, Ausgabe. Frankfurt am Main

Duda D (1982) Die Hamburger Armenfürsorge im 18. und 19. Jahrhundert. Eine soziologisch-historische Untersuchung. Weinheim

Fögen MT (1974) Der Kampf um Gerichtsöffentlichkeit. Berlin

Gladen A (1974) Geschichte der Sozialpolitik in Deutschland. Wiesbaden

Gömmel R (1991) Merkantilstaatliche und kommunale Sozialpolitik. In: Pohl H (ed) Staatliche, städtische, betriebliche und kirchliche Sozialpolitik vom Mittelalter bis zur Gegenwart. Stuttgart

Habermann N (1976) Die preußische Gesetzgebung zur Herstellung eines frei verfügbaren Grundeigentums. In: Coing H, Wilhelm W (eds) Wissenschaft und Kodifikation des Privatrechts im 19. Jahrhundert, vol 3. Frankfurt am Main, pp 3–43

Hardtwig W (1997) Genossenschaft, Sekte, Verein in Deutschland. Vom Spätmittelalter bis zur französischen Revolution, vol 1. Munich

Härter K, Stolleis M (eds) (1996/1998/1999) Repertorium der Policeyordnungen der Frühen Neuzeit, vol 1, 1996: Deutsches Reich und geistliche Kurfürstentümer (Kurmainz, Kurköln, Kurtrier). Frankfurt am Main, vols 2/1, 2/2: Simon T (ed) (1998) Brandenburg-Preußen mit Nebenterritorien (Kleve-Mark, Magdeburg und Halberstadt). Frankfurt am Main, vols 3/1, 3/2: Schilling L, Schuck G (eds) (1999) Wittelsbachische Territorien (Kurpfalz, Bayern, Pfalz-Neuburg, Pfalz-Sulzbach, Jülich-Berg, Pfalz-Zweibrücken). Frankfurt am Main

Hedemann JW (1930) Die Fortschritte des Zivilrechts im XIX. Jahrhundert, vol 11/1. Berlin

Heffter H (1969) Die Deutsche Selbstverwaltung im 19. Jahrhundert. Geschichte der Ideen und Institutionen, 2nd edn. Stuttgart

Heidenreich U, Kohlmann W (1983) 150 Jahre Das Rauhe Haus 1833-1983 "Brunnenstube" der Inneren Mission. Hamburg

Hesse H (1971) Die sogenannte Sozialgesetzgebung Bayerns Ende der sechziger Jahre des 19. Jahrhunderts. Munich

Hollerbach A (1981) Das Staatskirchenrecht in der Rechtssprechung des Bundesverfassungsgerichts. Archiv für öffentliches Recht 106:218–283

Howard J (1780) Über Gefängnisse und Zuchthäuser. Leipzig

Howard J (1784) The state of the prisons in England and Wales with preliminary observations and an account of some foreign prisons and hospitals. London

Howard J (1791) Nachrichten von den vorzüglichsten Kranken- und Pesthäusern in Europa. Leipzig

Huber ER (1978/1986) Dokumente zur deutschen Verfassungsgeschichte, vol 1/2, 3rd edn. Stuttgart

Huber ER, Huber W (eds) (1983) Staat und Kirche im 19. und 20. Jahrhundert. Dokumente zur Geschichte des deutschen Staatskirchenrechts, vol 3, no 126. Berlin

Isensee J (1995) Die karitative Betätigung der Kirchen und der Verfassungsstaat. In: Listl J, Pirson D (eds) Handbuch des Staatskirchenrechts der Bundesrepublik Deutschland, vol 2, 2nd edn. Berlin

Iserloh E (1975) Die soziale Aktivität der Katholiken im Übergang von caritativer Fürsorge zu Sozialreform und Sozialpolitik, dargestellt an den Schriften Wilhelm Emanuel von Kettelers. Stuttgart

Jütte R (1984) Obrigkeitliche Armenfürsorge in den deutschen Reichsstädten der frühen Neuzeit. Städtisches Armenwesen in Frankfurt am Main und Köln, Cologne

Jütte R (1995) The causes of poverty: the European context. In: Scribner R, Ogilvie S (eds) Germany: a new social and economic history, vol 1. London, pp 1450–1630

Jütte R (1996) Syphilis and confinement. Hospitals in early modern Germany. In: Finzsch N, Jütte R (eds) Institutions of confinement. Cambridge

Kleinschrod GAK (1789) Über die Strafe der öffentlichen Arbeiten. Würzburg

Koselleck R (1967) Preußen zwischen Reform und Revolution. Allgemeines Landrecht, Verwaltung und soziale Bewegung von 1791–1848. Stuttgart

Kreiker S (1997) Armut, Schule, Obrigkeit. Armenversorgung und Schulwesen in der evangelischen Kirchenordnungen des 16. Jahrhunderts. Bielefeld

Liese W (1922) Geschichte der Caritas, vol I. Freiburg im Breisgau

Lindemann M (1990) Patriots and Paupers, Hamburg 1712–1830. New York

Macfarlan J (1785) Untersuchungen über die Armuth, Aus dem Englischen übersetzt und mit einigen Anmerkungen und Zusätzen begleitet von Christian Garve. Leipzig
Maier H (1980/1986) Die ältere deutsche Staats-und Verwaltungslehre, 2nd edn (1980), 3rd edn (1986). Munich
Malthus R (1798) An essay on the principle of population, as it affects the future improvement of society. London
Marperger PJ (1733) Wohlmeynende Gedanken aber die Versorgung der Armen, Wes Standts, Alters, Leibs- und Unglück-Constitution nach selbige auch seyn möchten. Leipzig
Marx K, Engels F (1969) Manifest der Kommunistischen Partei. Stuttgart
Miller S (1974) Marie Juchacz. Neue Deutsche Biografie 10:633
Mors A (1986) Die Entwicklung der Schulpflicht in Deutschland. Dissertation. Tübingen
Münsterberg E (1887) Die Deutsche Armengesetzgebung und das Material zu ihrer Reform. Leipzig
Münsterberg E (1903) Das Elberfelder System. Leipzig
Neukamm KH (1987) Diakonie. In: Evangelisches Staatslexikon, vol 1, 3rd edn. Stuttgart, pp 610–618
Nipperdey T (1976) Verein als soziale Struktur in Deutschland im späten 18. und frühen 19. Jahrhundert. In: Gesellschaft, Kultur, Theorie. Gesammelte Aufsätze zur neueren Geschichte. Göttingen, pp 174–205
Padoa-Schioppa A (ed) (1997) Legislation and justice. The origins of the modern state in Europe, 13th–18th century. Oxford
Palme R (1991) Städtische Sozialpolitik bis zum 16. Jahrhundert. In: Pohl H (ed) Staatliche, städtische, betriebliche und kirchliche Sozialpolitik vom Mittelalter bis zur Gegenwart. Stuttgart
Pauli CW (1838) Was kann unter uns wider das zunehmende Branntweintrinken geschehen? Lübeck
Peitzsch W (1968) Kriminalpolitik in Bayern unter der Geltung des Codex Juris Criminalis Bavarici von 1751. Munich
Preu P (1983) Polizeibegriff und Staatszwecklehre. Die Entwicklung des Polizeibegriffs durch die Rechts- und Staatswissenschaften des 18. Jahrhunderts. Göttingen
Quaritsch H (1986) Souveränität. Berlin
Ratzinger G (1868) Geschichte der kirchlichen Armenpflege. Freiburg im Breisgau
Reicke S (1932) Das deutsche Spital und sein Recht im Mittelalter. Stuttgart
Roeck B (1993) Außenseiter, Randgruppen, Minderheiten. Göttingen
Röhrich W (1972) Sozialvertrag und Bürgerliche Emanzipation von Hobbes bis Hegel. Darmstadt
Röper U (ed) (1998) Die Macht der Nächstenliebe. 150 Jahre Innere Mission und Diakonie. Berlin
Roscher W (1894) System der Armenpflege und Armenpolitik. Stuttgart
Saam G (1936) Quellenstudien zur Geschichte des Deutschen Zuchthauswesens bis zur Mitte des 19. Jahrhunderts. Berlin/Leipzig
Sachße C, Tennstedt F (1980/1988) Geschichte der Armenfürsorge in Deutschland, vol 1, 1980; vol 2: Fürsorge und Wohlfahrtspflege 1871 bis 1929. 1988. Stuttgart
Scheller B (1987) Die Zentralwohlfahrtsstelle. Der jüdische Wohlfahrtsverband in Deutschland. Eine Selbstdarstellung. Frankfurt am Main
Scherner K-O (1979) Das Recht der Armen und der Bettler im Ancien Regime. Savigny-Zeitschrift für Rechtsgeschichte (Germanistische Abteilung), pp 55–99
Schilling L, Schuck G (eds) (1999) Repertorium der Policeyverordnungen der frühen Neuzeit, vols 3/1, 3/2: Wittelsbachische Territorien (Kurpfalz, Bayern, Pfalz-Neuburg, Pfalz-Sulzbach, Jülich-Berg, Pfalz-Zweibrücken). Frankfurt am Main
Schlumbohm J (1997) Gesetze, die nicht durchgesetzt werden - ein Strukturmerkmal des frühneuzeitlichen Staates? Geschichte und Gesellschaft, pp 647–663
Schott C (1978) Armenfürsorge, Bettelwesen und Vagantenbekämpfung in der Reichsabtei Salem. Bühl

Schubert E (1983) Arme Leute, Bettler und Gauner im Franken des 18. Jahrhunderts. Neustadt an der Aisch

Schuck G (1995) Überlegungen zum Verhältnis von Arbeit und Policy in der Frühen Neuzeit. Ius Cummune: pp. 12ff

Schulze W (1987) Gerhard Oestreichs Begriff der "Sozialdisziplinierung in der frühen Neuzeit". Zeitschrift für Historische Forschung 14:265–302

Schulze W (ed) (1988) Ständische Gesellschaft und soziale Mobilität. Munich

Schwennicke A (1993) Die Entstehung der Einleitung des Preußischen Allgemeinen Landrechts von 1794. Frankfurt am Main

Simon T (ed) (1998) Repertorium der Policeyverordnungen der frühen Neuzeit, vols 2/1, 2/2: Brandenburg/Preußen mit Nebenterritorien (Kleve-Mark, Magdeburg und Halberstadt). Frankfurt am Main

Steindl H (1984) Entfesselung der Arbeitskraft. In: Steindl H (ed) Wege zur Arbeitsrechtsgeschichte. Frankfurt am Main, pp 29–135

Stolleis M (1976) Die bayerische Gesetzgebung zur Herstellung eines frei verfügbaren Grundeigentums. In: Coing H, Wilhelm W (eds) Wissenschaft und Kodifikation des Privatrechts im 19. Jahrhundert, vol 3. Frankfurt am Main, pp 44–117

Stolleis M (1990) Sozialrecht. In: Erler A, Kaufmann E (eds) Handwörterbuch zur Deutschen Rechtsgeschichte, vol 4. Berlin, columns 1730–1733

Stolleis M (1992) Geschichte des öffentlichen Rechts in Deutschland, vol 2 (1800–1914). Munich

Stolleis M (ed) (1996) Policey im Europa der Frühen Neuzeit. Frankfurt am Main

Stolleis M (1997) Die "Idee des souveränen Staates". Der Staat. Suppl 11:63–85

Uhlhorn G (1895) Die christliche Liebesthätigkeit, 2nd edn. Stuttgart

von Meyer PAG (1859) Corpus juris Confoederationis Germanicae, part II, 3rd edn. Frankfurt am Main

von Moeller E (1906) (reprint 1972) Die Elendenbrüderschaften. Ein Beitrag zur Geschichte der Fremdenfürsorge im Mittelalter. Leipzig

von Reitzenstein F (1887) Die ländliche Armenpflege und ihre Reform, Verhandlungen des deutschen Vereins für Armenpflege und Wohltätigkeit. Freiburg im Breisgau

von Willard P (ed) (1997) "Mitten im Aufbruch". 300 Jahre Franckesche Stiftungen Halle an der Saale 1698–1998. Halle an der Saale

Wagnitz HB (1791–1794) Historische Nachrichten und Bemerkungen über die merkwürdigsten Zuchthäuser in Deutschland, 2 vols. Halle an der Saale

Weinacht P (1968) Staat. Studien zur Bedeutungsgeschichte des Wortes. Berlin

Wichern JH (1849) Die innere Mission der deutschen evangelischen Kirche. Eine Denkschrift an die deutsche Nation im Auftrage des Centralausschusses für die innere Mission. Hamburg

Wollasch H-J (1978) Der Deutsche Caritasverband: Entwicklung und Aufgaben. In: Wollasch H-J (ed) Beiträge zur Geschichte der Deutschen Caritas in der Zeit der Weltkriege. Freiburg im Breisgau, pp 1ff

Wright WJ (1977) Reformation contributions to the development of public welfare policy in Hesse. Journal of Modern History (On-Demand-Supplement) 49:1145–1179

Zacher HF (1993) Grundfragen des internationalen Sozialrechts. In: Zacher HF (ed) Abhandlungen zum Sozialrecht. Heidelberg, p 433

Ziekow J (1997) Über Freizügigkeit und Aufenthalt. Tübingen

III. Social Policy in the Empire: The Insurance Solution

1. The Idea of Insurance

One of the basic human experiences is that membership in a group affords greater protection. Children, the weak and sick, the poor and the elderly have always depended on solidaristic support from the immediate or extended family as well as their neighbors. This has given rise to a great diversity in forms of aid and support of every kind. Industrial society at the beginning of the twenty-first century also knows this diversity, and it grounds its functions more or less consciously in these early efforts. However, there is a growing number of living arrangements involving single adults living on their own (probably historically unprecedented in this form) without clear group membership, though their existence depends, of course, on the functioning of many public institutions. The taxes, fees, and contributions generated also by these "singles" help to keep these institutions operating and viable.

Equally as old as the forms of security arising from the family unit are the solidaristic protections of particular endangered groups, especially seamen and miners. Since antiquity there has existed the idea and practice of "coffers" that are maintained by moderate contributions from those affected, which create a fund that is able to cushion the occupation-specific risks of the individual ("all for one"). The payment of such contributions presupposes an economic and social model that has writing, money, and ordered legal conditions, which allow for a higher level of organization that is grounded in institutional confidence. In this way, the typical risks of life (illness, inability to work, old age) or the risk of dangerous work can be economized and spread out among the respective community of solidarity. The individual who joins or is born into such a community agrees tacitly or explicitly to

Previously published in English in the following publication: Stolleis: Origins of the German Welfare State (German Social Policy, Vol. 2), Springer, Berlin/Heidelberg, 2013.

M. Stolleis, *History of Social Law in Germany*, 29
DOI 10.1007/978-3-642-38454-7_3, © Springer-Verlag Berlin Heidelberg 2014

a certain "pact": one pays into an institution borne by all in order to transform individual risk into collective risk and thereby make it bearable. Thus, the central point is not the equivalence of what one receives from the insurance relative to one's own contributions, but the amelioration of the "vagaries of life" that is "bought" by these contributions.

The origins of communities of solidarity forged together by dangers communally endured are unknown. Departing soldiers or ship crews who promised mutual aid as sworn religious bands could be identified as the first traces, as could the groups united to operate common institutions (defense installations, mills, wells, dikes). That is also where we find the first examples of a monetarization of obligatory services. There also emerged occupational groups brought together by a shared education, interests, and religious and feast day rituals. Here, too, we find the basic idea that the common pursuit of certain goals is more effective, that the division of labor and the shift of typical risks onto an institution jointly maintained is advantageous.

2. Old Forms of Security and the Industrial Revolution

This simple idea spawned throughout the European Middle Ages a vast number of orders, guilds, corporations, brotherhoods, confraternities, and the like. In the life of a society that did not know the modern institutional state, they formed—alongside the house community—the real core elements of the human community. The shared exercise of religion was substantially carried by them, but so were the trades, mining, seafaring, and other common activities that were related to work driven by shared dangers (Stradal 1971, pp. 1522–1527; 1687–1692; Brand 1998, pp. 1792–1803; Oexle 1982; Brück 1994). The early modern period, under the influence of growing secularization and commercialization, saw the emergence of associations, societies, cooperatives, and unions. Each word was part of a different, historically mutable semantic field. There were regular primary and secondary purposes, and the latter usually included caring for members in cases of accidents and in old age. The reason for this is obvious: because members belonged together and felt responsible for each other, this also included solidarity in cases of need.

Although the tradition of these institutions can still be detected today, it has been visibly weakened by the primary trends of modernity—secularization of values and the industrialization of production, and sometimes its traces have been lost entirely. Monasteries and lay congregations, guilds and journeymen associations, where they still exist at all, are marginal phenomena of society. Their function of providing security for broader segments of the population has disappeared. White-collar employees and self-employed tradesmen are today covered by social security. Members of religious orders occasionally find themselves in a situation where their order or the church has to provide supplemental insurance, because the orders are no longer able to take on the task of providing for old age (Schulin 1980; Listl 1994, pp. 841–863). In general, one can observe that the task of the older forms of solidarity of providing security to their members has passed to social insurance. Where these older institutions still exist, they serve the commercial or cultural life as foundations, societies, cooperatives, and associations in the legal forms of the nineteenth century, but they no longer play a central role for the protection of their members against illness and old age. The larger community of solidarity that is the general social insurance system has been superimposed upon and has displaced the older, autonomous forms of security provided by smaller entities.

This shift from smaller to larger entities is a socio-historical and socio-legal process that cannot be clearly dated. But there are reasons to situate the qualitative rupture between the older and the modern forms of protection at the end of the eighteenth and the beginning of the nineteenth century. Of course, the transitions were fluid, nor could it be any other way with transformations that encompass the entire society. Thus, during the last three decades of the eighteenth century there were still countless "cooperative" institutions of the kind mentioned above, but many of them were in crisis. The religious orders—to the extent that they had turned into institutions providing social care—saw themselves threatened by the Enlightenment, the emancipation of the bourgeoisie, and changing ideas about the role of women. At the same time, the rapidly changing economy, which was trying to shake off the mercantilist regime of Absolutism, was destroying many smaller forms of security that originated within the trades. The guilds themselves were ossified and defended themselves as best they could against the rise of economic liberalism. Manorial lordship and landholding in the countryside were being unsettled by demands for reform, and one sensed that the end of personal ties also involved the existing mechanisms of social protection. Clear-sighted conservatives tried to use that argument to prevent all-too-deep ruptures in the existing system. Reformers were willing to accept the social damages, where these could be foreseen at all, in order to attain what they regarded as the more important goal of personal liberation and the mobilization of the land. As a result, the traditionally organized trades, agriculture, and the lay organizations of the church slid into a parallel crisis, one that also affected the equally traditional systems of "sickness, burial, and aid funds" which had arises out of cooperative self-help. In other words: the last remnants of personal networks from the Middle Ages no longer proved adequate when the Ancien Régime ended, by revolution or evolution, and the Industrial Revolution got under way on a larger scale.[1]

It was thus several, parallel developments of revolutionary character that ruptured the connection to the older forms of protection. The Enlightenment weakened the transcendental relationship between group formation and mutual care; the place of Christian charity and sworn solidarity was taken increasingly by the expected utility and a relationship of financial equalization. The emerging agrarian reform, with its elimination of the three-field system and the commons, ended the

[1] The legal-historical literature can be found in Stradal (1971), "Gilde," Lentze (1971), "Handwerk," and Luther (1971), "Innung," all in Erler, Adalbert, Kaufmann, Ekkehard (eds.), Handwörterbuch zur Deutschen Rechtsgeschichte, vol. 1 (1971).

dependency of those who worked the land on the manorial lord or landowner. Split ownership (Obereigentum—primary ownership, and Nutzungseigentum—usufruct ownership or copyhold) was fused into a single concept of property by bourgeois society. With this the hierarchy of estates in the microcosms of rural labor also tended to disappear. The place of the social bonds that tied families in hereditary serfdom was taken by contractual bonds under civil law. The traditional "house" as an economic entity and a unit of life was dissolved into a bundle of work contracts. Workers coming from the countryside flocked to the emerging industrial centers of the textile industry, mining, and steel manufacturing (Hahn 1998). They worked for exceedingly low wages and with minimal social protections. In this way, without knowing or intending to, they provided the real economic boost to the Industrial Revolution. Henceforth, the "workers' question" that arose from this and would accompany the entire nineteenth century also formed the starting point for the counter-forces. Finally, political revolution also destroyed the traditional legitimacy by the Grace of God; its place was taken by the newly legitimated "Caesarian" rule, or by power that was derived from the will of the people. Both forms promised a trend toward material and legal equality, even if they had different views of political participation.

With the reforms of the Napoleonic and post-Napoleonic period, these developments became intertwined. The social consequences of the economic and political upheavals, of wars on the one side and the new machines (spinning machines, looms, steam machines) on the other, the collapse of the system of rural bonds, and the migratory movement from the countryside into the new centers, formed the starting point of the "social question." The abolition of old forms of social community, which brought enormous gains in terms of economic and personal freedom, the latter flanked by the newly won constitutional guarantees of human and civic rights (Schmale 1997), always entailed losses, as well. They were losses of a sense of responsibility, which, even if it may have been present only in rudimentary form in individual cases, was able, embedded in a religious context, to develop a certain power that restrained egoism. Added was the shift of all processes of social exchange into a law of obligations that was shaped by Roman law. Labor and wages were contractual goods. Initially there was little room for secondary obligations that could have softened the harshness of the exchange, or for limitations on and transformations of contracts through public law. Nineteenth-century legal "Germanists" whose allegiance was to "German law" always lamented the reduction of service relationships and other forms of exchange to the quality of a commodity, and Karl Marx confirmed that this was happening in his own way and with his analytical tools. But what Germanists called upon was an unhistorical, romanticizing transfiguration of older legal conditions. Still, the diagnosis that the "prevailing Roman law" at that time favored the tendencies to reduce social relationships to contractual ties was correct. Of course, modern Romanistic scholarship points out that casting the work relationship as a relationship of obligation also brought advantages, for example in the case of the continued payment of wages if it was the employer's fault that work could not be performed (Mayer-Maly 1967; Söllner 1967). All these factors that were at work added up to a problem that threatened the entire society. The population more than doubled in the course of the nineteenth century. The number of people working and living off the land declined steadily. Traditional crafts came under pressure from the new commercial freedom and let workers go. The masses flocked to the cities and industrial centers, unless they had chosen to emigrate (Henning 1978; Zöllner 1981; Tennstedt 1983). It was only around the middle of the century that a gradually solidifying awareness of belonging to a common class took shape within the wage-dependent population. In 1848, the emerging fourth estate already constituted a considerable potential, even if it was not yet able to articulate itself in parliamentary terms.

In March 1848, workers in Berlin demanded from the Prussian King "a ministry for workers, though it may be composed of employers and workers, and its members may be elected only from within these two circles themselves" (Valentin 1947, p. 421). In the Frankfurt *Vorparlament* [Pre-Parliament], Gustav von Struve presented a socio-revolutionary program, whose core demands likewise included remedying the misery of the working class and the middle class, as well as a "ministry of labor" that would secure for labor "its share of the profits of work" (Valentin 1947, p. 472). Although the Left at the Paulskirche could not agree on the details, the welfare of the working classes had been recognized, as the Saxon delegate Berhard Eisenstuck put it, "as the true and great national question of the present time." The Berlin delegate Nauwerck demanded a "right to maintenance" for "those who could no support themselves by their own power." All these efforts on the national and individual state level failed along with the revolution as a whole. But with these demands, with the Communist Manifesto (1848), and with the *Allgemeine deutsche Arbeiter-Verbrüderung* [General Fraternization of German Workers] of the same year, which preserved also in its name the old idea of a sworn union, the social movement had constituted itself out of the working class, just as the bourgeois social reforms in favor of the working class would henceforth devote themselved continuously to the new problem.

The *Allgemeine deutsche Arbeiter-Verbrüderung* was outlawed in 1854 when the old powers staged a comeback. But it was precisely this suppression that consolidated the workers' movement (Grebing 1966). In 1863, Ferdinand Lassalle founded the *Allgemeiner Deutscher Arbeiterverein* [General German Workers' Association], the Social-Democratic Workers' Party took shape in 1869, and in 1875 the two camps merged. With this, the transition to the level of participation at the political—especially parliamentary—level had been carried out.

The reactions of the state and society to the "social" or "workers' question" were initially uncoordinated and aimed at various points. The old charity of the churches was now supplemented with better-organized activities, for example, by church-affiliated aid organizations to combat the dissipation of the youth, alcoholism, and prostitution, by the Kindergarten movement, by "Internal Mission," activities that promoted thrift and savings, and much more. This was essentially an attempt, through mobilizing the willingness of bourgeois circles to help, to directly attack the social harms of the Industrial Revolution without questioning the social order in a fundamental way. These harms presented themselves as the "poverty" of entire social classes. This was not only a threat to bourgeois safety through crime and tensions in everyday life, but also a profound danger to the entire social order. It meant a lack of work and little pay, unhealthy and "immoral" living conditions, a lack of health care for women in childbed, child labor in mines and factories with undesirable consequences for school attendance and the physical health of future recruits. Anyone who wanted to help solve these problems in the nineteenth century typically founded an "aid association" [*Hülfsverein*] or a foundation for which money then had to raised, for example, through charitable events. These were activities that emanated from the middle of society.

The legal forms that were used for that purpose were derived from the "common law" that was in force throughout the nineteenth century, that is, the existence side-by-side of various codes (Bavarian Codex Maximilianeus, Allgemeines Landrecht für die Preußischen Staaten, Code Civil, Austrian Allgemeines Bürgerliches Gesetzbuch, Saxon Bürgerliches Gesetzbuch) (Schlosser 1996, pp. 96ff.), individual laws, and "pandect law" that was regarded as valid law in legal teachings and judicial decisions and was implemented in practice (Wieacker 1967, §23–24). These were the organizational forms of private-law organizations, which grouped around the universal freedom of action that had just recently been won, and by means of which reformers were trying to mitigate the harm that was done by this very freedom, specifically in the form of contractual freedom. Mitigation is all it could be, since the underlying principle of liberty could not be threatened. To that extent it was unavoidable that the efforts at self-healing by a society that regarded itself in principle as liberal could only have a limited reach. They had a built-in brake in the respect for the free market (Wieacker 1953 [in 1974, pp. 9–35] and 1966 [ibid, pp. 55–78]). However, the ability of the market to function depended in turn, as it was subsequently discovered, on the market not destroying its own foundation, that is, avoiding mass misery, and supporting a state that oversaw with sovereign guidance at least the core areas.

Germany in the nineteenth century, however, saw neither a renaissance of the absolutist welfare state, nor the establishment of a purely free-market society. Instead, what is characteristic are transitional forms: from agrarian to industrial production, from Absolutism to parliamentary democracy, and from the state-guided economy to more or less free markets. The dominant forces in the state and society in Germany were by no means supporters of a dogmatic liberalism. The enlightened Absolutism of the second half of the eighteenth century, which was responsible for the welfare of its subjects, was still present in a myriad of ways. In the constitutional battles of the early nineteenth century, the liberal powers still confronted defenders of the Ancien Régime. Though the latter used the catchwords of the day, politically they defended the "monarchic principle" and "legitimacy." The transformation of the princely state into the modern institutional state occurred only gradually. Between 1815 and 1848, as well as in the decade after 1848, bourgeois society was politically fairly unfree and patronzied by the state. To be sure, there were considerable differences between constitutional and non-constitutional states, between small and large states, between more liberal "states under the rule of law" and late-absolutist administrative states. And a burgher class that glossed over these differences, thought and acted in larger contexts, and was accustomed to the responsibility of governing, did not exist in sufficient strength. Even in times when economic liberalism seemed dominant (1845/1850 to 1873), the "solicitously patronizing" state had not in fact pulled back. No different from the eighteenth century, it looked after the economy by creating investment incentives, holding fairs, setting up *Realschulen* and technical colleges, or stimulating improvements in quality and "design" (Kaufhold 1982; Gessner 1982). Even state-funded industrial espionage abroad occurred.

In this setting, it appeared self-evident to preserve the old forms of social protection for the time being, to expand and adjust them to the new challenges. It seemed especially sensible to first use the existing potential of the support funds and to expand the circle of the beneficiaries. After the gilds had already fallen in 1810/1811 with the introduction of commercial freedom, Prussia in 1848 allowed journeymen, assistants, and factory workers to preserve existing or create new aid funds, and envisioned compulsory enrollment by journeymen and assistants through local ordinances. Since 1849, local communities, using the organizational forms of the old gilds (where they had not disappeared with the introduction of commercial freedom), were able to compel the self-employed to enroll and pay contributions to help "journeymen and helpers who were looking for work, sick, or needy for other reasons," or aid in the "continuing education of apprentices, journeymen, or helpers."[2]

State compulsion to protect the socially dependent within trades and profession was, of course, not very successful, even when in Prussia the right to exert that compulsion passed into the hands of the district governments (1854) and the possibility of compulsory enrollment was extended to workers. Communities had been reluctant to order compulsory enrollment. The system of work-based aid funds was stagnant. The regulatory history of this system, from the commercial code of the North German Confederation (June 21, 1869) to the final Aid Fund Act of April 7, 1876,[3] shows a vacillating approach that wavered between interventionism and liberalism. Compulsory enrollment for those ensured and competition between compulsory funds and voluntary funds stood side by side. A comprehensive system of compulsory insurance was still opposed as much by the liberalism that dominated economic theory and the top echelons of the Prussian civil service, as by the reluctance on the part of the working class itself. The latter was understandable: the exclusive financing of the fund system from wage contributions would have further depressed living standards, while the financing from other sources raised fears about new dependencies.

[2] "VO betr. die Errichtung von Gewerberäthen und verschiedene Änderungen der allgemeinen Gewerbeordnung v. 9 February 1849," PrGS, 93 f. (§57).

[3] "Gesetz über die eingeschriebenen Hülfskassen v. 7. April 1876," BGBl. des Norddeutschen Bundes, 125. On the influence that the *Verein für Socialpolitik* exerted in this law see Töpfer (1970, p. 163), Plessen (1975).

The situation was more favorable in mining.[4] Since mining had always been a special area of production and was accordingly endowed with special characteristics in societal law, labor law, and social law, it provided ideal openings for a development that was tending toward the universal insurance of workers. A Prussian law of April 10, 1854, ordered the establishment of Miners' Associations for all workers in mines, smelting works, saltworks, and processing plants, where these did not already exist.[5] In the form this regulation was then given in the Prussian General Mining Law of June 24, 1865, it became exemplary for compulsory insurance, for the public-law status of social insurance, characterized by the autonomy to issue statutes and the guarantee of self-administration, and for the system of participation by employees and employers and the duty of employers to hand over the contributions. That is why the most important parliamentary initiative before the actual legislation on social insurance, the 1878 resolution by the delegate v. Stumm on the introduction of disability and old-age funds that was supported by the Conservatives and the Center Party, copied the model of the funds for miners.[6]

A survey of the socio-political landscape in the 1870s reveals extraordinary shortcomings, an assessment also generally shared by contemporaries. The system of aid funds, the system of guild sickness funds, work-based provision that was taking shape only in major industry (Krupp, Zeiss, Stumm), the incomplete liability in cases of accidents in the workplace ("Reichshaftpflichtgesetz vom 7. Juni 1871")—all of this together did not form an adequate protection against the misery and risks faced by factory workers. Commercial self-help was still in its infancy. The discriminatory poor relief and the slowly spreading church-based work of charity fought merely the symptoms, and because of their underlying motivation alone—reflecting in part the authoritarian state and in part a mixed political-charitable interest—they were not able to attack the causes of the workers' misery at their core.

3. Reform Attempts

In the wake of the first large miners' strike in Lower Silesia (1869), Bismarck, as the Prussian Minister President, thought about "giving those new formations that are presently—following the elimination of the old, defunct commercial corporations—crystalizing out of the mass that is now in flux, once again a

[4] A comprehensive account of the development of mining law in the nineteenth century is given by Winkler (1979); on social protection in mining law see Thielmann (1960), Lingnau (1965).

[5] "Preußisches Gesetz betr. die Vereinigung der Berg-, Hütten-, Salinen- und Aufbereitungs-Arbeiter in Knappschaften, für den ganzen Umfang der Monarchie, v. 10. April 1854," PrGS, 139.

[6] As already in *Drucksache des Reichstags des Norddeutschen Bundes 1869*, No. 132 d, which led to the "Reichshaftpflichtgesetz" of June 7, 1871. The bill was presented again in 1878 (*Reichstags-drucksache 1878*, No. 9) and debated on February 27, 1879. A year later, Stumm once again requested a response from the government (*Reichstagsdrucksache 1880*, No. 17).

corporative form, to the extent possible, and place them into a reciprocal exchange with corresponding organs of the state."[7] This was aimed at reviving the old system of cooperatives, which was now intended as an entity representing equally employers and employees. It was to be tied as closely as possible to the state, for example, through state factory inspectors. This approach was not only thwarted by the Franco-Prussian War of 1870, but it also encountered resistance at home.[8]

Still, the issue was pondered further in spite of the founding of the Reich. There were discussions about measures against the Socialist "International" and about improving the condition of the workers. Bismarck was hoping that "with the proper intervention by the state it will be possible at this time to reconcile the majority of the workers with the existing order of the state, and to bring the interests of workers and employers once again into harmony."[9] But there was disagreement and controversy over how to get there. While some, like Bismarck's advisor Hermann Wagener, opted for vigorous state intervention, others sought to limit state measures to the absolute minimum in order to stimulate the self-organization and self-help of the working class (Th. Lohmann) (Rothfels 1927; Machtan 1995). But at least a consensus emerged about a long catalog of urgent issues.[10] In November 1872, Prussia and Austria talked about their positions at a conference. But the *Kulturkampf* soon overshadowed the constructive elements of social policy, especially since Bismarck believed that he could detect the "collaboration of Jesuit and Socialist agitation."[11] With that, Bismarck could not hope for the Center Party as his allies. Moreover, the repressive forces in penal and commercial law, labor law, the law of assembly and association vis-à-vis the growing social democratic movement led to a further alienation of the working class.

After the outbreak of the economic crisis of 1873, the doubts about economic liberalism, the so-called Manchester Theory, grew stronger. The "state" once again moved into the center. It was to intervene preemptively, on behalf of both the affected sectors of industry and the workers, to prevent social unrest. The "state Socialist" Hermann Wagener now pushed for a "genuine solution to the social question."[12] As he saw it, the state should seize the leadership in economic and social policy and not relinquish the field to big capital.[13] State intervention, long known and practiced in Germany in any case, no longer seemed out of the question, but the forms it would take were still unclear. There were discussions about creating

---

[7] Born et al. (1993–1997). Quellensammlung zur Geschichte der Deutschen Sozialpolitik 1867 bis 1914, 18 volumes. Quote from vol. 1, p. 182. An extensive review is by Ritter (1997).

[8] Officials within the Prussian Ministry of Trade were concerned about competition between the commercial cooperatives and the existing aid funds. See the verdict by the Minister of Trade v. Itzenplitz on April 2, 1870, in *Quellensammlung Sozialpolitik*, vol. I, 1, pp. 188–197.

[9] Bismarck to Itzenplitz, November 17, 1871, *Quellensammlung Sozialpolitik*, vol. I, 1, p. 249f.

[10] "Denkschrift Stüve," *Quellensammlung Sozialpolitik*, vol. I, 1, pp. 253–256.

[11] Decree by Bismarck dated January 27. 1873, *Quellensammlung Sozialpolitik*, vol. I, 1, p. 436.

[12] "Denkschrift Wagener v. 31 Juli 1873," *Quellensammlung Sozialpolitik*, vol. I, 1, pp. 457ff.

[13] "Denkschrift Wagener v. 1. November 1875," *Quellensammlung Sozialpolitik*, vol. I, 1, pp. 465ff.

jobs through state contracts, the intensification of communal building activities, and protective tariffs, on the one hand, and through a fundamentally new, "positive" social policy, on the other. Although the latter was only beginning to emerge in rough outline, it became increasingly urgent as mass job cuts were exacerbating the situation of the workers (Spree 1978).

Bismarck exploited the two attempts on the life of Emperor Wilhelm I in May and June of 1878 in truly Machiavellian fashion to immediately step up the repression of the social democratic movement, though he simultaneously activated the idea that these measures had to be supplemented in a "positive" way. The Geheime Regierungsrat Robert Bosse articulated this idea,[14] and via the Prussian government it made it into the center of the deliberations, which already revolved around a new economic, agricultural, and social policy. Yet a new political program became feasible only within a new constellation of the political parties, especially through the incorporation of the Center Party.

Essential driving forces behind the new direction came from the sectors of the economy that were suffering. In opposition to the free-trade camp, a protective tariff was demanded, which was regarded as a temporary aid during the start-up phase, until national industry was strong enough to stand up to the competition of global trade. Advocates believed that the country would simply have to put up with the losses in the export economy. Bismarck, who now also took over the Prussian Ministry of Trade, was charting a course of "moderate, sensible state socialism,"[15] specifically for old-age and disability provision of the working class. He believed that the monopoly on tobacco was suitable as a source of financing.

Objections from the liberals came immediately: by opening himself up to state socialism, they charged, he was preparing the way for Socialism—his talks with Lassalle were brought to mind. He was creating a "centralistic state bureaucracy," a "state insurance juggernaut," and a "system of state pension" for do-nothings. All that seemed antiliberal, patriarchal, and incompatible with the principles of progress and freedom. Moreover, critics argued that the financing was unsound and that the risks were not manageable in actuarial terms.

The latter point was certainly true from the private-sector perspective. However, if one pursued a cooperative solution that administered the risks of sickness, accident, and old age separately, incorporated the affected groups of workers gradually, raised benefits carefully, and worked with state subsidied, as Albert Schäffle proposed,[16] the enterprise did seem feasible. Thus, industry, as well, pushed for the introduction of compulsory old-age and disability insurance for all factory workers, "on the model of the miners' associations."[17]

---

[14] *Quellensammlung Sozialpolitik*, vol. I, 1, p. 504.

[15] *Quellensammlung Sozialpolitik*, vol. I, 1, p. 598.

[16] *Quellensammlung Sozialpolitik*, vol. I, 1, p. 676.

[17] Interpellations by Freiherr v. Stumm-Halberg, September 11, 1878, and February 12, 1879. On this see Hellwig (1936, pp. 185ff.).

A better solution to the stagnating system of aid funds also seemed increasingly important. The transformation of the older aid funds into "enrolled aid funds" was not really progressing. Evidently it was more than local communities could handle if the local industrialist did not favor this solution. Moreover, the communities of solidarity were too small and thus vulnerable to risk. Finally, the Reich Liability Law of 1871, with its obsolete focus on personal "fault," had not stood the test of time. In the case of industry-typical accidents, jurists and social politicians therefore advocated the principle of "liability," until the breakthrough to the modern principle of strict liability around 1880 (Esser 1969; Barta 1984). In 1880, Bismarck, after reading a "well-written memorandum from Kommerzienrath Baare in Bochum," stated that one would have to take the path of an "insurance", indeed one would have to "arrive at the proposal of a Reich or state insurance."[18] In that sense it is accurate to see the real beginning of social legislation not in the Anti-Socialist Law (October 21, 1878) or in the Emperor's Message (November 17, 1881), but in the problems with cases of harm in industry that had been articulated since 1868.[19]

4. Bismarck's Social Insurance

a) The Political Background

It was thus the interaction of various factors from social, economic, and political-institutional history that made Germany the pioneer in state-initiated and state-guaranteed social insurance. Heavy and textile industries, the agrarian world, the workers' movement, the churches, scholarship, and—above all—the ministerial bureaucracy in Prussia and the Empire had been influencing one another since the 1860s, and against the backdrop of changing party constellations they created the climate in which the decision to seek a "large," primarily state-determined solution could arise. As time has passed, scholarship has described this interaction in ever greater detail.[20] A large edition of documents added a wealth of new information in recent years.[21] All this had made it a good deal easier to interpret these events, as the picture we have of them has become sharper and many a legend has been exploded. Still, the interpretation depends crucially on the questions that are asked. The hypothesis shapes the perception, just as conversely, fundamental a priori attitudes influence the articulation of hypotheses. Much depends on whether one sees Bismarck's social legislation as a clever political maneuver against the socio-revolutionary workers'

[18] Stürmer (1978, p. 169f.). Bismarck was referring to Baare (1880). On Baare see Däbritz (1953).

[19] *Quellensammlung Sozialpolitik*, vol. I, 2 (1993), p. XXI.

[20] Craemer (1940), Vogel (1951), Ritter (1983, 1998b), Mommsen (1993, pp. 624–665), Wehler (1995, pp. 907–915).

[21] See also *Quellensammlung Sozialpolitik*.

movement, or as an expression of welfare state, Christian paternalism, or whether one sees it as an element of the "inner founding of the Reich," a historically "necessary" transition to "organized capitalism" and thus a mutual supportive action on the part of capitalism and constitutional monarchy. It is also crucial what weight is accorded the social and economic conditions and interests, the creative power of the ministerial bureaucracy and the party apparatuses, and, finally, the dominant statesman of the age, Bismarck—provided this kind of "weighting" is methodologically articulated instead of being implicitly packaged within value judgments.

b) "Idea" and Motive

"Bismarck's workers' insurance" combined very heterogeneous motivations and driving forces, something that is quite evident from the laws themselves. Yet the laws were always conceived of as a single entity, as expressed by the Emperor's Message of 1881. To be sure, the genesis of this bundle of laws[22] shows many obstacles and stoppages, specifically on accident insurance, and the original intentions of Bismarck, but also of Lohmann, were in the end not attained. Still, after initial uncertainties, it was a project that was based on a stabilizing "idea," but it did not rule out a variety of secondary purposes. The idea that it was imperative, in the wake of two attempts on the life of Wilhelm I in 1878, to supplement the intensified repression of the party of the workers' movement with something "positive," for example, with a reform of the commercial code, the system of aid funds, and protection against occupational accidents, appeared from the fall of 1878 and gradually grew stronger. In the spring of 1879, Bismarck himself was finally determined to take this path. What followed were planned campaigns against free trade and the Progressive Party. In 1880, Bismarck, using the accusatory word of his political opponents, argued in favor of a "moderate, reasonable state socialism."[23] The shrugged off warnings from the liberal side against too much state influence; on the contrary: he was precisely interested in the influence of the state. He wished to demonstrate that the repressive state, which he did not want to yield even an inch, was perfectly compatible with controlled "state socialism." That is why, unlike Theodor Lohmann, he argued against too much self-help and self-participation. What he envisioned was the worker as a materially secure "small state pensioner." He would have preferred to do away entirely with contributions from the workers.

The project was conceived as "the completion of the laws to protect against the social-democratic strivings,"[24] and as the Imperial Message of November 17, 1881, put it, it was borne by the conviction "that the healing of the social harms will have

[22] Peters (1978), Rückert (1990), Köhler (1990).

[23] *Quellensammlung Sozialpolitik*, vol. I, 1, p. 598.

[24] Opening speech in the Reichstag, 4th legislative period, IV. Session 1881.

to be sought not exclusively through the repression of social-democratic excesses, but equally so through the positive promotion of the welfare of the workers."[25] The basic idea of removing from the state the odium of class rule and blunting socio-revolutionary efforts by providing material security characterized the bundle of laws that was passed between 1883 and 1889. In that regard, social insurance was a "response" in several directions. It reacted to the domestic political pressure exerted by the social-democratic movement through the ballot box and strikes, but also to the needs of industry, which wanted a predictable solution that was shaped with input from its organizations. It drew the lesson from the experiences with the fragmented system of sickness funds, the visible shortcomings of accident protection, and the lack of old-age and disability insurance for industrial workers. The feeling of entering unknown territory is palpable among all the actors. Still, official government rhetoric emphasized the traditional, the connection between the laws and Christianity, which commanded positive help for the weak and the needy, and with the previous system of poor relief—indeed, it was said "the measures that can be taken to improve the state of the unpropertied class are, in truth, merely a further development of the idea underlying the state system of poor relief."[26] However, this statement conceals the fundamental innovations that had now been introduced: a shift from the old system of poor relief to future pension rights backed by a legal entitlement, from voluntariness to compulsory participation, from the communal to the Reich level. Very different from before, the "state" now became the focus—or more precisely: the social monarchy in the sense of Lorenz von Stein (Blasius 1971; Forsthoff 1972, pp. 549ff.; Saile 1958). As a neutral power, this monarchy was supposed to smooth out class differences, to take a step toward modernity in order to preserve itself. In this appeal, "monarchy" was a metaphor and its political neutrality a fiction; the king was to take the initiative and set a worker-friendly development in motion. That view was in line with the constitutional situation. The government depended on the king, not on the political powers in parliament. In that regard, Lorenz von Stein, who wanted to achieve social progress, was aiming in the right direction. Of course, in real political terms the monarchy was neither neutral nor independent. Within the spectrum of party politics, it was oriented toward a slice ranging from the old-Prussian Conservatives to the National Liberals.

The Social Democrats were completely familiar with this perspective, which is why they were also suspicious of this policy. Bismarck's intent of driving a wedge between the social democrats and the workers was obvious. The policy of repression had not been abandoned, it had not even been moderated. The unions were not recognized and the instruments of civil and criminal law to contain labor struggles continued to be used. The fact that the workers' movement was right in seeing in

---

[25] Tennstedt (1981, pp. 663–710). The original printing of the draft and the message in *ZSR* (1981): 711–728, 730–735. See also Kafka's literary treatment in Kafka (1961). On Kafka as a jurist of social insurance law see Kafka (1984).

[26] "Amtliche Begründung zum 1. Entwurf eines Unfallversicherungsgesetzes 1881," *Reichstagsdrucksachen* 1882, p. 31.

Bismarck, who had never made a secret of his deep aversion to the political and social emancipation "from below," not a true ally, but a Machiavellian arch-conservative, made them look at this entire endeavor with suspicion. Since its intent was to divide the working class and the political party, workers' insurance remained, at least during the process that gave rise to it, an undertaking of the ruling class.

The bourgeois camp became increasingly receptive to reformist ideas that affirmed the capitalist economic system, but wanted to cushion its negative social consequences through state interventionism. These ideas had to defend themselves against both dogmatic Liberalism and the still predominantly Marxist social democratic movement, and in 1872 they created a widely regarded platform for themselves in the *Verein für Socialpolitik* [Association for Social Policy] (Gustav Schmoller, Lujo Brentano, Adolph Wagner, Wilhelm Roscher, Albert Schäffle, and others) (Töpfer 1970; Lindenlaub 1967). In 1874 the *Verein* published expert opinions and the resolution "On old-age and disability funds for workers," 1879 saw the publication of Brentano's work "Die Arbeiterversicherung gemäß der heutigen Wirschaftsordnung" ["Old-age insurance in line with the economic system today"], and in 1881 came his piece that was sharply opposed to Bismarck, "Der Arbeiter-Versicherungszwang. Seine Voraussetzungen und seine Folgen" (Berlin, 1881). The topics discussed by the *Verein* in the first decade (1872–1882) and its connections to members of the legislature[27] show how general the conviction had become that unfettered economic liberalism was a threat to the system by provoking revolutionary pressure from below.

There was an unavoidable blending of motivations (Born 1960). A social ethos grounded in the role of the territorial ruler and in Christianity, the visible failures in the police suppression of the social democratic movement, and the promise of "positive" social legislation that Bismarck gave when the anti-Socialist laws were enacted in 1878, the switch of the formerly free-market farmers and their parliamentarians to a policy of protective tariffs (1879), finally, the publications of the liberal press, the churches, and the economists mentioned above—all of this, taken together, made possible the bundle of insurance laws that constitute, alongside the Civil Code, the most important legislative achievement of these years.

The appeals to the Reichstag to come together and pass "positive" social legislation extends from the King's Speech in February 1879,[28] to the King's Speech in February 1881,[29] to the actual Imperial Message on November 17, 1881. The latter, carefully edited by Bismarck (Tennstedt 1981, pp. 663–710), reiterated once again the basic idea that "the healing of the social harms will have to be sought not exclusively through the repression of social-democratic excesses, but equally so through the positive promotion of the welfare of the workers. We regard

[27] Töpfer, "Verhandlungen," 158ff. The economist Albert Schäffle was directly involved in the social insurance legislation.

[28] *Stenographischer Bericht Reichstag 4. Legislaturperiode*, 2. Session 1979, vol. 1, pp. 1–3.

[29] *Quellensammlung Sozialpolitik*, I, 2, p. 550.

it as out imperial duty to once more recommend this task warmly to the Reichstag." The legislative program was now: revising the draft of March 8, 1881, for accident insurance and the bill about the "consistent organization of the commercial system of sickness funds." "But also those," the text continued, "who become unfit to work through age or disability have a justified claim against the whole for a higher degree of state care than could be provided them until now." This open formula was supposed to make it possible to pursue various options, though the text went on to single out among them the unification of the "real powers" of national life "in the form of corporative cooperatives under state protection and promotion" as the goal. This was a reassuring signal for those who had previously spoken out against a purely "state-socialist" direction.

c) The Constitutional Situation and the Social Question

The constitutional dimensions of what transpired are impossible to miss. National and social questions clashed in a half-finished state structure[30] and necessitated an intensive linkage of domestic and foreign policy. Observers rightly pointed out that the "incompleteness and uncertainty, the ongoing problems of the new Reich, the dangers it faced at home and abroad" (Rothfels 1962: 166) led to the typically Bismarckian "policy of external risk, and the creation of internal alliances of heterogenous forces internally through the ostracism of a minority" (Hofmann 1977/1986, pp. 77ff.). In spite of the broad support of the middle class for the establishment of the Reich and the legitimacy it conveyed, Bismarck always remained conscious of the fragility of the entity that was created in 1871. In the end, he left unresolved the fundamental problems of the German Reich, which had become apparent in 1878 in concentrated form: "the internal dynamic of the unfinished nation state, the discrepancy between economic-political modernization and a lack of democratization, and the strain on European politics that flowed from Germany's role as a great power" (Stürmer 1978, p. 45f.; Stürmer 1983).

This attempt at bringing together the "social monarchy" in the sense of Lorenz von Stein (Stolleis 1990) with the new interventionist forces from industry, church-based social work, and the reformist middle class, while at the same time preserving the idea of corporative self-help, was quite a balancing act. It demanded a lot from everyone involved: the Liberals had to give up their cherished basic principles, the economy had to accept being tied into and co-financing a state-dominated system of social protection, and the Center Party had to cooperate with a state which had just now relented in the *Kulturkampf*. Concessions also had to be made by champions of Christian-motivated corporative self-help, like Theodor Lohmann, or advocates of

---

[30] See Rodbertus (1880, p. 84) who stated that the Paris Commune was "a providential warning that the German state is called upon to address also the social question after it has solved the national one."

the idea of a corporative organization of the economy, like Albert Schäffle. In the end, nobody was quite happy; indeed, Bismarck himself regarded the result as a "parliamentarian and privy-councilor changeling" disfigured by the bureaucracy. It was no coincidence, Lothat Gall concluded, "that Bismarck, in his memoirs, did not say one word about this complex of laws, which was completed in 1889 with passage of old-age and disability insurance, and which represented in substance the most important legislative accomplishment of the last decade of his term in office" (Gall 1980, p. 648).

In spite of the verdict that social insurance was a failure because it did not achieve Bismarck's goal, the political integration of the working class, social insurance has unquestionably become a monumental achievement (Zacher 1979; Köhler and Zacher 1981). The path that was embarked upon at that time has held up for a long time. The institutions erected by it and thanks to it have survived two World Wars and two periods of ruinous inflation. Over the past century the effects it triggered, the medicalization of society along with an extension of the average life expectancy by around a generation, the drastic cut in industrial accidents through the work of the occupational cooperatives, finally, the securing of the greatly extended old age of broad segments of the population, have taken deep roots in the social structures. Without a doubt: a state-guaranteed compulsory insurance of dependent workers, whose assets are administered separately from the state budget, was obviously the appropriate response to the typical side-effects of the Industrial Revolution as they manifested themselves in Germany from the middle of the nineteenth century. The forms of labor had an enormous effect on social structures (Hahn 1998). The bonds and forms of support typical of agrarian societies—the family, neighbors, the village community—eroded, just as the independent protections of the trades (guilds, "aid funds") proved too weak and fragmented. Moreover, the help that the entire society mustered, especially through the churches, was based too much on voluntariness and good sentiments to be sufficiently effective in and resistant to crisis. Finally, the system of state poor relief that was tied to the local communities and rural districts (*Landkreise*) was not suitable for solving the great problem of the "social question." In that sense, the social insurance created between 1881 and 1889, for all its diversity in detail, was a uniform response to a socio-political challenge.

d) Modernity and Traditionalism

By European standards, that response was especially early. That is surprising, since Germany is considered a "latecomer nation" [*verspätete Nation*] (Plessner 1969) when it comes to industrialization and national unity. But that seeming contradiction dissolves if one considers that this step into modernity could succeed only because elements of pre-liberal statehood were better preserved in Germany than elsewhere. Here, solicitous coercion, on the one hand, and self-organization, on the other, came together in a way that is also evident in Bismarck's system of government itself. This leads us back to the deeper roots of Prusso-German history.

Modern scholarship on the "older state and administrative doctrine" (Maier 1986; Härter 1993) of the Ancien Régime has shown how intensively the traditions of the princely state articulated there had been carried over beyond the French Revolution well into the nineteenth century. The pronounced Christian notion of office and service, the expectation toward authority that it would ensure the realization of "happiness" and "good order," the penchant, finally, to reform the administrative apparatus rather than overthrow the state—all this did not really change even in the age of liberalism. If we look at the history of public law, we can see, also after the transition to the nineteenth century, the dominance of the administrative theorist over the state theorist, the continuation of "*Policeywissenschaft*" [science of public policy] as part of legal education, and the combination—so typical of Germany—of state administration and self-governance, federal structures, and a pronounced sense of social responsibility.

To be sure, this current of tradition was influenced by the Enlightenment and the constitutional movement after 1818, but it retained its characteristic in so far as the rigid reduction of the state's tasks to "security and order" was not fully accepted in theory, let alone practiced. *Policey* was slowly subjected to the constraints of the *Rechtsstaat* [state under the rule of law], but until the middle of the century it remained comprehensively in charge of "welfare," it preserved the link with politics and the general sciences of the state, and it showed a particular openness to social questions, at least until the so-called Gerber-Laband Positivism carried the day (Scheuner 1977). In the work of Lorenz von Stein and his conception of the "social monarchy," this way of thinking carried on even to the beginning of the twentieth century, specifically in Austria (Forsthoff 1972; Schnur 1978).

In nineteenth-century national economics, as well, the lines of connection to eighteenth-century thinking were never fully severed (Winkel 1977). To be sure, the ideas of Adam Smith were received in the first two decades of the nineteenth century (Chr. J. Kraus, G. Sartorius, A. F. Lueder, G. Hufeland, J. F. E. Lotz, K. H. Rau), and Liberalism was considered the "dominant doctrine." But everywhere one could see state-economic modifications of Smith's position, modifications that sought to do justice to tradition, to the conditions created by a patchwork of small states, and to the unchanged, strong role of the state in economic life. Even in the liberal, Prussian-led *Zollverein* [Customs Union], the champions of free trade (Deutscher Freihandelsverein 1847, Kongreß Deutscher Volkswirte 1857) were never completely triumphant (Hentschel 1975). Practitioners, even those who can be considered Smithians, the likes of P. Ch. Beuth in Prussia, engaged in an intensive promotion of industry (Henderson 1958; Ritter 1961; Mieck 1965; Fischer 1962). The theory and practice of protective tariffs remained alive and well. The originally Romantic criticism of enlightened Liberalism culminated in part in theological blueprints (A. Müller, F. X. v. Baader), but in part it was also translated, supported by the idea of the nation state, into a national economic program that sought to combine free trade, the promotion of industry, and economic unity (F. List). Even in the years from 1860 to 1873, at the height of Liberalism, we find notions of the "common weal," and the representative of the Historical School of Economics (W. G. F. Roscher, K. G. A. Knies, G. v. Schmoller) underscored the importance of state intervention in the sense of mercantilism.

Finally the Socialist literature that emerged on a broad front after 1848 offers a substantial corrective to the notion that Liberalism "ruled" nineteenth-century economics. Especially the state socialists and the champions of the idea of the "social monarchy"—such varied thinkers as Johann Karl Rodbertus-Jagetzow, Victor Aimé Huber, Hermann Wagener, Ferdinand Lassalle, Lorenz von Stein, Albert Schäffle, and others—formed an important counterweight. They managed to get social legislation off the ground, indirectly via the state-socialist wing of the Social Democratic movement, and directly via the *Verein für Socialpolitik* and the bureaucracy.

This continuity is meant when observers speak of Germany's special "state-economic tradition."[31] It appears in the historical-philosophical guise of the Historical School, of Right-wing and Left-wing Hegelians, and as the Christian philosophy of Stahl and Gerlach. Always, the state and not society retains the final responsibility for economic life and social conditions. The state becomes (secularized) "God on earth," the "greatest moral institution for the education of mankind" (G. v. Schmoller), the height of cultural evolution. It is not only the guarantor of security or the distributor of material benefits, but also a Christian-moral state. In the face of these traditions, Bismarck's embrace of "state socialism," which seems so sudden and unexpected at first glance, contains clear elements of a return to principles that had by no means been forgotten.

e) The Decision in Favor of Compulsion

The orientation toward the state that is typical of the German tradition, moderated and rendered bearable through the ethical bonds of its roots in Christianity or transcendental philosophy, suggest the call for the "state" in situations of crisis. Under the conditions of the constitutional monarch, "state" referred primarily to the monarchy—"if it could only decide to become a social monarchy" (Lassalle).[32] The state or monarchy should answer their social calling, they should above all impose limits on unfettered private autonomy. The industrialist Harkort wrote in 1844: "[T] he state must intervene to prevent further ruination, so that the stream of pauperism, growing incessantly, does not disastrously deluge the blessed pastures of the fatherland... We demand of the state that it not only command, but also step in to help and promote" (Schraepler 1964, p. 87f.). Four decades later it sounded like

[31] Treue (1970, p. 529).

[32] Letter of February 24, 1864 to Victor Aimé Huber, in Mayer (1911, p. 192).

an echo when Bismarck declared: "The state must take the matter into its hands."[33] This principle was accepted by line that stretched from the Conservatives to the Lassallians, within the bureaucracy (stripped of its liberal top echelons), and in broad segments of the middle class, while orthodox Liberals, the revolutionary wing of the Social Democrats, large entrepreneurs, and segments of the Center Party were opposed for varied reasons of their own.

Still open was the question of whether this appeal to the state would invariably lead to compulsory insurance. The debate that was carried on reveals the dilemma of the Liberals: to affirm the purpose of social protection while rejecting the compulsion necessary for achieving it. Characteristically enough, no consensus on this point was possible also within the *Verein für Socialpolitik* (Lindenlaub 1967, vol. 1, pp. 85ff.). After the issue of compulsion had already been contested over the factory inspection law (§139f. GewO),[34] National Liberals spoke once again of "state omnipotence" and "state bureaucratism" (von Treitschke 1874, pp. 67–110, 248–301), and they pointed to the contradiction between a liberal commercial order and compulsory protection (Brentano 1881); indeed, they saw Bismarck and the ministerial bureaucracy as "already mired in Socialism up to their shoulders."[35] As the Liberal Hirsch put it: "The compulsory fund is the direct path to Communism" (Hirsch 1875, pp. 11, 38).

Bismarck had early on given this slogan a positive turn: "Many of the measures we have taken are socialist, and as it is, the state in our Reich will have to get used to a little more Socialism."[36] He reminded his audience that "the socialist element is nothing new, and the state cannot exist without a certain Socialism,"[37] and of the everyday reality and positive effects of compulsion in the past, as with the liberation of the peasants, in poor relief, and in compulsory school attendance. He sought historical points of connection in Frederich the Great's policy of protective tariffs and to Freiherr von Stein. State compulsion seemed to be the historically more lasting and more successful political instrument.[38] At the *Verein für Socialpolitik* he received backing from Albert Schäffle with the likewise historical reference to the

---

[33] Rothfels (1925, p. 398); Bismarck in the Reichstag on March 15, 1884: "Does the state have the obligation to care for its helpless citizens, or does it not? I assert that it does have this obligation, and not just the Christian state, as I ventured to suggest once with the words 'practical Christianity,' but every state in and of itself."

[34] In this case, Bismarck, contrary to his support for compulsion when it came to social insurance, opposed compulsion. Theodor Lohmann, meanwhile, who otherwise tended to reject compulsion, was in favor based on the experiences to date, and his position carried the day in the government draft of 1878 and the final bill.

[35] Ludwig Bamberger in the Reichstag on May 12, 1884, *Verhandlungen Reichstag*, vol. 75, p. 546.

[36] Bismarck in the Reichstag on June 12, 1882; see also his Basic Speech on Socialism on March 15, 1884, *Verhandlungen Reichstag*, vol. 75, pp. 72ff.

[37] Bismarck in the Reichstag on March 15, 1884, *Verhandlungen Reichstag*, vol. 75, pp. 72ff.

[38] Bismarck in the Reichstag on June 14, 1882, *Stenographischer Bericht 5. Legislaturperiode II. Session*, 437.

abolition of feudal dues on the land. Compulsion (to preserve liberty), he argued, was "not a new and unheard-of intervention of public law;" for "voluntariness alone is a rope by which especially the masses in need of help are not able to pull themselves out of the morass of economic misery" (Schäffle 1884, pp. 10, 112). The new compulsion could thus be situated within the traditional dialectic of subordination and protection, of freedom vs. security. Against a weakly rooted Liberalism, the fundamental willingness of conservative thinking to overlay the freedom of the contract with bonds of ethics and public law remained the predominant tendency.

When it came to sickness insurance, the existing organizational substructure was complemented with the principle of compulsion, and agreement extended well into the liberal camp, since the previous voluntariness had quite clearly proved inadequate.[39] On accident insurance it was the very issue of compulsion that led to a break between the rather liberal Lohmann and Bismarck, who was pursing a different, vague idea, namely to develop the commercial occupational cooperatives into a "parliament" organized by estates to take the place of the Reichstag that was a thorn in his side. However serious one might judge this idea to have been, it is evident that the issue of compulsion, specifically, remained controversial within the bureaucracy. The "state socialists" and Bismarck opted for compulsion, while the opposing party would go only as far as "indirect compulsion." The front lines were similarly drawn within the Reichstag. That is also why the principle of compulsion carried the day on pension insurance with a slim majority, which was created only by splitting up the Center Party.

To explain the eventual triumph of the principle of compulsion, it is not enough to point to the bad experiences with voluntariness: for if voluntariness had truly been an incontrovertible tenet of faith, there would no doubt have been a greater effort to come up with positive incentives to get workers to enroll in the insurance. But voluntariness was *not* such a tenet. The liberal era had lasted barely more than a decade in Germany. Liberalism was not the real political force, especially since it was internally divided. The Prussian civil service, the army, the land-owning nobility, and the church were nearly all conservative through-and-through. That meant, however, that a willingness to engage in social reform was more widespread among them than among the economic liberals (Schmoller 1874, p. 342). What flowed together here were the welfare-state tradition of the eighteenth century, the Lutheran ethic of service, and a mistrust that existed among the noble leadership strata toward the new powers of industrial capitalism. The liberal Ludwig Bamberger could thus declare in the Reichstag, with an undertone of resignation: "[I]f this idea was feasible anywhere in the world, it would be Germany. What is called the social monarchy, the connection between a strong sovereign power – resting on a strong army – and socialist view and endeavors, if it were feasible anywhere in the world, that much I admit, it would be in Germany."[40]

[39] This is how Theodor Lohmann justified the draft of the sickness insurance bill. See Rothfels (1927, p. 54).

[40] Reichstag, *Protokolle*, 70th session on May 18, 1889, 1839.

f) Bureaucracy and Parties

One of the classic analyses of the process that gave birth to social insurance concluded that the ministerial bureaucracy, influenced in many ways by science, could "be seen, on the whole, as the real bearer of the social legislation" (Vogel 1951). It is in fact true that it functioned not only as the coordinating link for the various impulses coming from Bismarck, industry and its new organizations, and the parties; rather, it was substantially involved itself, for example, through the likes of Hermann Wagener, Robert Bosse, and Theodor Lohmann. As it was, the role of the ministerial bureaucracy was particularly important within the constitutional monarchy, because it knew it had the backing of the "monarchical principle" and was independent of parliament. Since the eighteenth century, Prussia, and thus also the Reich that was so closely intertwined with it, was in a special sense an "administrative state;" it was governable and capable of integration only thanks to its excellent, vaunted administration. The rebuilding of the country after the catastrophe of 1806 took place through administrative reforms "from above." Between 1815 and 1848, the administration was seen as a kind of replacement for a constitution. And now, after the founding of the Reich, specific conditions were added that strengthened the self-confidence of the growing Reich administration (Morsey 1957). Bismarcks's repeated attempts to put pressure on the Reichstag and the Bundesrat, for example with respect to the representation law [*Stellvertretergesetz*], protective tariffs, and the anti-Socialist laws (Binder 1971), indirectly boosted the power of the ministerial bureaucracy. By seeing itself as the instrument of the monarchy, it partook in the latter's claim of being above the parties. What was "irreconciled" in parliament, it could attempt to bring together again in a "social policy of reconciliation" (Th. Lohmann).

Even if the parties (like the Center Party), the Prussian conservatives, the *Verein für Socialpolitik*, and other groups had provided significant stimuli, on the whole it remains true to say: The bearer of social reforms in their entirety was—as in Prussia at the beginning of the nineteenth century—the upper civil service (Treue 1970, p. 515), but a civil service that was directed rather forcefully in a new direction by Bismarck. At first the Prussian Ministry of Trade was dominant, later the Reich Office of the Interior.

The importance that the ministerial officials had in this area can be seen indirectly also in the influence exerted by industry and private insurance companies, for it was precisely the officials that provided a successful point of access, and not the Reichstag. And so the industrialist Louis Baare sketched the basic outlines of the accident insurance law in an 1880 memorandum, Tonio Bödiker, the first president of the Reich Insurance Office, continued his career with Siemens & Halske, and the shape of pension insurance in the Prussian *Volkswirtschaftsrat* [National Economic Council] was substantially influenced by Johann Friedrich Jencke, the Director General at Krupp and expert on social policy in the Central Association of German Industrialists (Althoff 1940, p. 181). To be sure, many lines of connection also ran between the parties in the Reichstag and the bureaucracy.

That is true above all for the Conservatives, the Christian Socialis under Stoecker, the conservative wing of the *Verein für Socialpolitik* (A. Wagner, G. v. Schmoller, A. Schäffle, G. Schönberg) and the variant of "state Socialism" advocated there.[41] It also holds—though with qualifications—for the National Liberals and the Center Party. Early and independent impulses for social policy came especially from the Center Party, and in modified form they were able to become part of Bismarck's body of laws.[42] The accident insurance law, for example, came about as a clerical-conservative compromise (Ritter 1997, p. 700). The Social Democrats, however, remained decidedly opposed, to the extent that at the time the current around Bebel and Liebknecht was dominant, and not the reformist group (Auer, Grillenberger) that become stronger only later. To them, State Socialism was the attempt by the bourgeoisie to do what Lassalle had counseled, namely, "to open the valves in time to preempt an explosion." The obvious intent was to separate the working class from its political leadership. The SPD's resolution on State Socialism in 1892 was still very firm: "Social Democracy is by its nature revolutionary, State Socialism is conservative. Social Democracy and State Socialism are irreconcilable opposites" (Domann 1974; Martiny 1976). The left Liberals, led by Richter and Bamberger, acted out of different motivations but ended up taking the same oppositional stance (Kelsch 1933; Mueller 1952).

Far more important in this regard than the direct contacts between the bureaucracy and the parties was probably the fact that the ministerial bureaucracy tailored its draft bills ahead of time to the positions of the parties to give them a chance of passage. The parties were the constitutional eye of the needle on social legislation, and they made intensive use of that function, especially on accident insurance. The Center Party had a key role in the debate over self-administration and state subsidy. This relativizes the claim about the dominance of the bureaucracy: it did not remain unaffected itself, since Bismarck removed its most important liberal leaders, and it was open in various directions to influence from the organizations of industrial entrepreneurs, the Verein für Socialpolitik, and the parties. But the heart of the observation that the bureaucracy played a leading role remains true, especially against the background of the traditionally important role of the administration in Germany and the theoretical and practical traditions reaching back to Federick the Great's Prussia and still in place in the nineteenth century.

---

[41] Rothfels (1935, p. 59): "Society, shaped by the state, and the framework of the state filled in by a well-structured social body, these are the basic ideas of so-called State Socialism." On Hermann Wagener see Saile (1958).

[42] See, for example, the proposal by Count v. Galen on March 19, 1877, *Reichstagsdrucksache* No. 74, 274, on worker protection (Sunday rest, protection of trades, factory worker protection, restrictions on youth and women's work, and so on), freedom of movement, and liability. See also Vogel (1951, pp. 58ff.). Moenning (1927), Eickhoff (1932), Reiss-Vaseck (1934), Quandt (1938), Bauer (1974).

g) Self-Administration

The real counterweight to the use of compulsion by way of public law in social insurance was to be the idea of self-administration. This was an effort to integrate a principle that had unparalleled success in the course of the nineteenth century. "Self-administration" signaled independence from the absolutist "state administration," democratic participation, and the autonomous organization of society (Stolleis 1990). The Historical School connected it to the memory of the "Germanic" principle of the free association of groups [*Genossenschaft*], and it elevated the opposition between centralized political power [*Herrschaft*] and *Genossenschaft* into a structural characteristic of history. The principle became accordingly important in the communal government after the Prussian City Code of 1808, in Humbold's university reform after 1810, in the reorganization of the trades after the abolition of guild constitutions, and in the Lutheran state churches, which already during the nineteenth century were emancipating themselves from the control of the church by the territorial ruler and gradually arriving at self-administration (Heffter 1969).

It therefore made sense to employ this central institution, which mediated between state and society, also for social insurance to anchor this new form of protection with those at whom it was directed, and to make them aware that they were administering their own "patriconium" with it. The Center Party and the Christian Socials were also open to this. At the same time, one could use it to ease the distrust of Liberalism against "State Socialism."

Bismarck's attitude toward self-administration was not very decisive. On the one hand, he was moved by the idea of integrating the working class, but already accident insurance set up self-administration only for the industrialists in the form of the "Occupational Cooperatives" [Berufsgenossenschaften]—at the suggestion of Schäffle and against Lohmann.[43] When it came to sickness insurance, the adoption of the strongly decentralized institutions of self-administration (1885: 17,511 funds) was motivated more by the idea of feasibility and the hope of winning the support of the Center Party, than by a fundamental commitment to self-administration. Additional impulses may have come from sensitivity to the liberal concern over "state omnipotence" and "bureaucratism," but also from a specifically Prussian tradition of Freiherr von Stein's idea of self-administration and from a conception of British "selfgovernment" as mediated by Rudolf von Gneist (von Gneist 1869; Hahn 1995). At any rate, through its position outside of the sovereign administration, the social administration retained the historical connection to organized social self-help.[44]

Of course, self-administration was part of an entirely different historical context at the end of the nineteenth century. The separation of state and society, which had

[43] Schäffle (1905, vol. 2, pp. 143ff.); Rothfels (1927, p. 57). On the limited participation by Schäffle overall see also Oncken (1906, p. 254f.).

[44] See Bieback (1976) on the organization of social insurance in the form of public law entities (sickness funds, occupational associations) and of public-law institutions with corporative elements (Pension Insurance Funds).

once been part of its very essence, was beginning to dissolve again with the move toward the interventionist state (Menger 1983). With Industrial Revolution and population growth, communal self-administration became once again dependent on state support, and in this way it got caught up in a process that hollowed out its competencies and finances, a process that would intensify into the "crisis of self-administration" in the 1930s (Köttgen 1931). Occupational self-administration also changed into a system of compulsory public-law associations with reduced autonomy and narrow legal parameters (Chambers of Trades, Industry, and Commerce, Chambers for the Healing Professions, Lawyers, and Notaries). The self-administration practiced there was more like a mixture of state administration (including the expertise of those who worked there) and the preservation of particular group interests. In a comparable way, the "self-administration" of social insurance has developed over time into a large bureaucracy removed from the insured, in which the decision-making spheres left to self-administration have become occupied by the associations of the parties to collective bargaining that emerged around the same time (Bogs 1973).

Already the contemporary verdict on self-administration within social insurance was not favorable, no doubt also because observers were comparing it, consciously or unconsciously, with other models of self-administration. The enlightened-liberal and simultaneously national pathos of the reformers of 1806 is something we look for in vain at the end of the nineteenth century. Workers were neither inclined nor able to assume in this idealized way the self-administration of their own material provision granted to them by the state, nor was Bismarck willing to convey the impression, by emphasizing self-administration too much, that the state no longer had anything to do with social insurance. The important thing was precisely the positive connection to the state. For that reason, self-administration in the sense of a genuine participation by the working class stood from the outset on weak ground, even if the self-administration in the sickness insurance gave the SPD the chance to survive in the face of the repressive anti-Socialist laws. To Bismarck's disappointment, the hoped-for integration effect did not happen, and it probably could not happen, since the idea of bridging the class differences through self-administration was not viable. In the emerging mass society, self-administration could no longer be created by a legislative act, unless the older traditions still existed and could be revived, as was the case with sickness insurance. The latter saw the emergence of the so-called "rule of Social Democracy in sickness insurance" (Möller 1908; Tennstedt 1976, p. 390; Tennstedt 1991).

h) State Subsidy

The basic idea of social insurance was thus to deal with the social question through statist solutions "from the top down," and in so doing bring about the integration of the working class into the new state. Along this line, Bismarck's advocacy of state subsidies for the accident and sickness insurance was only consistent. He wanted what he had seen in France: "state pensioners" who would, if push came to shove, vote for the continuation of their pension, that is, conservative. The workers, as Hermann Wagener had put it in an earlier memorandum to Bismarck, were to be "won over to the idea of the Reich and bound to it through the benefits of the Reich."

With equal consistency, Liberals and the Center Party fought against state subsidies as the core of the Bismarckian "State Socialism" and managed to get it dropped from accident insurance. The state subsidy for pension insurance became a symbol of the emerging interventionist state, in the eyes of the Center Party a "very dangerous piece of Communism" (F. Hitze), in the eyes of industry a "fatal gift [*Danaergeschenk*]," a "legal title for an excess of policy."[45] Lujo Brentano believed the interventionist state was bringing the "downfall of political liberty and the nation's civilized behavior," and eventually the "ruination of culture" (Brentano 1881, p. 108f.). What explains the intensity of the debate over the state subsidy—especially in the Reichstag debates of April 1–4, 1881, and March 13–15, 1884—is not only party-political differences, but also the realization that it would mean a significant loss of ground for Liberalism. The factual arguments—as laid out by Schäffle, for example—thus no longer took, not even the economic argument that the state subsidy lowered the social contributions of industry, which should have been in its interest.

In retrospect, one can say that Bismarck overestimated the integrative effect of a state subsidy as much as his opponents did its effect as a "pacemaker into state Socialism." The liberal middle class affirmed state help for the working class in principle, but it wanted to hold on to its own material and political position without any losses and at the same time prevent the power of the state from growing. The revolutionary wing of the workers' leadership was hostile to or at least suspicious of the "little material concessions" from the bourgeoisie (August Bebel, in Domann 1974, p. 120). Given its social structure, Prussian conservatism, which was pushing for a state solution to the social question, would hardly have been open to a Bonapartist pact with the working class against the bourgeoisie (Hofmann 1977/1986). Such plans were unrealistic; Bismarck, too, seems to have employed them more as a conceptual model and an instrument of blackmail.

5. Sickness, Accident, Disability

"Bismarck's social insurance," a label it rightly deserves in spite of the complexity of the process that produced it, came into being through three major laws in 1883, 1884, and 1889.[46] This process was a difficult one. Accident insurance, originally

[45] As said by the Association of German Millers in 1882, in Vogel (1951, p. 42).

[46] "Gesetz betr. die Krankenversicherung der Arbeiter v. 15. Juni 1883" (amended April 10, 1892, supplemented June 30, 1900); "Unfallversicherungsgesetz v. 4. Juli 1884" (expanded May 5, 1886, and July 13, 1887), and "Gesetz betr. Unfall- und Krankenversicherung der in land- und forstwirtschaftlichen Betrieben beschäftigten Personen v. 5. Mai 1886;" "Alters- und Invaliditätsversicherungsgesetz v. 22. Juni 1889" (amended July 13, 1899).

intended as the first law, ran into considerable parliamentary opposition.[47] As a result, sickness insurance, which comprehensively restructured the already existing system of funds, moved to the head of the line, and it retained that place also in the *Reichsversicherungsordnung* [Social Insurance Act] of 1911. Finally, disability and old-age insurance, which, like accident insurance, was venturing into uncharted territory, was particularly controversial; the real process of debate began on November 17, 1887, with a memorandum from the Reich Office of the Interior and ended with the final vote in the Reichstag on May 18, 1889 (Rückert 1990: margin numbers 8–24).

a) Sickness Insurance

The sickness insurance for workers,[48] enacted by law on June 15, 1883, was the culmination of a long prehistory and opened up a new—at the time still unforeseeable—development. In no other sector of social insurance did the tradition of cooperative self-help reach back as far as in the case of sickness insurance. The traditional "sickness, aid, and funeral funds" of the guilds, fraternities, unions, and miners' associations still existed, even if in modified form: the association of individuals that carried these funds had gradually dissolved into the industrial proletariat, while the external forms of the funds, with their cooperative structure and self-administration, continued (Höffner 1956). Though they had survived even the abolition of the guilds between 1806 and 1848, they were unable to cope with the problems of industrial society. They incorporated only a fraction of the workers, were unequally distributed regionally, and quickly exhausted their capacity. Membership numbers stagnated, the poorest were excluded from them, and voluntariness was not working. In Prussia in 1845, communities were given the initiative to compel journeymen and shortly thereafter also factory workers (1849) to join the funds, and to compel their employers to pay half of the contributions. However, the communities proved too weak to push through the funds over the opposition of factory owners. Even when lawmakers moved to the higher levels of district governments (1854), the fund system did not come together in a way that provided real geographic coverage. By 1874, only about 5 % of the population was insured in a fund. When the private funds that had sprung up by 1876 were given a semi-public status through the Law Regarding Registered Aid Funds, only about two million of eight million workers were insured, and the fund system was bewilderingly complex and not very effective, especially since the funds had not yet formed a union of solidarity with a corresponding balancing of risks (Zöllner 1981, p. 81).

---

[47] Tennstedt and Winter (1993), Tennstedt (1995). The entire process of discussion can now be retraced in the two volumes of *Quellensammlung Sozialpolitik*, Part 1, vol. 2 (1992), and Part 2, vol. 2.1 (1995).

[48] "Gesetz betr. die Krankenversicherung der Arbeiter v. 15. Juni 1883," *RGBl.*, pp. 73–105, went into effect on December 1, 1884.

It was clear that something had to be done: problems were growing, and the working class was becoming radicalized and politically organized. Sickness became a mass phenomenon of industrial society. The old causes of disease were joined by the factory with its stresses, poisons, and accidents. A poor diet and the infamous living conditions in working-class neighborhoods were breeding diseases. Sickness, in turn, did not mean primarily physical suffering, which one endured or cured as best as possible, but the loss of income that threatened the family.

Yet the liberal state was still being cautious. The Aid Fund Act of 1876 did not help much. The number of funds barely increased, and the system remained confusing, inefficient, and plagued by glaring differences in benefits and services. Everything was therefore pushing toward a grand solution, which contemporaries began to look for in the direction of a universal compulsory insurance for industrial workers. Models existed especially in the mining industry. Beginning in 1878, this grand solution seemed to be moving within reach, though the plan was for an accident insurance, while sickness insurance was accorded only a supplementary function.

The Imperial Message of November 17, 1881, thus promised a bill "that takes a standardized organization of the commercial system of sickness funds as its task." Since the creation of accident insurance was being delayed, sickness insurance was split off in 1882. The hope was that it could be advanced most readily, since the commercial system of sickness funds could be presupposed. The decision was now made in favor of broad compulsory insurance, which means that the existing structures were completed both organizationally and in terms of the principle of compulsion. That principle laid down obligatory insurance for three large groups of workers and white-collar employees (up to an annual income of 2,000 RM) in mining, industry, the railroads, inland steam navigation, trade, and commerce, and allowed the expansion to further groups, especially in the transportation sector, home-based industry, as well as agriculture and forestry. With that, nearly all wage-dependent workers had compulsory insurance in one of the already existing or newly set up sickness funds (communal, local, work-based, guild-based, miners', and registered funds), and they received, for a maximum of 13 weeks, the costs for doctors and medications, half of a day-laborer's wage as sick pay, maternity benefits, and funeral benefits. This applied also in case of sickness from an accident in the workplace, which facilitated the adoption of accident insurance. In case of unemployment, the beginning of separate unemployment insurance was created as an annex to the sickness insurance (Koch 1971; Tennstedt 1977; Aribas 1981; Tons 1983; Frank 1994). The financing of sickness insurance was divided—against Bismarck's intention—such that workers and employees paid two-thirds and employers one third. What explains the relatively weak parliamentary opposition to the law on the part of the Liberals and the Social Democrats is that a well-known institution was merely rounded out on the Reich level and made compulsory. This was not a genuine break with tradition.

The new compulsory insurance led rapidly to a doubling in the number of enrollees. In the self-administration, the workers, in accordance with their contribution, received a preponderance of two-thirds over employers, a situation that would prove consequential over the long term. The benefits of sickness insurance after 1883 were modest by today's standards. There was sick pay of half the wage starting on the third day and up to a maximum of 13 weeks, free medical treatment from "district" doctors under contract with the funds, and material benefits. Mothers in childbed received 4 weeks of support. Measured against the previous conditions, however, this was satisfactory, and it soon rooted sickness insurance deeply within the public's consciousness. The more members it had, the financially stronger it got. By 1913, including family members, about 62 % of the population was already insured. Benefits rose, but so did contributions. By the turn of the century, the number of doctors had doubled, while the population had grown by 11.5 %. There was plenty of work for all medical professions, since sickness insurance had opened up an enormous market for the relevant services.

When it came to the distribution of this market, the collective power of the association soon pushed aside the individual. As in the working world, the years after 1894 saw the emergence, in rapid succession, of associations, first those of the sickness funds, and then, on the other side, the German Medical Association [*Verband der Ärzte Deutschlands*, the so-called *Hartmann-Bund*]. Shortly before the First World War, there was a clash of interests. Until then, the funds hired doctors to provide services to the insured. It was their decision who received such a contract. Doctors who did not participate in this system felt threatened, especially since competition had already grown keener within the medical profession. The goal of the Hartmann-Bund was to abolish the two-class system among doctors and to give all of them the opportunity to treat insured patients. This was achieved only in 1913 through the threat of a general strike by doctors. The subsequent "Berlin Agreement" brought not only a regulated procedure for licensing sickness fund doctors, but also a ratio that was favorable to the medical profession: one doctor per 1,000 insured patients.[49] With that, the system in place to this day had been created, with all its advantages and disadvantages: it moved the costs incurred by the individual out of his view and left it to the associations to settle them. Doctors' fees, hospital per diems, costs for medications and services need not concern the patient. Behind this stands the humane notion of providing to the individual what he truly needs without fear about the costs. The flipside of this setup were and are the abstractness and anonymity of the process, which provides little incentive to the parties involved to keep down costs.

[49] The debates were heavily politicized: "Social Democratic sickness funds" confronted "bourgeois" doctors, while the "Social Democratic Association of Doctors" (founded in 1913) stood between the two camps by advocating the right of doctors to organize. See Hansen et al. (1981).

b) Accident Insurance

A year later, on July 6, 1884, the protracted process that gave rise to the accident insurance law—with a first Emperor's Speech urging its accelerated adoption[50]—reached its conclusion. The means of common law, by which the worker had to prove the fault of the employer in cases of accidents in the workplace, were no longer able to solve the problem of the enormous number of accidents that were occurring. The regulations in the Prussian *Landrecht* and in the Law on Domestics, which contained stronger elements of care, proved inadequate. This was also true of the areas using French law, even though the latter contained a liability by factory owners also for those acting on his behalf. And since 1838, the Prussian Railroad Law of November 3, 1838,[51] included tougher liability, which, by reversing the burden of proof, was heading in the direction of an "absolute liability." After the establishment of the North German Confederation, there were efforts to both improve liability under civil law and to make progress by expanding the Commercial Code. This gave rise to the "Law Concerning Obligatory Compensation for Deaths and Bodily Harm Caused by the Operation of Railroads, Quarries, Mines, and Factories, 7 June 1871," the Reich Liability Law. Under this law, as well, the "entrepreneur" could escape liability by invoking a higher power or maintaining that the employee himself was at fault. He was liable for those acting on his behalf only if they were at fault. Nobody could be happy with this regulation, neither the employees, who were forced to engage in costly procedures to prove fault, nor employers, who, for reasons of cost, preferred to see the problem of rising rates of accidents solved by way of insurance.

Still, the breakthrough to the (public law) idea of insurance proved difficult, especially since even the expert Theodor Lohmann was arguing only in favor of tightening liability. By the time the delegate Karl Ferdinand Stumm repeated his motion of 1869 on September 11, 1878, demanding obligatory old-age and disability funds for all factory workers, political conditions had changed. The breakthrough came with a memorandum by the Bochum industrialist Louis Baare (Baare 1880, pp. 31ff; Tennstedt and Winter 1993, pp. XXV–XXVIII). Bismarck decided to abandon civil law liability and embraced compulsory insurance, for which—and this was important to him—workers did not have to pay any contributions. This did away with the previous necessity of directing the worker to pursue civil legal action against his employer, which was practically tantamount to a denial of justice. The principle of an individual settlement of damages in accordance with the principle of liability for fault was replaced by the "social" principle of absolute liability with a simultaneous pooling of the risk. The benefits of accident insurance complemented those of sickness insurance, but it did not cover all accidents, only those "that happened in the workplace," and only those that impaired a person's ability to engage in gainful employment.

---

[50] Emperor's Speech on February 15, 1881. Text in *Quellensammlung Sozialpolitik* 1, Section 1, Volume 2 (1993), No. 203. For a detailed account of how the law came to be see Quandt (1938).

[51] PrGS 1838, p. 505.

The political problem of accident insurance lay in the diverging opinions about whether it should be a genuine, state-independent insurance financed by premiums, or an institution carried by the Reich through state subsidies. The first draft, which envisioned a Reich institution as well as employer contributions and a Reich subsidy, revealed the faultlines: the Reichstag wanted a federal structure of the organization, contributions from workers, and no state subsidy. When it failed, the Imperial Message of November 17, 1881, urged the Reichstag to take the task "to heart again" and promised a revision of the draft. But the second version—not combined with sickness insurance—also failed, with the result that only the separation of sickness insurance (1882) and the revamping of accident insurance achieved the breakthrough in the third attempt (Quandt 1938; Wickenhagen 1980, pp. 38ff., 44ff.; Tennstedt et al. 1995). The carriers of accident insurance would now be the public-law "Employers'" or "Trade Associations" in which the entrepreneurs of the insured companies had joined together. The state subsidy so urgently desired by Bismarck was gone. The insurance was financed through a pay-as-you-go (unfunded) scheme through contributions from employers. The funds, as the explanation of the third draft put it, should be raised "not in accordance with the principles of private law, but those of public law."[52] The organizational part of the Accident Insurance Law of July 6, 1884, took effect on July 9, 1884, the entire law did so on October 1, 1885. With the previous resistance having been overcome, the law could be rapidly expanded. A first "expansion law" (postal service, telegraph, railroad, naval, and military administrations) was already passed between December 1884 and June 1885. This was followed in 1886, after some opposition, by enterprises in the agricultural sector and in forestry, with lake navigation and the construction industry following suit in 1887.

The insurance now covered workers and white-collar employees (up to an annual income of 2,000 RM). As a benefit they received medical treatment starting in the 14th week. What became particularly important over the long term, however, was the task of accident prevention that was assigned to the Trade Associations. In this area, they created bodies of regulation that were gradually implemented through the pressure tools of higher contributions, higher danger classes, and monetary fines, and which did in fact bring down the accident rates (Wickenhagen 1980, pp. 63ff.). The merger of these associations into a single one in 1887 contributed to the coordination of these efforts throughout the Reich. With this, the Trade Associations took on a part of the regulatory risk prevention that was originally supposed to be the sole purview of the factory inspectors of the Trade Supervisory Office.

On the occasion of the creation of accident insurance, a Reich Office of Social Insurance [*Reichsinstanz der Sozialversicherung*] was also set up. It was the highest decision-making and supervisory body of the Reich Insurance Office [*Reichsversicherungsamt*] and existed from 1884 to 1945.[53] Under its first president, Tonio

[52] *Reichstagsdrucksache*, IV. Session 1884, No. 4.

[53] Wickenhagen (1980, pp. 57–79), Tennstedt (1984, pp. 47–82), Bogs (1977, pp. 195ff.), Bogs (1979, pp. 3–23), Stolleis (1990: cols. 801f.).

Bödiker (1884–1897), it was initially under the authority of the Reich Chancellor, after the First World War under that of the Reich Ministry of Labor. Its tasks were gradually expanded to all of social insurance: first Accident Insurance (1884) and Disability Insurance (1889), then also Sickness Insurance (1913), White-Collar Employee and Miner's Insurance (1922/1923), as well as Unemployment Insurance (1927). The year 1919 saw the addition of the Reich Provisioning Court [*Reichsversorgungsgericht*], which was responsible for looking after war victims and was linked to the Reich Insurance Office in that the same person was president of both.

Characteristic of the activity of the Reich Insurance Office was the competency for the entire area without a separation of powers; that is to say, the exercise side-by-side of supervisory, administrative, and legal decision-making tasks. When it came to the latter, representatives of the employers and employees were consulted—as is still the practice today. Even certain law-making powers were in place. The legal process was three-tiered: from the Insurance Offices to the State Insurance Offices and then to the top. Although the functions were institutionally connected, the Reich Insurance Office developed de facto into a Reich Court for Social Insurance. It was therefore only consistent with this development that the members of the Reich Insurance Office (and of the Reich Provision Court [*Reichsversorgungsgericht*]) formed the basic personnel of the new social jurisdiction after 1945 (Stolleis 1979).

c) Disability Insurance

The discussions over the third core area of social insurance began with the publication of "Rudiments of Old-Age and Disability Insurance for Workers, along with a Memorandum" on November 17, 1887. Scholars and associations, parties and the public took up the draft bill, which came from the Bundesrat to the Reichtsag, where it was repeatedly deliberated and revised. At the end of this unusually intensive process stood the "Law Concerning Disability and Old-Age Insurance of June 22, 1889" [*Gesetz, betr. die Invaliditäts- und Altersversicherung vom 22. Juni 1889*], a law, incidentally, that was opposed by the Social Democrats, the left-leaning Liberals, and the majority of the Center Party. It introduced compulsory insurance for wage-earners who made less than 2,000 RM per year. As with the Sickness Insurance, white-collar employees were now included. In cases of disability, which was determined solely by the public legal authorities, a disability pension—and starting at age 70, an old-age pension—could be applied for; the disabled person must have paid regular contributions for 5 years, the 70-old for 30 years. The pension he received was a "security supplement to his livelihood," not a guarantee of his living standard (Rückert 1990; Fisch and Haerendel 2000). Because the insurance for disability and old-age could be expected to relieve the system of government poor relief, the state from the beginning supported pension insurance with subsidies.

Bismarck had originally sought a Reich institution and at least a visible state contribution to the financing. That proved impossible to implement, at least not in the form of the "tobacco monopoly" as Bismarck had planned. For one, industry resisted the transfer of the new branch of insurance to the Trade Associations. For another, the federal states, working through the Bundesrat, changed the central "Reich Office" that was planned into state insurance offices. Finally, the Reichstag limited the state subsidy from one-third of the total costs to a fixed sum of 50 Reichsmark per pension. The principle had thus been preserved, but Bismarck's real intent of having the Reich bear the full burden had been distorted: the perspective of the insured and the public was dominated by contributions paid by both workers and employers. Disability and Old Age Insurance thus seemed like a construct in which personal contribution and state compulsion and state subsidy were balanced. This dual character has persisted to this day. It also finds a constitutional echo in the question to what extent the entitlement to a pension is based on personal contributions and thus falls under the constitutional-legal notion of property. Accordingly, an increase in the state's share through subsidies to pension insurance from tax revenues would reduce the personal share and in a sense get closer again to Bismarck's intention, if for very different reasons.

An appreciation of this tripartite insurance edifice as it presented itself in 1889 has come for the most part from retrospectives on its anniversaries. From the perch of what had been accomplished in the meantime, these retrospectives were "exhibitions of achievements," though occasionally also accompanied by the anxious question of how this path could be continued under the changed social and economic background conditions. Contemporaries took a different view: Bismarck himself was disappointed after the long struggles in parliament; he had not achieved his political goal. His middle class supporters followed his cue and paid relatively little attention to social insurance. It seemed, at least in the first few decades, more like a byproduct in the great man's accomplishments. After Bismarck's departure from the political stage, Social Democrats gradually came to recognize the high value of this entity, institutionalized, partially uncoupled from its founding motives, and primed for growth. To be sure, the initial dimensions were modest: sickness insurance began with an insured share of the population of less than 10 %, and it paid an average of 11.20 Reichsmark annually per covered person (Wehler 1995: 914). Accident Insurance began to get traction only after 1886, and over the long term its accident prevention measures took decades to take effect. The benefits of Old-Age and Disability Insurance with their average payments of 155 RM per year were not intended to replace wages. In 1900/1910, only 27 % of all men reached the retirement age of 70.[54] However, this body of laws meant that a threshold had been crossed—something of which contemporaries became aware more or less quickly, depending on their "class situation." The condition of the working class improved, also through the relatively continuous rise in real wages. The state had changed its role: it had become an interventionist state, that is to say, it now derived its legitimacy also from the functioning of these institutions, indeed, it became clear that social security and

[54] Ibid. Here one must consider, though, that the average age at retirement in 1905 was 56.3, and that life expectancy was higher for those who entered the working world and paid contributions (men: 46.7, women: 49). See Ritter (1991, p. 92), Kaschke (2000).

"mass loyality" would henceforth have to be related one to the other. The state had created a system of compulsory insurance whose conditions it controlled. This system worked in the context of a society that had long since ceased to be predominantly agrarian, but was instead a powerfully industrialized one. In the economy, gigantic enterprises had formed and become interconnected through association structures and cartels. The Social Democrats and the unions had pushed to the fore via the twofold path of parties and associations; pure repression as during the time of the anti-Socialist laws was now out of the question. The approval by the Majority Socialists of the war bonds of 1914 also rested in this slow change of the political climate since Bismarck's resignation.

6. Supplementary Laws and Further Development Down to the First World War

Although the two-and-a-half decades between Bismarck's resignation and the outbreak of the First World War were filled with growing political uncertainties and profound changes in intellectual history, in economic and socio-political terms they constituted a growth phase in which the structural change toward an industrial and service society and the expansion of the group of white-collar employees took place. Social protection mirrored this, initially with a series of laws that expanded upon and amended the social insurance.[55] The circle of the insured was expanded, especially in Sickness Insurance, which was revised in 1892 to strengthen the principles of non-cash benefits, and to create the possibility of including family members at the level of the community, the workplace, and the guilds (RGBl., p. 379). The intended side-effect was the displacement of the voluntary aid funds of the workers which were oriented toward cash benefits. The result was that the number of persons covered by sickness insurance had doubled by 1900. In Tennstedt's assessment, the amended law of 1892, with its strengthening of the principle of non-cash benefits, contributed substantially to the de facto recourse to doctors and hospitals by the workers, that is, to the "medicalization" of broad segments of society (Tennstedt 1991, p. 226).

After 1884, Accident Insurance broadened horizontally through the inclusion of other types of businesses, and vertically through the incorporation of higher-earning white-collar workers (up to 3,000 RM per year). This in turn had a positive effect on

[55] For example: the laws of August 28, 2885, RGBl., p. 159, and of May 5, 1886, RGBl., p. 132, on the expansion of sickness and accident insurance; the laws of march 15, 1886, RGBl., p. 53, of July 11, 1887, and July 13, 1887, RGBl., pp. 287, 329, on the expansion of accident insurance; laws amending sickness insurance of April 10, 1892, RGBl., p. 379, and May 25, 1903, RGBl., p. 233; laws amending accident insurance of July 5, 1900, RGBl., p. 573; laws amending disability and old-age insurance of July 13, 1899, RGBl., p. 463; for reasons of space, an account of the additional provisioning for the public sector is not included here. See the historical comments in Hautmann (1984, pp. 6–17).

the possibilities of accident prevention, which was systematically pursued after 1886, and on the benefits of the insurance.

A growth in enrolled members also allowed Disability Insurance to loosen the strict preconditions for the existence of disability; initially there was no pension payment if and as long as there was still the strength and ability to engage in any kind of work. What was supposed to matter now was the "reasonableness" of this work, and this represented a very decisive step in the direction of a decision that respected the individual case. At the same time, however, this also became a source of disputes. The interest of the insurance to avoid the case of inability to work as much as possible, simultaneously stimulated the efforts to grant treatment and stays at spas of their own. The commitment of insurance companies in financing clinics and homes for the insured was the correct calculation: the result was economically more favorable than pension payments. Since the average life expectancy around 1900 was still below fifty, the burden from pension because of old-age disability was small, to begin with. This led to the rapid accumulation of capital stock, which made it possible to pay for the above-mentioned treatments and spa stays. Moreover, since 1899 it was possible to use some of the contributions to financially balance the State Insurance Agencies, which in turn supported the construction of workers' apartments. The financial compensation, in turn, was the precondition for being able to keep the contribution and benefit levels uniform across the Reich. Of course, the level of services was so low that no workers could live off the pension, and there was no security for the widow (Dreher 1978).

Yet the picture of placid development should not cause us to overlook the fact that the end of the Bismarck era coincided with a domestic political crisis. The laws dealing with workers' insurance had been completed in 1889, but it had taken a lot of effort to do so. The political forces were shifting, and the party cartel on which Bismarck had been relying collapsed. In May of 1889, a large miners' strike in Westphalia was quashed. But the majority in the Reichstag no longer believed that the workers' movement could be tamed by repression. The unlimited renewal of the anti-Socialist laws asked for by the government failed. The Reichstag elections of February 20, 1890, documented the new situation. The Free Conservatives and the National Liberals had suffered a catastrophic defeat, while the Social Democrats, the Left Liberals, and the Center Party achieved a landslide victory. Bismarck quickly embraced a new reformist line of social policy. Surprisingly enough he agreed with the young Emperor Wilhelm II that protective labor legislation was necessary. These were half-hearted rearguard battles. The policy of repression toward the workers' movement had failed. The anti-Socialist laws were abrogated on September 30, 1890. Social insurance had been achieved, though it could unfold its positive effects only over the long term. By contrast, protective labor legislation, for which there was a pent-up need, could be enacted fairly quickly.

a) Protective Labor Law

What Wilhelm II had in mind in 1890 was another step in a direction that had been conspicuously neglected since the founding of the Reich (Reichold 1990). The word *Arbeiterschutz* [worker protection], which came into common use in the 1870s, referred to limits on working hours, the protection of women (especially women who were pregnant or in childbed), youths, and children against hard labor, as well as protection from dangers in the workplace. This was an issue that incorporated social policy and health policy motives as much as the intent of the traditional defense against dangers by good public policy, which, under the conditions of industrialization, had to deal with entirely new phenomena. Its means were largely the sovereign prohibition, the relevant control, and sanctions for violations.

In this sense, regulations to prevent dangers had already existed in the manufactures of the eighteenth century. Enlightened Absolutism had no qualms about issuing directives and prohibitions if they deemed it appropriate to protect workers, who were simultaneously also subjects and potential recruits. However, the beginning of occupational safety is usually dated to when the Prussian state, rattled by reports from the military inspectors, began to fear for the health of the youth; at the same time, it recognized that compulsory schooling had a lot of gaps in its implementation. The well-known Prussian directive of March 9, 1839, about the employment of young workers in factories generally prohibited the employment of children under the age of 9 years and of youths over the age of 16 for more than 10 h a day (Wickenhagen 1980, pp. 11ff.). This was within the tradition of health regulations, the ordered school system, and the protection of churches, which urged the sanctification of Sunday and religious, catechumen, and confirmation classes. A law of 1853 continued along this line by raising the general age of protection to 12 (PrGS, pp. 225–227).

In the following years—when economic liberalism was at its height—signals in this direction were fairly rare. The regulations on continued payment of wages and protection against dismissal for clerks in the *Allgemeines Deutsches Handelsgesetzbuch* [General German Commercial Code] of 1861 remained marginal and exerted no influence as a model. The liberal commercial code that was drawn up in 1869 for the North German Confederation, with which Bismarck ended the Prussian constitutional conflict politically and brought the Liberals into the coalition he needed to establish the Reich (and which lasted until 1878), contained only the incontrovertible points: protective regulations for adults, especially for women, did not exist at all (except for the prohibition against payment of wages in kind); children under the age of 12 were in principle not allowed to work in factories, 12–14 year-olds could work 6 h, 14–16 year-olds up to 10 h. Night and Sunday work was permissible only from age 16 on. The restriction of these regulations to factory work and their inadequate policing by factory inspectors,[56] the local policy, or

[56] "Gesetz über Fabrikinspektoren v. 16. Mai 1853," 225. State factory inspectors were made obligatory throughout the Reich only by the Reich law of July 17, 1878, p. 199.

volunteer citizens meant that the traditional use of children in cottage industry and agriculture remained untouched. The year 1871 saw the addition of the Reich Liability Law with regulations on accident prevention that were limited and soon recognized as ineffective (Wickenhagen 1980, pp. 21ff., 29ff.). Thus, until 1871, a systematically conceived and effective occupational safety law existed only in its rudiments. The problem was recognized and also frequently articulated, but this did not give rise to a political will that was capable of garnering a majority.

The history of legislation dealing with occupational safety between the founding of the Reich and the end of Bismarck era is therefore a history of failure. While social insurance from about 1874 developed a model that was very progressive compared to the rest of Europe, German fell behind other countries on labor protection, especially England and Switzerland. Even though all significant social forces—from the Social Democrats to the Conservatives, from the Center Party to the *Kathedersozialisten* [academic Socialists]—agreed that something had to be done, Bismarck consistently blocked all attempts at legislative improvements. The personal biases of the estate owner Bismarck and his aversion to too much bureaucracy factored into this as much as the fact that it was precisely the workers' movement that was advocating for labor protection. It was one of his basic beliefs that one should not lead workers too much by nose as they pursued their material interests. Finally, he regarded protective measures as an impediment with a view toward foreign competition. He used the differences of opinion among supporters to split them apart: some were more strongly in favor of the normal working day (10 h) and the prohibition against payment in kind, others of prohibitions against work by youths, pregnant women, and mothers in childbed, and against night and Sunday work. There was also disagreement over the means to be employed: stricter enforcement of the laws by factory inspectors, strengthening of occupational safety by intensifying individual regulations and/or by expanding the circle of protected individuals and the circle of workplaces that are covered by the law.

The result was that initiative followed initiative.[57] They began with a draft by the *Allgemeiner Deutscher Arbeiter-Verein* [General German Workers' Association] in 1876, continued with a draft bill on the Commercial Code by Theodor Lohmann in 1876 (Ayaß 1996, introduction to No. 89), a Social Democratic blueprint of 1877, and a plan by the Center Party in 1885. Within the ministerial bureaucracy it was once again especially Hermann Wagener and Theodor Lohmann (Lohmann 1878; Tennstedt 1994) who advocated workplace protection in factories, specifically by reviving the institution of factory inspectors, which was standard throughout the Reich after 1878, but also through large-scale inquests into women and child labor in the factories (1875/1876).[58] Bismarck, who was angry not only about a ministerial administration that was pressing him with draft laws, but also about a brave factory

[57] A very good overview is offered by Ayaß (1996) in his introduction to Arbeiterschutz, vol. 3, pp. XIX–XXXIX.

[58] *Ergebnisse der über die Frauen- und Kinder-Arbeit in den Fabriken auf Beschluß des Bundesrats angestellten Erhebungen, zusammengestellt im Reichskanzler-Amt* (Berlin, 1877).

inspector at his paper mill in Varzin, blocked all efforts towards occupational safety in 1877. As a result, the only thing that was achieved was a minor amendment to the Commercial Code on July 17, 1878. Following the English mode, it introduced Commercial Supervisory Offices throughout the Reich, which had the authority of a local policing authority (§139 b GewO). With that, business inspections could also be carried out at night. Moreover, a general duty of the employer to ensure "workplace safety" [*Betriebssicherheit*] (§120 a GewO) was laid down in the law. Finally, maternity leave limited to 3-weeks was introduced for female factory workers, namely without protection against dismissal and continuing payment of wages. All told that was a meager result, one that meant Germany lagged behind by international standards. All areas outside of factory work were unprotected. The essential demands for restrictions on work hours, night work, child labor, and maternity rights remained unfulfilled, especially since activists were not able to attach improvements in workplace protection to the social insurance legislation. Only factory inspection, the future *Gewerbeaufsicht* [Industrial Supervision], had gotten under way and was supplemented after 1884 by the preventive work of the Trade Associations of the accident insurance (Umlauf 1980).

The tide seemed to be turning again in 1890. Bismarck had once again stymied plans to improve workplace protection laws and thus contributed to his political downfall (Rothfels 1921, pp. 267ff.; Grebe 1937; Gall 1980). Hopes for a new beginning in social policy were revived under the young Emperor Wilhelm II, who was looking for an area of domestic politics in which he could make a name for himself. But after the Emperor's two decrees of February 4, 1890, which Bismarck had still drafted but did not want to publish, his interest in this subject matter flagged again. The one decree led to the—essentially unsuccessful—International Berlin Conference on Workplace Protection in 1890 (Stolleis 1931, p. 11f.), the other to the "socio-political reform legislation of the Berlepsch era" (von Berlepsch 1987; Mommsen 1995, pp. 105ff.). Its measures aimed at improving the structures within businesses without questioning the rights of entrepreneurs, for example, the obligation to issue factory codes. The first possibility of voluntary employee representation in the workplace appeared in 1891 (Rückert and Friedrich 1979, pp. 22ff., 117ff.). However, these beginnings of codetermination within companies were also accompanied by impediments to the right to strike, for example, by the prohibition against "breach of contract," that is, leaving the workplace.

In the foreground, however, stood the improvement in workplace protection. It was inserted into an amendment of Part VII of the Commercial Code. This law, the so-called Work Protection Law of June 1, 1891, incorporated a number of older demands: the general prohibition against Sunday work in industry and its restriction to 5 h in trade and commerce, the introduction of the maximum workday of 11 h for women, and the prohibition against night work for women and youths under the age of 16.[59] Added to this were different break regulations for youths under the age of

[59] "Gesetz über die Neufassung des Titel VII der Gewerbeordnung v. 1. Juni 1891," RGBl., p. 262. See Kaufhold (1991).

16; during these breaks, they were prohibited from being in the working areas. But special protective regulations also applied beyond the age of 16 up to the age of majority. For example, businesses had to keep a "work book for underage industrial workers," which was intended chiefly to strengthen the familial authority vis-à-vis the underage person (§§107ff., GewO). Male and female workers under the age of 18 were encouraged to attend the "continuing education school" [*Fortbildungsschule*] (§106 GewO). These regulations were then supplemented by the Reich Law concerning Child Labor in Industrial Enterprises of March 30, 1903 (RGBl., p. 113). The law distinguished between the employment of children that were part of the family for one's own commercial business, the employment of own children at home but for a third party, and the employment of other children. The maximum work time was tiered accordingly: as a rule, other children could be employed for only up to 3 h a day, during vacations up to 4 h, but not before morning school hours and only 1 h after the end of afternoon classes. A distinction was also made as to whether the children were employed in workshops, in commercial businesses, in "public theatrical performances and other public shows," in inns and taverns, or whether they delivered goods or ran errands. Sunday work, where it was not completely prohibited, could not prevent attendance of the main church service. Regulations concerning the protection of apprentices had already been inserted into the Commercial Code in 1900 (Jacobi 1924, pp. 75–89).

The Law on Work at Home of December 20, 1911, now also created—supplementary to the stipulations of §§618 BGB, 62 HGB, 120 a ff. GewO—regulations about occupational health and safety for so-called "home-workers" [*Heimarbeiter*] (RGBl., p. 976). The elaboration of the law that was actually in effect in all these areas came to a large extent under the regulatory authority of the Bundesrat, which in this way acquired the position of an important mediating organ for federal social policy. Moreover, the "law actually in effect" depended on the work of the factory inspectors who were being used with growing frequency (Ritter and Tenfelde 1992).

b) Labor Law

The work protection law was genuine public law in the spirit of the "good public policy" that warded off dangers. Its primary instrument was the prohibition, an interventionist special regulation to suspend general contractual freedom. By contrast, the labor law of the late nineteenth century was derived substantially from common law, though one must not overlook the fact that important traditional currents existed in the special laws in mining (Strätz 1974), the trades (Ebel 1964; Ogris 1967), and the law dealing with domestics (Schröder 1992). Following concepts in Roman law, dependent work was referred to as "*Dienstmiete*" (locatio conductio operis) [hired service]. The textbooks on pandectics devoted little space to the topic, less because Roman law did not offer any starting points, and more because of the underlying social consensus that the establishment of a working relationship was the subject of a voluntary agreement (Coing 1989, vol. 2, pp. 185ff.; 194ff.; Becker 1995).

The principle of liberty had turned in the French Revolution against anti-free market, "exclusive" organizations of citizens in the same profession (Simitis 1989). It was hostile above all to the traditional organizations of the guilds. Under the banner of economic liberty, the nineteenth century had begun to "de-juridify" the working world. Estate-based barriers, not the estates themselves, were removed: "Every nobleman is authorized to engage in any common trade, without any disadvantage to his estate; and every burgher or farmer is entitled to move from the estate of farmers into that of the burghers, and from the estate of burghers into that of the farmers," declared the Prussian Edict of October 9, 1807. Beginning in 1810, the Law on Domestics was based only on work contracts. In principle, all citizens now had legal capacity and the ability to engage in business and commerce, had equal rights of property and inheritance, and were subject to the civil law code.

While the economic forces unleashed by this contributed to launching Germany into the industrial age, they also produced misery on a massive scale—the "social question." Legal freedom allowed employers in the first phase of industrialization to dictate the price of labor and its conditions. The creation of a counterforce by workers through organization was outlawed, as in the Prussian Commercial Code of 1845 (Huber 1969, vol. 4, pp. 1134ff.; Lorenz 1991). This did not prevent the emergence of unions, especially since the Janus-headed principle of liberty could also be invoked to justify "freedom of association" (Kögler 1974; Hardtwig 1997). The Commercial Code of the North German Confederation of 1869 allowed "agreements and associations for the purpose of achieving favorable wage and working conditions, especially by means of the cessation of work and the dismissal of workers" (§152), but it denied legal protection to coalition agreements and prohibited forcible measures against those who do not wish to join an organization. At least there was now a possibility of setting up collective self-help organizations by industrial workers, which means that the year 1869 forms in retrospect the real beginning of collective labor law and the unions.[60] The great waves of strikes in 1869, 1872/1873, and 1889/1890 were no longer able to rattle the freedom of association in principle, though the state certainly did attempt to contain the repercussions of the new instruments, especially by blunting the strikes that were a necessary corollary of the freedom of association through restrictions under civil law, criminal law, and commercial law. Attempts to restrict the freedom of association and the freedom to strike by means of penal law included an initiative to make "breach of contract" a criminal offense. In the end, the public debate over this merely led to the solidarization of the worker's movement. The liberal main current from the founding phase of the North German Confederation grew weaker again around 1874. The state opted for repression, but it did not dare abolish the right of association. Notwithstanding, the union movement continued to grow steadily. Between 1890 and 1900, the total number of organized

[60] Schönhoven (1987), Ramm (1978), Schröder (1988), especially pp. 250ff. on the possibilities of the judicial system to deal with the new forms (strikes, lockout, boycott, "breach of contract," collective bargaining agreements) on the basis of civil and penal law. For a summary account see Bieber (1998).

workers rose from just under 280,000–680,000; by 1914, the number had risen again to 2.5 million. Since employers' associations were also set up at this time (Kessler 1907; Blaich 1979; Ullmann 1981), by the end of the nineteenth century the two camps faced off on the organizational level. Until 1914, however, the state could not be prevailed upon to guarantee the parties to collective bargaining a legally secured sphere in which to develop, to recognize collective wage agreements, and thereby institutionalize the social conflict (Ayaß et al. 1997; Huber 1969, vol. 4, pp. 1223ff.; Schlickum 1978), even if the Reich Court decided in 1910 to regard collective bargaining agreements as binding (RGZ 23, 100). But at least the restrictions in association law that dated back to the Prussian period of repression in 1850 were partially repealed by the Reich Association Law of April 19, 1908 (RGBl., p. 151). Now, agricultural workers could also organize and membership of women and youths was allowed.

It is against this background that one must see the sharp criticism already by contemporaries that the Civil Code did not deal with the law concerning modern mass labor relations (Wieacker 1967, pp. 481, 549f.; Benöhr 1997). It was not until 1900 that the labor contract was interpreted as a special kind of contract (Lotmar 1902–1908; Rückert 1992a, b; Gasser 1997). This gradual uncoupling of material labor law from civil law corresponded, in terms of legal procedure, to the creation of special courts characterized by particular expertise. On the Reich level these were the Commercial Courts [*Gewerbegerichte*] introduced on July 29, 1890: they were set up by the turn of the century, and their equal representation from both sides also hinted at the trend toward a special labor and social jurisdiction in the twentieth century (Brand 1990; Weiss 1994; Kraushaar 1995).

In this way, modern labor law became a special law motivated by social policy and working with the instruments of state intervention.[61] Everything that was called "progress" as it developed had been wrested from the countervailing forces of economic liberalism. That such interventions invariably entail restrictions on the freedom of all concerned comes as no surprise. Rather, it is part of the core problem of how the economic interests of the few strong members of society should be balanced against the need for self-actualization and need for protection on the part of many. This can succeed now and then and it requires constant rebalancing.[62]

The opposition of interests thus indicated is paradigmatically revealed by the emergence of the great camps of coalitions of organized workers and employers' associations, in which the self-regulation of the basic social conflict was practiced as an "epochal alternative to state regulation" (Bender 1984, 1991). The result was the formation of intermediary powers, which the state of the early modern period had just recently eliminated in a long process of monopolizing state power (Willoweit 1978).

The first collective wage agreement in 1873, initially still suppressed by the state, began the long history of its success in Germany and the neighboring

[61] The literature since 1945 was exhaustively compiled by Rückert (1996).

[62] With a slightly divergent view, Rückert (1998).

countries in Western Europe (Ullmann 1977; Coing 1989, vol. 2, §31, pp. 201–206; Englberger 1995). That success was very rapid after 1899: shortly before the First World War, there were 12,369 collective wage agreements for 193,000 enterprises with about 1.8 million employees (Hueck and Nipperdey 1963, p. 12). These agreements were regarded as a special kind of legal contract between the workers' and employers' association, or between a union and a single company. At the same time, however, it was recognized that in addition to the legal-contractual relations between the two parties (obligation to maintain social peace), there were also normative repercussions for the individual employment relationship (wage, work time). The distinction between the obligatory and the normative part of the collective wage agreement was beginning to take shape. Many details were contested, especially the immediate effect of the normative part (Imle 1905; Rundstein 1906; Sinzheimer 1907–1908). It was not only constructive difficulties that prevented the assumption that the agreement was directly obligatory for the individual employment relationship. Rather, a doctrine that was impregnated with individualism resisted constraints on the employer's freedom from a norm negotiated by his association. While the solving of conflict by societal forces was accepted, the "non-state" law-making that developed from it was not.[63]

c) Social Insurance Law Down to 1914

aa) Expansion

From the beginning of the so-called Posadowsky Era (1899–1907), the prevailing tendency is social insurance law was toward expansion and external rounding off (Real 1958; Huber 1969, pp. 1237ff.), parallel to the economic process of ongoing industrialization and urbanization. Growing prosperity and shorter working hours, population growth and an increase in the ratio of workers (especially white-collar workers) against a declining ratio of self-employed, as well as an increasing presence of women in the labor market were the essential characteristics of the development (MG Schmidt 1998, p. 36f.; Suhr 1930; Frevert 1979). Social insurance was by now established and was accepted by the broadest circles. The focus here, unlike in the law on collective wage agreements or in codetermination in the workplace, was on building out and rounding off what existed. In addition to the expansion of the groups covered by accident insurance (1900) and the temporal extension of the general protection of the sickness insurance from 13 to 26 weeks (1903), this was evident above all in the introduction of insurance of surviving family members (Dreher 1978).

[63] Huber (1969, p. 1256), sees in the gradual development of the law-creating function of the Trade Associations their emergence as an "element of statehood." For him, the setting of norms through collective wage agreements is therefore delegated by the state. That is in line with the views at the time, which was also the basic assumption underlying the final Decree on Collective Wage Agreements, Workers' and White-collar employees' Committees, and the Mediation of Labor Disputes, December 23, 1918: RGBl., p. 1456.

In the area of social insurance, legislators got that far only in accident insurance. In pension insurance, the premiums that were paid in were refunded if the insured person died before reaching retirement. That was clearly inadequate, especially for the worker's widow with children who had previously not been gainfully employed. As a result, politicians agreed in 1902, in a peculiar coupling with a higher customs tariff, to set up a modest insurance for surviving family members within a decade, though only for a widow who was not self-insured and disabled. As long as a worker's widow was able to continue working no pension was forthcoming, while the widows of white-collar workers were not exposed to this dilemma, as the middle class parties believed that it would be too much to ask of them. The widows' pensions that were paid beginning in 1912, "stood at 87 million RM a year. That corresponded to 47 % of the average level of disability pension, and 9 % of the average annual earned income" (Zöllner 1981).

bb) Insurance for Salaried Employees

A second innovation with far-reaching socio-political repercussions was the creation of an Insurance Law for Salaried Employees on December 20, 1911 (Bichler 1997). This law did justice to the fact that white-collar workers had established themselves within a short period of time as a separate social group between workers and civil servants (Croner 1962; Engelsing 1967; Kadritzke 1975; Kocka and Prinz 1983). The previously uninsured salaried employees who earned between 2,000 and 5,000 RM pushed for a parallel insurance that was separate from workers' insurance. This goal was achieved with relative ease: the new insurance demanded higher contributions, but it also provided more benefits whose level was clearly above that of the pension insurance for workers (Zöllner 1981, p. 111). This higher benefits imparted to this insurance the a "pace-maker function" in social policy (Zöllner 1981, p. 111). The motive behind these enhanced benefits was "to immunize salaried workers against the agitation by Social Democrats and the socialist Free Unions and win them over to the state or one's own party" (Ritter 1998a, p. 94f.). That also accorded with the intentions of salaried employees, who tended to define themselves as "bourgeois" and formed a salary-dependent middle class. The bourgeois parties wooed this group of so-called "private civil servants." That was also why the previously "petty salaried employees" (below 2,000 RM) were also included in the new insurance, without exempting them from the workers' insurance. A strong motive for a separate insurance for salaried employees was also that this obviated the need to raise the state subsidy for old-age and disability insurance for workers.

cc) Reich Insurance Code

Of great significance, finally, was the unification of the three main pillars of social insurance into a single law code, the Reich Insurance Code [*Reichsversicherungs-ordnung*] on July 19, 1911 (Rother 1994; Fuchs 1998). This had been preceded by various debates about a restructuring, for example, the unification of the various insurances under one roof, or at least the combining of sickness or accident insurance with old-age insurance. Beginning in 1903, then, the dominant idea was that of an "organic linkage."

This was the path of adding together the codifications of autonomous-remaining parts and bracketing them with a General Part. The Introductory Act issued on the same day repealed the existing laws on social insurance in the same way that the Law of December 20, 1911 also abrogated the old 1876 law about registered Aid Funds [*Hilfskassen*]. Although this did not create a comprehensive code of social law, the part of social law that was characterized by strong inner homogeneity and was most important in practice was arranged in a coherent way and opened up to scholarly treatment. Technically, the purpose of the Reich Insurance Code was to update the law in an area that had evolved in stages and to restructure the procedural pathways. Politically, it was intended to contain the influence of the SPD and the Free Unions in the sickness insurance and to eliminate from the latter funds that were too small (Ritter 1983, p. 57f.). Yet it was "modern" in the sense that, completely emancipated from the common law, it regulated an area that had been unknown only a generation earlier.

The division into a General Part and six special "books" corresponded to the structure of the Civil Code enacted in 1896. The *Reichsabgabenordnung* [German Tax Code] that was drawn up in 1919 also followed this pattern. With this, social insurance, civil law, and tax law had been organized in a way that nineteenth-century legal science had envisioned following the codification controversy of 1814. The fact that the summarizing codes of social insurance and tax law came about fairly quickly[64] also has to do with the standard of jurisprudential work attained by pandectics. All jurists involved had been trained in the common law, from where they derived their inspiration in terms of the degree of abstraction in the General Part, the parsimonious use of unspecified legal concepts, and the conciseness of expression, or the method of citation.

Substantively, the Reich Insurance Code did not offer anything that was in principle new. It specified and reformed the existing state of legislation and the practice it had given rise to over 20 years. During that time, social insurance had above all expanded, both by pulling in new circles of the insured and instituting an insurance for surviving family members that was attached to the disability insurance, and by increasing benefits (Peters 1978, pp. 78–80). By now, domestics and workers in agriculture and forestry were included in sickness insurance, the latter in the so-called *Landkrankenkasse* [Rural Sickness Fund]. Disability insurance for the first time had a pension for widows—if a widow was herself disabled.

However, bringing the laws together into a code made it more obvious than before that the social insurance laws had imparted to the state a new quality overall. What might have seemed historically as the return to welfare-state concepts from the

[64] The first draft of the Code in 1909 became the second draft of 1910, which was then adopted on May 31, 1911. The parts then went into effect gradually between 1912 and 1914.

eighteenth century, what had been intended politically as a means of fighting Social Democracy and had failed on the whole in its goal, had now become a financially strong institution with a considerable dynamic of its own. The most important risks in life had been collectivized and insured against by the state, "compulsion" was legitimized by its purpose and was no longer regarded as a scandalous deviation from the doctrines of economic liberalism. The Social Democratic movement, which had long since embarked on the road to changing from a party of revolution into a party of reform, appreciated the practical advantages of the new system and secured for itself in the self-administration a certain share of public functions which had been closed off to it within the state prior to 1918.

It was only in the 1920s and 1930s that observers, looking back, realized that it was not so much protective tariffs or minor stipulations of social protection (such as the prohibition against usury) that marked the real entry into the interventionism of industrial society, but social insurance. It occupied an "intermediate space" between state and society: it was close to the state but "self-administering," it was largely financed by "contributions" and was therefore a benefit generated by the productivity of society and dedicated to a specific purpose. That is why social insurance can also be seen as an institution with a cushioning function, one that mediated between the statist impulse and cooperative self-help. In this way, typical risks of life (sickness, accident, disability, and old age) could be moved from the realm of the individual into a special public system without directly affecting the state. Special systems also develop special responsibilities, and thus they relieve the state both financially and politically. At the same time, they relieve families from providing services and material and cash benefits. Of course, over the long term this also results in families being no longer able or willing to generate these things. Thus, with the waning of responsibility comes also a waning of the capacity for self-help. Accordingly, the number of children, once seen as a kind of insurance policy for the survival of the family, declines, while life expectancy simultaneously increases.

In this area, too, we see the above-mentioned development of an "intermediary" sphere that was to be guided by the interaction of employers and workers, though in this case with a good deal more weight and guiding powers on the part of the state. Still, cooperation between employers and employees was also practiced here. Not only was there agreement in the collective wage negotiations, the two sides also cooperated in the committees of social insurance, the work of the Trade Associations, factory inspection, and judicial decisions. Over the long term, this cooperation, while it did not cause the opposing camps in the class warfare to disappear, blunted their edge and contributed to the emergence of the later "social partnership."

In terms of domestic politics, social insurance—as was already evident before 1914—was shifting the centers of gravity. It reinforced the existing trend toward Reich administration (Reich Office of the Interior, Reich Insurance Office), and it favored the trend—already visible in its early stages—whereby the ministerial bureaucracy, associations, and social insurance arrived at agreements that circumvented parliament. Within Germany's federal structure, social insurance now formed a financially and politically important special bureaucracy that cut across the federal states. That corresponded to the logic of migration movements in industrial society.

Finally, we can note that social insurance had been created because the political forces agreed that the "state" was responsible; however, because it was visibly successful, it reinforced this trait—so characteristic of Germany—of a social-state statism. Once the starting situation with the fragmented system of funds, inadequate liability, and the all-but absent protection against old age had been overcome and the standardizing superstructure of the Reich Insurance Code had been erected, a return to the status quo ante had become in every way unthinkable.

Imperial Germany did not move significantly beyond the state of social insurance that had thus been achieved. Leaving aside the outbreak of the First World War, the balance of political power also did not suggest any substantial changes. Wilhelm II's embrace of big industry, Germany's entry into the politics of international imperialism (colonies and trade treaties, expansion of the navy), and the renewed struggle against the re-invigorated social democratic movement in Prussia and Saxony stifled the beginnings of a renewal of social policy. Paradoxically enough, this was especially true for the period after 1912, when the Social Democrats had become the strongest party but did not constitute the government. In this constellation, progressive social policy carried the stain of giving in to the opposition. In addition, the Social Democratic movement itself had moved into a phase of wait-and-see and consolidation (Domann 1974).

d) The Municipal Level

Below the level of politics on the big stage, living conditions and administrative tasks changed during the Wilhelmenian era especially within the municipalities (Steinmetz 1993). A first large wave of incorporations created new administrative structures in the conurbations. The water supply and sewage disposal were centrally organized on a large scale or modernized, street lighting emerged, public baths, slaughter houses, transportation enterprises, modern hospital facilities, parks, and cultural institutions were created. In substance—but not yet in its later name—municipal *Daseinsvorsorge* [governmental provision of essential public services] came into being. "With the takeover of numerous private enterprises by the cities and municipalities," Ferdinand Schmid wrote in 1909, "we have, in the opinion of many, already in fact entered into the age of a partial state and municipal Socialism" (Schmid 1909, p. 205). In fact, the establishment of journals and annuals dealing with issues of municipal administration reveals the degree to which Germans, stimulated by the English municipal Socialism of the "Fabians" (Grunwald 1897; Hugo 1897), were becoming attuned to these phenomena. From around the turn of the century there also emerged a so-called *Kommunalwissenschaft* [science of municipal administration]. One of its most important tasks was to take note of the growing social problems of the large urban landscapes. There was more and more discussion about the social tasks of the cities (Adickes and Beutler 1903; Hugo 1901/1906; Sohnrey 1907; Thissen and Trimborn 1910; Damaschke 1922), especially in the areas of the health care system and public health, education, and youth care. The growing understanding for the special needs of young people against the backdrop of the culture-critical "Youth Movement," and the growing pressure of problems on the ground led to the replacement of the Prussian Compulsory Education Law of 1878 with the new Law for the Corrective Training of Minors [*Gesetz für die Fürsorgeerziehung Minderjährigerl*] of July 2, 1900 (Petersen 1907). Step by step, the still politically discriminatory poor relief and the non-discriminatory public services to care for young people took divergent paths.[65] The context of wider attention—supported by statistical surveys—to the condition of children and young people since 1900 also included the Reich Law Concerning Child Labor in Commercial Enterprises [Child Protection Law] of March 30, 1903, which outlawed factory work and night work outright and allowed it only on a limited basis in trade and commerce (Agand 1902). When it came to poor relief itself, the political harmfulness of an across-the-board denial of suffrage and other public rights was recognized, and one tried to cast off ballast without giving up the principle. As a result, certain benefits and services were defined out of poor relief on the ground that their absence did not harm the essential principle.[66]

References

Adickes F, Beutler G (1903) Die sozialen Aufgaben der deutschen Städte. Leipzig

Agand K (1902) Kinderarbeit und Gesetz gegen die Ausnutzung kindlicher Arbeitskraft in Deutschland. Jena

Althoff H (1940) Erinnerungen aus den Anfängen der Invalidenversicherung. Zentralblatt für Reichsversicherung und Reichsversorgung

Aribas N (1981) Die Entwicklung der landwirtschaftlichen Krankenversicherung in Deutschland. Dissertation. Bonn

Ayaß W (ed) (1996) Arbeiterschutz, vol 3. In: Born KE, Henning H-J, Tennstedt F (eds) 1993–1997: Quellensammlung zur Geschichte der Deutschen Sozialpolitik 1867–1914. I. Abt. Von der Reichsgründung bis zur Kaiserlichen Sozialbotschaft (1867–1881). Stuttgart

Ayaß W, Nickel K-H, Winter H, Czaplinski M, Roeder E (eds) (1997) Arbeitsrecht, vol 4. In: Born KE, Henning H-J, Tennstedt F (eds) (1993–1997) Quellensammlung zur Geschichte der deutschen Sozialpolitik 1867–1914. I. Abt. Von der Reichsgründung bis zur Kaiserlichen Sozialbotschaft 1867–1881. Darmstadt

Baare L (1880) Gesetzentwurf betreffend die Einrichtung einer Arbeiter-Unfall-Versicherungskasse nebst Motiven. Elberfeld

Barta H (1984) Entstehung und Funktion der sogenannten Theorie der wesentlichen Bedingung. Der Weg vom frühen zivilen, industriell/gewerblichen Haftpflichtrecht zur öffentlichrechtlichen Gefährdungshaftung der Arbeiter(unfall)versicherung. In: Steindl H (ed) Wege zur Arbeitsrechtsgeschichte. Frankfurt am Main, pp 205–249

[65] "Reichsgesetz betr. die Einwirkung von Armenunterstützung auf öffentliche Rechte v. 15. März 1909," RGBl., p. 319.

[66] The Law Concerning the Effect of Poor Relief on Public Rights ["Gesetz betr. die Einwirkung von Armenunterstützung auf öffentliche Rechte v. 15. März 1909"], RGBl., p. 319, removed sickness support, institutional care for the disabled, benefits of youth care, education, and vocational training, benefits to ease a temporary emergency, and funeral benefits as non-discriminatory.

Bauer C (1974) Georg von Hertling als Sozialpolitiker. In: Carlen L, Steinegger F (eds) Festschrift für Nikolaus Grass. Innsbruck, München, pp 187–203

Becker M (1995) Arbeitsvertrag und Arbeitsverhältnis in Deutschland. Vom Beginn der Industrialisierung bis zum Ende des Kaiserreichs. Frankfurt am Main

Bender G (1984) Strukturen des kollektiven Arbeitsrechts vor 1914. Ein Beitrag zu den historischen Grundlagen der rechtsförmigen Steuerung des industriellen Konflikts. In: Steindl H (ed) Wege zur Arbeitsrechtsgeschichte. Frankfurt am Main, pp 251–293

Bender G (1991) Die schwierige Koalitionsfreiheit. Eine Studie zu Rechtsprechung und Gesetzgebung im Jahrzehnt der Reichsgründung. In: Mohnhaupt H (ed) Rechtsgeschichte in den beiden deutschen Staaten (1988–1990). Frankfurt am Main, pp 466–490

Benöhr H-P (1997) Fast vier Tropfen sozialen Öls — Zum Arbeitsrecht im BGB. In: Köbler G, Nehlsen H (eds) Festschrift für Karl Kroeschell. Munich, pp 17–38

Bichler B (1997) Die Formierung der Angestelltenbewegung im Kaiserreich und die Entstehung des Angestelltenversicherungsgesetzes von 1911. Frankfurt am Main

Bieback K-J (1976) Die öffentliche Körperschaft. Berlin

Bieber H-J (1998) Die Rolle von Gewerkschaften und Wirtschaftsverbänden bei der Entstehung des Arbeitsrechts. In: Nutzinger H-G (ed) Die Entstehung des Arbeitsrechts in Deutschland. Marburg, pp 15–69

Binder H-O (1971) Reich und Einzelstaaten während der Kanzlerschaft Bismarcks 1871–1890. Eine Untersuchung zum Problem der bundesstaatlichen Organisation. Tübingen

Blaich F (1979) Staat und Verbände in Deutschland zwischen 1871 und 1945. Wiesbaden

Blasius D (1971) Lorenz von Steins Lehren vom Königtum der sozialen Reform und ihre verfassungspolitischen Grundlagen. Der Staat 10:33–51

Bogs H (1973) Die Sozialversicherung im Staat der Gegenwart. Berlin

Bogs W (1977) Das Bundesversicherungsamt im Rückblick. In: Schewe D (ed) Die Praxis des Bundesversicherungsamtes. Bonn-Bad Godesberg, pp 195ff

Bogs W (1979) Sozialrechtspflege vor Einführung der Sozialgerichtsbarkeit. In: Deutscher Sozialgerichtsverband: Festschrift 25 Jahre Bundessozialgericht, vol 1. Cologne

Born KE (1960) Die Motive der Bismarck'schen Sozialgesetzgebung. In: Die Arbeiterversorgung 62

Born KE, Henning H-J, Tennstedt F (eds) (1993–1997) Quellensammlung zur Geschichte der Deutschen Sozialpolitik 1867–1914, founded by Rassow P, 18 vols. Stuttgart (1997: Darmstadt). I. Abt. Von der Reichsgründung bis zur Kaiserlichen Sozialbotschaft (1867–1881), vol 1 (1994) Tennstedt F, Winter H, Ayaß W, Nickel K-H (eds) Grundfragen staatlicher Sozialpolitik. Die Diskussion der Arbeiterfrage auf Regierungsseite vom preußischen Verfassungskonflikt bis zur Reichstagswahl von 1881. Stuttgart et al; vol 2 (1993) Tennstedt F, Winter H, Domeinski H (eds) Von der Haftpflichtgesetzgebung zur Ersten Unfallversicherungsvorlage, Stuttgart et al; vol 3 (1996) Ayaß W (ed) Arbeiterschutz. Stuttgart et al; vol 4 (1997) Ayaß W, Nickel K-H, Winter H, Czaplinski M, Roeder E (eds) Arbeiterrecht. Darmstadt.; Abt. II. Von der Kaiserlichen Sozialbotschaft bis zu den Februarerlassen Wilhelm II. (1881–1890); vol 2/1 (1995) Tennstedt F, Winter H, with Domeinski H, Roeder E (eds) Von der Zweiten Unfallversicherungsvorlage bis zum Unfallversicherungsgesetz vom 6. Juli 1884. Stuttgart

Brand J (1990) Untersuchungen zur Entstehung der Arbeitsgerichtsbarkeit in Deutschland, vol 1/1. Pfaffenweiler

Brand J (1998) Zunft, Zunftwesen. Handwörterbuch zur Deutschen Rechtsgeschichte, vol 5, columns 1792–1803

Brentano L (1881) Der Arbeiter-Versicherungszwang. Berlin

Brück T (1994) Korporationen der Schiffer und Bootsleute. Untersuchungen zu ihrer Entwicklung in Seestädten an der Nord- und Ostseeküste vom Ende des 15. bis zum Ende des 17. Jahrhunderts. Weimar

Coing H (1989) Europäisches Privatrecht 1800–1914, vol 2. 19. Jahrhundert. Munich

Craemer R (1940) Bismarcks Erbe in der deutschen Sozialversicherung. Berlin

Croner F (1962) Soziologie der Angestellten. Cologne

Däbritz W (1953) Baare. Neue Deutsche Biographie 1:477
Damaschke A (1922) Aufgaben der Gemeindepolitik, 10th edn. Jena
Domann P (1974) Sozialdemokratie und Kaisertum unter Wilhelm II. Die Auseinandersetzung der Partei mit dem monarchischen System, seinen gesellschafts- und verfassungspolitischen Voraussetzungen. Wiesbaden
Dreher W (1978) Die Entstehung der Arbeiterwitwenversicherung in Deutschland. Berlin
Ebel W (1964) Quellen zur Geschichte des deutschen Arbeitsrechts. Göttingen
Eickhoff AF (1932) Georg von Hertling als Sozialpolitiker. Cologne
Engelsing R (1967) Die wirtschaftliche und soziale Differenzierung der deutschen kaufmännischen Angestelltenschaft 1690–1900. Zeitschrift für die gesamten Staatswissenschaften 123:347–380
Englberger J (1995) Tarifautonomie im Deutschen Reich. Berlin
Esser J (1941/1969) Grundlage und Entwicklung der Gefährdungshaftung, 1st edn. 1941. Munich Berlin. 2nd edn. 1969. Munich
Fisch S, Haerendel U (eds) (2000) Geschichte und Gegenwart der Rentenversicherung in Deutschland. Berlin
Fischer W (1962) Der Staat und die Anfänge der Industrialisierung in Baden 1800–1850, vol 1. Berlin
Forsthoff E (1972) Lorenz von Stein. Frankfurt am Main
Frank A (1994) Die geschichtliche Entwicklung der gesetzlichen Krankenversicherung. Dissertation. Munich
Frevert U (1979) Vom Klavier zur Schreibmaschine - weiblicher Arbeitsmarkt und Rollenzuweisungen am Beispiel der weiblichen Angestellten in der Weimarer Republik. In: Kuhn A, Schneider G (eds) Frauen in der Geschichte. Düsseldorf, pp 82ff
Fuchs M (1998) Bewertung der Arbeit von Klaus Rother: Die Reichsversicherungsordnung 1911. Das Ringen um die letzte große Arbeiterversicherungsgesetzgebung des Kaiserreichs unter besonderer Berücksichtigung der Rolle der Sozialdemokratie. Zeitschrift für neuere Rechtsgeschichte 160–163
Gall L (1980) Bismarck. Der weiße Revolutionär. Frankfurt am Main, pp 684–708
Gasser CA (1997) Philipp Lotmar (1850–1922), Professor der Universität Bern. Sein Engagement für das Schweizerische Arbeitsrecht. Frankfurt am Main
Gessner D (1982) Die Industriealisierung, staatliche Gewerbepolitik und die Anfänge des industriellen Ausstellungswesens in Deutschland. In: Mai E, Pohl H, Waetzold S (eds) Kunstpoltik und Kunstförderung im Kaiserreich. Berlin
Grebe P (1937) Bismarcks Sturz und der Bergarbeiterstreik vom Mai 1889. Historische Zeitschrift 157:84–97, with futher references
Grebing H (1966) Geschichte der deutschen Arbeiterbewegung. Munich
Grunwald M (ed) (1897) Englische Sozialreformer. Leipzig
Hahn E (1995) Rudolf von Gneist 1816–1895. Ein politischer Jurist in der Bismarckzeit. Frankfurt am Main
Hahn H-W (1998) Die Industrielle Revolution in Deutschland. Munich
Hansen E, Heisig M, Leibfried S, Tennstedt F (1981) Seit über einem Jahrhundert.... Verschüttete Alternativen in der Sozialpolitik. Cologne
Hardtwig W (1997) Genossenschaft, Sekte, Verein in Deutschland. Vom Spätmittelalter bis zur französischen Revolution, vol 1. Munich
Härter K (1993) Entwicklung und Funktion der Policeygesetzgebung des Heiligen Römischen Reiches Deutscher Nation im 16. Jahrhundert, Ius Commune XX
Hautmann G (1984) Die Zusatzversorgung im öffentlichen Dienst und ihre Rechtsverhältnisse. Heidelberg
Heffter H (1969) Die Deutsche Selbstverwaltung im 19. Jahrhundert. Geschichte der Ideen und Institutionen, 2nd edn. Stuttgart
Hellwig F (1936) Carl Freiherr von Stumm-Hallberg. Heidelberg Saarbrücken
Henderson WO (1958) The state and the industrial revolution in Prussia. Liverpool
Henning FW (1978) Das industrialisierte Deutschland 1914 bis 1976, 4th edn. Paderborn

Hentschel V (1975) Die deutschen Freihändler und der volkswirtschaftliche Kongress 1858 bis 1885. Stuttgart
Hirsch M (1875) Die gegenseitigen Hülfskassen und die Gesetzgebung. Berlin
Höffner J (1956) Sozialpolitik im deutschen Bergbau. Münster
Hofmann H (1977/1986) Das Problem der cäsaristischen Legitimität im Bismarckreich. In: Hofmann H (ed) Recht - Politik - Verfassung. Studien zur Geschichte der politischen Philosophie. Frankfurt am Main, pp 181–205
Huber ER (1969–1984) Deutsche Verfassungsgeschichte seit 1789, vols 4 (1969), 5 (1978), 6 (1981, rev 1993) and 7 (1984). Stuttgart
Hueck A, Nipperdey HC (1959/1963) Lehrbuch des Arbeitsrechts, vol 1, 6th edn, 1959; 7th edn, 1963. Berlin
Hugo C (pen name Hugo Lindemann) (1897) Städteverwaltung und Municipal-Sozialismus in England. Stuttgart
Hugo C (pen name Hugo Lindemann) (1901/1906) Die deutsche Städteverwaltung. Ihre Aufgaben auf dem Gebiet der Volkshygiene, des Städtebaus und des Wohnungswesens, Stuttgart, 2nd edn. unter Lindemann, 1906. Stuttgart 100 Jahre Carl-Zeiss-Stiftung (1989). Jena
Imle F (1905) Gewerbliche Friedensdokumente. Jena
Jacobi E (1924) Einführung in das Gewerbe- und Arbeitsrecht, 4th edn. Leipzig
Kadritzke U (1975) Angestellte - Die geduldigen Arbeiter. Zur Soziologie und sozialen Bewegung der Angestellten. Frankfurt am Main
Kafka F (1961) Eine kaiserliche Botschaft. In: Kafka F(ed) Die Erzählungen. Frankfurt am Main
Kafka F (1984) Amtliche Schriften. Edited by Hermsdorf K, with Poßner W, Louezil J (eds). Berlin
Kaschke L (2000) “Nichts als Bettelgelder?” Wert und Wertschätzung der Alters- und Invalidenrenten im Kaiserreich. Historische Zeitschrift 48 (2)
Kaufhold KH (1982) Fragen der Gewerbepolitik und der Gewerbeförderung. In: Mai E, Pohl H, Waetzold S (eds) Kunstpolitik und Kunstförderung im Kaiserreich. Berlin, pp 95–109
Kaufhold KH (1991) Die Diskussion um die Neugestaltung des Arbeitsrechts im Deutschen Reich und die Novelle zur Reichsgewerbeordnung 1891. Zeitschrift für Arbeitsrecht 277–322
Kelsch W (1933) Ludwig Bamberger als Sozialpolitiker. Dissertation. Jena
Kessler G (1907) Die Deutschen Arbeitgeberverbände. Leipzig
Koch P (1971) Von der Zunftlade zum Grossbetrieb. Kleine Geschichte der privaten Krankenversicherung. Karlsruhe
Kocka J, Prinz M (1983) Vom “neuen Mittelstand” zum angestellten Arbeitnehmer. Kontinuität und Wandel der deutschen Angestellten seit der Weimarer Republik. In: Conze W, Lepsius MR (eds) Sozialgeschichte der Bundesrepublik Deutschland. Stuttgart, pp 210–255
Kögler P (1974) Arbeiterbewegung und Vereinsrecht. Berlin
Köhler PA (1990) Entwicklungslinien der 100jährigen Geschichte der gesetzlichen Rentenversicherung. Die Zeit von 1891–1957. In: Ruland F (ed) Handbuch der gesetzlichen Rentenversicherung. Neuwied Frankfurt am Main
Köhler PA, Zacher HF (eds) (1981) Ein Jahrhundert Sozialversicherung in der Bundesrepublik Deutschland, Frankreich, Grossbritannien, Österreich und der Schweiz. Berlin
Köttgen A (1931) Die Krise der kommunalen Selbstverwaltung. Tübingen
Kraushaar M (1995) Die Gewerbegerichte im Deutschen Reich und Vorläuferinstitutionen. Arbeit und Recht 1995: 313–317
Lentze H (1971) Handwerk. In: Erler A, Kaufmann E (eds) Handwörterbuch zur Deutschen Rechtsgeschichte, vol 1. Berlin
Lindenlaub D (1967) Richtungskämpfe im Verein für Sozialpolitik. Wiesbaden
Lingnau J (1965) Das System sozialer Hilfeleistungen für die Bergarbeiter in der Knappschaftsversicherung des Ruhrbergbaus 1767–1961. Cologne
Listl J (1994) Die Ordensgemeinschaften und ihre Angehörigen in der staatlichen Rechtsordnung. In: Listl J, Pirson D (eds) Handbuch des Staatskirchenrechts der Bundesrepublik Deutschland, vol 1, 2nd edn. Berlin, pp 841–863
Lohmann T (1878) Die Fabrik-Gesetzgebungen der Staaten des europäischen Kontinents. Berlin

Lorenz R (1991) Zur rechtlichen Regelung der Arbeitsverhältnisse in Preußen in der Zeit zwischen Reformen und Revolution (1800–1848). Ein Beitrag zur Vorgeschichte des Arbeitsrechts. In: Mohnhaupt H (ed) Rechtsgeschichte in den beiden deutschen Staaten (1988–1990). Frankfurt am Main, pp 491–513

Lotmar P (1902–1908) Der Arbeitsvertrag nach dem Privatrecht des Deutschen Reiches, 2 vols. Leipzig

Luther R (1971) Handwerk. In: Erler A, Kaufmann E (eds) Handwörterbuch zur Deutschen Rechtsgeschichte, vol 1. Berlin

Machtan L (ed) (1995) Mut zur Moral. Aus der privaten Korrespondenz des Gesellschaftsreformers Theodor Lohmann, vol 1 (1850–1883). Bremen

Maier H (1980/1986) Die ältere deutsche Staats-und Verwaltungslehre, 2nd edn (1980), 3rd edn (1986). Munich

Martiny M (1976) Integration oder Konfrontation? Studien zur Geschichte der sozialdemokratischen Rechts- und Verfassungspolitik. Bonn

Mayer G (1911) Unbekannte Briefe Lassalles. Archiv für Geschichte des Sozialismus und der Arbeiterbewegung 1:176–197

Mayer-Maly T (1967) Römische Grundlagen des modernen Arbeitsrechts. Recht der Arbeit 281–286

Menger CF (1983) Entwicklung der Selbstverwaltung im Verfassungsstaat der Neuzeit. In: von Mutius A (ed) Selbstverwaltung im Staat der Industriegesellschaft. Festgabe für Georg Christoph von Unruh. Kiel, pp 25–40

Mieck I (1965) Preußische Gewerbepolitik in Berlin 1806–1844. Berlin

Moenning M (1927) Die Stellung der deutschen katholischen Sozialpolitiker des 19. Jahrhunderts zur "Staatsintervention" in der sozialen Frage. Dissertation. Münster

Möller W (1908) Die Herrschaft der Sozialdemokratie in der deutschen Krankenversicherung. Berlin

Mommsen W (1993) Das Ringen um den nationalen Staat. Die Gründung und der innere Ausbau des Deutschen Reiches unter Otto von Bismarck 1850 bis 1890. Berlin

Mommsen W (1995) Bürgerstolz und Weltmachtstreben. Deutschland unter Wilhelm II. 1890 bis 1918. Berlin

Morsey R (1957) Die oberste Reichsverwaltung unter Bismarck, 1867–1890. Münster

Mueller R (1952) Die Stellung der liberalen Parteien im deutschen Reichstag zu den Fragen der Arbeiterversicherung und des Arbeiterschutzes bis zum Ausgang des 19. Jahrhunderts. Dissertation. Jena

Oexle OG (1982) Die mittelalterliche Zunft als Forschungsproblem. Blätter für Deutsche Landesgeschichte 118:1–44

Ogris W (1967) Geschichte des Arbeitsrechts vom Mittelalter bis in das 19. Jahrhundert. Recht der Arbeit 186–197

Oncken H (1906) Albert Schaffte, Lebenserinnerungen. Historische Zeitschrift 243–258

Peters H (1973/1978) Die Geschichte der sozialen Versicherung, 3rd edn (1978) Bonn

Petersen J (1907) Die öffentliche Fürsorge für die hilfsbedürftige Jugend. Leipzig

Plessen M-L (1975) Die Wirksamkeit des Vereins für Sozialpolitik von 1872–1890. Studien zum Katheder- und Staatssozialismus. Berlin

Plessner H (1969) Die verspätete Nation, 5th edn. Stuttgart

Quandt O (1938) Die Anfänge der Bismarckschen Sozialgesetzgebung und die Haltung der Parteien. Berlin

Ramm T (1978) Die Arbeitsverfassung des Kaiserreiches. In: Triffterer O (ed) Festschrift für Walter Mallmann. Baden-Baden, pp 191ff

Real W (1958) Die Sozialpolitik des neuen Kurses. In: Berges W, Hinrichs C (eds) Zur Geschichte und Problematik der Demokratie. Festgabe für Hans Herzfeld. Berlin, pp 441–457

Reichold H (1990) Der "Neue Kurs" von 1890 und das Recht der Arbeit - Gewerbegerichte, Arbeitsschutz, Arbeitsordnung. Zeitschrift für Arbeitsrecht 5–41

Reiss-Vaseck E (1934) Zentrum und Sozialpolitik zur Zeit Bismarcks. Gelbe Hefte 10:590

Ritter UP (1961) Die Rolle des Staates in den Frühstadien der Industrialisierung. Berlin

Ritter GA (1983) Sozialversicherung in Deutschland und England. Entstehung und Grundzüge im Vergleich. Munich

Ritter GA (1991) Der Sozialstaat. Entstehung und Entwicklung im internationalen Vergleich, 2nd edn. Munich

Ritter GA (1997) Sozialpolitik im Zeitalter Bismarcks. Historische Zeitschrift 265:683–720

Ritter GA (1998a) Über Deutschland. Die Bundesrepublik in der deutschen Geschichte. Munich

Ritter GA (1998b) Bismarck und die Entstehung der deutschen Sozialversicherung. Pforzheim

Ritter GA, Tenfelde K (1992) Arbeiter im deutschen Kaiserreich. 1871 bis 1914. Bonn

Rodbertus JC (1880) Briefe und sozialpolitische Aufsätze. Berlin

Rother K (1994) Die Reichsversicherungsordnung 1911. Das Ringen um die letzte große Arbeiterversicherungsgesetzgebung des Kaiserreichs unter besonderer Berücksichtigung der Rolle der Sozialdemokratie. Aachen

Rothfels H (1921) Zur Bismarck-Krise 1890. Historische Zeitschrift 123

Rothfels H (1925) Otto von Bismarck. In: Der Staat; ausgewählte Dokumente

Rothfels H (1927) Theodor Lohmann und die Kampfjahre der staatlichen Sozialpolitik (1871–1905). Nach ungedruckten Quellen. Berlin

Rothfels H (1935) Prinzipienfragen der Bismarckschen Sozialpolitik. Königsberg

Rothfels H (1962) Prinzipienfragen der Bismarckschen Sozialpolitik. In: Rothfels H (ed) Bismarck, der Osten und das Reich. Darmstadt, p 166

Rückert J (1990) Entstehung und Vorläufer der gesetzlichen Rentenversicherung. In: Ruland F (ed) Handbuch der gesetzlichen Rentenversicherung. Neuwied, pp 1–50

Rückert J (ed) (1992a) Philipp Lotmar, Schriften zu Arbeitsrecht, Zivilrecht und Rechtsphilosophie. Frankfurt am Main

Rückert J (1992b) "Frei" und "Sozial". Arbeitsvertrags-Konzeptionen um 1900 zwischen Liberalismen und Sozialismen. Zeitschrift für Arbeitsrecht 23:225–294

Rückert J (ed) (1996) Beschreibende Bibliographie zur Geschichte des Arbeitsrechts mit Sozialrecht, Sozialpolitik und Sozialgeschichte. Baden-Baden

Rückert J (1998) Die Verrechtlichung der Arbeitsbeziehungen in Deutschland seit dem frühen 19. Jahrhundert. In: Nutzinger H-G (ed) Die Entstehung des Arbeitsrechts in Deutschland. Aktuelle Probleme in historischer Perspektive. Marburg, pp 213–229

Rückert J, Friedrich W (1979) Betriebliche Arbeiterausschüsse in Deutschland, Großbritannien und Frankreich im späten 19. und frühen 20. Jahrhundert. Eine vergleichende Studie zur Entwicklung des kollektiven Arbeitsrechts. Frankfurt am Main

Rundstein S (1906) Die Tarifverträge und die moderne Rechtswissenschaft. Eine vergleichende Untersuchung. Leipzig

Saile W (1958) Hermann Wagener und sein Verhältnis zu Bismarck. Tübingen

Schäffle A (1884) Der korporative Hülfskassenzwang, 2nd edn. Tübingen

Schäffle A (1905) Aus meinem Leben, vol 2. Berlin

Scheuner U (1977) Robert von Mohl, Die Begründung einer Verwaltungslehre und einer staatswissenschaftlichen Politik. In: Festgabe 500 Jahre Eberhard-Karls-Universität Tübingen. Tübingen, pp 515ff

Schlickum G (1978) Die Tariffähigkeit der Arbeitnehmer-Organisationen in der Weimarer Republik. Dissertation. Frankfurt am Main

Schlosser H (1996) Grundzüge der Neueren Privatrechtsgeschichte, 8th edn. Heidelberg

Schmale W (1997) Archäologie der Grund- und Menschenrechte in der Frühen Neuzeit. Munich

Schmid F (1909) Über die Bedeutung der Verwaltungslehre als selbständiger Wissenschaft. Zeitschrift für die gesamten Staatswissenschaften 65:193ff

Schmidt MG (1998/2005) Sozialpolitik in Deutschland. Historische Entwicklung und internationaler Vergleich, 2nd edn (1998) 3rd edn (2005). Wiesbaden

Schmoller G (1874) Die soziale Frage und der preußische Staat. Preußische Jahrbücher 342

Schnur R (ed) (1978) Forsthoff, Lorenz von Stein; Staat und Gesellschaft. Studien über Lorenz von Stein. Berlin

Schönhoven K (1987) Die deutschen Gewerkschaften. Frankfurt am Main

Schraepler E (1964) Quellen zur Geschichte der sozialen Frage in Deutschland, vol 1, 3rd edn. Göttingen

Schröder R (1988) Die Entwicklung des Kartellrechts und des kollektiven Arbeitsrechts durch die Rechtsprechung des Reichsgerichts vor 1914. Ebelsbach

Schröder R (1992) Das Gesinde war immer frech und unverschämt. Gesinde und Gesinderecht vornehmlich im 18. Jahrhundert. Frankfurt am Main

Schulin B (1980) Fragen der gesetzlichen Krankenversicherung bei Ordensleuten. Vierteljahresschrift für Sozialrecht 8:165–167

Simitis S (1989) Die Loi le Chapelier: Bemerkungen zur Geschichte und möglichen Wiederentdeckung des Individuums. Kritische Justiz 157–175

Sinzheimer H (1907–1908) Der korporative Arbeitsnormenvertrag, 2 vols. Berlin

Sohnrey H (1907) Aus der sozialen Tätigkeit der preußischen Kreisverwaltungen. Berlin

Söllner A (1967) Ohne Arbeit kein Lohn. Archiv für die civilistische Praxis 167:132

Spree R (1978) Wachstumstrends und Konjunkturzyklen in der deutschen Wirtschaft von 1820–1913. Göttingen

Steinmetz G (1993) Regulating the social. The welfare state and local politics in imperial Germany. Princeton

Stolleis E (1931) Das internationale Arbeiterschutzrecht. Kallmüntz

Stolleis M (1979) Entstehung und Entwicklung des Bundessozialgerichts. In: Deutscher Sozialgerichtsverband (ed) 1979: Sozialrechtssprechung. Verantwortung für den sozialen Rechtsstaat. Festschrift zum 25-jährigen Bestehen des Bundessozialgerichts. Cologne

Stolleis M (1990) Sozialrecht. In: Erler A, Kaufmann E (eds) Handwörterbuch zur Deutschen Rechtsgeschichte, vol 4. Berlin, columns 1730–733

Stradal H (1971) Genossenschaft. In: Erler A, Kaufmann E (eds) Handwörterbuch zur Deutschen Rechtsgeschichte, vol 1. Berlin, columns 1522–1527

Strätz H-W (1974) Bergmännisches Arbeitsrecht im 15. und 16. Jahrhundert. In: Ebert K (ed) Festschrift Nikolaus Grass. Innsbruck, pp 533–558

Stürmer M (ed) (1978) Bismarck und die preußisch-deutsche Politik 1871–1890, 3rd edn. Munich

Stürmer M (1983) Das ruhelose Reich, Deutschland 1866–1918. Berlin

Suhr S (1930) Die weiblichen Angestellten. Berlin

Tennstedt F (1976) Sozialgeschichte der Sozialversicherung. In: Blohmke M, von Ferber C et al (eds) Handbuch der Sozialmedizin, vol 3. Stuttgart, pp 385–492

Tennstedt F (1977) Geschichte der Selbstverwaltung in der Krankenversicherung von der Mitte des 19. Jahrhunderts bis zur Gründung der Bundesrepublik Deutschland. Bonn

Tennstedt F (1981) Vorgeschichte und Entstehung der Kaiserlichen Botschaft vom 17. Nov. 1881. Zeitschrift für Sozialrecht 663–710

Tennstedt F (1983) Vom Proleten zum Industriearbeiter. Arbeiterbewegung und Sozialpolitik in Deutschland 1800 bis 1914. Cologne

Tennstedt F (1984) Das Reichsversicherungsamt und seine Mitglieder. In: Deutscher Sozialrechtsverband, Wannagat G (eds) Entwicklung des Sozialrechts, Aufgabe der Rechtsprechung. Festgabe aus Anlass des 100jährigen Bestehens der sozialgerichtlichen Rechtsprechung. Cologne, pp 47–82

Tennstedt F (1991) Der Ausbau der Sozialversicherung in Deutschland 1890 bis 1945. In: Pohl H (ed) Staatliche, städtische, betriebliche und kirchliche Sozialpolitik vom Mittelalter bis zur Gegenwart. Stuttgart, pp 225–243

Tennstedt F (1994) Sozialreform als Mission. Anmerkungen zum politischen Handeln Theodor Lohmanns. In: Kocka J, Puhle HJ, Tenfelde K (eds) Von der Arbeiterbewegung zum modernen Sozialstaat. Festschrift für Gerhard A. Ritter. Munich, pp 538–559

Tennstedt F (1995) "Nur nicht privat mit Dividende und Konkurs". Der deutsche Weg zum Sozialstaat - auch eine Folge von Bismarcks Ansichten über private Unfallversicherungsgesellschaften. In: Heinze M, Schmitt J (eds) Festschrift für Wolfgang Gitter. Wiesbaden, pp 993–1004

Tennstedt F, Winter H (1993) "Der Staat hat wenig Liebe - activ wie passiv". Die Anfänge des Sozialstaats im Deutschen Reich von 1871 - Ergebnisse archivalischer Forschungen zur Entstehung der gesetzlichen Unfallversicherung. Zeitschrift für Sozialrecht 39:362–392

Tennstedt F, Winter H, Domeinski H, Roeder E (eds) (1995) Von der Zweiten Unfallversicherungsvorlage bis zum Unfallversicherungsgesetz vom 6. Juli 1884, vol 2/1. In: Born KE, Henning H-J, Tennstedt F (eds) 1993–1997: Quellensammlung zur Geschichte der Deutschen Sozialpolitik 1867–1914. Abt. II. Von der Kaiserlichen Sozialbotschaft bis zu den Februarerlassen Wilhelm II (1881–1890). Stuttgart

Thielmann H (1960) Die Geschichte der Knappschaftsversicherung. Bonn

Thissen O, Trimborn C (1910) Soziale Tätigkeit der Stadtgemeinden, 4th edn. Mönchengladbach

Tons H (1983) Hundert Jahre gesetzliche Krankenversicherung im Blick der Ortskrankenkassen. Bonn

Töpfer I (1970) Die Verhandlungen des Vereins für Sozialpolitik und die Rechtspolitik der späten Bismarck- und Wilhelminischen Zeit. Dissertation. Frankfurt am Main

Treue W (1970) In: Gebhardt, B (ed) Handbuch der deutschen Geschichte, vol 3, 9th edn. Stuttgart

Ullmann P (1977) Tarifverträge und Tarifpolitik in Deutschland bis 1914. Entstehung und Entwicklung, interessenpolitische Bedingungen und Bedeutung des Tarifvertragswesens für die sozialistischen Gewerkschaften. Frankfurt am Main

Ullmann H-P (1981) Unternehmerschaft, Arbeitgeberverbände und Streikbewegung 1890–1914. In: Tenfelde K, Volkmann H (eds) Streik. Zur Geschichte des Arbeitskampfes während der Industrialisierung. Munich, pp 194–208

Umlauf J (1980) Die deutsche Arbeiterschutzgesetzgebung 1880–1890. Berlin

Valentin V (1947/1998) Geschichte der deutschen Revolution von 1848–1849, vol 1. Berlin. Reprint 1998: Weinheim Berlin

Vogel W (1951) Bismarcks Arbeiterversicherung, ihre Entstehung im Kräftespiel der Zeit. Braunschweig

von Berlepsch H-J (1987) "Neuer Kurs" im Kaiserreich? Die Arbeiterpolitik des Freiherrn von Berlepsch 1890 bis 1896. Bonn

von Gneist R (1869) Verwaltung, Justiz, Rechtsweg, Staatsverwaltung und Selbstverwaltung nach englischen und deutschen Verhältnissen. Berlin

von Treitschke H (1874) Der Socialismus und seine Gönner. Preußische Jahrbücher 34:67–110, pp. 248–301

Wehler H-U (1987/1995/2003/2008) Deutsche Gesellschaftsgeschichte: Von der "Deutschen Doppelrevolution" bis zum Beginn des Ersten Weltkrieges 1849–1914, vol 1–5. Munich

Weiss J (1994) Von den Gewerbegerichten zu den Arbeitsgerichten. Die Arbeitsgerichtsbarkeit 7587

Wickenhagen E (1980) Geschichte der gewerblichen Unfallversicherung. Wesen und Wirken der gewerblichen Berufsgenossenschaften. Munich

Wieacker F (1953) Das Sozialmodell der klassischen Privatrechtsgesetzbücher und die Entwicklung der modernen Gesellschaft. In: Wieacker F (ed) 1974: Industriegesellschaft und Privatrechtsordnung. Frankfurt am Main, pp 9–35

Wieacker F (1966) Pandektenwissenschaft und Industrielle Revolution. In: Wieacker F (ed) 1974: Industriegesellschaft und Privatrechtsordnung. Frankfurt am Main, pp 55–78

Wieacker F (1967) Privatrechtsgeschichte der Neuzeit, 2nd edn. Göttingen

Willoweit D (1978) Struktur und Funktion intermediärer Gewalten im Ancien Regime. Der Staat. Suppl 2. Gesellschaftliche Strukturen als Verfassungsproblem. Berlin, pp 9–27

Winkel H (1977) Die deutsche Nationalökonomie im 19. Jahrhundert. Darmstadt

Winkler W (1979) Die Entwicklung des Bergrechts im 19. Jahrhundert. In: Coing W (ed) Wissenschaft und Kodifikation des Privatrechts im 19. Jahrhundert, vol 4. Eigentum und industrielle Entwicklung. Frankfurt am Main

Zacher HF (ed) (1979) Bedingungen für die Entstehung und Entwicklung von Sozialversicherung. Berlin

Zöllner D (1981) Ein Jahrhundert Sozialversicherung. Landesbericht Deutschland. In: Köhler P, Zacher HF (eds) Ein Jahrhundert Sozialversicherung. Berlin, pp 57ff

IV. The First World War

Germany's entry into the First World War changed the constitutional situation—in addition to all circumstances of everyday life. The Bundesrat was empowered "to order, during the time of the war, such measures as may prove necessary to remedy economic harms" (RGBl., p. 327, §3). The Reichstag stepped back as the legislator during normal times and conceded extra-parliamentary legislation to the Bundesrat, which inundated all of economic and social life with a total of 825 Bundesrat Decrees. With numerous other "legislators," including the Supreme Army Command, contributing, the result was a Special War Law that spread out over all areas of the law. Not only did it bridge the conventional separation of private law and public law, but is also massively restricted legal protections.

1. Adjustments

Since this war was for the first time less a war of militaries than of productive capacities, labor and social law were deployed equally to concentrate society's forces and to stabilize the domestic political situation.[1] These were "adjustments to the special conditions of the war" (Preller 1949/1978, p. 59), but also much more, namely the continuation of a movement that had already begun before the war, namely to bind the world of economics to political goals "from the outside" and "from the inside" (Feldman 1974). In practical terms this meant: loosening workplace protection where it was a hindrance to military production; making it more difficult to freely change jobs and—especially significant—introducing a state-issued certificate of employment; exempting skilled workers from military service;

Previously published in English in the following publication: Stolleis: Origins of the German Welfare State (German Social Policy, Vol. 2), Springer, Berlin/Heidelberg, 2013.

[1] Kahn (1918), Heymann (1921), on the economic and labor-policy questions see Feldman (1966); for a comparative analysis see Williams (1972).

DOI 10.1007/978-3-642-38454-7_4, © Springer-Verlag Berlin Heidelberg 2014

shifting workers into military production; protecting workers from garnishment of wages and dismissal; and lowering the retirement age in the workers' pension insurance to 65, where it already was for white-collar workers. When it came to social insurance, furthermore, it was necessary to guarantee that soldiers did not suffer any disadvantage from contributions they missed and that the social insurances themselves did not collapse from the massive loss of contributions. Wartime production drew in women as workers on a large scale, which made the number of the insured rise again.

2. The *Vaterländischer Hilfsdienst* [Patriotic Auxiliary Service] and Collective Labor Law

As the war intensified in 1915/1916, the military demanded greater access to the civilian population, especially through the introduction of the obligation to work, initially for men and women, then only for men. This gave rise to the Law on the Patriotic Auxiliary Service of December 5, 1916, which was a compromise between the private sector, unions, the government, and the military (RGBl., p. 1333). Far-reaching and forward-looking socio-political concessions were made to compensate for the fact that public law was being superimposed upon contractual freedom with this obligation to work. Participants in the Auxiliary Service were covered by social insurance,[2] service in the military and the Auxiliary Service were counted for eligibility,[3] the benefits for orphans were increased, and, as previously mentioned, the age of retirement was lowered from 70 to 65.[4] In part these measures were simple adjustment processes, in part reactions to acute problems, and in part politically achieved improvements that carried on older lines of development.[5] More important still was the fact that long-defended positions in collective labor law were abandoned: the parties to collective bargaining were included when it came to obligatory service and decisions about a change of jobs. All workers were explicitly granted the right to form clubs and the right of assembly, which amounted to an indirect recognition also of the right of association and the right to strike. Committee of Workers and Salaried Employees became obligatory in all commercial enterprises with a workforce of 50 or more, which was tantamount to a breakthrough for co-determination in the workplace. In this way, the unions,

[2] "VO über Versicherung der im vaterländischen Hilfsdienst Beschäftigten v. 24 February 1917," RGBl., p. 171.

[3] "Gesetz betr. Erhaltung von Anwartschaften aus der Krankenversicherung v. 4. August 1914," RGBl., p. 334; "Bekanntmachung über die Anrechnung von Militärdienstzeiten und die Erhaltung von Anwartschaften in der Invaliden- und Hinterbliebenenversicherung v. 23. Dezember 1915," RGBl., p. 845.

[4] "Gesetz betr. Renten in der Invalidenversicherung v. 12. Juni 1916," RGBl., p. 525.

[5] As for example the "Gesetz über Bezüge von Sozialrentnern v. 18 Juli 1922," RGBl. I, p. 649.

whose main currents (Free Unions, Christian Unions, Hirsch-Dunker's Trade Unions) were now working in unison, were integrated into the model of the emerging cooperative social state.[6]

3. War Relief and Unemployment Benefits

Eventually, the war-waging state not only had to win over workers for military production and pacify the "home front" with the help of the parties to collective bargaining and social insurance, it also had to address unemployment and mass poverty caused by the war. Before the war, initiatives in the direction of support in case of unemployment had been unsuccessful, both because of the opposition from the private sector and because unemployment was not seen as an urgent crisis affecting society as a whole. Depending on the constellation, it was either "fate" or an instrument of repression against the political pressure from the working class. That situation change when unemployment rose rapidly in the fall of 1914 (Sachße and Tennstedt 1988, p. 46f.). A jobless and unsupported proletariat at home would have magnified the threat from outside. As a result, initial steps were taken—within the framework of welfare—to find jobs for workers in the communities, and unemployment benefits were paid out at the municipal level, financed for the first time by the Reich (Faust 1986; Führer 1990).

At first the families of men drafted into the military had to be looked after. This was done through benefits that depended on demonstrated need, but which were different from welfare and charity in that the recipients were legally entitled to them. The state tried hard in other ways, as well, to distinguish these benefits of "war relief" funded by the Reich, which were also joined by special help for women in childbed as part of sickness insurance (Kleeis 1928, pp. 221ff.), from poor relief.[7] Voluntary benefits from the communities supplemented "war relief" with *Kriegswohlfahrtspflege* [wartime welfare]. Families received rent subsidies, and landlords were expected to lower the rent. The disputes this created went before the "Rent Tribunals" [*Mieteinigungsamt*]. As a result, there arose, beyond poor relief, a much more modern second system, which in turn influenced poor relief: "a uniform Reich law, a uniform administrative organization and efficient associations, cost-sharing by the Reich, states, and communities, replacement of the complicated principles of residential relief [*Unterstützungswohnsitz*] by the normal place of residence, no discrimination" (Sachße and Tennstedt 1988, p. 51).

Finally, the unemployed and needy family members were joined by disabled veterans and surviving dependants of servicemen. They were the recipients of care benefits as well as supplemental relief measures, which were regulated after the war

[6] Huber (1978, vol. 5, pp. 110–115).

[7] "Gesetz betr. die Unterstützung von Familien in den Dienst eingetretener Mannschaften v. 28. Februar 1888 i.d.F.v. 4. August 1914," RGBl., p. 332; Sachße and Tennstedt (1980/1988, p. 50f.).

through decrees and laws.[8] Since that time, the Reich and the states were financially involved also in the area of the formerly purely communal welfare.

All in all, in this area, as well, we can see an almost inescapable assumption of overall responsibility by the state. Poverty and unemployment under the conditions of the war pushed the state into the role of the great guarantor. Although the war also precipitated an enormous increase in voluntary welfare and charity, which in turn prompted a response by the state in the area of collection of charitable giving and to the creation of a National Women's Service [*Nationaler Frauendienst*] (Sachße and Tennstedt 1988, pp. 56–63), the dominant characteristic was the trend toward state regulation. Only the state was in a position to guide the social dynamic triggered by the war. The material differences between civil servants, while-collar employees, workers, and the self-employed in the trades and retail diminished noticeably. The supply problems leading to ration cards for food, the establishment of the "people's kitchens" and the production of staples by the communities themselves, widespread deficiency diseases, and the social problems in the wake of neglect and crime essentially affected all strata of society. If the state wanted to administer the shortage evenhandedly and have the greatest possible pacifying effect, traditional class barriers had to fall when it came to distribution, while efforts were made at the same time to avoid the discriminatory effects of "poor relief."

When it comes to the repercussions of the war for all spheres of life, I will look at them only as they related to social policy. In this area the *dirigiste* state took what it needed—workers, war-essential raw materials, food. It devoured individual freedom and replaced it with the sovereign order. But since the complex constitutional monarchy, which was to a significant degree directed also by associations and parties, could not simply be commandeered, the social forces made up for their losses through concessions, for example, the recognition of the parties to collective bargaining and of labor action. Modern wars of material and national economies, which are waged by exhausting all reserves of raw material and human labor, could be fought only with the utmost consideration for the workers and the organizations representing them. As a result, even more so than before the war, semi-public forces inserted themselves between state and society, which shaped the legislature in terms of substance, but which could not do without it when it came to the translation of substance into normative programs. Parallel processes were evident in efforts to resolve emergency situations below and outside of social insurance: since the war pushed broad strata also of the middle class to the poverty line, the state had to intervene on the level of the Reich and the federal states, coordinate, and draw up a scale of values. War casualties and surviving dependants ranged at the top, in the middle were the self-employed, civil servants, and salaried employees who had fallen on hard times, followed by the working class, and at the bottom the previous

---

[8] "VO über die soziale Kriegsbeschädigten- und Kriegshinterbliebenenfürsorge v. 8. Februar 1919," RGBl., p. 187; "Gesetz über die Kosten der Kriegsbeschädigten- und Kriegshinterbliebenenfürsorge v. 8. Mai 1920," RGBl., p. 1066.

population of the poor. Similar to the way in which the insurance for salaried workers had exerted a socio-political pull on insurance for workers, one could now observe a gradual convergence of war relief and poor relief. This also led to a new quality of cooperation between organizational forms of the state, local communities, the churches, and society at large. The "new, non-discriminatory style of relief" (Sachße and Tennstedt 1988, p. 65), not least via the medium of the integration of women's labor and through growing professionalization, spread across all efforts to combat poverty. Finally, there was the war "as the great pacemaker of social policy" (Preller 1978, p. 85; Schmidt 1998, pp. 41–46). There is little doubt that the socio-political advances of the Weimar Republic in collective labor law, in the equalization of protections for salaried employees and workers, in unemployment insurance, in maternity benefits, in tenant law, in youth welfare law, and in the welfare system would not have been achieved so quickly without the upheavals of the war. The state vastly expanded its activities, but the more it did so, the less it could be a dictatorial state. The social state of industrial society that was now emerging lived from cooperation and the formation of consensus on social policy.

4. Provisioning

"Individual rights and advantages by members of the state must be secondary to the rights and duties for promoting the common weal, if there is a genuine contradiction (collision) between them "Conversely, the state is obliged to compensate the person who is compelled to sacrifice his rights and advantages for the good of the common entity." These two famous maxims from the introduction to the *Allgemeines Landrecht für die Preußischen Staaten* [General Laws for the Prussian States] of 1794 contain the principle of burden-sharing. The precedence of the common weal, one of the most venerable and fragile formulas in European legal history (Stolleis 1987), implies the subordination of individual rights, in return for which the community itself, "for the sake of justice," promises to offer compensation.

In this abstract sense, the principle covers a whole host of constellations of intervention and compensation.[9] Not all have the character of social law: for when it comes to equalization of "special victims" or "intolerably" grave interventions via legal instruments such as expropriation and sacrifice, the social status of those affected should not matter. But when one speaks of the function and conception of

---

[9] Whether the so-called "public-law compensations" are part of social law or, because of their retroactive compensatory function, they constitute merely a compensatory annex to the law of the state's activities, is a question that is of more theoretical than practical interest (see the discussion in VVDStRL 28 [1970], pp. 270ff.). The fact that these two areas are related is evident in the care given to disabled war veterans: conventionally considered part of social law, it grants "compensation" for thee harm done by the state. On this see also the umbrella term "compensation system" suggested by Zacher (1970, p. 6) and Zacher (1972, pp. 461ff.).

social law, that very status is a crucial criterion as the material foundation of socio-legal norms. Thus, the present discussion will address as social provisioning law in the narrower sense only those norm that were intended to equalize social shortcomings or prevent them (provisioning as equalization for special sacrifices, maintenance-"pension" as the equivalent of services rendered, mitigation of inequalities in the distribution of opportunities in concrete cases and generally through long-term changes in social structures).

a) Civil Service, General Conscription, War Victims

These norms initially regulated cases in which the community as a whole granted compensation for special burdens that constituted untypical irruptions into the life of an individual: that is, help during catastrophes, acts of nature, famine, epidemics, and above all war. In addition, they regulated cases of need in groups or individuals that were typical, continuously recurring, or at least common in certain social formations. Here, the state compensated groups that bore a "special" burden relative to others. A similar motivation in terms of social policy lies behind state aid to compensate for the unequal life chances and opportunities for self-development for the mentally and physically disabled, and among those of equal abilities within an educational system that contains inequalities and either fails to dismantle them or produces them in the first place.

b) The Legal Development

However, the basic notion of compensation for special sacrifices mentioned above also gave rise to an area of the law that seems to have very little to do with social law: provision for civil servants and judges. The early modern state gradually created means of "providing" for its functional elite in the form of a "salary" [*Besoldung*]. The professional civil servants who had thus become dependent, and who now also represented the state (Wunder 1982), secured itself by striving for life-time jobs and maintenance through a "salary," which distanced itself already terminologically from the "pay" for services. This area moved systematically into public law (Wunder 1978; Hattenhauer 1993, pp. 195ff.), along with its maintenance according to position and service and including care for widows and orphans.[10]

In the course of the nineteenth century, this current established itself in all German states (for Baden see Wunder 1989). It was completed with the Prussian

[10] Wunder (1985); more basic, Gönner (1804, §425); Gönner (1808). On this see Hattenhauer (1993, pp. 204ff.); on Gönner see Schaffner (1964) and Stolleis (1995, p. 242).

Law on the Pensioning of Direct Civil Servants of March 27, 1872, and translated onto the Reich level with the Law on Reich Civil Servants of March 31, 1873 (Zacher and Ziegler 1984, pp. 7–13). Whatever peculiarities still existed on a state level were then removed during National Socialism through the Civil Servant Law of 1937. As far as "maintenance" was concerned, that law also remained essentially within the existing tradition.

c) Maintenance of Soldiers and the Law on the Consequences of War

"Maintenance" of soldiers developed along partly parallel, partly divergent lines. This had to do with the fact that soldiering in the early modern period, once it had replaced the armies based on the medieval feudal system, tended to be characterized more like risk-conscious entrepreneurship up to the Thirty Years' War. Whoever went to war provided his own equipment, had to "risk his neck," and was accordingly interested in booty. Absolutism subsequently set up standing armies, gave them uniforms, and put them in barracks, which automatically brought with it an obligation on the part of the state to maintain them. Here, too, discipline and maintenance proved to be two sides of the same coin. Since then, the state took on the maintenance and "re-socialization" of soldiers returning from the war, support for widows and orphans, reconstruction, and compensation for those affected as secondary phenomena of the war. The monopolization of war and peace in the modern sovereign state (Hofmann 1967) also entailed in the state's responsibility for the consequences. Henceforth, it was no longer the family or kinship units, the community, or the *Landschaft* but the territorial lord who was responsible for war and its effects. He provided for veterans through compensation (the Prussian "*Gnadentaler*"), settlement as farmers, or employment as trainers of recruits, teachers, and other low-level civil servants ("*Zivildienstschein*"), he granted tax breaks and privileges, and set up manufactures. Prime examples are the policy of Maximilian I of Bavaria after the Thirty Years' War (Doeberl 1904), the measures taken by Brandenburg-Prussia from the Great Prince Elector to Frederick the Great, and the maintenance of the Napoleonic veterans.

Within the law that evolved in this way, oriented toward war and its consequences, two lines of development are evident, first, in the emergence of a civil-service like mechanism of maintenance for the professional army, and, second, in the increasing impact on the civilian population:

The first line, which extends to the prevailing law, included the regulations pertaining to the pay and pension entitlements of professional soldiers, including the maintenance in case of disability and the care of widows and orphans. The basis of these benefits is the service relationship in the broader sense. The purpose of the benefits is to keep the army intact and to safeguard psychologically the readiness of soldiers to go to war. Functionally, then, these regulations can be sufficiently separated from social law.

In the seventeenth and eighteenth centuries, these regulations included numerous pension provisions for disabled officers, the Prussian "Military Pension Regulation" of 1825, but especially the Reich Law Concerning the Pensioning and Maintenance of Military Personnel of the Reich Army and the Imperial Navy, and the Grants for the Dependants of Such Persons of June 27, 1871 (RGBl., p. 275). After 10 years of service, professional officers were now provided for like civil servants, non-commissioned officers and common soldiers after 18 years. In addition, both groups were entitled to maintenance in case of injuries sustained on the job; the waiting period of 8 years originally stipulated was eliminated in 1906 (RGBl., pp. 565, 593). Additional improvements came with the Military Survivor Law of May 17, 1907 (RGBl., p. 214), the Capital Compensation Laws for Enlisted Men and Officers of July 3, 1916 and July 26, 1918 (RGBl., p. 680; 1918, p. 994), and the Compensation Law for Re-enlisted Men and Officers of September 13, 1919 (RGBl., pp. 1654, 1659). After the Weimar Constitution stated: "The inviolability of the acquired rights and the option of legal recourse for proprietary claims are guaranteed especially to the professional soldier" (Article 129, Section 4) (Anschütz 1933, p. 596), the practical consequences of this for the soldiers of the Reichswehr were drawn through the Military Law of March 23, 1921 (RGBl., p. 329) and the Wehrmacht Maintenance Law of August 4, 1921 (RGBl., p. 993; 1925, p. 349). Interestingly enough, disputes over maintenance involving soldiers were "supposed" to be settled through the normal legal channels, but what exactly established itself was the legal channel that ended with the *Reichsversorgungsgericht* [Reich Maintenance Court] and was part of social law. National Socialism did not depart from this line in principle, at least as far as the maintenance of the Wehrmacht through the Wehrmacht Welfare and Maintenance Law of August 26, 1938, was concerned (RGBl. I, p. 1077). Of course, the parallel "maintenance" of the "old fighters" [*Alte Kämpfer*] (RGBl. I, p. 133) and of the members of the Reich Labor Service (RGBl. I, p. 1158; RGBl. I, p. 1631) who were deployed like soldiers was in line with the nature of the political system.

It was in the second line of development, managing the immediate consequences of the war, that social law in the narrower sense took shape. In part this was the traditional poor relief that filled in the gaps in the maintenance law. Well into the nineteenth century, poor relief was the final stop for disabled soldiers, especially if they had to endure a waiting period in cases of service-related disabilities. However, these were the developmental stages of the provision for professional soldiers.

The situation was different for citizen subject to conscription. Early forms of an "obligatory military service" with the community subsequently assuming responsibility for the consequences had already existed in medieval cities, in which the community of citizens defended and cared for itself as a group. But modern conscription emerged only in the wake of the mass levies of the French Revolution. Ever since, it was "nations" that took up arms. The "cabinet wars" became national wars, in which for the first time the opposing nation was identified as an enemy to be defeated. This could not but lead to a comprehensive ideologization, but also to a blurring of the distinction between civilians and fighting troops, since both were parts of the nation. Accordingly, the state had to offer regulations of provision and compensation for those citizens who, as "conscripts," had to bear a special sacrifice for the nation as a whole. Likewise, dependents who lost their "breadwinner" made a special sacrifice. The price for the ideologization of entire nations was the protection of all citizens against the consequences through social legislation. "Patriotic" war also imposed an obligation on the fatherland. The promised "gratitude of the fatherland" in the form of later care and provision at least for dependents was to make the sacrifice of the individual easier and overcome reluctance in the mobilization of the entire nation. This motivation applied to all soldiers; however, with respect to the legal justification of provision, one must distinguish the above-described current of civil service law for professional soldiers, and the current of social law for conscripts. In that sense, the notion of provision also split: providing for civil servants, judges, and professional soldiers is a functional equivalent for services rendered, while providing for those who are forced to bear the burden of war is compensation—at least similar to social law—for a special sacrifice.

It is obvious that it was especially the socio-legal elements of the law dealing with the consequences of war that gained greatly in importance in the privations of the First World War and the postwar period. There were 1.5 million disabled veterans and 1.7 million surviving dependents. Two hundred-and-twenty-one government-run army hospitals had to be dismantled: the patients had to be discharged as "healed," many of whom most definitely were not, and the personnel had to be let go or moved to different jobs. The old legal foundations of the provision law before 1914 were obsolete for the simple reason that they had emphasized the distinctions in rank between enlisted men and officers in a way that was now felt to be outdated.[11] That is why the whole complex was newly regulated in the Reich Provision Law of May 12, 1920, which came in the wake of the Decree on Social Provision for Disabled Veterans and Surviving Dependents of February 8, 1919. These legal foundations for the benefit of the affected civilian population were supplemented by the Act on Harm to Persons from the War of July 15, 1922 (RGBl. I, p. 620). Creations on the institutional side were Social Welfare Offices [*Versorgungsämter*], which decided on the ground about pension applications, Main Social Welfare Offices [*Hauptversorgungsämter*], which served as an oversight authority, and procedural law.[12]

On this basis, the authorities approved not only about 2.5 million pensions, but also curative treatments, orthopedic care, and stays at health spas utilizing the facilities of the sickness funds. Much more so than before, the socio-political engagement was now focused on regaining or boosting gainful employment, job

[11] "Gesetz über die Versorgung der Personen der Unterklassen des Reichsheeres, der Kaiserlichen Marine und der Kaiserlichen Schutztruppe v. 31. Mai 1906," RGBl., p. 593; "Gesetz über die Pensionen der Offiziere v. 31. Mai 1906," RGBl., p. 565.

[12] "Gesetz über die Versorgungsbehörden v. 15. Mai 1920," RGBl., p. 1063; "Gesetz über Verfahren in Versorgungssachen v. 10. January 1922," RGBl. I, p. 59.

placement, and integrative measures for surviving dependents (*Kinderhilfswerke* [Children's Charities], stays in the countryside, institutional care). Social distinctions based on rank were not to exist any more, but there was a gradation derived from income and previous social status.

Like all other social benefits, those for soldiers, disabled veterans, and surviving dependents got caught in the maelstrom of inflation. The Social Welfare Offices, which had suffered a drastic personnel reduction of about two-thirds, now granted inflation adjustments, which were later, after the inflation, converted into a need-based "supplementary pension." So as not to get close again to welfare based entirely on need, the basic pensions were raised in 1925 and the supplementary pensions were reduced. Then, beginning in 1919, the provisioning law, half-way stabilized and only slowly waning in terms of its practical importance, was hit by the general benefits cuts as part of the consolidation policy of the presidential cabinets.[13]

References

Anschütz G (1933) Die Verfassung des Deutschen Reichs vom 11. August 1919, 14th edn. Berlin

Doeberl M (1904) Innere Regierung Bayerns nach dem Dreißigjährigen Krieg. Munich

Faust A (1986) Arbeitsmarktpolitik im Deutschen Kaiserreich. Stuttgart

Feldman GD (1966) Army, industry and labor in Germany 1914–1918. Princeton

Feldman GD (1974) Der Organisierte Kapitalismus während der Kriegs- und Inflationsjahre 1914–1923. In: Winkler HA (ed) Organisierter Kapitalismus. Voraussetzungen und Anfänge. Göttingen, pp 150–171

Führer KC (1990) Arbeitslosigkeit und die Entstehung der Arbeitslosenversicherung in Deutschland 1902–1927. Berlin

Gönner NT (1804) Deutsches Staatsrecht. Landshut

Gönner NT (1808) Der Staatsdienst aus dem Gesichtspunkt des Rechts und der Nationalökonomie betrachtet. Landshut

Hattenhauer H (1993) Geschichte des Beamtentums, 2nd edn. Cologne

Heymann E (1921) Die Rechtsformen der militärischen Kriegswirtschaft als Grundlage des neuen Industrierechts. Marburg

Hofmann H-H (ed) (1967) Die Entstehung des modernen souveränen Staates. Cologne

Huber ER (1969–1984) Deutsche Verfassungsgeschichte seit 1789, vols 4 (1969), 5 (1978a), 6 (1981, rev 1993) and 7 (1984). Stuttgart

Kahn R (1918) Rechtsbegriffe der Kriegswirtschaft. Ein Versuch der Grundlegung des Kriegswirtschaftsrechts. Munich

Kleeis F (1928/1981) Die Geschichte der sozialen Versicherung. Berlin. Reprint 1981. Berlin

Preller L (1949/1978) Sozialpolitik in der Weimarer Republik. Reprint 1978. Stuttgart

Sachße C, Tennstedt F (1980/1988) Geschichte der Armenfürsorge in Deutschland, vol 1 (1980); Fürsorge und Wohlfahrtspflege 1871 bis 1929, vol 2 (1988). Stuttgart

Schaffner L (1964) Gönner. Neue Deutsche Biographie 6:518f

Schmidt MG (1998/2005) Sozialpolitik in Deutschland. Historische Entwicklung und internationaler Vergleich, 2nd edn (1998), 3rd edn (2005). Wiesbaden

[13] "Zweite VO des Reichspräsidenten zur Sicherung von Wirtschaft und Finanzen v. 5 Juni 1931," RGBl. I, p. 279.

Stolleis M (1987) Besatzungsherrschaft und Wiederaufbau deutscher Staatlichkeit 1945–1949. In: Isensee J, Kirchof P (eds) Handbuch des Staatsrechts, vol 1, § 5. Heidelberg (3rd edn, 2003, § 7)
Stolleis M (ed) (1995) Juristen. Ein biographisches Lexikon. Munich
Williams J (1972) The home fronts. Britain, France and Germany 1914–1918. London
Wunder B (1978) Privilegierung und Disziplinierung. Die Entstehung des Berufsbeamtentums in Bayern und Württemberg (1780–1825). Munich
Wunder B (1982) Hof und Verwaltung im 17. Jahrhundert. Daphnis 11:5–14
Wunder B (1985) Pfarrwitwenkassen und Beamtenwitwen-Anstalten vom 16.-19. Jahrhundert Die Entstehung der staatlichen Hinterbliebenenversorgung in Deutschland. Zeitschrift für Historische Forschung 12:429–498
Wunder B (1989) Die Stellung der Subalternen und Unterbeamten in Baden während des 19. Jahrhunderts. Jahrbuch für Europäische Verwaltungsgeschichte 1:187–206
Zacher HF (1970) Entschädigungssysteme. Die Öffentliche Verwaltung 6
Zacher HF (1972) Zur sozialen Programmatik der Bayerischen Verfassung. Festschrift zum 25jährigen Bestehen des BayVerfGH. Munich, pp 95ff
Zacher HF, Ziegler T (1984) Die Versorgung der Beamten, Richter und Soldaten. Heidelberg

Stolleis M (1987) Besatzungsherrschaft und Wiederaufbau deutscher Staatlichkeit 1945–1949. In: Isensee J, Kirchhof P (eds) Handbuch des Staatsrechts, vol I, 3. Heidelberg (3rd edn. 2003), § 7

[illegible]

V. The Weimar Republic

The economic and social situation was desperate after the war. The situation could no longer be managed with the traditional poor relief. Before the war, the basis of welfare provisioning had been "that one is dealing with non-economic entities" who were unable "to find their place in life on their own" and "to fulfill their task in economic life and society" (Klumker 1918, p. 25). Six million soldiers and more than three million surviving dependents and disabled veterans now had to be integrated. They were joined by impoverished service members and other unemployment casualties of the conversion from wartime to peacetime production. National income had been cut in half. The state and local government were in debt and a rising inflation, which would destroy savings, seemed only a matter of time. In this way, the relatively contained strata of the "poor" (Klumker 1918, pp. 10ff.) from before the war had become a menacingly broad stratum, which was filled not only by victims of the war, but also by a middle class stripped of their assets.

In spite of the exceedingly difficult economic situation, conditions were not unfavorable for the Republic, as long as one looked at the given institutional structure. The Republic inherited from the Empire not only the legal system and the institutions, but also a professional civil service vaunted as exemplary. The same is true of the local communities and communal organizations. Traditionally, they were the locus of a majority of the tasks at hand (poor relief and youth care, the creation of jobs and housing, communal health policy, social infrastructure). Since they were closest to the social problems, it was there that the powers for overcoming them were most likely to emerge. Voluntary charity continued to be present and organized into the large associations (Sachße and Tennstedt 1988, pp. 152–172): (1) *Centralausschuß für die Innere Mission der deutschen evangelischen Kirche*, (2) *Deutscher Caritas-Verband*, (3) *Zentralwohlfahrtsstelle der Juden*, (4) the *Deutsche Rote Kreuz* [German Red Cross], (5) *Fünfte (Deutsche*

Previously published in English in the following publication: Stolleis: Origins of the German Welfare State (German Social Policy, Vol. 2), Springer, Berlin/Heidelberg, 2013.

DOI 10.1007/978-3-642-38454-7_5, © Springer-Verlag Berlin Heidelberg 2014

Paritätische) Wohlfahrtsverband, (6), *Hauptausschuß für Arbeiterwohlfahrt*, and (7) *Zentralwohlfahrtsausschuß der christlichen Arbeiterschaft*, all—with the exception of the Arbeiterwohlfahrt—united in the *Deutsche Liga der freien Wohlfahrtspflege* [German League for Charitable Welfare].

And more: the social insurances for workers and salaried employees were financially weakened, but they were institutionally intact. Wartime Welfare [*Kriegsfürsorge*] could be continued. The "Weimar Coalition" (Social Democrats, Center Party, German Democratic Party), which was particularly progressive on social legislation, dominated the National Assembly. Women's right to vote (Art. 22 WRV) imparted to this current a far broader democratic legitimacy. The denial of voting rights to welfare recipients had also be repealed on November 29, 1928, by a decree from the Council of People's Representatives. The number of workers organized in unions grew from 3.9 million (1918) to 13.3 million (1922) (Preller 1978, pp. 180ff.). The new constitution of August 11, 1919, gave the Reich the legislative authority for "welfare for the poor and migrants," "population policy, welfare for mothers, infants, children, and youths," "labor law, insurance and protection of workers and employees as well as certification of employment," and "welfare for servicemen and their dependents" (Art. 7 WRV). To the extent that there was a need for the enactment of uniform regulations, the Reich also had the legislative authority for the "welfare system" (Art. 9 WRV). Together with the basic principles of social policy (partly programmatic in nature, partly possessing the character of basic law) in the second main section of the Constitution (Articles 109, 119, 122, 151, 155, 161–163), these norms formed the constitutional basis for a wide-ranging social legislation with which the Republic, endangered from the very beginning, could set out to deal by means of social policy with the misery of the war, inflation, and depression (Henning 1978, pp. 64ff.; Büsch and Feldman 1978; Feldman 1984, 1993).

Although these starting conditions seemed good, problems quickly proliferated. German society and its political system were unsettled by the defeat in the war and the humiliation in foreign policy, the hitherto ruling classes were partly overthrown, partly disoriented. The symptoms of intellectual unrest and a quest for meaning, which had been multiplying already since the end of the nineteenth century and were an indicator for a crisis-driven transformation of social conditions and attitude towards life that went with it, were now at times condensing into the experience of catastrophes. The most difficult phases (1920–1923, 1929–1932) and their political events have been closely studied and described (Bracher 1971; Kindleberger 1973; Möller 1997; Winkler 1993). That is also true of the social policy that was realized during these phases (Deutsche Sozialpolitik 1918–1928 (1929); Preller 1978; Abelshauser 1987).

War and inflation shifted the basic direction of social policy. While in the Empire it had aimed primarily at industrial workers and had simultaneously sought to pacify them politically by providing material security, the consistent expansion of social insurance was already pointing in the direction of a slowly emerging national insurance. However, that trend asserted itself fully only when entirely new segments of the population became involuntarily dependent upon the state in the postwar period. The number of the needy quadrupled between 1913 and 1924, and the need for state support per capital grew eightfold (Sachße and Tennstedt 1988, p. 81). Since the number of industrial workers stagnated, while that of salaried employees and the socially needy strata increased, what became evident here was the transition from a more simply structured class society to a more complex, modern mass society. In that society, those who had jobs gained a relatively secure place, thanks to guarantees and protections from associations, while the unemployed and many other groups gradually turned into the "poor," without being able to fight against it in any organized form. These groups, which were now also voters, could not be pacified by pointing to traditional welfare. The trend and potential was forever broader strata to become recipients of social services and benefits, which would lead invariably to an intertwining of the various special systems and to an ever more refined balancing of "equality." That is also the reason why the equality clause in Article 109 of the Constitution experienced an extraordinary growth in importance (Anschütz 1933: Art. 109).

Other areas of politics, too, were seized in this way by the ubiquitous notion of "the social." Every political measure that affected a nation sorely oppressed by dire circumstances had to take the social element into considerations. Thus, social law in the broader sense included the Reich Settlement Act [*Reichssiedlungsgesetz*] and Reich Homestead Act [*Reichsheimstättengesetz*], legal regulations to protect renters and tenants, regulations to eliminate the housing shortage, steps to hold down rent increases, and the entire social housing construction of the 1920s and 1930s. Socially motivated in this broadest sense was also the fight against inflation.

1. Welfare [*Fürsorge*]

The welfare measures occasioned by the war had placed alongside the old poor relief an "elevated welfare," the War Welfare [*Kriegswohlfahrtspflege*]. That created two classes of welfare recipients: the traditional poor, who had to be supported "by virtue of their existence," were joined by the "special victims" of the war, whom one did not wish to burden with the odium of poor relief. This concerned primarily family support for the wives and children of conscripted soldiers, care for disabled veterans and their families, and provisions for surviving dependents (widows and orphans), as well as special care for those groups so badly damaged economically by war and inflation that they had to become welfare recipients. This new "welfare" dominated by the notion of special sacrifice gave rise to ideas that were no longer compatible with the old poor relief: the end to political discrimination, legal entitlement to benefits, the individualization of aid, professionalization, and a socio-political guiding intent that was very different from the traditional "poor policy." As a result, the older system of poor relief receded into the background to the same degree that the new systems of protection took shape. Nevertheless, it continued to be indispensable as a subsidiary system. Welfare was the supplementary system when other protections failed or did not provide adequate benefits. However, this clean separation was not really accomplished, especially since the goal was to combine organizationally all welfare benefits "into one hand" of the district and state welfare associations. For example, the differentiation between poor relief and "elevated welfare" could be achieved only through different benefit levels and by not including the social security pension or other benefits. Notwithstanding all efforts at drawing distinctions, "welfare" [*Fürsorge*] became the dominant term. All recipients of social benefits who wanted to escape the negatively-freighted status of the "poor" saw themselves cast back into this status in the post-war period and the crisis years of the Republic—whether they were disabled veterans or surviving dependents, members of the middle class wiped out by the devaluation of the money, recipients of very small pensions from social insurance, or unemployed who fell outside of the protection of insurance. The bitterness this generated became one of the essential causes behind the instability of the Republic (Winkler 1972; Möller et al. 1993).

Public welfare had traditionally been the domain of local communities and the federal states (Castell-Rüdenhausen 1991). The Reich level had to be used at most to regulate such central questions as that of the *Unterstützungswohnsitz* [residential relief system]. During the war, as we have seen, the Reich took on those special areas of "elevated welfare" that ran parallel to poor relief, were financed or subsidized by the Reich, and at the same time were supposed to remain clearly separated from poor relief. That line was continued after the war. The Residential Relief Act [*Unterstützungswohnsitzgesetz*] of 1870 remained in force (in the version of July 7, 1908) and the Reich was initially active in areas that lay aside poor relief. These were: communal unemployment relief, co-financed by the Reich and the states, which could be means-tested and demand work in return, but which was not poor relief[1]; welfare for surviving dependents and disabled veterans[2]; welfare for recipients of very small pensions and social security retirees[3]; child and youth welfare (Sachße and Tennstedt 1988, pp. 99ff.); health care, including care for women in childbed[4]; and housing welfare (Sachße and Tennstedt 1988, pp. 138ff.). These continuously growing areas began to divide and break down into more specific and detailed areas of welfare. They were in part emergency measures to deal with the consequences of the war, dominated by the basic notion of the "special sacrifice," and in part the expression of an engagement by the welfare state that had moved far away from the older notions of "good order." The endeavor to maintain

[1] "VO über die Erwerbslosenfürsorge v. 13. November 1918", RGBl., p. 1305; Sachße and Tennstedt (1980, pp. 94ff.).

[2] "VO über die soziale Kriegsbeschädigten- und Kriegshinterbliebenenfürsorge v. 8. Februar 1919", RGBl., p. 187; Sachße and Tennstedt (1988, pp. 98ff.)

[3] "Reichsgesetz über Notstandsmaßnahmen zur Unterstützung von Rentenempfängern der Invaliden- und Angestelltenversicherung v. 7. Dezember 1921," RBGl., p. 1533; "Gesetz über Kleinrentnerfürsorge v. 4. Februar 1923," RGBl. I, p. 104; Sachße and Tennstedt (1988, pp. 92ff.).

[4] This area was separated from sickness insurance, since this was not insurance law, but organizationally nothing changed. See the "Gesetz über Wochenfürsorge v. 9. Juni 1922", RGBl. I, p. 502; Sachße and Tennstedt (1988, pp. 114ff.).

social harmony by means of social policy was crisis management intended to prevent an internal political collapse. The state, which had laid claim since the World War to overall responsibility for the reliable performance of societal processes, or at least was not able to rebuff the corresponding ascription of this kind of responsibility, now carried on the sovereign guidance it had rehearsed during the war: in part through financial subsidies, which tended to turn local communities into "paying offices of the Reich" (Sachße and Tennstedt 1988, p. 87), in part through laws that created the framework, through laws that exerted direct guidance on areas assigned by the competency system of the Reich Constitution, and by (emergency) decrees, "basic principles," or "recommendations." No strict system was pursued in the process. The Reich regulated what could be regulated within the framework of what was politically and financially possible, and developed the organizational forms that went along in a very pragmatic fashion (Berg 1985, §8, pp. 231ff.). Or to put it more clearly: there "emerged a de facto highly fragmented, difficult-to-grasp tangle of special types of welfare, each with different legal foundations and financing modalities, different administrative organization, and unequal benefit levels" (Sachße and Tennstedt 1988, p. 142f.).

Thus, as long as the Reich, out of tradition and a supraordinated perspective, devoted itself to the areas of "elevated welfare," aid to the poor through public welfare remained a matter for the states. The state laws that were now passed[5] were "organizational laws intended to standardize and stabilize the developments of communal welfare that had begun during the Wilhelmenian period. The goal was to ensure that all institutions, both public and private, followed uniform, planned, and deliberate procedures, to prevent a fragmentation of efforts and expenditures, and gain professionally trained personnel to carry out the newly defined tasks" (Sachße and Tennstedt 1988, p. 87).

Parallel to this development, however, as the welfare system was transferred from the Reich Ministry of the Interior to the Reich Labor Ministry in October 1918 on the basis of the new constitution, ideas about a "Reich Poor Law" that had been floating around in the *Deutscher Verein für öffentliche und private Fürsorge* [German Association for Public and Private Welfare] since 1912 became more concrete. Out of the initially modest plans to replace the *Unterstützungswohnsitz* with the *Aufenthaltsprinzip* [the principle that aid is given wherever a person happens to be living], to grant a legal entitlement to aid, and to have the Reich bear more of the costs than it did before, grew plans for a more comprehensive codification of social law. It was to encompass not only all areas of welfare, but also insurance law. Of course, given how recently the Reich Insurance Code of 1911 had been codified, this was not very realistic. That is why the plans were limited to a statutory regulation for all "poor" groups, including youth welfare, that is to say, an integrative "Reich Welfare Law" with legal entitlement and an emphasis on the

[5] Especially: Saxony ("Gesetz über die Wohlfahrtspflege v. 30. Mai 1918"), and Thuringia ("Wohlfahrtsgesetz v. 20. Juni 1922"), but also in nearly all other city states and smaller states. See Sachße and Tennstedt (1988, p. 88).

principle of individualization. Finally, even more restrictive was a continuation of the existing poor law that excluded youth welfare but included the "elevated welfare." As infeasible as a total codification of social law may have seemed, this idea did express the tendency to interconnect all social benefits, which had emerged under the pressure of war and the post-war miseries. Henceforth, the modern welfare state realized itself in a network of social benefits with a tendency to encompass all groups.

And so, all that seemed possible in 1923 was a small solution. It was the year of the inflation, the occupation of the Ruhr region, martial law for the Reich territory, unrest in Saxony and Thuringia, Bavaria's conflict with the Reich, and the Hitler putsch. At the end of the year, the parties agreed to an Enabling Act of December 8, 1923, which would run for 10 weeks (RGBl. I, p. 1179; Huber 1984, vol. 7, pp. 451ff., 458ff.) It provided the basis for a third Emergency Tax Decree on February 14, 1924 (RGBl. I, p. 74). Paragraph 42 of that Decree transferred various areas of social care from the Reich to the states and eliminated the Reich subsidies that had been given until then. The added burden on the state was covered via financial equalization.

In spite of this transfer, the Reich reserved for itself the right to pass more specific decrees under Reich law. And those decrees appeared in the Reich Law on the Responsibility to Provide Social Welfare Assistance [*Reichsverordnung über die Fürsorgepflicht*] of February 13, 1924 (RGBl., p. 100), the first Reich-wide regulation of the core area of welfare provision. As an aside, this path was also used to adjust the contribution and benefits of social insurance, extend working hours, enact the so-called "Emmingerian reform of the judicial system" (1924; Claussen 1985), and pass a series of financial measures.

The Reich law primarily regulated the carriers of public welfare assistance. It replaced the old Associations of Local and State Poor and appointed the State and District Welfare Associations as the new carriers (§1), through the specific form they would take was left to the states. Important for the relationship to the system of voluntary charity was not only the possibility of delegating state tasks, but above all the statement: "The Welfare Associations are not to create their own institutions where suitable institutions of voluntary charity exists in adequate numbers" (§5, Sect. 3). For one, this was intended to prevent inefficient overlapping and competing offerings, for another, it reflected recognition that broad sections of welfare were occupied by social forces, and that these forces should now be given preference as the status quo. This stipulation (§17, Sect. 3, SGB I) has been seen to this day as the basic rule for the division of labor and as an expression of mutual respect and support in the area of social work. Historically it is also a reflection of the strong position of the Center Party and the Caritasverband within the spectrum of socio-political forces in the Weimar Republic.

Public welfare assistance now comprised the following: social assistance for disabled veterans and surviving dependents, assistance for the disabled and for salaried employees who had no insurance protection,[6] assistance for recipients of

[6] Law of December 7, 1921, RGBl., p. 1533, newly promulgated on July 22, 1922, RGBl. I, p. 675.

small pensions,[7] assistance for the severely disabled and those seriously impaired in their ability to work through job procurement, assistance for needy minors, maternity benefits, and—listed only at the very end—assistance for the poor. To set the last-named apart from "higher level welfare," officials resorted to the instruments of material differentiations, whether by granting higher direct benefits, not counting certain income when means-testing, or accepting untouchable "*Schonvermögen*" [exempted personal assets] for those living on social security pensions or very small pensions. After fierce political debates, a new §33a of the Reich Principles stipulated in 1925 that the target levels for "higher level welfare" should be at least one quarter above those for subsistence assistance granted by general welfare for the poor. The difficulties that emerged here reveal how the notions of compensation for special sacrifices and of social equalization became intermixed. Public welfare assistance became the catch-all for those who dropped out of their special systems of social protection and now found themselves in the company of those who became welfare recipients solely because of their poverty. With this, essential special areas of welfare had been once again subsumed under one roof and at a higher level than before. Welfare tasks that occurred at the local level "should by all means be taken on by the same office" (§3).

To be sure, the Reich Decree left it to the states to specify the criteria for the receipt of welfare benefits, define the goals, and decide how the benefits would be delivered. But here, too, the Reich reserved for itself the right to issue "fundamental principles," which then came into force in 1924/1925 (RGBl. I, p. 765). The fundamental principles were based on preliminary work done by the German Association for Public and Private Welfare, especially a memorandum of 1919, which was continued in another memorandum issued by the Reich Labor Ministry on February 14, 1923. They contained a clearly thought-through General Part of welfare law and represented, in terms of substance, the most important codification in this area. They were in force until the passage of the Federal Welfare Act [*Bundesozialhilfegesetz*] in 1961; in fact, they are valid to this day as a material part of this law. Their intellectual concept, strongly shaped by the socio-political tradition of political Catholicism, existed in the previously mentioned memorandum. It stated the following: "Welfare should create values instead of merely preserving them. Its noblest goal must be to strengthen the will and power of the need person such that he can hold his own through his own skill, effort, and productivity. It must not paralyze the self-responsible work, especially not the fulfillment of one's obligations towards one's own family. It must take effect in time and adequately, and, where the need exists, also intervene preemptively. Formally it must respect human dignity. It must not help in a uniform manner, but must probe into the peculiarity of the emergencies and on that basis select the means to remedy them. It should no longer put the giving of cash in the center, but help from one human being to another."[8]

[7] Law of February 4, 1923, RGBl. I, p. 104.

[8] Deutsche Sozialpolitik 1918–1928 (1929), 241.

The essential principles of social assistance today are spelled out in these brief words: what is presupposed is an image of the person that is focused on earning a living through work. That means, conversely, that "asocials" and "work shirkers" ranged at the lowest end of the scale. In case of "uneconomical conduct," social assistance should "test in the strictest way and restrict the kind and measure of social assistance to what is indispensable for getting by." Persons "who stubbornly act against the legitimate directives from the relevant authorities" were disciplined in this way and stood under the threat of being committed to a "work house" (§20, RGBl. I, p. 770). Thus, the work ethic and repression thus lay closely side by side—as they already had throughout the entire modern period and continue to do so to this day.

What this meant was: "normally," everyone should use his own strength and means, should ask his family members for help and seek out aid "form other sides." Only when all of that failed was a person "needy." If that was indeed the case, as verified by a means test involving question about income and living circumstances, the state itself responded "in a timely manner" without an application from the person in need of help and covered the "necessities of life."[9]The state should look to providing work and provide assistance to the needy person in such a "lasting" way that he will be able to get back on his feet again ("help to self-help"). Job procurement thus ranked ahead of cash benefits, lasting help seemed more economical than a never-ending chain of small payments. Following the principle of individualization, the decision about which measure was appropriate was left to the discretion of the authorities: "The assistance that should be granted in each individual case within the framework of the necessities of life must be guided by the peculiarities of the case, namely, the type and duration of the need, the person who is in need, and local conditions."[10] Help was thus to be assistance for the individual, should due justice to the individuality of the person receiving it, and determine his life situation very precisely in order to offer targeted aid. In addition, however, there were also "institutions" of social assistance, to the extent that standardized help seemed more useful or cheaper.

The latter is already an indication that the principle of individualization could not be sustained. Everything was pushing toward standardization, not least the maxim of equality. There were strong regional differences in the aid granted by rural district [*Landkreise*] and cities, the lines of demarcation between general and

[9] "The necessities of life include

a. subsistence, especially housing, food, clothing, and nursing care;
b. sickness assistance and help to restore the ability to work;
c. assistance for pregnant women and maternity benefits, moreover
d. educating minors and enabling them to be gainfully employed,
e. enabling the blind, deaf-mute, and disabled to be gainfully employed.

If necessary, funeral costs shall be paid." (§6 Reichsgrundsätze). For a contemporary voice on this see Arendsee (1932). On this author see Cemy (1992, p. 17).

[10] Compare today §3, Section 1 of the BSHG (Federal Welfare Act).

"elevated" social assistance had to be specified, and the mass nature of the administrative processes called for unified national regulation. As a result, "guidelines" [*Richtsätze*] established themselves, even as the Reich shifted costs almost entirely to the states and local communities, while at the same time having stripped those communities of essential source of income through the Erzbergian Financial Reform of 1920. The *Richtsätze* [today referred to as *Regelsätze*] had a homogenizing effect on the practice of social assistance and also lifted its level. But that precisely caused an accumulation of socio-political dynamite. The communal level bore a growing burden of social assistance, while the previously possible differentiation of benefits according to local conditions and possibilities became increasingly impossible (Sachße and Tennstedt 1988, pp. 175ff.). At the end of the Weimar Republic, local communities across the board were deeply in debt, not least because they had to shoulder the costs of welfare benefits, which became oppressive precisely during a time of crisis. When benefits were cut in 1930, the homogenization previously achieved through the *Richtsätze* revealed its downside to those affected.

To be sure, the Basic Principles did not establish an actionable legal claim to general welfare, which began to establish itself in legal decision after 1949 and became law in 1961 (§4 Federal Welfare Act). Yet such legal claims certainly did exist with the "elevated social assistance," and beginning in 1926 it was also possible to challenge the denial of benefits and the determination of their kind and level. But the protection by the administrative court failed: one was dealing with a discretionary decision, and there was a consensus that it followed from the "historical development of public welfare measures, from poor relief, from the Residential Assistance Act, and the Reich Law on the Responsibility to Provide Social Welfare Assistance of February 13, 1924, that the person in need of assistance never has a legally actionable claim against those obligated."[11] Where a material claim does not exist, the failure of public assistance does not constitute a violation of the individual's legal positions.

In this way, the system of public assistance during the Weimar period reflected the achievements and setbacks of the Republic. Thanks to the preliminary work done before the war, it was possible fairly quickly to reform the organizational foundations, give public assistance a uniform framework throughout the Reich, and provide it also with viable guiding ideas in the "Principles." The "special assistances" that had been developing along their own tracks were to some extent brought back into general public assistance. The professionalization of those working in public assistance made rapid progress especially in the 1920s, namely on both sides of the dual system, the communal assistance bureaucracy and charitable welfare (Sachße and Tennstedt 1988, pp. 202ff.). Consequently, the individuals working in these areas were incorporated into social insurance. But

[11] "Urteil des Preus. Kompetenzkonflikt-Gerichtshofs v. 20. Juni 1931," in *Nachrichtendienst des Deutschen Vereins für öffentliche und private Fürsorge 1954*, 133. On the qualification of this claim as a *Reflexrecht* see already Jellinek (1905, p. 73).

the expanding system of public assistance as the final protection against material privation invariably came under enormous pressure when the fallout from the war had to be deal with, when inflation destroyed savings, and when the global economic crisis once again threw millions out of work. The expenditures for public assistance weighed heavily on local budgets and thus closed the fateful circle of political hopelessness.

Although the system of charitable welfare, which encompassed more than 10,000 institutions of closed assistance and nearly 19,000 institutions of open assistance on the eve of the war, had expanded and professionalized itself to an astounding degree, it still had to wage the same battle against inflation as all other structures and it did not receive from the state the kind of support in keeping with its function. The subsidies for the work it did declined continuously also in the economically favorable years of the Republic (1924–1929). In the end, charitable welfare was not able to cushion the shortcomings that had developed in public assistance.

2. Youth Welfare

Parallel to the development of public assistance, and in part preceding it, "youth social law" came into its own. Such a special area tailored specifically to an age group had never before existed. To be sure, the state in the nineteenth century had reacted in an age-specific way with the gradual curtailment of child labor after 1939, with the enactment of obligatory school attendance, with aid to orphans under poor relief law, and with regulations pertaining to guardianship, but this was not driven by a self-contained social policy for the benefit of "young people." Such a policy was absent especially in the reactions of criminal law and of corrective training [*Fürsorgeerziehung*], which varied from state to state and could be imposed by the criminal judge.

Beginning in 1900, however, a number of factors changed. The Civil Code standardized family law, especially the stipulations regarding maintenance, guardianship, and adoption. It established a threshold for state intervention with "child welfare [*Kindeswohl*]" (§§1666, 1838 BGB). In addition, for the purpose of preventing "utter moral dissolution," the "compulsory education of minors" that was possible since 1871 was made feasible at the state level.[12]

In Prussia, this led to the separation of local poor relief and supralocal public assistance education (*Fürsorgeerziehung*) administered by the provincial associations.[13] The states now also began to set up a system of youth welfare separate from poor relief. It included, in addition to oversight of foster care, the institution of official guardianship (*Amtsvormundschaft*), through which—different

[12] Article 135 "Einführungsgesetz zum BGB" (EGBGB).

[13] "Gesetz für die Fürsorgeerziehung Minderjähriger v. 2. Juli 1900," PrGS, 264–269.

from the individual guardianship of the Civil Code—an official agency was employed for a community's orphans (Art. 136 EGBGB) (Keidel 1929, pp. 357ff.).

While the relevant local authority still combined task related to policing, poor relief, and youth welfare between 1900 and 1910, a process of differentiation began: for example, in 1900 in Mainz with a special deputation for youth welfare (Schmidt 1907), with "Committees for Youth Welfare" in Prussia's Rhenish Province and in Westphalia, or in 1910 with the creation of the first Youth Office in Hamburg (Hasenclever 1978, p. 31). Henceforth, services to youth people were no longer supposed to have the politically discriminatory effects of poor relief.[14] The same period saw the beginning of the youth court movement, which was based on the realization that juvenile delinquency had specific causes and called for a specific response. Preliminary work for a "Youth Court Law" commenced in 1908, born by the hope of incorporating as many pedagogical elements as possible into penal law.

Behind these varied approaches stood the bourgeois Youth Movement and the Workers' Youth Movement, though the latter was looked upon with suspicion by the Wilhelmenian state and was excluded from government support.[15] In order to maintain political control in this area, Prussia initiated a patriotically oriented leisure time education for boys in 1911, after 1913 also for girls.

The First World War on the one hand interrupted the reformist approaches, while on the other hand intensifying the aspect of public assistance and oversight. Young people were subject to the reach of the military administrative apparatus (obligation to work, prohibition against entering taverns, compulsory savings, etc.); at the same time, they were recognized as national "capital" in need of active, non-discriminatory care. Embracing the promotion of young people could thus have military, nationalistic, idealistic-reformist, or socialist motives. All of these currents presupposed "youth" as a separate phase of life, and the demand for a separate "youth law" was accordingly raised for the first time in 1916 (Simon 1916).

With the revolution of 1918 and the work of the National Assembly in 1919, a standardized national regulation of public youth welfare through Youth Offices seemed possible, indeed, supporters were hoping for a major Reich Youth Law (Felisch 1917; Gräser 1995). The new constitution stipulated the parents' right and obligation "to raise their children to bodily, spiritual, and social fitness" and the authority of the state to supervise it (Art. 120 WRV). It further promised equality for "children of our wedlock" and the protection of youth "against exploitation and against moral, spiritual, or bodily dissipation" (Articles 121, 122 WRV). Large families now had a "claim to compensatory social welfare" (Art. 119, Section 2 WRV).

---

[14] "Reichsgesetz betreffend die Einwirkung von Armenunterstützung auf öffentliche Rechte v. 15. März 1909," RGBl., p. 319.

[15] See §17 of the "Vereinsgesetz v. 19. April 1908," which prohibited young people under the age of 18 not only from being members in political organizations, but also from attending public political gatherings.

The hope was that a Reich law on youth welfare could be quickly created on this basis. But the Kapp Putsch and the financial concerns of the states slowed the National Assembly. The legislative process resumed only after an interpellation by 33 women from all parliamentary groups in the Reichstag, led by Marie Elisabeth Lüders (DDP), Gertrud Bäumer (DDP), Agnes Neuhaus (Zentrum), and Marie Juchacz (SPD), pushed for its acceleration (Hasenclever 1978, pp. 52–58). Although many reformist hopes from the pre-war period were not considered, the Reich Law for Youth Welfare of July 9, 1922, did guarantee for the first time a "right to an education to bodily, spiritual, and social fitness" (§1), recognized the primacy of the parents and the principle of subsidiarity between the family and the state, emphasized the "unity of youth welfare" against certain centrifugal tendencies, and, finally, regulated the position of public youth welfare toward private, charitable youth welfare (RGBl. I, pp. 633, 647).

In the loss column was the fact that there was no supreme Reich agency and that youth jurisdiction remained separated from youth welfare. The tension—visible to this day—between state youth welfare (official guardian ship, local orphans' council, protection of foster children, corrective training [*Fürsorgeerziehung*] and the largely charitable *Jugendpflege* [care for the youth]) persisted. The demarcation between youth law and social assistance law, toward the Kindergarten and school system, toward disability law and health care required several more decades of efforts in practice and legal decisions. Finally, youth welfare saw its sphere of action curtailed again almost immediately.[16]

In spite of all the compromises and curtailments (Neundörfer 1923), however, the Youth Welfare Law was an outstanding legislative achievement by the young Republic, a balancing act between the "socialization of youth welfare" and the bourgeois-confessional "protection of the family." It installed throughout the Reich the communal "Youth Office" as a new agency staffed with professionals. It carried out the shift from thinking in categories of warding off dangers toward a pedagogically motivated "protection of the youth," no doubt also in consideration of the increasingly important function of the private, charitable *Jugendpflege*, which attained considerable influence through the participation of the laity. It became the framework law for the youth work by the states,[17] individualized youth assistance, and asserted the latter's "unity" with respect to assistance and care.[18]

The subsequent years also saw strong discrepancies between an advanced professional discussion and the political possibilities of a Republic wracked by crises. Apart from the politicians in the Reichstag, it was especially Gertrud Bäumer, Christian Klumker, Wilhelm Polligkeit, Hans Muthesius, and Hermann

[16] "Verordnung über das Inkrafttreten des RJWG v. 14.2.1924," RGBl. I, p. 110; "Einführungsgesetz zum Reichsgesetze für Jugendwohlfahrt i. d. F. v. 14. Februar 1924," RGBl. I, p. 110.

[17] Hasenclever (1978, pp. 98ff.); Friedeberg and Polligkeit (1930, pp. 47ff.). The implementing laws for the Reich Youth Law after 1923 can be found in von Staudinger (1929), EGBGB, 356f.

[18] Weaknesses of the Law summarized in Hasenclever (1978, p. 85f.).

Nohl who advanced the practice and who did the conceptual work. What was created in spite of the short and problem-ridden time was still impressive: the legislator now regulated across the Reich the "religious majority" of children and youths that was stipulated in the constitution.[19] Criminal law witnessed the same kind of differentiation as social law through the emergence of a "youth social law." In preparation since 1920, the Youth Court Act was passed in 1922.[20] It contained new thresholds for the age of criminal responsibility and allowed for a response to young people based on their "capacity of discernment." In fact, it generally followed the trend to consider the developmental processes in young people in the kind of punishments handed down, in the register of convictions, and in the cooperation with charitable youth aid and the Youth Offices (so-called Youth Court Assistance). To be sure, the corrective training that had just recently been eliminated from youth assistance law, and which was still considered indispensable, had moved into youth penal law as an instrument of educational discipline in the hands of the judge. Eventually, the legislators responded preventively with the Movie Theater Law of May 12, 1920, to the real or presumed dangers of the new medium, a trend that continued with the December 18, 1926 law—highly controversial in terms of cultural policy—to combat harmful publications.[21] Other "protective" initiatives, including also those to improve workplace safety, failed.

A summary of the legislative and practical developments in youth welfare during the Weimar Republic is not easy. There were considerable delays and other shortcomings in implementation, but at the same time a move toward professionalization and the incorporation of women as youth welfare workers, combined with the mobilization of voluntary forces. The same kind of professionalization occurred in the work of organizations, in which socialist, charitable, reform-pedagogical, and nationalistic patterns emerged. Needless to say, there were heated debates, for example about the inadequate and scandal-ridden corrective training, which was to be transformed—if possible—from a tool resembling penal incarceration into an effective pedagogical institutions, while the Left argued that it should be abolished altogether. The fact that corrective training was reduced during the final phase of presidential dictatorship, over the objection from professionals, and the young people in this program added to the already catastrophic number of unemployed youths, was a bitter ending to the controversy.[22] In the end there were efforts to ward off a catastrophe, for example through the creation of the voluntary labor service after 1929 and an "Emergency Organization for German Youth" (1932), efforts that were unsuccessful given the dire financial straits of public budgets and the radicalization of the youth that had already occurred.

[19] "Gesetz über religiöse Kindererziehung v. 15. Juli 1921," RGBl., p. 939. See Kammerloher-Lis (1994).

[20] "Jugendgerichtsgesetz v. 16. Februar 1923," RGBl. I, pp. 135, 252.

[21] Petersen (1995, pp. 50ff. [Movie Theater Law], 56ff. [Harmful Publications Law]).

[22] "VO des Reichspräsidenten über Jugendwohlfahrt v. 4. November 1932," RGBl. I, p. 522; "VO des Reichspräsidenten über Fürsorgeerziehung v. 28. November 1932," RGBl. I, p. 531.

3. Housing Policy

Although some measures of government housing policy had already been taken during the world war, this area gained new importance only under the conditions of the Weimar Republic. The steps taken during the war to support the social peace on the "home front" (tenant protection, rent control, publicly-run housing, promotion of housing construction) could be expanded and built upon under the provisions of Article 155 of the Weimar Constitution. With that article, state care for housing made its way into the catalog of public tasks by way of constitutional law. It stipulated that that state should secure "healthy housing to all Germans, and to all German families, especially those with many children, housing and an economic homestead in accordance with their needs." War veterans were to be given "special consideration in the homestead law that is to be written." Of course, this stipulation, too, was only a guideline for the legislators and therefore—as Gerhard Anschütz put it in his leading commentary—"lex ferenda, not lex lata" (Anschütz 1933, p. 723). Still, important reform projects in this area fell into the period 1918–1933. Initial measures were already taken even before the constitution took effect. The situation in the housing market was exacerbated especially by the return of many veterans and the concentration of workers in a few centers of the armaments industry. Added to this was the fact that housing construction had virtually ground to a halt during the war. With the national economy focused on war industry, construction materials and workers were hard to come by. At times there were even thoughts of prohibiting all construction activity that did not serve military interests through the general commands (Bunte 1995, p. 23). The capital market for housing construction had collapsed; compared to war bonds, housing construction was barely profitable for investors; the construction of company housing and construction programs for employees by the Reich, the states, and the local communities had ceased, except for the erection of barracks for armaments workers. While the net gain in housing units had been at 200,000 in 1913, by 1918 it had dropped to only 8,000 (Bräunche 1997, pp. 23ff.; Bunte 1995, p. 24). Estimates put the housing shortfall in 1918 at 700,000–800,000 units, and it nearly doubled again by 1923 (Peters 1984, p. 60; Stratmann 1976, p. 40; Witt 1979, p. 392). The reasons lay in the immediate fallout from the war. An army of a million had to be demobilized, refugees from Alsace-Lorraine had to be absorbed,[23] soldiers from the dissolved garrisons flooded the housing market, and the establishment of households and families surged in the first years after the war.[24] The housing crisis, which was latent in many parts of the Reich also before 1914, could no longer be shunted aside. The Frankfurt City

[23] A total of 32,000, who were looked after by the "Reich Office of Care for Expellees from Alsace-Lorraine" in Freiburg i. Br. Bräunche (1997, p. 25). Karlsruhe had 6,000 resettlers from Alsace (Bräunche, ibid.), Frankfurt am Main about 4,500 (Stratmann 1976, p. 52).

[24] In the *Standesamtsbezirk* Karlsruhe, the number of marriages was well below 1,000 during the war years, rose to 1,877 by 1919, and to 2,155 by 1920. For the repercussions on the housing market see Dommer (1926).

Construction Councilor [*Stadtbaurat*], Ernst May, expressed the general sentiment: "The war and its consequences – the Revolution – have sharpened the authorities' sense of responsibility for pacifying the people with healthy housing" (Stratmann 1976, p. 53).

The response of the legislature on the Reich level to the growing crisis lay largely in expanding protection for tenants. The "Law on Tenant Protection and Rent Tribunals" of June 1, 1923 (RGBl. I, p. 353) created special regulations for the old housing stock (the cutoff date for that list was July 1, 1918), exempting the units owned by the public, non-profit Housing Construction Association. The right to terminate a lease was essentially revoked; there was merely the possibility of an action requesting a modification of legal status, the success of which depended on the existence of certain reasons for the termination of lease (personal use, arrears in rent, improper use of the rented space, or nuisance to the landlord). The legal enforcement of an order to vacate could occur only with the consent of the Rent Tribunals. Moreover, if a rental agreement was terminated, the tenant had to be provided with housing of equal quality.

A year earlier, the Reich Rent Law of March 20, 1922, had introduced nation-wide rent control, the enforcement of which was placed into the hands of the communal Rent Tribunals. Prussia already had a corresponding regulation since the Maximum Rent Decree of December 9, 1919 (PrGS, 59). But tenants, too, had to accept restrictions, specifically on the basic right of freedom of movement (Article 111 WRV). In addition to the fight against food shortages, the fight against the housing shortage played a major role in this area. Thus, the Proclamation about Measures against the Housing Shortage of September 23, 1918 (RGBl., p. 1353), in its last version as the "Housing Shortage Act" of July 26, 1923 (RGBl. I, p. 751), was in force throughout the Weimar Republic. The result of these regulations during the period of inflation was that the rents that were fixed lagged the erosion in the value of the money. At times, the rent amounted to merely 1 % of net wages.[25]

Another response to the general misery was passage of the Reich Homestead Act on May 10, 1920 (RGBl., pp. 962, 1218). It picked up the homesteading idea that had been spreading to Germany from America since the 1880s, and which, in addition to pursuing certain goals of population policy, was aimed primarily at improving the economic situation of socially weaker groups.[26] Under the leadership of the Prussian land reformer Adolf Damaschke, the "Main Committee for Soldiers' Homesteads" was founded in 1915, whose goal was to strengthen the morale of the fighting troops; the soldier, as Damaschke put it, should "fight like a man who is defending his own homestead" (Schildt 1998, p. 154). As in so many cases, it was only the control economy of the war that made possible long-delayed interventions

[25] Bunte (1995, p. 30). Case studies in Stratmann (1976: Frankfurt) and Bräunche (1997: Karlsruhe).

[26] On the homesteading idea see *Der Große Brockhaus*, vol. 8, 13th edn. (Leipzig, 1931), "Heimstättenwesen," 328; Damaschke (1922, pp. 262–298).

by the social state. The Reich Homestead Act of 1920 distinguished so-called Residential Homesteads (the family's house and vegetable garden for suburban and rural conditions), and economic homesteads (for farm or truck gardens), which were handed out by the Reich, states, local communities, and community associations (§1). The status as a homestead had to be entered into the land register (§5). When a homestead was sold, the issuer had the first right of refusal (§11), and in the case where "the homesteader does not himself permanently occupy or work the homestead, or if he engages in gross mismanagement," the issuer had the right to reclaim it (§12). A mortgage on the homestead required the approval of the issuer (§16), a foreclosure because of the homesteader's personal indebtedness was not permissible (§20). In line with Article 155 of the Weimar Constitution, veterans and war widows should be given preference in the distribution of homesteads.

Of course, all of these measures could do no more than "administer" the existing shortages and misery. A fundamental change would have required a reinvigoration of construction activity. Especially the shortage of private capital as well as building land, and not least the significantly higher building costs (in 1920 they were about 15 times higher than before the war) (Bunte 1995, p. 32), prompted the public authorities in 1918 to embark on the path of promoting housing construction. Five hundred million Marks were set aside to create housing, especially for large families and socially weaker segments of the population (Bunte 1995, p. 34). These subsidies served to compensate for the higher building costs, but they offered so little incentive for economical construction that the straight subsidy program was replaced with construction loans starting with the 1920 budget. The "Law Concerning the Temporary Promotion of Housing Construction" of February 12, 1921, obligated the states to spend at least 30 Marks per resident in fiscal 1921/1922 for the public promotion of housing construction, with most of the money—totaling about 1.8 billion Marks—advanced by the Reich. The financing of this measure was largely provided by the "Law Concerning the Levying of Tax for the Promotion of Housing Construction" of June 26, 1921, which required the owners of housing completed before July 1, 1918, including renters, to pay 5 % of the pre-war user value (calculated as of July 1, 1914) (RGBl., p. 773). That program came to an end during the inflation summer of 1923, when the receipts, in spite of higher rates (up to 90,000 % higher), no longer covered even the expense of collecting them. All told, the balance sheet of those years up to 1923 was not very positive. The net addition of around 560,000 housing units covered merely a third of the shortfall, which had risen once again during the period of inflation (Bunte 1995, p. 37). The promise of at least temporary relief came from the creation of makeshift and small dwellings, whereby the public authorities increasingly took the lead as the builder. Settlements for disabled veterans and expellees were erected with "emergency" dwellings of varying quality, sometimes also in former barracks (Bräunche 1997, p. 27). In this way 60,000 units were created in the German Reich in 1919, but we certainly cannot speak of a standardized process. Construction activity was more intensive in cities where the workers' movement had achieved influence through the workers' and soldiers' councils.[27] But the city as the builder remained the exception; for the most part, the state's direct influence was exerted by way of housing taxes, loans, and rent regulations.

It was only the introduction of the Rentenmark and the stabilization of the currency from 1923/1924 that made possible a new policy of promoting housing on the basis of precise budgeting. At the same time, the voices demanding a radical change of course toward the unfettered housing market of the pre-war period grew louder.[28] The Reich government, too, regarded the low rents (depending on the states, between 25 and 40 % of the peacetime rents in 1913) as a problem. There were discussions in the Reich Labor Ministry about bringing rents slowly up to the pre-war level, but to collect the differences in taxes and channel it into housing construction (Ruck 1997, p. 41). That was the thrust of the Emergence Tax Decree of February 14, 1924 (RGBl. I, p. 74). This decree levied a "monetary depreciation compensation tax on built-up land" from states and local communities, one tenth-of which had to be spent on promoting housing construction. Since this levy was referred to in Prussia in short as the *Hauszinssteuer* [House rent tax], people spoke in view of the public construction activity that soon began of the "*Hauszinsteuer* era."[29]

With the introduction of this tax, the urgently needed housing construction was financially secured for the foreseeable future; local communities now had the possibility of pursuing housing policy on a larger scale and implementing the settlement measures. Comprehensive planning concepts in the form of "general construction plans" emerged in all large cities. Within the framework of this "new building" there arose new settlements still regarded as exemplary today, such as the "Römerstadt" in Frankfurt am Main (Ernst May), the "Hufeisensiedlung" in Berlin (Bruno Taut), or the "Jarrestadt" in Hamburg (Fritz Schumacher).[30] In the area of public construction and "urban sanitation," as well, long-delayed projects could be carried out, such as schools, libraries, and public swimming pools.[31] This era came to an abrupt end at the beginning of the 1930s: the receipts from the *Hauszinssteuer* dropped by half from 1930 to 1933, and even these reduced funds were used for the general consolidation of the budgets.

[27] Five hundred units were built in Berlin in 1919, but twice as many in much smaller Frankfurt am Main; the city was the direct builder for two-thirds of them, one-third were erected by Construction Associations and Savings Associations. Stratmann (1976, p. 53).

[28] For example, the request by Paul and comrades (DNVP) on October 9, 1924, *Reichstags-drucksache* No. 566, for a "precisely delineated program for dismantling tenant protection and rent control."

[29] The fundamental work on the *Hauszinssteuer* era is Ruck (1987, pp. 91–123), Ruck (1988, pp. 150–200).

[30] For a comprehensive contemporary overview see Adler (1931/1998).

[31] Margold (1931/1998); on the example of Munich see Rudloff (1999).

4. Social Insurance and Labor Law Confront New Challenges

a) Dealing with the Fallout from the War and the Further Development of the Classic Branches of Social Insurance

The historical retrospectives that were written in 1981 and 1989 for the one hundredth anniversary of social insurance strongly emphasized and praised its continuity.

That perspective was perfectly understandable, and in terms of institutional history and personnel there was little to argue against it: "During the Weimar Period, the five branches of the classic social insurance, sickness, accident, and disability insurance, insurance for salaried employees, and miners' insurance preserved their traditional form grounded in the principle of self-administration" (Huber 1981/1993, p. 1097). But it is equally undeniable that social insurance entered into a new political constellation after the revolution and with the new constitution. The constitution proclaimed an active social policy. The Republic began with a majority, the so-called "Weimar Coalition," that was especially open-minded toward social policy. In the founding act of the Republic, the "social" was the element that bound together the workers' movement, the center, and the liberals. Social insurance, as the most important system of protection, had now once and for all ceased being an instrument of domestic politics that was only partially parliamentarized; instead, it was a policy that had been removed from the Ministry of the Interior and handed over to the new Reich Labor Ministry (Rindt and Saffert 1968, p. 13f.), and was fully dependent on the vote of the electorate, which now also included women. That meant more "politics" in the sense of a more active management of the social problems. For the first time it was now also possible to push through by parliamentary means the demands of the women's movement.[32] But there was also "more politics" in the sense of a quicker and less filtered reaction to government crises and economic miseries of the Republic. Especially the inflation of 1923, which devoured not only the citizens' savings but also the reserves of the social insurances, constituted a deep economic rupture from which the various branches of the insurance recovered at different rates. To keep up with the galloping inflation, the capital cover system had to be abandoned at times. Moreover, adjusting the contribution rates and the benefits to the inflation consumed a large portion of the legislative energy (Mügel 1927).

In other words: social policy, which was inescapably also societal policy on a large scale, was the Achilles heel of the young Republic. Its capacity to defuse

[32] Gerhard (1990, p. 342f.) list the Law on Religious Child Rearing (1921), the Reich Youth Welfare Act (1922), the Law on the Admission of Women to Legal Offices and Professions (1922), the Home Work Act (1924), and the Law for the Protection of Women Before and After Giving Birth (1927), and the Reich Law to Combat Sexually Transmitted Diseases (1927).

social conflicts would decide the fate of the state. That was not only the constellation of the years after a lost war and a new beginning marked by uncertainties; it also reflected the long-term trend in the development of the western and central European states since the nineteenth century. The industrial revolution had gotten under way in these states through the unleashing of capitalism and with the enormous human sacrifices that constituted the "social question." But the political pressure emanating from the "social question" and the rising productivity of industrialization also allowed for the creation of large collective system of security, the expansion of worker protections, and the legal regulation of the clash of interests in collective labor law. In all areas, the state abandoned its paltry role as merely a "night watchman" focused on warding off threats and assumed the position of a comprehensive guarantor. It became a "welfare state," initially still in the sense of fighting off threats that could arise for the body politic from mass poverty and class warfare, but then increasingly as a agency for the distribution of the national income that was intertwined in multifarious ways with the societal forces. Those forces were now organized into associations, and in cooperation and competition with the other parties and the ministerial bureaucracies, they were especially intent on getting their hands on the rudder of legislative activity. Everything now depended on the viability of this changed state: the ability for political action, on the one hand, and the productivity of the economy, on the other.

The functionality specifically of the large systems of social insurance was, in turn, linked to the existence of "work." Only jobs brought contributions to the insurance funds, which could in turn benefit others. Conversely, unemployment meant a financial burden and political extremism. There was good reason why the Weimar Constitution promised special and comprehensive social protection for labor (Articles 157–163), and declared that every German "shall be given the opportunity to earn his living by economic labor" (Article 163). The central place of the factor "labor" is also evident in the fact that the organizations of employees and employers, ever since their recognition in the constitution (Articles 159, 165), also dominated the participation of the insured in the social insurance scheme. "Work" and "joblessness" were the two dominant themes of the Republic. That led to an intensive reshaping of individual and collective labor law and to the introduction of a separate labor court jurisdiction. It touched indirectly on social insurance, whose basic pillar was a work relationship subject to compulsory contributions; thus, every measures aimed at the labor market also altered the background conditions for the accessory social insurance. Finally, the classic social insurance was broadened by a bold innovation—a Law on Job Placement and Unemployment Insurance of 1927 that combined job placement and real insurance against joblessness. The fate of the Weimar Republic was "work." It owed its creation to a workers' movement that was largely moderate, and it was eventually undone by rampant unemployment.

For the first time there existed a Reich Labor Ministry.[33] It was also in charge of the "comprehensive insurance system" guaranteed by the constitution, with crucial

[33] "Erlaß v. 4. Oktober 1918," RGBl., p. 1231. The removal of the Reich Insurance Office from the Reich Ministry of the Interior had been pursued in vain by the Republic's first president. See Tennstedt (1984, pp. 47ff.).

contributions by those insured, "to maintain health an the ability to work, to protect motherhood and prevent the economic consequences of old age, weakness, and the vicissitudes of life" (Article 161). These words in the constitution referred to the existing branches of social insurance, while the "critical contribution of the insured" had been limited in 1911. It was "critical" only for sickness and miners' insurance, weaker for insurance for disability, salaried employees, and unemployment, and completely absent for accident insurance. However, 1928 saw the first joint social elections of the insurances for workers and salaried employees and for miners' insurance.[34] The core of the legal foundation of social insurance continued to be the Reich Insurance Code of 1911, which was revised and newly issued.[35] It was joined by the Salaried Employees' Insurance Act (1911/1924) and the Reich Miners' Act (1923).[36]

There were some characteristics that all of the various branches of social insurance in the Weimar Republic shared (Kleeis 1928/1981; Bogs 1981): a generally higher level of democratic legitimacy and a more intensive dependence on politics and party politics that came with that; the functionalization of social insurance in dealing with the consequences of the war, inflation, and the global economic crisis; the expansion of the circle of the insured and of insurance benefits (with a countervailing tendency of frantic cuts through emergency decrees); and, finally, the growing intertwinement of the systems of protection into an overall entity called the "welfare state" [*Wohlfahrtsstaat*].[37]

The latter had clear downsides in the every growing complexity of the set of norms of social insurance. A fundamental reorientation did not take place, even though there were suggestions in that direction. Not even the obvious merger of disability insurance and insurance for salaried employees succeeded. But under the pressure of the circumstances, social insurance law had to be changed and amended so many times that even specialists threw up their hands (Preller 1978, p. 283). That was not only a shortcoming of praxis, but also a structural problem with which social policy has had to wrestle to this day: a legal system with a high degree of complexity into which external political impulses must be continually incorporated is no longer able to gauge the side-effects on the subsystems, effects that can occasionally cascade. Accordingly, the preferred method is to work with the "tentative" introduction of innovations, experimental legislation, or time-limited regulations. Decisions are made on the basis of "equity" by by-passing statutory law

---

[34] "Gesetz über die Wahlen nach der Reichsversicherungsordnung, dem Angestelltenversicherungsgesetz und dem Reichsknappschaftsgesetz v. 8. April 1927," RGBL. I, p. 95; Tennstedt (1977).

[35] "Reichsversicherungsordnung in der Fassung v. 15. Dezember 1924," RGBl., p. 779; "Reichsversicherungsordnung (Drittes, Fünftes und Sechstes Buch) i. d. F. v. 9 Januar 1926," RGBl. I, p. 9.

[36] "Angestelltenversicherungsgesetz i. d. F. v. 28. Mai 1924," RGBl. I, p. 563; "Reichsknappschaftsgesetz v. 23. Juni 1923," RGBl. I, p. 431, "Neufassung v. 1. Juli 1926," RGBl. I, p. 369.

[37] On the history of the word itself see Stolleis (1998).

that has ceased to be meaningful. Above all, the scientific permeation of a field suffers if the latter proves so unstable that any attempt at systematization is soon thwarted by countervailing political impulses.

aa) Sickness Insurance

The legislative changes in the area of sickness insurance reflect societal developments that, in turn, constitute reactions to the existence of functional sickness insurance. I am referring here to the medicalization of society—which now also reached the rural areas—through health reforms, the women's movement and its fight to decriminalize abortion (Gerhard 1990, pp. 366ff.), care for families, and the growing ratio of doctors to the population. The following groups were insured between 1919 and 1923: employees in public corporations, those engaged in home-based commercial work, workers in child-rearing, education, social assistance, nursing, and welfare—in other words, groups that were until then believed to be protected by special social relationships, but which had long since lost this special protection or wished to exchange it for an anonymous-institutional protection for their sake of their own autonomy. Equally important was the inclusion of a "breadwinner's" dependents: they were granted the "family assistance" that was derived from the main contribution payer and legally guaranteed in 1927. The unemployed were also covered by insurance in 1927, a necessary and important innovation intended to prevent gaps in insurance protection from a temporary hiatus in work. In addition, new sickness insurance for sailors was created, carried by a Professional Maritime Association [*Seeberufsgenossenschaft*] (RGBl. I, p. 337). The result of all these expansions was that about 60 % of the population was insured in the statutory sickness funds at the end of the Weimar Republic. If we add all the other funds, sickness insurance at that time was already de facto a "national insurance." With that, a base had been created that was able to carry the complex system of doctors, pharmacists, hospitals, rehabilitation facilities, and the medical, pharmaceutical, and hygiene industries.

Fights over how this important segment of the national income would be divided up were inevitable. Especially doctors who advocated the free choice of a physician and higher fees found themselves at the receiving end of the patronizing power of the sickness funds, particularly since the latter were showing a tendency to set up their own "outpatient clinics" (Hansen et al. 1981). On the one hand, physicians were losing private patients to the compulsory insurance funds, on the other hand, the income base for all physicians broadened. Following a major physicians' strike in 1920, the Reich Labor Ministry brokered an agreement about an approval procedure to provide care as a fund-approved physician.[38] Physicians and sickness funds now negotiated in a "Reich Committee" that guided the shape of the

[38] On the development of the so-called Berlin Agreement of 1913, which was to run for 10 years, see Hansen et al. (1981, pp. 152ff.).

agreements through "guidelines."[39] The conflict had thus been shifted into a corporative institutions operating in a semi-authoritarian fashion, not untypical of the zeitgeist, which could not decide on either the free market approach or a state-run, planned health care service, but preferred "self-responsible guidance." This did not really resolve the conflict: physicians, organized into the Hartmannbund, continue to oppose state guidance of medical care and especially against the possibility of disciplining physicians who were practicing in an "uneconomical" way and even exclude them from working as fund-approved doctors for 2 years.

The Emergency Decree of December 8, 1931, then regulated the question in such a way that the sickness funds paid a flat fee to the Association of Fund-Physicians for every treatment reported to them (RGBl. I, p. 699). The latter, a public law body with compulsory character, in turn distributed the funds to the doctors. One physician was to be responsible for 600 insured patients.

bb) Accident Insurance

Here, too, one can see the pervasive tendency toward an expansion of the individuals covered, the risks that were insured against, and the benefits. For example, it turned out to make sense to insure not only the workers on the factory floor, but also those in the sales and administrative departments closely connected to actual production. Outside of businesses emerged groups that were either new (lab technicians) or previously unprotected (actors), and especially those that were active in the public interest and especially "vulnerable to dangers" (firemen, rescuers, those providing nursing care and welfare assistance).[40]

But accident insurance also expanded the "sphere" of possible accidents by including the way to and from the workplace,[41] and by broadening the notion of a "work" accident by including the operation of tools, for example for the purpose of repair and maintenance. Finally, it went beyond the restriction to "accidents" suggested by its label and protected against occupational diseases that were indicated on an initial list. Thereafter, there was an ongoing, particular discussion—dominated by medical expertise—about an expansion of that list.[42]

However, since the consequences of accidents or occupational diseases extended far beyond medical recovery, the professional associations now also saw to restoring or boosting the ability of victims to return to gainful employment.[43] That

[39] "Verordnung über Ärzte und Krankenkassen und die Krankenhilfe VO v. 30. Oktober 1923," RGBl. I, p. 1051; RGBl. (1932), I, p. 19.

[40] "Drittes Gesetz über Änderungen in der Unfallversicherung v. 20. Dezember 1928," RGBl. I, p. 405f.

[41] "2. Gesetz über Änderungen in der Unfallversicherung v. 14 Juli 1925," RGBl. I, p. 97.

[42] "1. Berufskrankheiten VO v. 12. Mai 1925," RGBl. I, p. 69; expanded by a decree of February 11, 1919, which recognized another 11 occupational diseases.

[43] "2. Gesetz über Änderungen in der Unfallversicherung v. 14. Juli 1925," RGBl. I, p. 97.

included help in finding new work. This led to almost unavoidable frictions with sickness funds and physicians, because the accident insurance began to care for "its" patients in its own facilities. An agreement between the professional associations and physicians in 1926 sought to find common ground.

Finally, the preventive work of accident prevention was from the beginning among the tasks of the professional associations, especially since these efforts also had the effect of lowering costs. That sector was now further strengthened, both through training and codes for businesses, and through the creation of a central office for accident prevention.

cc) Disability Insurance

Disability and old-age insurance would prove the most vulnerable component of social insurance during the crisis years of the Weimar Republic. Although their principles remained unchanged, the First World War already increased the burden by more than tenfold between 1913 and 1924 (Tennstedt 1981, p. 436). At the same time, the inflation caused a catastrophic devaluation of pensions. In spite of frenetic legislative changes,[44] there was simply no longer any equivalence between contributions paid in gold Marks and the benefits paid out in the inflation year of 1923. Rather, the certificate handed out to those entitled to a pension was the prerequisite for the provisions of the somewhat increased *Sozialrente* [social security pension] to kick in.

Since inflation had annihilated the capital of the disability insurance funds, the capital cover system had to be abandoned. A gradual consolidation was achieved by 1929 with the help of the "average premium method based on pay-as-you-go principles" (Prämiendurchschnittsverfahren nach Umlagegrundsätzen), of which was used to move away from the rigid principle of Mark = Mark. Still, by that time pensions had not yet reached the level of truly securing a person's livelihood in old age.

Important was the elimination of the double insurance of "low-level salaried employees" in both the workers' and salaried employees' insurance schemes, a result of the way these had come about.[45] While this was an organizational disentangling, by virtue of the simultaneous de facto adjustment it followed the general trend of leveling out the old distinctions conceived in "statist" terms. Anyone who moved between the insurance schemes for workers and salaried employees had his contributions counted. The separate systems also moved more closely together thanks to the fact that beginning in 1922, the Reich Insurance

[44] See "Notgesetz v. 24. Februar 1924," RGBl. I, p. 147 ("AusführungsVO betr. Preistreiberei, Ausfuhrverbote, Handelsbeschränkungen, Verkehr von Vieh und Fleisch, Notstandsversorgung, Preisprüfung, Auskunftspflichten, Wucherverbote," RGBl. [1924] I, p. 699).

[45] "Gesetz v. 10. November 1922," RGBl. I, p. 849.

Office and its legal decisions was equally responsible for workers' insurance and salaried employees' insurance (Bogs 1979, pp. 3ff., 9).

dd) Insurance for Salaried Employees

After 10 years, the separate insurance for salaried employees that had been in existence since 1911 first underwent a thorough amendment (RGBl. I, p. 849) and revision through the Salaried Employees' Act.[46] It defined more precisely that term "salaried employee" [*Angestellter*] stipulated in 1911,[47] expanded self-governance, and—as in the other branches of social insurance—it included new occupational groups from the area where independent and dependent work overlapped (musicians, midwives, nurses). After inflation had been tamed, the restructuring of this insurance scheme sought a model of graduated contribution rates that combined certain uniformity with the principle of contribution equivalence. That model was found by combining a basic rate for all and five different income classes for contributions.

ee) Miners' Insurance

During the Weimar Republic, the insurance law governing the mining sector retained its age-old special status, though it did not rule out a close legal interlocking with the Reich Insurance Code. It found its final codification on the Reich level in the Reich Miners' Law of June 23, 1923, which was revised once more in 1926 (RGBl. I, pp. 431, 760; RGBl. [1926] I, p. 369). The Miners' Insurance, carried by the Reich Miners' Association, uniformly protected workers and salaried employees as "employees" [*Arbeitnehmer*] in the area of sickness, pension, disability, and salaried employees' insurance—incidentally, at more favorable conditions than other schemes (Geyer 1987).

[46] "Gesetz v. 28. Mai 1924," RGBl. I, p. 563. It was only in 1923 that the Reich Insurance for Salaried Employees was given its own building. See Bonz (1989, pp. 138–141).

[47] "Bestimmung der Berufsgruppen der Angestelltenversicherung v. 8. März 1924," RGBl. I, pp. 274, 410.

b) From Social Assistance for the Jobless to Insurance Against Unemployment

aa) The Risk of Joblessness

That unemployment was one of life's risks in industrial society was certainly apparent in the last third of the nineteenth century, but more like an "affliction" and as such also a domestic political problem, and not as a cyclically returning, "typical" problem, and therefore one that was amenable to an actuarial approach (von Schanz 1895, 1897; Molkenbuhr 1902). The dogma of contractual freedom under private law was simply too dominant (Wieacker 1953; Mayer-Maly 1998), the countervailing interests of employers was too strong, and the political establishment after Bismarck was not very willing to embark once again on a path of intervention that was difficult to grasp with actuarial tools (Faust 1986). What was known seemed sufficient, namely, certain progressive protections by individual companies (Carl-Zeiss-Stiftung, Jena 1889) (Auerbach 1925; *100 Jahre Carl-Zeiss Stiftung*, 1989), communal insurance initiatives ("Insurance Fund against Unemployment in the Winter," Cologne, 1896; "Ghent Model") (Ritter 1983, p. 61), union benefits to the unemployed, small insurance solutions for salaried employees, or work procurement measures and emergency labor schemes. State assistance and self-help setups still seemed adequate, as well. The Reichstag examined the issue in 1902 and established a commission of inquiry, which in 1906 presented a report that compared Germany to other countries. The government hesitated about whether to follow the English example of an unemployment insurance (1911), but in the end decided not to.

The World War, however, forced the state to act because unemployment numbers surged. As early as December 1914, the communal unemployment assistance [*Erwerblosenfürsorge*] was set up, which was supposed to support individuals who were able and willing to work and had become unemployed and in need of help as a result of the war. Politically important in this process was drawing a line between this and the discriminatory poor relief; those made jobless by the war did not want to and should not find themselves on the same level as those who, in the prevailing opinion at the time, had created their situation by their own improvident behavior. This gave rise to the already mentioned doubling of "public assistance" and "elevated public assistance."

This doubling remained in place during the demobilization following the end of the war. The proclamation by the Council of the People's Representatives on November 12, 1918, highlighted the "support for the unemployed" as a special point. The following day saw the publication of the Decree on Unemployment Assistance, which explicitly prohibited the local communities from according the new branch of assistance, the "*Arbeitsfürsorge*," "the legal character of poor relief" (RGBl. I, p. 1305). Half of the funds came from the Reich, one-third from the respective state, and one-sixteenth from the local communities. Assistance was given to those individuals above the age of 14 who were able and willing to work and "who find themselves in a situation of need from unemployment caused by the war." This was joined by a first attempt to curtail these assistance measures again through emergency labor schemes (RGBl. [1919], I, p. 1827, subparagraph 5). The unemployment assistance kicked in after a 1 week waiting period and lasted 6 weeks. As would become evident during the difficult years that followed, that was not enough, and so the decision was made in 1926 to follow this up with the grant of "emergency assistance." By the standards of systematic social law, this represented a hybrid interim solution. The Reich once again bore the main burden of this subsidy, three-quarters, while the respective local communities had to provide one quarter (RGBl. I, p. 489). Moreover, as with poor relief, there was a means test. On the other hand, there was a legal entitlement, and the committees of unemployment assistance were equally staffed by representatives of workers and employers. Both employers and workers/employees were to pay contributions as supplements to their sickness fund premiums. At this state one can therefore still observe the existence side by side of characteristic of welfare, social insurance, and public assistance. If there were such a thing as an "evolutionary theory of social law," this would be the prime example for the transition from a benefit granted by sovereign authority to the needy to an insurance solution based on social solidarity (Faust 1987).

This transition was facilitated by the centralized employment agencies from the World War, which one could now use in peace time. Job-placement ranked ahead of unemployment insurance; ever since, the "linkage of job placement and unemployment insurance" shaped the thinking.[48] The first two drafts of such a dual law (1920, 1921) failed largely for financial reasons in the inflation of 1923. The undertaking was then brought to fruition in the years 1925–1927 thanks to a fairly broad consensus across parties. The "Law on Job Placement and Unemployment Insurance" of July 7, 1927 (RGB. I, pp. 187, 320; Führer 1990) now assigned protection against the risk of unemployment to the state's sphere of responsibility. It encompassed the insured individuals from the classic insurance branches, but it left out more people than were covered there. Financing followed the model of pension insurance: i.e., employers and employees each paid half of the contributions, with contributions that were very small borne by employers alone. The benefit was "unemployment assistance" for 6 months. After that, "emergency assistance" kicked in for another 6 months as welfare-like assistance in cases of need. Once that had been exhausted, public assistance would be available to the long-term unemployed.

Organizationally, the state now created employment agencies, state employment offices, and a Reich Office for Job Placement and Unemployment Insurance as a public law body. Both the dominant insurance principle and the creation of these independent structures made clear that unemployment was not an individual "fate" or "failure," but a risk typical of a large and continually growing segment of the population in an industrialized world in which production was based on the free market.

[48] "Arbeitsnachweisgesetz v. 22. Juli 1922," RGBl. I, p. 657.

The new insurance, however, stood on shaky ground. Already the initial assumptions about the number of the unemployed and the length of assistance (estimated at 3 months), were off. The insurance had barely been set up when reserves had to be drawn on. Because of the harsh winter of 1928/1929 and the global economic crisis, the number of unemployed rose from 1.4 million (1928) to 3.4 (1930), then 5 (1931), and eventually 6.2 (1932). In the end, about one third of the population was below the poverty line (welfare unemployed), and in the insurance was bringing in an ever shrinking number of contributions. The Reich Office was presiding over an enormous deficit. In the political quarrel over how to restructure it, the last truly democratic parliamentary government of the Weimar Republic was undone by its internal contradictions. Those on the side of industry (German People's Party) wanted cuts in benefits, while the Social Democrats wanted to preserve them and contemplated an emergency payment by all those on fixed wages and salaries, a raise in contributions of one half percent, and tax increases. In and of themselves these were negotiable positions, but in the crisis of the Weimar Republic they turned into an existential problem, even though a compromise carried by the Center Party, the German People's Party, and the German Democratic Party was on the table. The SPD parliamentary group abandoned its chancellor, which left the government no choice but to relinquish power (Huber 1984, pp. 718ff., 724ff.). From the perspective of economic policy, the social state might have seemed at the time and now as an obstacle to the hoped-for recovery (Borchardt 1976; Sommariva and Tullio 1987, p. 5; Berringer 1999), but politically the end of parliamentarism was an unmitigated catastrophe: not only because it de facto paved the way for the anti-parliamentary dictatorship, but also because the multi-party state's "inability to compromise" became engraved in political memory.

bb) State Intervention Against Unemployment

However, the state sought to solve—or at least ameliorate—the problem of a lack of jobs not only through unemployment assistance, job placement, and unemployment insurance. It deployed other means as well. On the constitutional level, a "right" to work had its counterpart in a "moral obligation" to work (Article 163, WRV). To make that right a reality, the state, which saw itself immediately after the war as an interventionist state authorized to pursue all emergency measures, at first pursued coercive means. It acted through demobilization commissioners and intervened when companies were in danger of shutting down, thus placed severe restrictions on employers.[49] War veterans had to be given preference in hiring (Huber 1981, p. 1091).

[49] "Verordnung betr. die Einstellung und Entlassung von Arbeitern und Angestellten während der Zeit der wirtschaftlichen Demobilmachung v. 3. September 1919," p. 1,500, in the version of Febuary 12, 1920, RGBl., p. 218; "Verordnung betr. Maßnahmen gegenüber Betriebsabbrüchen und –stillegungen v. 12. November 1920," RGBl., p. 1901; "Verordnung über

An especially important law regulated the hiring of the severely disabled. Since the job market was not readily open to them, given the excess of workers, coercion was also used here. The Law on the Employment of the Severely Disabled of April 6, 1920,[50] could be seen as a special implementation of the right to work (Article 163, WRV). It stipulated that all private and public employers with more than 20 employees were obligated to hire Germans disabled by war or accident and with at least a 50 % reduction in their ability to work.[51] All told, 2 % of all jobs were to be made available for the severely disabled. This was achieved through the classic sovereign instruments, the imposition of an obligation to take affirmative action, secured by the right of oversight and inspection on the part of the authorities, and the requirement that the main assistance-providing agencies approve job terminations. All in all, this mechanism has proved effective, and in principle it was also retained over the following decades.

But in an effort to preserve jobs, the legislator could also work through individual and collective labor law, for example, by expanding the protection of home-based work, maternity rights, and protection against dismissal (§§621–624, 626–628 of the Civil Code) in favor of older workers.[52] The Work's Council could now also raise the objection of "social detriment" to dismissals and force the employer to seek mediation, failure of which would then compel the court to decide.

In this way, the state guided the number of work contracts that had to be signed, it favored certain groups out of general political and social considerations, it laid down the framework conditions for the individual work contract, and in imposed a prohibition on job terminations or at least provided the workers' representation in the workplace with the procedural tools to make such terminations more difficult. One of the main points of this interventionism was the introduction of the eight-hour day for workers and salaried employees outside of agriculture, which was a social achievement for the unions and the Social Democrats, but also an impediment in economically unusually difficult times (Preller 1978, pp. 253ff., 304ff.).

Betriebsstillegungen und Arbeitsstreckung v. 15. Oktober 1923," RGBl. I, p. 983. See also Huber (1981, pp. 1093f.).

[50] RGBl., p. 458, in the version of January 12, 1923, RGBl. I, p. 58.

[51] This created a certain overlap with the activities of the professional associations of accident insurance, which were also intent on making it possible for the victims of accidents to return to the labor market.

[52] "Hausarbeitsgesetz (1911 in der Fassung vom 30 Juni," RGBl. I, p. 472; "Gesetz über die Fristen für die Kündigung von Angestellten v. 9. Juli 1926," RGBl. I, p. 399; "Gesetz über die Beschäftigung vor und nach der Niederkunft v. 16. Juli 1927/29. Oktober 1927," RGBl. I, pp. 184, 325.

cc) Changes in Labor Law and the Response of Jurisprudence

The First World War and the Revolution of 1918 led to "fundamental changes in labor law" (Hueck and Nipperdey 1959, p. 13), which later observers regarded as the "transition from individual to collective labor law" (Görlitz 1974, p. 42). While there had already been numerous collective bargaining agreements prior to 1914, especially in areas with a structure centered on small and mid-size businesses, it was only the union's *Burgfrieden* policy that led to their acceptance as the "appointed representatives of the workers." This found expression in the Central Working Group Agreement between Employers' and Workers' Organizations on November 15, 1918 (Blanke et al. 1975, vol. I, pp. 181ff.). The Agreement, named the "Stinnes Legien Agreement" after its most prominent signatories, was submitted to the Council of the People's Deputies the very same day it was signed; the Council gave its emphatic approval and had the Agreement officially published immediately.[53] Although this did not grant the Agreement the character of a formal law, it did provide it with political sanction; for public sector enterprises, it assumed the binding character of an administrative order (Huber 1978, p. 771). In addition to a recognition of the unions, the central stipulations were that the labor conditions for all workers were to be set through collective bargaining agreements with the professional organizations of the employers, and that restrictions on the freedom of assembly for workers be prohibited (Weiss 1998). This led to a triumphal march of the collective bargaining contract in all areas of labor law, with the result that the year 1922 saw 10,768 collective agreements that applied to 890,000 businesses with 14.3 million employees (that is, 75 % of all workers) (Hueck and Nipperdey 1963, p. 19). The "Decree on Collective Agreements, Workers' and Employees' Committees, and the Settlement of Labor Disputes" of December 23, 1918 (RGBl. I, p. 1456; Blanke et al. 1975, p. 19) boosted the legal effectiveness of collective bargaining contracts. Labor contracts that deviated from the norms of collective agreements were declared invalid and replaced with the standard regulations (§1 of the Decree). In addition, the Reich Labor Office that was established in October 1918 (under the leadership of its first head, the Social Democratic union leader and future Reich Chancellor, Gustav Bauer) was given the authority to declare collective agreements as generally binding upon request (§2).

From among the postwar legislation one should mention, not least, the relevant stipulations in the Weimar Constitution of August 11, 1919. They guaranteed freedom of association (Article 159) and assigned to the Reich the jurisdiction for the entire area of Labor Law (Article 7, Subsection 9). Alongside stood the design of an entire system of social and economic co-determination, composed of Works' Councils, District Worker Councils, a Reich Workers' Council, as well as District Economic Councils and a Reich Economic Council.[54] In that spirit, Article

[53] *Reichsanzeiger*, November 18, 1918.

[54] On the economic constitution of the Weimar period see Huber (1981, pp. 1023ff.). On the forces, motives, and concepts that led to the anchoring of the council system in Article 165 of the Weimar Constitution see Ritter (1994); on the Reich Economic Council see Glum (1930).

165 declared that "workers and employees are called upon to participate, on an equal footing and in cooperation with the employers, in the regulation of wages and working conditions as well as in the economic development of productive forces." However, with the exception of Section 6, Article 165 was only "a legislative program, that is, future law" (Anschütz 1933, p. 747). All that was implemented were the temporary Reich Economic Council through a decree of May 4, 1920 (RGBl., p. 858) and the establishment of Works' Councils.[55]

A year later, then, the Works' Councils Act of February 4, 1920 (RGBl., p. 147; Blanke et al. 1975, pp. 211ff.), called for the establishment of works' councils in all enterprises with at least 20 employees. Their primary tasks were to support the "enterprise management with advice, in order thereby to ensure, along with it, the highest possible level of economic performance of enterprise management," agreement about joint official work regulations within the framework of collective contracts, and the promotion of "concord among the workers and between them and the employer" (§66). In addition, they had the right to participate in a preliminary capacity in the appeal procedure in cases where workers were dismissed. Paragraph 84 allowed for an appeal to the Workers' or Employees' Council, among other reasons, if there was a suspicion that the dismissal was based on a person's political, confessional, or union activity or membership, and in cases of dismissals that "did not represent a hardship brought on by the conduct of the worker or employee or the circumstances of the enterprise." If no agreement could be reached with the employer, both the Works Council and the affected worker could take the case to court, initially to the Commercial Court [*Gewerbe- oder Kaufmannsgericht*], after 1927 the Labor Court (Huber 1981, p. 1092f.). The Works' Councils Act was flanked by the so-called Corporate Balance Sheet Act of February 5, 1921, which obligated businesses to reveal their annual balance sheet to the Works Council (RGBl., p. 159), and by the Law Concerning the Delegation of Employees to the Supervisory Board of February 15, 1922 (RGBl. I, p. 209), a precursor to co-determination in the workplace (Bieber 1998).

The Decree Regarding the Mediation System of October 30, 1923 (RGBl. I, p. 1043; Blanke et al. 1975, pp. 230ff.) and the related Second Mediation Decree of December 29, 1923 (RBGl. I, p. 9), reorganized the state's mediation system, which had been regulated until then by the collective bargaining code. A distinction was made between private (voluntary) and state mediation bodies. Within their sphere of jurisdiction, the voluntary bodies had precedence over the state mediation offices (§3 Mediation Code) and were set up by the parties to collective bargaining agreements; if their activity did not end with a collective bargaining relationship, the jurisdiction of the state mediation organs took effect. Depending on the nature of the dispute in collective bargaining, the mediation authorities were the Mediation

[55] On the reasons for the "failure" of this legislative program, which must be sought above all in the decay of the council movement, in the strengthening position of employers, the fragmentation of the workers' movement, and the defeat of the Weimar coalition in the Reichstagelections of 1920, see Ritter (1994, p. 108f.), who also pointed to the "open" nature of Article 165 as a reason behind its "failure."

Committee, the mediators, and, at the highest level, the Reich Labor Minister, all of which acted as state authorities.

At least until 1928/1929, the unions, too, were interested in avoiding labor disputes, with the fundamental idea of autonomy in collective bargaining predominating. But the Leipzig Professor of Labor Law, Lutz Richter, also expressed a widespread belief when he stated that "the generality, the population as a whole, the state because of the consumer need for the products of labor and because of the political dangers that can arise from idle means of production and the misery of masses of workers, must place value on settling the labor struggle and restoring orderly working conditions" (Richter 1928, p. 104). As a result of the shift in the power relationships in the economic crisis, state mediation, originally intended as the exception, became more and more the norm—and it did so at the urging of the unions, who would have been at a disadvantage in their dealings with employers without the support of government mediation (Bieber 1998, p. 59).

The discipline of labor law develop in parallel to the fundamental changes brought on by industrialization and the World War, which turned "work" into the fateful issue of the Weimar Republic (Mestitz 1984; Nutzinger 1998). It was cultivated in the legal departments and continuing education programs of the workers' organizations and unions (Bieber 1998, p. 15ff.), but increasingly also at the universities. Its pioneers were Philipp Lothmar, Hugo Sinzheimer, Ernst Fraenkel, Otto Kahn-Freund, Franz L. Neumann, Erwin Jacobi, Heinrich Potthoff, Walter Kaskel, Wilhelm Herschel, Alfred Hueck, Erich Molitor, and others.[56] Their starting point was largely private law, on the basis of which they dealt not only with the individual labor contract with all its "public law" restrictions, but also with "collective labor law," which presented itself as a separate entity constituted by the interaction of social forces under state oversight. Needless to say, the new legal regulations of works' councils, the mediation system, the law on working hours, labor court jurisdiction, job placement, and unemployment insurance attracted the interests of those who wrote about the subject. The first analyses of the body of law (Neumann 1929; Kahn-Freund 1931) and the first textbooks appeared—the latter a sure indicator of the establishment of a subject within university teaching (Sinzheimer 1921/1927; Hueck 1922; Erdal 1923–1924; Meisbach 1923; Oertmann 1923; Groh 1924; Jacobi 1924; Kaskel 1920; Kaskel 1925/1932).

The discipline of "social law" experienced a parallel development, though the label is one we can assign only in retrospect. The consciousness that insurance for workers and employees, public assistance, the law on war victims, and the wealth of interventionist emergency measures by the state were held together by a common purpose had not yet formed at the time. The differences in the systematics, the institutions, and the still-modest approaches toward a scientific treatment of the field simply seemed to large. In the Weimar period, as well, legislating was a field of the ministerial bureaucracy, in this case the Reich Labor Ministry, the

[56] Rückert (1993a, b), Benöhr (1993), von Brünneck (1988), Ramm (1980), Däubler (1988). An indispensable reference work is Rückert (1996).

associations, and praxis. As during the Empire, scholarly contributions still came across the broad from academic outsiders. In the *Gründerjahre* (late 1860s, early 1870s), only the "law of workers' insurance" was taken note of, and it was still unclear whether it should be counted as part of private law or public law. Its character as an annex to the working relationship argued in favor of private law, its compulsory character and organizational forms argued in favor of public law. The law of occupation protection was the public law of warding of dangers, and poor relief was a special subfield of communal law. Thus, the conditions for the recognition of an overarching "social purpose" were not favorable.

One far-sighted founder of the field was the Freiburg public law jurist Heinrich Rosin (1855–1927). Not only did he make a very sophisticated contribution to dogmatics with his work *Die Rechtsnatur der Arbeiterversicherung* (Rosin 1908) [The Legal Nature of Workers' Insurance], which was in line with the then-current scholarly ideal of constructive jurisprudence, but he was also the founder of the first course on the science of insurance (Hollerbach 1993). And yet, a work that would have brought together the scattered pieces of "social" legislation and systematized them was still beyond the general horizon. The rapidly multiplying writings on social policy after 1919 were consistently aimed at the issue of how to reform special legal fields or at the creation of new areas, for example, youth welfare law. Only a few legal faculties set up lectureships for practitioners (Leipzig, Freiburg, Frankfurt a. Main), even though legislation was continually providing new material, the constitution had guaranteed a "comprehensive system of insurances based on the critical contribution of the insured" (Article 161), and the Reich Labor Ministry had all essential powers of social law in its hand. It was only in 1931 that the young Leipzig public law jurists Lutz Richter (1891–1945), a student of Erwin Jacobi's, succeeded in writing the first systematic account of social insurance law, including miners' insurance and the new insurance against unemployment (Richter 1931; Stolleis 2004, pp. 215ff., 297). There also appeared textbooks on public assistance and youth welfare law, and the categories of "Introductions" and legal commentaries also grew rapidly. Still, the various fields of the law remained strangers; their structural commonalities, which could have led to an overarching "General Part," were not yet apparent. One cannot really find fault with that, considering that even in the Federal Republic of West Germany, this kind of integrative perspective was only pursued in the 1960s and achieved in the 1970s.[57]

5. Labor Courts

The Labor Court Act of December 23, 1926 (RGBl. I, p. 507) took effect on July 1, 1927, nearly contemporaneous with the unemployment insurance. In this field, as well, we can observe a tendency toward organizational independence and the

[57] The great document of this change is Zacher (1980).

emergence of a separate scientific consciousness, of the kind that had already taken hold of material law (social law, labor law, tax law, economic administrative law). Of course, the practice of separating disputes over labor law from the ordinary justice system because of the strong personal and social elements involved was older. The medieval guild courts, the miners' and merchants' courts, but also the local commercial courts of the nineteenth century banked on the special expertise of those involved in that they were either entirely corporative courts or at least included assessors [*Beisitzer*] from the occupational field involved. The fragmentation of the courts became increasingly bothersome as estate-based differences vanished during the industrial revolution and the homogenous mass labor relationship began to dominate the landscape. As a result, there were voices already before the First World War that called for a standardized labor law and a system of courts to go along with it. This became more urgent when the fragmentation increased during the war through mediation committees, economic councils, and agricultural councils. In 1919, Reich Labor Minister Bauer (SPD) took the initiative. The Decree Concerning Collective Bargaining Agreements, Workers' and Employees' Committees, and the Mediation of Labor Disputes of December 23, 1918, was already in place when the Weimar Constitution promised "uniform labor legislation" (Article 157). A partial fulfillment of that promise was the previously mentioned Works' Councils Act of February 4, 1920. However, "uniformity" also meant the independence of the judicial system that went along with the legislation, especially since mistrust of the regular judicial system had remained alive within the workers' movement. As a result, it wanted a system of courts that was as friendly as possible to workers: participation by the parties to collective bargaining, no obligation to be represented in court by a lawyer (a stipulation intended to favor union officials), a preceding conciliation procedure, and low fees.

Resistance to this new system of courts from the ranks of employers, lawyers, the Association of Judges, and the German Lawyers' Association was considerable. The discussion of the four various blueprints was accordingly long, and it eventually produced a law that was adopted by the Reichstag with a large majority. The most important demands were met, except for independence, which existed only at the first layer of courts, while the State Labor Courts and the Reich Labor Court remained organizationally intertwined with the regular judicial system (Leich and Lundt 1987).

This branch of the judiciary began its work under difficult conditions. The courts were barely up and running when mass unemployment and wage cuts began. Burgeoning protest from the unions was repressed with reference to the "duty to maintain peace." In 1933, the anti-Semitic measures of the Nazi state affected especially the labor courts were severely. Their competencies were curtailed. "Trustees of labor" and "social honor courts" took over the regulation of troubles within an enterprise. Disputes arising from collective bargaining agreements and the Works' Councils Act vanished with the Law on Ordering National Labor of January 20, 1934 (Ramm 1983; Kranig 1983, 1984). As a result, the system of labor courts shrank during National Socialism and especially during the Second World

War to the point of being meaningless. But the basis idea behind the Labor Court Act of 1926 had ceased to be visible as early as 1933.

6. Crisis Management Without Parliament

When the Weimar Republic, in 1929, stumbled into the economic and political crisis that would prove its death struggle, the "Emergency Decree" based on Article 48 of the constitution was once again the instrument of political crisis management (Stolleis 1984). Beginning in July 1930, the "Weimar presidential system" (Huber 1984, pp. 731ff.), carried by the Reich President and a chancellor dependent on him, employed this instrument to deal with the economic and socio-political problems. Its application gradually exceeded the boundaries spelled out only vaguely in the constitution. What had now longer been possible through party compromises was now decreed without parliament: an increase in the contributions to unemployment insurance and in the Reich subsidy (RGBl. I, p. 311), wage and salary cuts in the public sector (RGBl. I, p. 517), and benefit cuts in unemployment assistance.

Sickness insurance had seen a rise not only in benefits, but also in the rate at which they were claimed. The cost pressure this created on the one hand drove contributions so high that the government had to take countermeasures through emergency decrees, and on the other led to measures that affected the sick. This included the co-payment for medications that first appeared in 1923, the sickness certificate fee, the waiting period, and a system of *Vertrauensärzte* [physicians who examine patients certified as long-term sick by their personal doctor] to be set up and funded by the sickness funds (RGBl. I, p. 311). Finally, the asset management by the sickness funds and the auditing of their books were regulated in greater detail. In accident insurance, pensions were eliminated in cases of minor impairments to earnings, and for the rest there were robust pension cuts averaging 10 % and further restrictions (RGBl. [1932] I, p. 273).

A particularly dramatic situation had to be confronted in pension insurance: a decline in revenue during the global economic crisis and a simultaneous increase in applications for pensions. Restrictions began with the Emergency Decree of December 8, 1931: the general cuts in pensions, an increase in the waiting period from 200 to 250 weeks (for those voluntarily insured even to 550 weeks), the elimination of the child subsidy and widow's pension from the age of 15 on, and cuts to the drawing of multiple pensions. All told, however, even these measures were not able keep pension insurance from falling into a deficit of more than 12 billion RM (1933). Pensions were too low to provide real security for old age. Addition cuts were not possible if one wanted to avoid pushing the mass of pensioners toward public assistance and thus increase the political risk of radicalization.

Benefit cuts in employees' and miners' insurance were not quite as severe. The continuing preferential treatment of salaried employees was expressed in the fact that only this insurance could afford to take 60 year-olds who had been unemployed for a year out of the labor market through early retirement (RGBl. [1929] I, p. 75). Although the miners' insurance also experienced benefit cuts, it was supported by Reich funds in a way that one could even doubt whether it was an "insurance" at all (Preller 1978, p. 470).

Where insurances failed because they were close to collapse, state assistance filled the gap at best it could. But the benefits of public assistance also had to be cut. The introduction of a crisis tax was intended to tap a new source of funds. There followed further cuts to social security pensions and *Versorgungsrenten* [supplementary pensions], a reduction in unemployment assistance by more than half (1932), a reduction in entitlement to 6 weeks, and a cut in emergency assistance to the point where it was practically a return to the old welfare. Whatever could still be gained in this way from a squeezed system was to be simultaneously invested in measures to reduce unemployment (RGBl. 1931, I, p. 537). The beginning of a Voluntary Labor Service picked up the old idea of "public works" (RGBl. 1931, I, p. 279). Two months later, the state decreed rent reductions by 10 % effective January 1, 1932, benefit cuts in sickness funds to "standard benefits", and benefit cuts in accident and pension insurance as well as in the area of public assistance (RGBl. 1931, I, p. 699). However, Brüning's austerity policy went too far with additional interventions in collective bargaining autonomy in favor of employers and with wage and salary cuts of up to 10 % in the entire public sector. Opposition came not only from the unions, but also from the state apparatus, which had already been hit disproportionately hard in the inflation of 1923.

To extricate themselves from these problems, the main actors in Berlin and Neudeck apparently believed that only another shift to the right would help. As Reich Chancellor, Franz von Papen initially continued the existing line on social policy, with further cuts in the area of social insurance, unemployment assistance, and provisioning down to the level of 1927. Once again, the public sector was hit up for a special sacrifice to benefit the unemployed. At the same time, however, tax increases and emergency work projects were to ease the pressure on the social institutions (Decree of June 5, 1931). It was only after an agreement about the de facto end to reparations was reached at the Lausanne Conference (June 16 to July 9, 1932) could the government embark on a policy of deficit spending. Simultaneously, it loosened the strictures of collective bargaining agreements to push new hiring by cuts in wages—a measure it abandoned again in December 1932 following union protests. To provide the economy with an incentive for investments and the hiring of new workers, the government used emergency decrees to provide tax breaks by issuing vouchers for tax payments, bonuses for additional jobs, and funds to invest in emergency work projects in the public sector (Decree of September 4, 1932, RGBl. I, p. 425, Decree of September 5, 1932, RGBl. I, p. 433; Preller 1978, p. 467f.). In December 1932, the government set up an "Emergency Organization for German Youth" (Hasenclever 1978, p. 123).

The other measures of social policy that were attempted in the winter of 1932/1933, after December 3 by the government of Chancellor Kurt von Schleicher, were symptomatic of the intractable situation: the regular administration was replaced with "commissioners" with special powers (Hintze 1941), in this case the Reich

Commissioner for Job Procurement (RGBl. I, p. 543). On January 28, 1933, a mere 2 days before Hitler's assumption to power, he was still given a credit of 500 million RM for job creation measures. "Winter aid" was set up for recipients of public assistance, which was to distribute meat, bread, and coal free of charge.

All of these attempts were no longer able to alter the political game that was favoring the leader of the most radical party. But the crisis management of the presidential governments (transition to deficit spending, emergency work projects and labor service, abolition of collective bargaining autonomy, winter aid) continued uninterrupted under the "Hitler cabinet", though now, of course, under the light of a "national revolution" and accompanied by countless violations of the law. The instruments themselves did not change substantially, except that the element of compulsion intensified and the question of the legal forms that were employed became irrelevant, but social policy now mutated on a large scale into an instrument of pacification and discipline wielded by a regime that was rapidly shifting its focus toward war.

References

Abelshauser W (ed) (1987) Die Weimarer Republik als Wohlfahrtsstaat. Stuttgart

Adler L (ed) (1931/1998) Neuzeitliche Mietshäuser und Siedlungen. Berlin. Reprint 1998, Berlin

Anschütz G (1933) Die Verfassung des Deutschen Reichs vom 11. August 1919, 14th edn. Berlin

Arendsee M (1932) Wieviel braucht der Mensch zum Leben? Proletarische Sozialpolitik 5(5)

Auerbach F (1925/1989) Das Zeisswerk und die Carl-Zeiss-Stiftung in Jena 1925, 5th edn. Jena

Benöhr H-P (1993) Hugo Sinzheimer (1875–1945). Mitbegründer des Arbeitsrechts. In: Heinrichs H (ed) Deutsche Juristen jüdischer Herkunft. Munich, pp 615–630

Berg W (1985) Arbeits- und Sozialverwaltung einschließlich Sozialversicherung und Reichsversorgung. In: Jeserich K, Pohl H, von Unruh GC (eds) Deutsche Verwaltungsgeschichte, vol 4, §8. Stuttgart, pp 231ff

Berringer C (1999) Sozialpolitik in der Weltwirtschaftskrise. Die Arbeitslosenversicherungspolitik in Deutschland und Großbritannien im Vergleich 1928–1934. Berlin

Bieber H-J (1998) Die Rolle von Gewerkschaften und Wirtschaftsverbänden bei der Entstehung des Arbeitsrechts. In: Nutzinger H-G (ed) Die Entstehung des Arbeitsrechts in Deutschland. Marburg, pp 15–69

Blanke T, Erd R, Mückenberger U, Stascheit U (eds) (1975) Kollektives Arbeitsrecht. Quellentexte zur Geschichte des Arbeitsrechts in Deutschland, vol 1 (1840–1933). Reinbek

Bogs W (1979) Sozialrechtspflege vor Einführung der Sozialgerichtsbarkeit. In: Deutscher Sozialgerichtsverband: Festschrift 25 Jahre Bundessozialgericht, vol 1. Cologne Berlin

Bogs W (1981) Die Sozialversicherung in der Weimarer Demokratie. Munich

Bonz H-J (1989) Berlin als Standort des zentralen Trägers der Rentenversicherung der Angestellten. In: Mitteilungen des Vereins für die Geschichte Berlins 85:138–141

Borchardt K (1976) Wachstum und Wechsellagen 1914–1970. In: Aubin H, Zorn W (eds) Handbuch der deutschen Wirtschafts- und Sozialgeschichte, vol 2. Stuttgart, pp 685–740

Bracher KD (1971) Die Auflösung der Weimarer Republik, 5th edn. Villingen

Bräunche E-O (1997) Zur Wohnungssituation in Karlsruhe vom Kriegsende 1918 bis zum Bau der Dammerstocksiedlung 1929. In: Franzen B, Schmitt P (eds) Neues Bauen der 20er Jahre. Karlsruhe, pp 23ff

Bunte T (1995) Überwindung der Wohnungsnot - Sieg der Wohnkultur. Gemeinnütziger Wohnungsbau in der Weimarer Republik am Beispiel der Ravensberger Heimstättengesellschaft m.b.H. Bielefeld

Büsch O, Feldman GD (eds) (1978) Historische Prozesse der deutschen Inflation 1914–1924. Berlin

Castell-Rüdenhausen A Gräfin z (1991) Kommunale Gesundheitspolitik in der Zwischenkriegszeit.Sozialhygiene und Rassenhygiene am Beispiel Gelsenkirchens. In: Frei N (ed) Medizin und Gesundheitspolitik in der NS-Zeit. Munich, pp 67–80

Cemy J (ed) (1992) Wer war wer in der DDR, 2nd edn. Berlin

Claussen K-E (1985) Justizverwaltung. In: Jeserich K (ed) Deutsche Verwaltungsgeschichte, vol 4. Stuttgart

Damaschke A (1922) Aufgaben der Gemeindepolitik, 10th edn. Jena

Däubler W (1988) Otto Kahn-Freund (1900–1979). Ideologiekritik und Rechtsfortschritt im Arbeitsrecht. In: Kritische Justiz: Streitbare Juristen. Eine andere Tradition. Baden-Baden, pp 380–389

Deutsche Sozialpolitik 1918–1928 (1929) Erinnerungsschrift des Reichsarbeitsministeriums. Berlin

Dommer J (1926) Wie man in Karlsruhe baut und wohnt. In: Behrendt O (ed) Karlsruhe, Das Buch der Stadt. Stuttgart

Erdal A (1923/1924) Das Arbeitsrecht, 2 vols. Leipzig

Faust A (1986) Arbeitsmarktpolitik im Deutschen Kaiserreich. Stuttgart

Faust A (1987) Von der Fürsorge zur Arbeitsmarktpolitik. Die Errichtung der Arbeitslosenversicherung. In: Abelshauser W (ed) Die Weimarer Republik als Wohlfahrtsstaat. Stuttgart, pp 260ff

Feldman GD (1984) Vom Weltkrieg zur Wirtschaftskrise. Studien zur deutschen Wirtschafts- und Sozialgeschichte 1914–1932. Göttingen

Feldman GD (1993) The great disorder. Politics, economics and society in the German inflation, 1914–1924. Oxford

Felisch P (1917) Ein deutsches Jugendgesetz. Berlin

Friedeberg E, Polligkeit W (1930) Das Reichsgesetz für Jugendwohlfahrt, 2nd edn. Berlin

Führer KC (1990) Arbeitslosigkeit und die Entstehung der Arbeitslosenversicherung in Deutschland 1902–1927. Berlin

Gerhard U (1990) Unerhört. Die Geschichte der deutschen Frauenbewegung. Reinbek

Geyer M (1987) Die Reichsknappschaft. Versicherungsformen und Sozialpolitik im Bergbau 1900 bis 1945. Munich

Glum F (1930) Der Reichsverwaltungsrat. In: Anschütz G, Thoma R (eds) Handbuch des Deutschen Staatsrechts, vol 1. Tübingen, pp 578–585

Görlitz A (1974) Arbeitsrecht. In: Görlitz A (ed) Handlexikon zur Rechtswissenschaft, vol 1. Reinbek, p 42

Gräser M (1995) Der blockierte Wohlfahrtsstaat. Unterschichtjugend und Jugendfürsorge in der Weimarer Republik. Göttingen

Groh W (1924) Deutsches Arbeitsrecht. Breslau

Hansen E, Heisig M, Leibfried S, Tennstedt F (1981) Seit über einem Jahrhundert.... Verschüttete Alternativen in der Sozialpolitik. Cologne

Hasenclever C (1978) Jugendhilfe und Jugendgesetzgebung seit 1900. Göttingen

Henning FW (1978) Das industrialisierte Deutschland 1914 bis 1976, 4th edn. Paderborn

Hintze O (1941) Der Commissarius und seine Bedeutung in der allgemeinen Verwaltungsgeschichte. In: Hintze O (ed) Gesammelte Abhandlungen, vol 1. Staat und Verfassung. Leipzig, pp 232–264

Hollerbach A (1993) Heinrich Rosin (1855–1927). Pionier des allgemeinen Verwaltungs- und des Sozialversicherungsrechts. In: Heinrichs H (ed) Deutsche Juristen jüdischer Herkunft. Munich, pp 369–384

Huber ER (1969–1984) Deutsche Verfassungsgeschichte seit 1789, vols 4 (1969), 5 (1978a), 6 (1981, rev 1993) and 7 (1984). Stuttgart
Hueck A (1922) Handbuch des Arbeitsrechts, 2 vols. Stuttgart
Hueck A, Nipperdey HC (1959/1963) Lehrbuch des Arbeitsrechts, vol 1, 6th edn, 1959; 7th edn, 1963. Berlin Frankfurt am Main
Jacobi E (1924) Einführung in das Gewerbe- und Arbeitsrecht, 4th edn. Leipzig
Jellinek G (1905) System der subjektiv-öffentlichen Rechte. Tübingen
Kahn-Freund O (1931) Das soziale Ideal des Reichsarbeitsgerichts. Eine kritische Untersuchung zur Rechtsprechung des Reichsarbeitsgerichts. Mannheim
Kammerloher-Lis S (1994) Die Entstehung des Gesetzes über die religiöse Kindererziehung vom 15. Juli 1921. Frankfurt am Main
Kaskel W (1920) Das neue Arbeitsrecht. Berlin
Kaskel W (1925/1932) Arbeitsrecht, 1st edn, 1925; 4th edn, 1932. Berlin
Keidel F (1929) EGBGB, 1. Teil. In: von Staudinger J (ed) Kommentar zum Bürgerlichen Gesetzbuch, vol 6, 9th edn. Munich, pp 357ff
Kindleberger C (1973) Die Weltwirtschaftskrise. Munich
Kleeis F (1928/1981) Die Geschichte der sozialen Versicherung. Berlin. Reprint 1981. Berlin
Klumker CJ (1918) Fürsorgewesen. Leipzig
Kranig A (1983) Lockung und Zwang. Zur Arbeitsverfassung im Dritten Reich. Stuttgart
Kranig A (1984) Arbeitsrecht im NS-Staat. Texte und Dokumente. Cologne
Leich S-H, Lundt A (1987) Zur Geschichte der Berliner Arbeitsgerichte. 10 Jahre Berliner Arbeitsgerichtsbarkeit 1927–1987. Berlin
Margold EJ (1931/1998) Bauten der Volkserziehung und Volksgesundheit (Reprint 1998). Berlin
Mayer-Maly T (1998) Vertragsfreiheit. Handwörterbuch zur Deutschen Rechtsgeschichte, vol 5, columns 855–858
Meisbach E (1923) Deutsches Arbeitsrecht. Berlin
Mestitz F (1984) Zur Wirkungsgeschichte des Arbeitsrechts. In: Steindl H (ed) Wege zur Arbeitsrechtsgeschichte. Frankfurt am Main, pp 1–28
Molkenbuhr H (1902) Zur Frage der Arbeitslosenversicherung. Die Neue Zeit 724ff
Möller H (1997) Weimar. Die unvollendete Demokratie, 6th edn. Munich
Möller H, Raulet G, Wirsching A (eds) (1993) Gefährdete Mitte? Mittelschichten und politische Kultur zwischen den Weltkriegen: Italien, Frankreich und Deutschland. Sigmaringen
Mügel O (1927) Das gesamte Aufwertungsrecht, 5th edn. Berlin
Neumann FL (1929) Die politische und soziale Bedeutung der arbeitsgerichtlichen Rechtsprechung. Berlin
Neundörfer K (1923) Widerstreitende Mächte in dem Reichsgesetz für Jugendwohlfahrt. Hochland 20:509–529
Nutzinger H-G (ed) (1998) Die Entstehung des Arbeitsrechts in Deutschland. Aktuelle Probleme in historischer Perspektive. Marburg
Oertmann P (1923) Deutsches Arbeitsvertragsrecht. Berlin
Peters K-H (1984) Wohnungspolitik am Scheideweg. Berlin
Petersen K (1995) Zensur in der Weimarer Republik. Stuttgart Weimar
Preller L (1949/1978) Sozialpolitik in der Weimarer Republik. Reprint 1978. Stuttgart
Ramm T (1980) Otto Kahn-Freund und Deutschland. In: Gamillscheg F (ed) In Memoriam Sir Otto Kahn-Freund. Munich, pp XXI–XXXII
Ramm T (1983) Nationalsozialismus und Arbeitsrecht. Kritische Justiz Der Unrechts-Staat. Recht und Justiz im Nationalsozialismus. Baden-Baden
Richter L (1928) Grundverhältnisse des Arbeitsrechts. Berlin
Richter L (1931) Sozialversicherungsrecht. Berlin
Rindt M, Saffert H (1968) Das Bundesministerium für Arbeit und Sozialordnung. Geschichte, Gestalt, Aufgaben. Berlin
Ritter GA (1983) Sozialversicherung in Deutschland und England. Entstehung und Grundzüge im Vergleich. Munich

Ritter GA (1994) Die Entstehung des Räteartikels 165 der Weimarer Reichsverfassung. Historische Zeitschrift 262:73–109

Rosin H (1908) Die Rechtsnatur der Arbeiterversicherung. In: Festgabe für Paul Laband. Tübingen. Reprint 1987: Staatsrechtliche Abhandlungen. Frankfurt

Ruck M (1987) Der Wohnungsbau - Schnittpunkt von Sozial- und Wirtschaftspolitik. Probleme der öffentlichen Wohnungspolitik in der Hauszinssteuerära 1924/1925–1930/1931. In: Abelshauser W (ed) Die Weimarer Republik als Wohlfahrtsstaat. Zum Verhältnis von Wirtschafts- und Sozialpolitik in der Industriegesellschaft. Stuttgart, pp 91–123

Ruck M (1988) Die öffentliche Wohnungsbaufinanzierung in der Weimarer Republik. Zielsetzungen, Erwartungen, Probleme. In: Schildt A, Sywottek A (eds) Massenwohnung und Eigenheim, Wohnungsbau und Wohnen in der Großstadt seit dem Ersten Weltkrieg. Frankfurt am Main, pp 150–200

Ruck M (1997) Das Karlsruher Finanzierungsmodell als Beitrag zur Reform der öffentlichen Wohnungsförderung Ende der zwanziger Jahre. In: Franzen B, Schmitt P (eds) Neues Bauen der 20er Jahre. Karlsruhe, p 41

Rückert J (1993a) Franz Leopold Neumann (1900–1954) - ein Jurist mit Prinzipien. In: Lutter M (ed) Der Einfluss deutscher Emigranten auf die Rechtsentwicklung in den USA und in Deutschland. Tübingen, pp 437–474

Rückert J (1993b) Philipp Lotmar (1850–1922). Römisches Recht, Rechtsphilosophie und Arbeitsrecht im Geiste von Freiheit und Sozialismus. In: Heinrichs H (ed) Deutsche Juristen jüdischer Herkunft. Munich, pp 331–353

Rückert J (ed) (1996) Beschreibende Bibliographie zur Geschichte des Arbeitsrechts mit Sozialrecht, Sozialpolitik und Sozialgeschichte. Baden-Baden

Rudloff W (1999) Die Wohlfahrtsstadt. Munich

Sachße C, Tennstedt F (1980/1988) Geschichte der Armenfürsorge in Deutschland, vol 1, 1980; vol 2: Fürsorge und Wohlfahrtspflege 1871 bis 1929. 1988. Stuttgart

Schildt A (1998) Wohnungspolitik. In: Hockerts HG (ed) Drei Wege deutscher Sozialstaatlichkeit. NS-Diktatur, Bundesrepublik und DDR im Vergleich. Munich, p 154

Schmidt G (1907) Das öffentliche Armenwesen der Stadt Mainz. Mit besonderer Rücksicht auf die im Jahre 1895 begonnene Neuordnung. Mainz

Simon H (1916) Das Jugendrecht. Berlin

Sinzheimer H (1921/1927) Grundzüge des Arbeitsrechts. Jena, 2nd edn, 1927. Gera

Sommariva A, Tullio G (1987) German Macroeconomic History 1880–1979. New York

Stolleis M (1984) Notverordnungsrecht. In: Erler A, Kaufmann E (eds) 1990/1998: Handwörterbuch zur Deutschen Rechtsgeschichte, vol 3. Berlin

Stolleis M (1998) Wohlfahrt. Handwörterbuch zur Deutschen Rechtsgeschichte, vol 5, columns 1486–1488

Stolleis M (2004) A history of public law in Germany 1914–1945. Oxford

Stratmann M (1976) Wohnungspolitik in der Weimarer Republik. Stuttgart

Tennstedt F (1977) Geschichte der Selbstverwaltung in der Krankenversicherung von der Mitte des 19. Jahrhunderts bis zur Gründung der Bundesrepublik Deutschland. Bonn

Tennstedt F (1981) Sozialgeschichte der Sozialpolitik in Deutschland. Vom 18. Jahrhundert bis zum Ersten Weltkrieg, Göttingen

Tennstedt F (1984) Das Reichsversicherungsamt und seine Mitglieder. In: Deutscher Sozialrechtsverband, Wannagat G (eds) Entwicklung des Sozialrechts, Aufgabe der Rechtsprechung. Festgabe aus Anlass des 100jährigen Bestehens der sozialgerichtlichen Rechtsprechung. Cologne, pp 47–82

von Brünneck A (1988) Ernst Fraenkel (1889–1975). Soziale Gerechtigkeit und pluralistische Demokratie. Kritische Justiz: Streitbare Juristen. Eine andere Tradition. Baden-Baden, pp 415–425

von Schanz G (1895) Zur Frage der Arbeitslosenversicherung. Untersuchungen. Bamberg

von Schanz G (1897) Neue Beiträge zur Frage der Arbeitslosenversicherung. Berlin von Staudinger J (1929) Kommentar zum Bürgerlichen Gesetzbuch, vol 6, 9th edn. Munich Berlin Leipzig

Weiss M (1998) Tarifvertrag. In: Erler A, Kaufmann E (eds) Handwörterbuch zur deutschen Rechtsgeschichte, vol 5. Berlin

Wieacker F (1953) Das Sozialmodell der klassischen Privatrechtsgesetzbücher und die Entwicklung der modernen Gesellschaft. In: Wieacker F (ed) 1974: Industriegesellschaft und Privatrechtsordnung. Frankfurt am Main, pp 9–35

Winkler HA (1972) Mittelstand, Demokratie und Nationalsozialismus. Die politische Entwicklung von Handwerk und Kleinhandel in der Weimarer Republik. Cologne

Winkler HA (1993) Weimar 1918–1933. Die Geschichte der ersten deutschen Demokratie. Munich

Witt P-C (1979) Inflation, Wohnungszwangswirtschaft und Hauszinssteuer. Zur Regelung von Wohnungsbau und Wohnungsmarkt in der Weimarer Republik. In: Niethammer L (ed) Wohnen im Wandel. Beiträge zur Geschichte des Alltags in der bürgerlichen Gesellschaft. Wuppertal, pp 385–407

Zacher HF (1980) Sozialpolitik und Verfassung im ersten Jahrzehnt der Bundesrepublik Deutschland. Berlin

VI. The Nazi State

1. Ruptures and Continuity

On January 30, 1933, the Hitler cabinet, on the outside a seemingly radical core surrounded by more moderate German Nationals and without a real majority, took over a virtually intact administrative apparatus. The civil service and the military, the leaders of the economy, and other bourgeois circles were in principle in agreement with the final abandonment of the parliamentary system, but they did not want to be delivered over to a "dictatorship of the street." They took a wait-and-see attitude, hoped for a speedy return of normal conditions, and were ready to put up with "excesses." Since the new regime was skillful at responding to their concerns, it won the loyalty of these groups, as well, especially after the spectacular murders that were part of the "Röhm putsch" in June of 1934, which were noted with a mixture of fear and relief. Moreover, there were few open differences as far as the content of policy was concerned. Even the approval for the programmatic points dealing with social hygiene extended well beyond the National Socialists. As for anti-Semitism, it was—of course, minus its murderous consequences—a more or less tolerated element of the bourgeois mindset, whose fear and envy in the economic crisis were now directed against a tiny minority. On foreign policy there was agreement over the struggle against the remnants of "Versaille", domestically the National Socialists lacked both a program and the requisite experts in nearly all areas. That applied to a high degree also to social policy.

The approaches that the new regime found in place were initially continued, in part unchanged, in part with much larger budget outlays, which could now be multiplied in a climate of nearly unchecked—if at first still concealed—deficit spending. This meant that the instruments familiar from the policies of the presidential dictatorships

Previously published in English in the following publication: Stolleis: Origins of the German Welfare State (German Social Policy, Vol. 2), Springer, Berlin/Heidelberg, 2013.

M. Stolleis, *History of Social Law in Germany*,
DOI 10.1007/978-3-642-38454-7_6, © Springer-Verlag Berlin Heidelberg 2014

(state contracts, direct and indirect subsidies to the economy, material incentives for individuals, qualified approvals and prohibitions with or without the reservation of permission) continued to be employed. This was now joined, after the downfall of the parliamentary system, parties, and unions, by massive intimidation and propaganda. This set in motion a mechanism by which the successes of this policy seemed greater and greater in those areas where the regime was working with a combination of propaganda and coercion. The conviction that "liberalism was finished," which ran across all strata of the population, and that nothing more could be achieved with voluntariness or the forces of the free market, injected further energy into a mechanism that tended toward a militarization of society. The recipe of the front line soldier and autodidact Hitler, that the "community of the nation fused together" out of the community of the front line was capable of overcoming all difficulties and that the previous enemies would yield demoralized, seemed to find confirmation. Everything seemed to be pointing toward a "triumph of the will."

All this led to an ambivalent relationship to the social policy experts and lawyers that were concentrated in the Reich Labor Ministry and on whom the new regime depended for legislation. The attitude of the party bigwigs was one of contempt for "experts," in most cases also fed by potent inferiority complexes. At the same time, however, the leadership agreed to leave the financing of state spending, for example, and labor market and social policy to the experts, if everything was done in line with the regime. If necessary, the regime could set its own accents through parallel or competing actions.

Accordingly, high-flying plans about a unification of social insurance into a single system that were initially entertained quickly dissipated. The Reich Labor Ministry, under German National leadership in the hands of the Stahlhelm chief Franz Seldte,[1] was as much opposed to a single insurance as were those party comrades who had moved swiftly into posts that were opening up in the various branches of social insurance and began to defend their turf (Zöllner 1981). Since the elimination of mass unemployment had the highest priority initially, if the regime wanted to consolidate itself by winning the loyalty of the masses (Narr and Offe 1975; Mason 1977, pp. 124ff.), social insurance was left untouched, once the "Führer principle" had been introduced there and self-administration had been eliminated. There was all the more cause for restraint when it became evident that the funds it had accumulated could be used as inconspicuous additional funding for rearmament.

If we turn our attention to the civil servants, specifically the top echelons of social policy, we can speak of an extensive continuity between the policy of the presidential cabinets and the Nazi state. But the ruptures become clear if we look at the workers and the workers' movement. The new regime not only quashed the

---

[1] Franz Seldte (1882–1847), founder of the "Stahlhelm," since 1929/1931 ("Harzburg Front") an ally of Hitler's, brought the Stahlhelm into the NSDAP on April 27, 1933, that is, he capitulated. He was simultaneously the Minister of Labor in Prussia. His letter of resignation in 1935 was rejected by Hitler. Berghahn (1966), Selig (1988).

unions, the freedom of association, and the right to strike, it also eliminated co-determination within enterprises, cut social benefits, dictated working conditions through the "Trustees of Labor," restricted job choice, and in this way gradually moved to a new kind of economy.

The place of the destroyed unions was taken by the German Labor Front (Deutsche Arbeitsfront, DAF) headed by Robert Ley (Schulz 1985), which officially became part of the NSDAP through a decree of October 24, 1934. However, after the installation of the "Trustees of Labor" on May 19, 1933, this organization was not able to simply carry on the previous union functions in the area of social policy. A "de-unionization" of the DAF became already apparent in the second half of 1933, and under the influence of Ley it increasingly put propagandistic functions in the foreground. At the end of 1933, the employers' associations also joined the DAF, which now united within itself the "pillars" of workers and salaried employees, of employers, tradesmen, and members of the independent professions. The "Appeal to all productive Germans" of November 27, 1933, signed by the Reich Labor Minister, the Reich Economics Minister, Hitler's Party Deputy for Economic Affairs, and the leader of the DAF defined the tasks of the organization as follows: "The great aim of the Labor Front is the education of all working Germans for the National Socialist state and for the National Socialist way of thinking" (Broszat 1988, p. 146). The Law on the Organization of National Labor enacted almost 2 months later, January 20, 1934, restricted the tasks of the Labor Front on matters relating to collective bargaining and labor contracts to a purely advisory role.[2] There was one innovation, however: §66, Section 3 introduced (free) legal counseling offices of the DAF for those going before the labor courts; these offices were to be set up separately for employers and for workers and salaried employees.

The material and political losses of the workers' movement were in part covered up and in part genuinely compensated for by propagandistically exploited actions [construction of the *Autobahn*, Reich Labor Service, Winter Aid (Tennstedt 1987), NS People's Welfare, One-pot Meal, Strength through Joy], by the staging of collective action-for-action's sake, and by a series of de facto improvements. It seemed that the new "National Community" was able to overcome the old class barriers, a perception that was aided in no small measure by the fact that the leading politicians were able to present themselves as "men of the people." What was labeled "German socialism" (Huber 1934, 1939, pp. 469ff.) consisted of an emasculation of the worker's movement combined with ideological and material gifts to the workers, of intact structures of the private sector economy (in fact, stronger now through the removal of the unions), combined with certain restrictions from the slogan "the welfare of the community over the welfare of the individual" [*Gemeinnutz vor Eigennutz*], though these did not affect the substance of the private

[2] RGBl. I, p. 45. On the final failure in 1935 of Ley's attempts to give the DAF greater weight on matters of social policy see Broszat (1988, p. 152f.). On the social planning of the DAF's Institute of Labor Science see Smelser (1991).

sector. Behind this stood a partly latent, partly implemented transition to a planned economy. This was a complex system of mutual toleration and reassurance, a mixture of "enticement and coercion" (Kranig 1983).

2. Race and Population Policy

For all the continuity, what set the social policy of the National Socialists apart was its racial components. Social law and social policy were no longer merely an "instrument for integrating the weak and disadvantaged, but served (also) to stabilize and intensify a racially defined inequality" (Ritter 1998; Ayaß 1999). The retention of the traditional systems thus took place in the shadow of the exclusion of significant groups like the Jews and other discriminated minorities from the system of social protection. This "biologization" of social policy began immediately after the Nazis assumed power in January of 1933. In the process, the National Socialists were able to link up with Social Darwinian and eugenicist doctrines that had attracted strong attention from the public in the final years of the Weimar Republic.[3] The goal of these doctrines was to reduce the procreation of "genetic lines unfit for or dangerous to preservation" and to promote the procreation of "genetic lines fit for preservation and of superior quality." On the negative side the preferred means were marriage counseling, voluntary and compulsory sterilization, especially of so-called "asocials, the sick, and the less able," and on the "positive" side tax breaks for "normal" families, economic and intellectual promotion of "gifted families" with many children, and measures to prevent the "highly talented" from not marrying and not having children. Scientific institutes of Eugenics existed in 1933 in places like London, New York, and Berlin (Kaiser Wilhelm Institute of Anthropology, Human Heredity, and Eugenics); textbooks and monographs were published and journals were established.[4] This went hand in hand with an unvarnished aversion to including broader circles into public assistance. For example, we read in the first issue of the journal *Eugenik* published by the German Society for Racial Hygiene (1933): "The system of public welfare and assistance contribute – the undesired side-effect of an irrefutable duty – to preserving the hereditarily ill and bringing them to procreate further. A crushing and constantly growing ballast of humans who are unfit and unworthy of living is maintained and cared for in institutions – at the expense of the healthy, hundreds of thousands of which are today without their own housing and millions of which are struggling without a job" (Ayaß 1995, p. 14).

---

[3] Hammerschmidt (1999, pp. 33–53); on the continuities of eugenicist ideas between the Weimar Republic and the Third Reich see Castell-Rüdenhausen (1991).

[4] See *Der Große Brockhaus*, vol. 15 (Leipzig, 15th edn., 1933), article "Rassenhygiene, Eugenik, Gesellschaftshygiene," 389, with additional references. On the history of Eugenics in Germany see Weingart et al. (1988).

Thus, the "measures" of the new regime did not require much advance work. One of the first legislative steps was the Law for the Prevention of Genetically Diseased Offspring of July 14, 1933 (Hereditary Health Law) (RGBl. I, p. 529). This was supplemented by an Implementing Decree on December 5, 1933 (RGBl. I, p. 1021), which spelled out the sterilization process in minute detail. It affected all those who were diagnosed with "hereditary feeblemindedness, schizophrenia, manic-depressive insanity, hereditary epilepsy, hereditary chorea, hereditary blindness, hereditary deafness, severe hereditary deformities, and severe alcoholism" (§1, Section 2). Those entitled to file an application were, in addition to the affected person or his or her legal guardian, "the official physician" and the "head of an institution for patients in a hospital, sanatorium, psychiatric hospital, or prison" (§3). The decision lay with the Hereditary Health Courts.[5] Parallel with this, university chairs and institutes of racial science were set up, which were tasked with writing numerous expert opinions on sterilization cases (Weindling 1991). For example, beginning in 1934, about 1,000 individuals were annually examined at the Frankfurt Institute for Hereditary Biology and Racial Hygiene, which was headed by Otmar Freiherr von Verschuer. At the top of the list was the diagnosis of "hereditary feeblemindedness," which accounted for about 50 % of the cases (Dorner et al. 1989, pp. 161ff., 168). For the Reich as a whole, 222,055 sterilization applications were filed in 1934, which turned into 84,330 requests for sterilization to the courts. Between passage of the law and the outbreak of the war, a total of about 430,000 such applications were submitted, three-fourths of which led to a sterilization decision, which almost always meant that an actual sterilization procedure was carried out.[6] To these approximately 300,000 sterilizations in the prewar period we must add another 60,000 during the war (Bock 1986, pp. 230–246). The organizational framework for a standardized and complete geographic implementation of the Hereditary Health Law was created by the Law on the Standardization of the Health Care System of July 3, 1934 (RGBl. I, p. 531), which provided for the establishment of state Health Offices as of April 1, 1935. In addition to performing the tasks of official and court physicians and independent medical examiners, which had previously been assigned to the public health officer by state law, to providing medical advice on personal hygiene and exercise, health care in schools, and counseling for mothers and children, the Health Offices were charged above all with making medical determinations and rendering expert opinions on questions related to public health policy, especially the "cultivation of heredity and race," including marriage counseling (Süß 1998: esp. 63). This organization, which was set up within a few years (in 1938 the state Health Offices already had more than 23,792 employees), registered broad segments of the population in its genealogical charts and hereditary files, not least through applications for marriage loans—the indispensable prerequisite for a widely applied selection activity. By 1942, no

[5] For a contemporary account see the report in the *Frankfurter Zeitung* of December 20, 1933, reprinted in Forsthoff (1935, p. 301; omitted from later editions).

[6] See the approving statement by the Archbishop of Freiburg, reprinted in Forsthoff (1942, p. 433).

fewer than 10 million file cards had been completed. In view of these activities, the NSDAP's Offices for Public Health could limit themselves to ideological oversight (Labisch and Tennstedt 1991).

The regulations of the Hereditary Health Law were substantively supplemented by the so-called "Marrital Health Law" of October 18, 1935 (RGBl. I, p. 1246). It contained prohibitions on marriage for those deemed to suffer from hereditary illnesses, for those placed under guardianship, and for individuals suffering from infectious diseases and in cases of "mental disturbances, ... that render marriage undesirable for the national community" (§1, Section 1). Only a few weeks earlier, the Law for the Protection of German Blood and Honor, part of the so-called Nuremberg Laws, had outlawed mixed marriages and prohibited "extramarital relations between Jews and citizens of German or kindred blood" (RGBl. I, p. 1146; Tarrab-Maslaton 1993, pp. 80–97).

The battle against "inferiors" [*Minderwertige*] and "non-Germans" [*Artfremde*] included additional far-reaching measures against so-called "asocials," that is, chiefly "loafers," alcoholics, beggars, prostitutes, and criminal offenders (Ayaß 1995, 1998; Hammerschmidt 1999). The "beggars' week" of September 1933, a raid against the homeless, led to the arrest of approximately several tens of thousands of individuals, most of whom were set free again after a few weeks of detention. The reason for this action was chiefly the goal of taking pressure off the Winter Relief Program. With the "beggars' week," the workhouses that had been half-empty since the end of the Weimar Republic also saw a rise in the number of their inmates. These measures found their legal basis (still) in the regulations of paragraphs 361 and 362 of the Reich Penal Code of May 15, 1871, which stipulated that those sentenced for vagrancy, begging, prostitution, procuring, refusal to work, and "self-caused" homelessness could be placed into a work house for another 2 years after serving their sentence. Those regulations were toughened by the Law Against Dangerous Habitual Criminals and About Measures of Security and Improvement of November 24, 1933 (RGBl. I, p. 995), which, as a form of the "dual track nature of criminal law", allowed lifelong placement in a work house. In this "new spirit", the communal welfare offices dealt with the recipients of public assistance with a more vigorous application of § 19 of the Reich Decree on Obligatory Assistance of February 13, 1924 (RGBl. I, p. 100), which allowed for making assistance benefits dependent on the recipient performing public service work. The same was true of §20, which allowed individuals who persistently refused to work to be placed in closed institutions, and of § 13 of the Reich Principles for the Decree of Obligatory Assistance (also passed in 1924 [RGBl. I, p. 765]), according to which "refusal to work" and "obvious uneconomical behavior" could lead to institutionalization. On the basis of a "creative legal" application of these norms, numerous cities now pursued the institutionalization of groups deemed "in need of maintenance." Behind this stood the notion that liberal ideas, which had hitherto prevented such interference in personal liberty, were now "overcome." These individuals were placed either in existing work houses (Frankfurt) or in (already) specially erected "camps for closed care" (Hamburg, Stuttgart). With the expansion of concentration camps after 1938, these camps lost importance; they were closed or converted to different uses. Since these measures were limited to recipients of social assistance, Welfare Office stepped up their efforts to have individuals who were living from their own earnings (esp. prostitutes) declared legally incompetent. Finally, the Decree on the Implementation of the Ordinance Regarding Unemployment Assistance of September 11, 1939, excluded "asocials" entirely from this benefit, since they could not be put to work (RGBl. I, p. 433). Particular weight was given to the fight against "asocial families:" not only were they excluded from certain supportive measures (marriage loan, child subsidy, child recreation), but the goal—especially after the outbreak of the war—as to break them up by housing parents and children in separate camps.

These measures reached an entirely new dimension in 1938 when the Reich began to actively combat these groups. In April, the Gestapo carried out a broad arrest sweep against "loafers," and the criminal police targeted chiefly the homeless (i.e. "vagrants, beggars, gypsies, and persons who move about like gypsies") with its "June action." With these sweeps the mass placement of "asocials" in concentration camps took on greater weight; political internees became the minority. Some of the internees were released again over the next 2 years, though some—to date the exact number has not been determined—fell victim to the euthanasia of prisoners and the "destruction through work" (Ayaß 1995, pp. 138ff.). There was little hesitation about sending Sinti and Roma to concentration camps. These groups were persecuted both socially and racially. As with the Jews, their persecution ended in genocide (Ayaß 1995, pp. 196ff.), the so-called "Final Solution," the culmination of the gradually intensifying measures of discrimination and expulsion (Peukert 1989; Härter 1998).

3. Job Creation and Labor Law

The new government needed a decline in the number of the jobless. Unemployment was the most important domestic political problem, and it would decide whether the acts of violence and breaches of the law during the first months could be compensated for by visible results (Sauer 1960, p. 799). As a result, the new regime focused on this issue, initially by continuing the approach of awarding public works that the Papen government had taken since the fall of 1932. A separate work-creation policy got under way with somewhat of a delay, starting in June 1933 (RGBl. I, p. 323). Now all conceivable means were deployed. The Reich spent a billion "*Arbeitsschatzanweisungen*" [long-term labor bonds] to finance public projects, for example, the previously planned but now accelerated construction of the *Autobahn* (RGBl. II, p. 509), other earth-moving works, and river control projects. The Reich Institute for Labor Placement and Unemployment Insurance also involved welfare recipients in this program (Frerich and Frey 1993, p. 254) and thereby reduced the burden on the heavily indebted communities. In addition, the 40-h week was introduced for 1 year to "stretch" the work. To free up jobs, the regime launched propaganda against "two-job holders", sought to place as many young women as possible either into domestic service jobs or encourage them to get married through marriage loans, loans that could also be repaid by the birth of children. Female civil servants had to give up their civil service status upon marriage (Thalmann 1982; Klinksiek 1982; Koonz 1991). Additional jobs were "opened up" by driving Jews, Social Democrats, Communists, and other undesirable groups from their. Their place was taken mostly by "old fighters" of the party or the SA, who had been waiting since the *Machtergreifung* to reap the reward for their service to the "movement."

As long as unemployment persisted, the regime continued to push employment through a bundle of measures: direct and indirect subsidies by way of tax breaks for certain jobs or things, and tax breaks for the rapid payment of taxes (RGBl. [1933] I, p. 651; Voß 1995, pp. 77–83). Added was the guidance of labor deployment to smooth out the over- or undersupply of workers (RGBl. [1934] I, p. 381). Finally, the reintroduction of conscription and 6 months of obligatory service in the Reich Labor Service for men and women between the ages of 18 and 25 helped to take pressure off the job market (RGBl. [1935] I, p. 609; RGBl. [1935] I, p. 769).

The successes achieved in this way were impressive. Unemployment, which had stood at just over six million at the peak, had already dropped to two million by 1935, and beginning in 1936 there was competition for skilled workers (especially for the purposes of armaments production), a typical feature of the Nazi years. Full employment was achieved around 1937.

If one judges the phase of work procurement based purely on its success and the approval ratings for the regime it generated, one can understand how the tackling of the first major problem boosted the government's self-confidence and impelled it to brush aside especially all financial concerns. Already by the end of 1934, the new regime had spent ten times on work procurement what the governments of Papen and Schleicher had expended. If one puts the armament goals—from the beginning explicit or not so latent—in the foreground, or if one criticizes the measures for not being "real" social policy (Mason 1977, pp. 126ff.), one probably comes close to Hitler's intentions, but misses the psychological state of the population. The formerly unemployed and their families credited the government with lifting the nightmare that had been weighing on them, even if they were still not doing well in material terms. And the willingness of medium-size businesses and industry to invest also rose in response to the regime's mantra—supported even by doctored statistics—that things were "looking up again." Thus, the approval rating for the regime spiraled upwards and created in Hitler and his supporters the illusion that every political goal could be achieved through "will," propaganda, repression, and a disregard for "bureaucratic" misgivings.

The model of a private market economy directed by politics that emerged only gradually in the process was not based on any real plan. Nor is it possible to reconstruct such a plan in retrospect. It was clear that rearming Germany would not be possible without cooperation from the economic sector, but that a guidance of production according to the "necessities of state policy" was in principle possible at the same time. And so the development, driven by the successes of deficit spending and the authoritarian setting of priorities, headed in the direction of a planned economy on a capitalist basis. In a climate that was anti-liberal in any case, freedom of movement and the free choice of work no longer played a role (Hachtmann 1989). The government therefore introduced the *Arbeitsbuch* [a booklet tracking a person's employment record] (1935), compulsory service for "tasks of special importance to state policy" (1938) (RGBl. I, p. 206), compulsory reporting of available jobs (1939) (RGBl. I, p. 444), and even outlawed the private placement of ads for jobs using box numbers. Under the pressure of the labor shortage that now began, the pendulum of women's policy also began to swing back (Frerich and Frey 1993, pp. 258–266): for example, young women who had taken jobs as domestics in the Netherlands were brought back in December 1938 with the threat of losing their citizenship (Henkes 1999).

Self-administration in unemployment insurance could not be reconciled with the anti-liberal principle of guidance for the entire labor market. The Reich took control of the entire labor administration, claimed the monopoly of job placement, and combined all labor-related assets into the public-law entity Reich Fund for Labor Deployment [*Reichsstock für Arbeitseinsatz*]. The contributions that were now flowing again because of the reduction in unemployment, and which were maintained at the existing level of 61/2 %, generated substantial surpluses, which were used both to support pension insurance and for rearmament purposes (Federau 1962; Peters 1978, pp. 120–122).

Since the policy of the regime generally followed an unprincipled calculus of accumulating power, this undifferentiated view of revenue was only consistent. Now that the organizing principles were reduced to what was "beneficial to the national community" (Stolleis 1974, pp. 127ff.), the world of tax law in a state governed by the rule of law became as meaningless as other legal forms, which could now be regarded merely as obstacles. That applied to the entire "labor constitution" (Wahsner 1994; Hachtmann 1998, pp. 27–54) that now emerged, but also to the social policy of the labor market that followed in its wake. Self-administration, civil liberties, and legal forms were negotiable if their opposed the current definition of utility.

The "order of national labor," as the new "basic law" of the National Socialist Labor Law of January 20, 1934 was called,[7] gave a spectacular boost to the position of employers and the state (Kranig 1983). "Trustees of Labor" took over the function of the parties to collective bargaining and of mediators (RGBl. I, p. 285; RGBl. I, p. 520). Enterprises were supposed to follow the model of "leader and followers." The place of the works' council was taken by an emasculated "council of trust." The NSDAP gained a foothold via the National Socialist factory cells and the Councils of Trust. Although the "enterprise leaders" were freed from the unions and the works' councils, they were subject to oversight by the Trustees and the (new) "social honor jurisdiction" [*soziale Ehrengerichtsbarkeit*] Labor jurisdiction

[7] RGBl. I, p. 45. Parallel to this for the public sector, but without Councils of Trust and "social honor jurisdiction", was the Law for the Order of Labor in Public Administrations and Enterprises of March 23, 1934, RGBl. I, p. 220.

remained formally intact, but it declined to the point of being meaningless (RGBl. [1933] I, p. 276).

The scholarly literature on labor law that accompanied these dramatic changes was severely decimated by the expulsion or silencing of a large number of well-known names from the Weimar period: H. Sinzheimer, E. Fraenkel, O. Kahn-Freund, F. L. Neumann, E. Jacobi, and others). Those who remained in Germany and commented on labor law took a position that was in principle positive, with the range of possible expressions ranging from reserved, positivist commentary to enthusiastic approval. In most instances the writers intensified the anti-liberal and anti-individualistic lines that had been previously present, interpreted the formula of the overcoming of class struggle by the national community in their own way, for example in reinterpreting the labor relationship as a "community relationship" or in concretizing the consequences of the notions of "enterprise community" and social "honor." Both the "Law on the Order of National Labor" and the new laws that refocused the protection of home-based work (1934/1939), working hours (1934/1938), youth protection (1938), and the procedures of labor courts (1938) toward the needs of the regime, were provided with extensive commentaries.

The theoretical elements that were developed in the process (Ramm 1968, p. 108; Rüthers 1970, p. 97; Hientzsch 1970) did not disappear with the end of the regime. Significant fragments of the theory of labor law reappear later in the labor law of the Federal Republic (Ramm 1994), but also in that of East Germany—in spite of an emphatic denial of this tradition and under a different ideological banner. There are good explanations for both phenomena. In the West it was the incontrovertible continuities of personnel and the circumstances of a rebuilding society focused on consensus and the avoidance of labor conflicts. In the East the crucial factor was a structurally comparable labor ideology, which, in spite of its vocal anti-capitalism, exploited the individual's labor power (and nature) for the benefit of a fictive community, disregarding civil rights in the name of this community and seeking to compensate this loss through a guaranteed job and welfare state-like care.

4. Social Insurance

The chroniclers of social insurance during the Nazi era agree that the structure of the traditional system was able to survive, in spite of many changes in specific details.[8] What is more: whatever the motives of the regime may have been, there was an expansion of the circle of those covered by insurance and the creation of

[8] For example, Peters (1978, p. 105): "The years 1933–1945 saw extensive changes in the area of social insurance. . . However, the foundations of social insurance were not shaken by the National Socialist legislation. Rather, social insurance in its old, classic sense was retained in its core, and its structure was not touched." Wannagat (1965, pp. 87ff.), Hockerts (1983), pp. 308ff., Gladen (1974), Hentschel (1983, p. 136), Lampert (1980).

new and an increase in traditional benefits. Moreover, the reduction in the number of sickness funds and the forced cooperation of institutions were supposedly reasonable and progressive moves. This verdict accurately reflects the institutional situation and the self-conception of the specialized civil servants in the Reich Ministry of Labor. The wishes for a "uniform insurance" and a "uniform administration" that initially emanated from the NSDAP were rebuffed, as was the 1940 "Ley Plan," which intended to replace the contribution-financed old-age insurance with a tax-financed model. Detlev Zöllner summed it up this way: "The development of social insurance during this time followed in essence the objectively logical exigencies of the previous development."[9] Of course, "in essence" is the crucial qualifier.

The defenders of the traditional system, represented by *Staatssekretär* Johannes Krohn in the Reich Labor Ministry (Tennstedt 1982), argued skillfully in the early phase that the diversity in the system created greater closeness to the insured, preserved the interests in "own" institutions, and was cheaper and more effective. To be sure, there were excesses of diversity and a harmful fragmentation, especially in the system of sickness funds, which is why one should carry out a measured reduction there, promote cooperation, and combine the whole thing "tightly toward the top."[10]

The defenders of social insurance thus took the approach of taking the measures toward simplification that seemed necessary and to present a restructured Reich insurance system without altering its substance. This was done through the "Law on the Structure of Social Insurance" of July 5, 1934 (RGBl. I, p. 577). For all its bold preamble—"To eliminate fragmentation and confusion in social insurance and to enhance its effectiveness through a uniform centralization…"—and the introduction of the *Führer* principle, what did *not* come about was precisely what had been wished for in party circles: a unitary insurance with unitary management and financing. Rather, the "Reich Insurance" (sickness, accident, and pension insurance), "Pension Insurance" (disability, salaried employees', and miners' insurance), and the renamed "Insurance for Labor Deployment" existed side by side. Seventeen decrees were passed between 1934 and 1942 to concretize the Social Insurance Law, which provided the framework. This led to the merger of sickness funds, and to various mergers and simplifications among the institutions that were operated in parallel by sickness funds and state insurance funds.

In spite of these continuities, especially with the policy of the presidential governments, a deep rupture occurred in terms of organization and personnel. The self-administration of the social insurance carriers, already reduced since 1929, was now completely eliminated. "Social elections" no longer existed. The tasks of the previous organs were taken over by the "heads" (§7 Social Insurance

[9] Zöllner (1981, p. 127). The ideas about reform concerning social insurance are documented in Schubert (2000).

[10] "Amtliche Begründung des Gesetzes über den Aufbau der Sozialversicherung v. 5. Juli 1934," RGBl. I, p. 577, quoted in Peters (1978, pp. 106–108).

Law).[11] On the "advisory councils" that existed alongside the heads but had no great significance sat "enterprise leaders" and workers/employees sent by the German Labor Front. The regime thus held the most important positions in its hands. It further reinforced this *Machtergreifung* in social insurance by carrying out a change in personnel with special propaganda fanfare. This was done on the basis of the Law for the Restoration of the Professional Civil Service of April 7, 1933 (Tennstedt 1979) and the Law on Honorary Posts in Social Insurance and the *Reichsversorgung* of May 18, 1933 (RGBl. I, p. 277). Under the slogan "war against the red boss rule [*Bonzentum*]," Jewish and Social Democratic civil servants, salaried employees, and unpaid officials, especially unionists, were stripped of their posts (e.g. Ronau 1933). Members of the SA and of the *Stahlhelm* as well as "old fighters" moved into the positions that were opening up and in so doing immediately morphed into defenders of the segmented system.[12] At the same time, the NS state stripped "non-Aryan," "Socialistic," and otherwise allegedly "subversive" doctors and dentists of their license to practice as sickness insurance physicians. The whole thing was accompanied by a corresponding wave of propaganda. The primitive and pornographic polemics against Jewish dentists, for example, which appeared in Julius Streicher's *Der Stürmer*, were among the lowest and vilest outgrowths of the regime.

The assets of the Pension Insurance and the Reich Insurance as a whole, parallel to Unemployment Insurance, participated in the economic upswing, but the de facto income of pensioners, which even in 1939 remained well below the average of the Depression years, did not. Thus, the growth could be distributed in other ways for the time being. The "Restructuring Law" (RGBl. 1933, I, p. 1039) repealed the earlier breakthroughs of the pay-as-you-go principle (RGBl. 1939, I, p. 793). State subsidies were expanded and a "Reich guarantee" provided that the state would step in if contributions and subsidies did not cover expenses (RGBl. 1937, I, p. 1393). Since the restrictions imposed between 1929 and 1933 were enforced and contributions were not reduced, the systems recovered fairly quickly. The remaining deficits were eliminated in 1937 by setting lower levels for new pensions and by "cleansing" the ranks of pensioners by having some declared fit to work following a purely administrative review.

The total assets of the social insurances had growth from 4.6 billion RM (1932) to 10.5 billion RM (1939) (Hentschel 1983, p. 144). This capital stock was also used to finance the war, namely through a simple decree of April 14, 1938 (RGBl. I, p. 398), which directed that half of the assets of pension insurance be invested in debt register claims of the Reich. Until that half was reached, at least three-quarters of the annual surplus funds would be skimmed off. Incidentally, this money was

[11] Hentschel (1983, p. 136) has rightly noted that the erosion of self-administration had already begun during the presidential governments.

[12] Leibfried and Tennstedt (1979) collected an abundance of material on this in the form of pamphlets and cartoons. The central text of this documentation in ZSR (1979), pp. 129ff., 184–191. Scheur (1967, pp. 61, 65).

used to finance the improvement in benefits that was believed to be necessary to maintain the public sentiment during the war.

a) Sickness Insurance

This insurance saw the most numerous dismissals of undesirable individuals, a reaction to the traditionally strong position of the Social Democrats and the unions, a strong reduction in the number of sickness funds (though the diversity of funds was retained), a new regulation of the statutory health insurance funds [*Ersatzkassen*], a takeover of the "community tasks" of the funds by the State Insurances, and a continuation of the old policy of expanding the circle of the insured. Compulsory insurance was now extended also to small groups of the self-employed, but especially individuals who were important to the regime (midwives and maternity care providers, surviving dependents of servicemen, and after 1941 the pensioners whose contributions were paid by the Pension Insurance) (Peters 1978, pp. 111–115). This, in turn, allowed for an improvement in benefits, for example, an expansion of nursing care, and an extension of the maternity allowance to 6 weeks before and 6 weeks after giving birth (Peters 1978, p. 114).

Parallel to these changes, the new state forced the most important carriers of the health care system into compulsory corporative entities, though without accounting for the corporative principle by granting self-administration. As elsewhere, the regime practiced authoritarian leadership. All doctors were made compulsory members in the Reich Association of Physicians. Licensing entitled them to the fees paid by the sickness funds, which were now distributed by the German Federation of Panel Doctors (a public law body), which stood between the doctors and the sickness funds. The institutions and payment procedures for dentists were set up in an analogous manner (Webber 1988, pp. 178ff.).

b) Accident Insurance

Initially, this insurance, like the others, was affected by the political transformations I have mentioned. Overall, however, it continued to develop along the traditional tracks, for example, by updating the list of occupational diseases, including accidents in vocational and professional schools, extending automatic coverage to emergency helpers in accidents, and expanding accident protection in the agricultural sector (Peters 1978, pp. 115ff.).

A less conspicuous but quite important change in principle was the transition of accident insurance from the previous insurance coverage for "enterprises" to insurance coverage for "employees" (RGBl. 1942, I, p. 107). This meant that the crucial factor for protection was no longer the particular hazard posed by an enterprise in which an individual worked, but the personal status of being insured.

Henceforth there were no longer "enterprise accidents" but "work accidents." One can see this as a long-overdue adjustment to the personal nature of the structures of the other kinds of social insurance, but also as a reaction to the changes in the modern conditions of production that were no longer invariably tied to enterprises. At any rate, this modernizing step, which was carried out during the war, is one example for the "objectively logical exigencies" (Zöllner) that were able to assert themselves in social insurance, for all the political oversight to which it was subjected.

c) Pension Insurance

Disability insurance, which was particularly ailing in 1933, but also the two other systems of old-age protection, insurance for salaried employees and miners' insurance, had to be initially propped up with higher state subsidies. The declining unemployment slowly provided them with more contributions, with the result that it was possible, over the long run, to switch from the pay-as-you-go method back to the capital-cover method (RGBl. 1933, I, p. 1039; Dobbernack 1933).

The goal of the restructuring, in conjunction with internal process of harmonizing the systems, was achieved in 1937 when excess funds of the unemployment insurance were redirected to pension insurance and the Reich not only paid large subsidies, but also assumed a general indemnity guarantee (RGBl. I, p. 1393). At the same time, the systems were opened to all Germans under the age of 40, including German nationals living abroad who wished to be insured voluntarily (RGBl. [1936], I, p. 1128). As a new occupational group, tradesmen were compulsorily enrolled in the salaried employees' insurance (RGBl. [1938], I, p. 1900), unless they were able to demonstrate that they had the right kind of life insurance. This was a piece of policy aimed at appeasing the *Mittelstand* (von Saldern 1985; Winkler 1977), but at the same time also the continuation of the most effective means of boosting revenue and diversifying risks by bringing in new members. The pull toward the dissolution of a society structured by occupational estates into a leveled mass society proved impossible to resist. A state that sought—with great propaganda fanfare—to dismantle class barriers in favor of the "national community," that wooed the workers by verbally placing the "*Arbeiter der Stirn*" [intelligentsia] and the "*Arbeiter der Faust*" [physical laborers] on an equal footing, invariably had to seek to dissolve also the "white-collar employees" as an "estate" (Prinz 1986; Ritter 1998, pp. 95, 267 note 53f.).

Thanks to restructuring measures and the expansion of the circles of the insured, the regime was able to raise benefits in some areas and eliminate the restrictions of the years 1929–1932 (e.g. RGBl. [1939], I, p. 739). Child subsidies and orphan benefits were once again paid up to the age of 18, there were higher child subsidies for large families, higher pensions for widows during wartime, and other improvements, behind which stood above all the goal of Nazi population policy and political sensitivities to the state of the war (RGBl. [1941], I, p. 443; Peters

1978, pp. 117–120). The old revenue collection system was also changed during the war: the literal "pasting" of contribution stamps was replaced by the withholding system implemented by employers. The sickness funds became responsible for collections overall (except for accident insurance). This innovation in 1942 no doubt reflected the practical needs of simplifications. But it was also symptomatic of the distance that had long since arisen between the insured person and "his" insurance, and of the de facto proximity of the social insurance contribution to a special tax on workers and employees, which was employed to siphon off funds that the regime by no means used only for social purposes.

5. Welfare and Provisioning

The area of public welfare [*Fürsorge*], whose legal form attained in 1924 was in principle retained, concerned the Nazi government only in so far as the burden of the assistance benefits to the long-term unemployed was weighing down the relief associations and the local communities. As unemployment declined, so did the importance of public assistance. A separate, positive interest in individuals unable to live up to the standards of productivity did not exist (Schleicher 1939; Hansen 1991). That the regime had no scruples in the end to free itself by force of "useless eaters" is evident from the so-called Euthanasia Action and the murder of "asocials" in the concentration camps.

Assistance and welfare were under a new banner: not humanity or altruism were the central concerns of Nazi national welfare, but national health, for which "constructive prevention" was the highest commandment. The guiding image was no longer an individualistic "sentimental compassion;" its place had been taken by "heroic strength" and "help to help oneself" (Vorländer 1988, pp. esp. 118ff.). In *Mein Kampf*, Hitler had denounced "charitable flim-flam" [*Wohlfahrtsduseleien*] and had attributed the traditional welfare policy to the hated Weimar state (Hitler 1940, I, p. 38). Nevertheless, since the twenties a self-help organization had emerged within the NSDAP (as in all other parties), which offered practical help in a more or less loose form to SA men in need. In addition, at the local level there were organizations like the "Brown Sisters" or the "Red Swastika Sisters." They found a new home in the National Socialist People's Welfare [*Nationalsozialistische Volkswohlfahrt*, NSV], which was founded in April 1933 as a registered association. A decree by Hitler on May 3, 1933, recognized it as the official welfare organization of the NSDAP.[13] The NSV very quickly achieved a membership of 16 million (1942), which made it the second-largest party organization behind the DAF with 24 million members (Vorländer 1988, p. 4). Its strong membership was the result not least of the restructuring of the system of charitable organizations in

[13] *Der Große Brockhaus*, vol. 21 (Leipzig, 1935), article "Nationalsozialistische Volkswohlfahrt," 573.

1933. According to the joint decree of the Reich Labor Minister and the Reich Minister of the Interior of July 25, 1933, only four Reich umbrella welfare organizations would be recognized henceforth: in addition to the NSV, these were the Protestant "*Innere Mission*" [Internal Mission], the "*Caritasverband*," and the German Red Cross. The latter, however, was restricted to task in the medical section of the Wehrmacht. The "*Arbeiterwohlfahrt*" was dissolved in 1933, the "*Paritätischer Wohlfahrtsverband*" was forcibly merged with the NSV, the "*Zentralwohlfahrtsstelle der Juden in Deutschland*" [Central Welfare Agency of the Jews in Germany] had to be incorporated into the Jewish self-governing bodies that were still authorized (Kaiser 1991). Among large segments of the population, the NSV stood for the NSDAP's competency on social matters and enjoyed considerable popularity. The organization found its main area of activity in street collections for the exceedingly popular "Winter-Relief Program of the Germany People" [*Winterhilfswerk des Deutschen Volkes*, WHV], in the aid program "Mother and Child," and in the "Support for Every Volk Comrade."[14] During the war a new activity was added, one that was very effective in terms of public relations: caring for the victims of the air raids on Germany's large cities. The "Brown Sisters" of the NSV distributed hot soup to those bombed out of their homes, arranged emergency shelter, and organized the "*Kinderlandverschickung*" (a program that sent children out of the cities into the countryside), which made them an indispensable element of Joseph Goebbels's "*Durchhaltepropaganda*," which called on Germans to stay the course.

Conflicts with the confessional welfare organizations were unavoidable, as the state's interference in the work of the churches increased steadily until 1941. Already during the preceding years, the regime, once more following its anti-liberal course, had displaced the churches and the private charities from competing for the donations collected from the people.[15] The NSDAP, its sub-organizations, and its affiliated associations were allowed to collect freely, all others were covered by a blanket prohibition that could be suspended with a special permit. In the struggle with the churches, even collections in churches were prohibited in 1937 and clergymen were sentenced for violations (Glenz 1936; Boos 1938; Kühn 1939). At the same time, the regime took over welfare services that were useful for propaganda purposes and expanded them into the large-scale actions referred to above (Vorländer 1988). It was only in the summer of 1941 that Hitler felt the need to reverse course to some extent. Concerned about the support of the part of the population that was loyal to the churches, he forbade party agencies (by means of the so-called "Stop Decree") to appropriate any more of the day-care centers and reformatories run by the churches (Hammerschmidt 1999, p. 447).

---

[14] *Der Große Brockhaus*, 21 (1935), "Nationalsozialistische Volkswohlfahrt;" on the work of the individual aid organizations see Hammerschmidt (1999, pp. 397ff.).

[15] RGBl. 1934, I, p. 1086, amended September 24, 1939, RGBl. I, 1943 and on October 23, 1941, RGBl. I, p. 654. The law was repealed only in 1966 by the Federal Constitutional Court (BverfGE 20, 150). See Rupp (1966), Hammerschmidt (1999).

The same pattern of preserving the legal foundations and instrumentalizing existing institutions and programs for the war-oriented political goals is also found in the law dealing with care of veterans and victims of the war. National Socialism did not add anything essential to the foundations created during the Weimar Republic (Reich Provision Law), except for a few amendments,[16] additions, and a summarizing reissue of the Reich Provision Law in April 1939 (RGBl. I, p. 633). The Law on War Damages to Individuals was changed (RGBl. 1934, I, p. 135), the Deployment Assistance and Deployment Provision Law and the Decree on Harm to Persons, both from 1939, were newly issued (RGBl. I, p. 1217. See Hudemann 1991, pp. 269ff.).

6. Social Policy in the War State

As during the First World War, social policy and social law were dominated by the "purpose" of winning the war. To be sure, even in times of peace social services and benefits are not provided for their own sake; they are always part of a matrix of political purposes and goals (Reidegeld 1998). Now, however, the goals of the war and of the regime's racial and population policy were turned into supportive social policy without impediment. The traditional social contentiousness between parties and organizations no longer functioned. A parliament no longer existed. The ministerial bureaucracy had largely lost its function of objectification and neutralization. The distance between state and society had been eliminated in favor of an authoritarian and anti-democratically led "national community." Protective civil rights, enforced by an independent judiciary, had ceased to exist. The Nazi state had incorporated the traditional systems of protection, "purged" them of real or presumed enemies, but had not—or had been unable to—change them structurally in any real way. Whether this can be seen as resistance from "tried-and-true institutions," as some liked to claim later, or whether the state simply made pragmatic use of them because of their effectiveness and adaptability, remains an open question. In the economic system that was characteristic of National Socialism, which H. D. Bracher has described as "a mixture of private and state capitalism, which under conditions of rearmament and a war economy were increasingly directed from above and outside, but which never became anti-capitalist or anti-monopolistic, let alone socialist" (Bracher 1979, p. 331), social policy played merely a subservient role to the extent that it offered propaganda material to provide psychological support for the "national community."

Social policy was thus "subservient" during the war in several ways (Recker 1985, pp. 17ff.; Recker 1991, pp. 245ff.). The remnants of a free choice of workplace and contractual freedom shrank rapidly (Linne 1995). The systems of

[16] RGBl. 1934, I, p. 541, amended on March 19, 1937, RGBl. I, p. 327, and on August 10, 1937, RGBl. I, p. 886.

sickness, accident, and pension insurance, as well as unemployment insurance were restructured, in part through the policy of job-creation driven by rearmament, in part through a diversion of funds, and in part through an increase in the Reich subsidies (the financing of which, though, was highly unsound). Restructuring, in turn, provided the opportunity to skim off funds to finance the war, and to increase benefits where the regime saw a need: population growth, care for the sick,[17] for workers feeling the strain, and for war victims.

There was certainly a method to all the contradictions within the Nazi social policy that we have seen. Within the context of the system, it was "rational" to free up positions in the social bureaucracy for "old fighters" in need of a job, to give in to pressure from "Aryan" doctors by eliminating their "non-Aryan" competition, and to politically instrumentalize the major insurance schemes under German-National leadership in the Reich Labor Ministry, but otherwise leave them unchanged. It was equally "rational" to continue to demand large contributions from the workers, to keep the real wage levels low, but to celebrate the "honor of work" and compensate the material deficits with propaganda. The restructured insurance assets could then be used in the ways described above. It would also have been "rational" to use the destructive and leveling energy that was unavoidable in the war to dismantle differences in social protection that were no longer justifiable and create a uniform system for all citizens. Such tendencies did exist in the so-called "Robert Ley Plan" (1940), which could even point to the NSDAP's party program of 1920 that had promised a "generous development of old-age insurance" (Point 15). These tendencies were less specific to National Socialism that it may have appeared later in the phase of rebuilding the classic social insurance. Those who after 1945 came out against a "uniform insurance" or even a system of security for citizens independent of contributions not only affirmed the intent of the experts whose views had been shaped by the traditional social insurance, but also signaled opposition to National Socialism and Communism, an important thing to do at the time. These plans were therefore swept away by a general verdict against anything associated with the National Socialists. Still, it is striking how much the Ley Plan paralleled the Beveridge Plan of 1942 (Beveridge 1942; Recker 1985). It is possible that the western industrial states, under the pressures of war and quite independent of fundamental ideological differences, had discovered a fundamental problem of modern social policy, which always seems to recur when traditional structures of social protection clash with dramatic changes in the world of work, a society's age structure, and the rhythms of life.

[17] For example, the decree of November 2, 1943, RABl. II, p. 485. The documents on the planned "Gesundheitswerk des Deutschen Volkes" 1940–1942 in Schubert (2000, pp. 586ff.).

References

Ayaß W (1995) "Asoziale" im Nationalsozialismus. Stuttgart

Ayaß W (1998) "Gemeinschaftsreform". Quellen zur Verfolgung von "Asozialen" 1933–1945. Koblenz

Ayaß W (1999) Rezension Gerhard Albert Ritter: Soziale Frage und Sozialpolitik in Deutschland seit Beginn des 19. Jahrhunderts. Zeitschrift für Sozialreform 890ff

Berghahn VR (1966) Der Stahlhelm. Düsseldorf

Beveridge W (1942) Social insurance and allied services. Her Majesty's Stationery Office. London (German: Der Beveridgeplan. Sozialversicherung und verwandte Leistungen, 1943. Zürich New York)

Bock G (1986) Zwangssterilisationen im Nationalsozialismus. Studien zur Rassenpolitik und Frauenpolitik. Opladen

Boos K (1938) Reichssammlungsrecht. Reichsverwaltungsblatt 59:129–136

Bracher KD (1979) Die deutsche Diktatur, 6th edn. Cologne

Broszat M (1988) Der Staat Hitlers, 10th edn. Munich

Castell-Rüdenhausen A Gräfin z (1991) Kommunale Gesundheitspolitik in der Zwischenkriegszeit. Sozialhygiene und Rassenhygiene am Beispiel Gelsenkirchens. In: Frei N (ed) Medizin und Gesundheitspolitik in der NS-Zeit. Munich, pp 67–80

Dobbernack W (1933) Die Finanzlage der deutschen sozialen Rentenversicherungen. Zeitschrift für das gesamte Versicherungswesen 275ff

Dorner C et al (1989) Die Braune Machtergreifung. Universität Frankfurt 1930–1934. Frankfurt am Main

Federau F (1962) Der Zweite Weltkrieg — Seine Finanzierung in Deutschland. Tübingen

Forsthoff E (1935) Deutsche Geschichte seit 1918. Leipzig

Forsthoff E (1942) Deutsche Geschichte 1918–1938 in Dokumenten, 3rd edn. Stuttgart

Frerich J, Frey M (1993) Handbuch der Geschichte der Sozialpolitik in Deutschland, vol 1. Munich

Gladen A (1974) Geschichte der Sozialpolitik in Deutschland. Wiesbaden

Glenz W (1936) Sammlungsgesetz und Sammelvermögen. Dissertation. Giessen

Hachtmann R (1989) Industriearbeit im "Dritten Reich". Untersuchungen zu den Lohn- und Arbeitsbedingungen in Deutschland 1933–1945. Göttingen

Hachtmann R (1998) Arbeitsverfassung. In: Hockerts HG (ed) Drei Wege deutscher Sozialstaatlichkeit: NS-Diktatur, Bundesrepublik und DDR im Vergleich. Munich, pp 27–54

Hammerschmidt P (1999) Die Wohlfahrtsverbände im NS-Staat. Die NSV und die konfessionellen Verbände Caritas und Innere Mission im Gefüge der Wohlfahrtspflege des Nationalsozialismus. Opladen

Hansen E (1991) Wohlfahrtspolitik im NS-Staat, Motivationen, Konflikte und Machtstrukturen im "Sozialismus der Tat" des Dritten Reiches. Augsburg

Härter K (1971–1998) Zigeuner. Handwörterbuch zur deutschen Rechtsgeschichte, vol 5, columns 1699–1707

Henkes B (1999) Heimat in Holland. Deutsche Dienstmädchen 1920–1950. Straelen

Hentschel V (1983) Geschichte der deutschen Sozialpolitik 1880–1980. Soziale Sicherung und kollektives Arbeitsrecht, Frankfurt am Main

Hientzsch U (1970) Arbeitsrechtslehren im Dritten Reich und ihre historische Vorbereitung. Marburg

Hitler A (1940) Mein Kampf, vol 1, 6th edn. Munich

Hockerts HG (1983) Sicherheit im Alter. Kontinuität und Wandel der gesetzlichen Rentenversicherung 1889–1979. In: Conze W, Lepsius MR (eds) Sozialgeschichte der Bundesrepublik Deutschland. Stuttgart, pp 296–323

Huber ER (1934) Die Gestalt des deutschen Sozialismus. Hamburg

Huber ER (1939) Verfassungsrecht des Großdeutschen Reiches. Hamburg

Hudemann R (1991) Kriegsopferpolitik nach den beiden Weltkriegen. In: Pohl H (ed) Staatliche, städtische, betriebliche und kirchliche Sozialpolitik vom Mittelalter bis zur Gegenwart. Stuttgart, pp 269ff

Kaiser J-C (1991) NS-Volkswohlfahrt und freie Wohlfahrtspflege im "Dritten Reich". In: Otto H-U, Sünker H (eds) Politische Formierung und soziale Erziehung im Nationalsozialismus. Frankfurt am Main, pp 78–105

Klinksiek D (1982) Die Frau im NS-Staat. Stuttgart

Koonz C (1991) Mütter im Vaterland. Frauen im Dritten Reich. Freiburg im Breisgau. American first edition 1987. New York

Kranig A (1983) Lockung und Zwang. Zur Arbeitsverfassung im Dritten Reich. Stuttgart

Kühn R (1939) Strafrechtliche Zweifelslagen zum Sammlungsgesetz. Deutsche Justiz 1939, p 1734

Labisch A, Tennstedt F (1991) Gesundheitsamt oder Amt für Volksgesundheit? In: Frei N (ed) Medizin und Gesundheitspolitik in der NS-Zeit. Munich, pp 36–66

Lampert H (1980) Staatliche Sozialpolitik im Dritten Reich. Hamburger Jahrbuch für Wirtschafts- und Gesellschaftspolitik 25:149–174

Leibfried S, Tennstedt F (1979) Berufsverbote und Sozialpolitik 1933. Die Auswirkungen der nationalsozialistischen Machtergreifung auf die Krankenkassenverwaltung und die Kassenärzte. Bremen

Linne K (1995) Die "innere Front". Deutsche Arbeitsfront und staatliche Sozialpolitik. Zeitschrift Geschichtswissenschaft 43:15–26

Mason TW (1977) Sozialpolitik im Dritten Reich. Arbeiterklasse und Volksgemeinschaft. Opladen

Narr W-D, Offe C (1975) Wohlfahrtsstaat und Massenloyalität. Cologne

Peters H (1973/1978) Die Geschichte der sozialen Versicherung, 3rd edn (1978). Bonn Bad Godesberg

Peukert D-J (1989) Rassismus und "Endlösungs" Utopie. Thesen zur Entwicklung und Struktur der nationalsozialistischen Vernichtungspolitik. In: Kleßmann C (ed) Nicht nur Hitlers Krieg: Der Zweite Weltkrieg und die Deutschen. Düsseldorf, pp 71–82

Prinz M (1986) Vom neuen Mittelstand zum Volksgenossen. Die Entwicklung des sozialen Status der Angestellten von der Weimarer Republik bis zum Ende der NS-Zeit. Munich

Ramm T (1968) Nationalsozialismus und Arbeitsrecht. Kritische Justiz 108–120

Ramm T (1994) Die Arbeitsrechtswissenschaft nach 1945. In: Simon D (ed) Rechtswissenschaft in der Bonner Republik. Studien zur Wissenschaftsgeschichte der Jurisprudenz. Frankfurt am Main, pp 449–528

Recker M-L (1985) Nationalsozialistische Sozialpolitik im Zweiten Weltkrieg. Munich

Recker M-L (1991) Sozialpolitik im Dritten Reich. In: Pohl H (ed) Staatliche, städtische, betriebliche und kirchliche Sozialpolitik vom Mittelalter bis zur Gegenwart. Stuttgart, pp 245ff

Reidegeld E (1998) Staatliche Sozialpolitik in Deutschland. Historische Entwicklung und theoretische Analyse von den Ursprüngen bis 1918. Opladen

Ritter GA (1998) Soziale Frage und Sozialpolitik in Deutschland seit Beginn des 19. Jahrhunderts. Opladen

Ronau C (1933) Die roten Hochburgen. Die Schuld der roten Sozialversicherung an Deutschlands Niedergang. Berlin

Rupp H-H (1966) Das Urteil des Bundesverfassungsgerichts zum Sammlungsgesetz. Neue Juristische Wochenschrift 2037–2040

Rüthers B (1970) Die Betriebsverfassung im Nationalsozialismus. Arbeit und Recht 97

Sauer W (1960) In: Bracher KD, Schulz G (eds) Die nationalsozialistische Machtergreifung. Studien zur Errichtung des totalitären Herrschaftssystems in Deutschland 1933/1934. Cologne Opladen

Scheur W (1967) Einrichtungen und Maßnahmen der sozialen Sicherheit in der Zeit des Nationalsozialismus. Dissertation. Cologne

Schleicher R (1939) Die Wandlung der Wohlfahrtspflege durch den Nationalsozialismus. Ludwigshafen
Schubert W (ed) (2000) Akademie für Deutsches Recht 1933–1945. Protokolle der Ausschüsse, vol X. Frankfurt am Main
Schulz U (1985) Robert Ley. Neue deutsche Biographie 14:424f
Selig W (1988) Franz Seldte. In: Benz W, Graml H (eds) Biographisches Lexikon zur Weimarer Republik. Munich, p 311
Smelser R (1991) Die Sozialplanung der Deutschen Arbeitsfront. In: Prinz M, Zitelmann R (eds) Nationalsozialismus und Modernisierung. Darmstadt, pp 71–92
Stolleis M (1974) Gemeinwohlformeln im nationalsozialistischen Recht. Berlin
Süß W (1998) Gesundheitspolitik. In: Hockerts HG (ed) Drei Wege deutscher Sozialstaatlichkeit: NS-Diktatur, Bundesrepublik und DDR im Vergleich. Munich, pp 54–97
Tarrab-Maslaton M (1993) Rechtliche Strukturen der Diskriminierung der Juden im Dritten Reich. Berlin
Tennstedt F (1979) Sozialpolitik und Berufsverbote im Jahr 1933. Zeitschrift für Sozialrecht 129–153
Tennstedt F (1982) Johannes Krohn. Neue Deutsche Biographie 13:69
Tennstedt F (1987) Wohltat und Interesse. Das Winterhilfswerk des deutschen Volkes. Die Weimarer Vorgeschichte und ihre Instrumentalisierung durch das NS-Regime. Geschichte und Gesellschaft 13:156–180
Thalmann R (1982/1984) Frausein im Dritten Reich. Munich Vienna (frz. Paris 1982)
von Saldern A (1985) Mittelstand im "Dritten Reich". Handwerker - Einzelhändler - Bauern, 2nd edn. Frankfurt am Main New York
Vorländer H (1988) Die NSV, Darstellung und Dokumentation einer nationalsozialistischen Organisation. Boppard
Voß R (1995) Steuern im Dritten Reich. Munich
Wahsner R (1994) Arbeitsrecht unter'm Hakenkreuz. Baden-Baden
Wannagat G (1965) Lehrbuch des Sozialversicherungsrechts, vol 1. Tübingen
Webber D (1988) Krankheit, Geld und Politik: Zur Geschichte der Gesundheitsreformen in Deutschland. Leviathan 156 (178ff)
Weindling P (1991) "Mustergau" Thüringen. Rassenhygiene zwischen Ideologie und Machtpolitik. In: Frei N (ed) Medizin und Gesundheitspolitik in der NS-Zeit. Munich, pp 81–97
Weingart P, Kroll J, Bayertz K (1988) Rasse, Blut und Gene. Frankfurt am Main
Winkler HA (1977) Der entbehrliche Stand. Zur Mittelstandspolitik im "Dritten Reich". Archiv für Sozialgeschichte 17:1–40
Zöllner D (1981) Ein Jahrhundert Sozialversicherung. Landesbericht Deutschland. In: Köhler P, Zacher HF (eds) Ein Jahrhundert Sozialversicherung. Berlin, pp 57ff

VII. The Post-War Period, the Federal Republic, and the German Democratic Republic

1. "Zero Hour" or Continuity?

The metaphor of the "zero hour" to describe the new beginning following Germany's capitulation on May 8, 1945, is both fairly accurate and misleading when it comes to social policy and social law. With respect to the human and physical devastation of the war, the Holocaust, the streams of refugees, and the paralysis of the power of the state, the assumption of "supreme authority" by the Allied military forces was in fact the end and a new beginning all at once.[1] Politically, militarily, and in terms of constitutional law, a point had been reached from which the only possible way was forward. A morally discredited regime had collapsed and its army had surrendered. Even the critics of the metaphor do not question that this was a indeed a "zero hour." But they point out that strong continuities existed in many other spheres of life, as work was simply resumed or carried on as best as possible. This is especially evident where specific material tasks had to be accomplished and the ideological cast of National Socialism could be thrown off or at least suppressed. Social law was such a sphere. The material hardships of the years after 1945 virtually cried out for a rebuilding of social protection, and the way this was accomplished, first in the occupation zones and then in the two German states, would have been unimaginable without the appropriately trained personnel, the structures that still existed, and what remained of the physical assets.

Thus, if one examines the continuity of personnel active in these spheres, the rapid reconstruction of the institutional framework, the nearly uninterrupted continuation of the concepts of welfare (*Fürsorge*) and youth welfare (*Jugendfürsorge*), the structured social security within the framework of the *Reichsversicherungsordnung* [Social Security Act of 1911] and of the provision for war victims, and, finally, even the transfer of case law from the Reich Insurance

[1] For the sphere of the law of the state see Stolleis (2003a, b). For a comprehensive account of the political and social situation see Zacher (2013).

M. Stolleis, *History of Social Law in Germany*,
DOI 10.1007/978-3-642-38454-7_7, © Springer-Verlag Berlin Heidelberg 2014

Office [*Reichsversicherungsamt*] and the Reich Provisioning Office [*Reichsversorgungsamt*] to the new Federal Social Court [*Bundesozialgericht*], talk of a "zero hero" has the effect of obscuring what actually happened.

The material situation was undoubtedly catastrophic. The reserves of Social Insurance, totaling about ten billion Reichsmark, had been invested in war financing,[2] any other assets had been largely destroyed. A "state" that might have been able to help existed initially only in the form of an emergency administration permitted by the military government of the Allies. Officials and employees of the Nazi state had been dismissed; their legal status had terminated as of May 8, 1945. Later, they had to pass through the winnowing process of "de-Nazification." Millions of refugees and expellees had to be admitted into the British and American occupation zones; the French zone opened up only when the first large waves of refugees had already arrived in the other two zones. The Soviet Occupation Zone embarked on its own road into a Socialist dictatorship—in the beginning it was still determined by strategic considerations, but then it became increasingly Stalinist in orientation.

As far as the blueprints of a future social policy were concerned, they were not at the forefront of attention, nor were the Western Allies able to take a uniform line, for the simple reason that they had such divergent traditions of social policy. The United States, already suspicious of models of centralized state control, had taken its first steps in the direction of a Continental European model of social protection only during Roosevelt's New Deal with the Social Security Act of 1935 (Davis 1986; Eichenhofer 1990, pp. 13ff.). Bismarck's statist approach to social insurance was alien to the Americans. By contrast, England embarked on a new path to a "national insurance" (Kaim-Caudle 1979, pp. 223–248; Ogus 1979, 1981) on the basis of the Beveridge Plan published on November 20, 1942 (Beveridge 1942). Fundamentally, that path had to lead toward a merger of the diverse insurance schemes into an omnium insurance. France, because of its strong liberal as well as ecclesiastical tradition, had devised a comprehensive *sécurité sociale* only in 1930, but because of the global economic crisis and World War II it did not set out to establish it until after 1945, starting over on the basis of the plans of the Résistance and extending it also to the French Occupation Zone (Saint-Jours 1981).

But the western powers did share a principled belief that the state had a responsibility to guarantee a minimum subsistence income and a "fair wage," protect against the elementary risks of life, and care for mothers and children. This found expression in both the Atlantic Charter (1941) and in Articles 22 and 25 of the UN's Universal Declaration of Human Rights (1948).

This constellation produced a tug-of-war in the Western occupation zones between reform impulses and the forces of continuity from within and outside. Internally, the carriers of structured social insurance and of a welfare system embedded in the state and local levels confronted the union-based social reformers.

[2] The regulation passed on April 14, 1938 (RGBl I, 398) had compelled insurance carriers to invest at least half of their assets in loans to the Reich. See Federau (1962, pp. 40, 48f.).

Given the memory of the recently vanished Nazi state and the communist-Soviet path, it was easy to denounce centralized models. This created a climate that was not exactly propitious for innovation. Moreover, the urgent and immediate needs were pushing people in the direction of leaving everything the way it had been for the time being, and to embark on something fundamentally new only when the time was ripe. As a result, the conservative forces prevailed on all essential points already before the establishment of the Federal Republic. An interesting parallel case is the attempt by the Allies to abolish or reform the "professional civil service," an institution alien to them. Here, too, the traditionalists were stronger and were able to enshrine this institution in the Basic Law (Article 33, Section 5) (Benz 1981; Wengst 1988).

In the Soviet Occupation Zone, after a brief orientation phase, fundamentally different decisions were made, decisions that incorporated both old demands of the workers' movement and Soviet guidelines.[3] The preliminary decisions were made in the Allied Control Council between 1946 and 1947. A reform concept developed in the Council for combining sickness, accident, and pension insurance under one roof, and for abolishing the distinction between blue-collar and white-collar workers, was defeated in the West by opposition from interest groups, but it was implemented on the Soviet side on February 1, 1947. When the Control Council ceased its operations in March 1948, the West retained its "structured system," while a "uniform insurance" was in place in the East. This political decision separated and accompanied the two German systems right up to the Unification Treaty of September 23, 1990.[4] In the West, the old experts of the Reich Labor Ministry and the Reich Insurance Office, the State Insurance Offices, the associations, and the unions were back in charge after 1947/1948. Especially the Bavarian ministerial bureaucracy in the American Occupation Zone worked on behalf of the "tried-and-true" system. The result was that the emphasis was on the reestablishment of the structures, not on their reorganization (something that could probably be implemented only "from above").

The development of the economy supported this waning of the reformist zeal: between 1948 and 1952, the European Recovery Program (ERP), the so-called Marshall Plan, injected subsidies totaling 1.39 billion dollars into the country and helped to jumpstart the economy (Abelshauser 1981; Knapp 1981). With that, contributions also flowed into the social insurance schemes, and taxes into tax-financed social benefits (welfare, provisioning, social housing, integration of refugees and expellees). The currency reform of June 21, 1948, drastically reduced the excess money supply that had been created by the war financing. All natural persons received 40 DM, later another 20 DM. Businesses and the self-employed received 60 DM per employee. Pensions were converted at the ratio of 1:1.

[3] For a comprehensive discussion see Schmidt (2012). Thanks to this very important essay, my own account can afford to leave out the GDR.

[4] Treaty of August 31, 1990, Agreement of September 18, 1990, and Law of September 23, 1990, BGBl II 1990, pp. 885ff. See there Article 30 and Appendix I, Chap. VIII, A–L.

Immediately afterwards, rationing was abolished for most everyday goods, which meant that the new money could really be put to work (Buchheim 1988).

On the whole, then, those in the West opted to revive the "tried-and-true systems." Since the experts in social policy carried on their collaboration, which often reached back into the Weimar period, they were not particularly interested in fixing basic decisions within the now emerging constitutional law. This explains why there were no fundamental differences about the future allocation of competencies on the road from the Economic Council via the Labor Offices of the Bizone and Trizone to the Parliamentary Council. Precise stipulations were also avoided in the Basic Law. The drafters were content to add the adjective "social" to the state (Article 20, Section 1, Article 28, Section 1), to reiterate the traditional social obligations of property (Article 14, Section 2), to list public welfare and social security (inclusive of unemployment insurance) among the competencies (Article 74, Nos. 7 and 12), and to specify the state subsidies in an obscure passage (Article 120). The Social Democrats, who strongly emphasized the "provisional" nature of the Basic Law and wished to avoid specifications that were too strong in the hope of an electoral victory, saw eye to eye on this with the Christian Democrats, who likewise rejected too strong a fixation of the social state, though of course for different reasons. On August 14, 1949, Adenauer won a narrow victory in parliament with 139 seats to the SPD's 131 seats. With that, as we now know, the general line had been laid down until 1967, regardless of all twist and turns of domestic politics.

2. From Welfare to Public Assistance

a) The Occupation Period

During the war and in its immediate aftermath, it was every man for himself in an effort to survive. To be sure, there were still remnants of National Socialist-shaped administrative activity until the spring of 1945, in fact, at times they functioned in an eerie way. But after the surrender on May 8, 1945, there was no such thing as state welfare for the time being. Government activity, to the extent that there was anything left alongside the National Socialist People's Welfare, was shut down, and it no longer had any resources at its disposal. The welfare law that had been simplified during the war[5] was abolished, as was all special National Socialist law, which meant that the old state of affairs of 1924 existed again: there was general and higher-level welfare, as well as assistance for disabled veterans and the surviving dependents of those killed in the war. In the first commentaries on welfare law, the writers, as though nothing had happened in the meantime, continued with

[5] "Erste Verordnung zur Vereinfachung des Fürsorgerechts vom 7. Oktober 1939," RGBl. I, 2002.

their commentary on the Reich Law on the Responsibility to Provide Social Welfare Assistance of February 13, 1924 (RGBl. 1924 I, p. 100) and the related Reich Principles on the Precondition, Nature, and Scope of Public Welfare of December 4, 1924.[6]

Conditions in the various occupation zones varied profoundly politically and economically, and most of all, poverty in the countryside was very different from poverty in the bombed-out cities. Everywhere, assistance for the victims of the war and the "dire vocational needs of young people" stood in the foreground. The regional and local differences, as well as the understandable tendency of welfare offices to shift needy cases to other agencies, quickly necessitated standardized arrangements. For that reason, the district and state welfare organizations in the British Occupation Zone passed a "Welfare Law Agreement [*Fürsorgerechtsvereinbarung*, FRV]" (Keese 1950, pp. 148ff.), which was revised on May 3, 1949. Drafted by welfare experts, it was joined by nearly all welfare associations of the US Zone and in 1950 also by those of the French Zone (Keese 1950, pp. 55ff.). The principle thereafter was that the welfare association on whose territory the emergency occurred was responsible for dealing with it. As a result, the distinction between provisional and final aid was usually moot.

After a certain legal unity had been achieved in the Bizone and then in the Trizone, especially through the regional mediation offices created by the welfare associations, the new Federal Republic initially added little that was new. "Public welfare" (*öffentliche Fürsorge*), as it was called in Article 74, Section 1, No. 7, of the Basic Law that had just gone into effect, was not the focus of interest in the wake of the currency reform. However, the characteristics that would become apparent later emerged early on: determining the level of the benefits was removed from the visible realm of politics by transferring it to the German Association for Public and Private Welfare (*Deutscher Verein für öffentliche und private Fürsorge*) (Orthbandt 1980). This achieved a kind of neutralization of the process, while at the same time securing local municipal influence over the bodies of the Association. In addition, from the outset the dual tracks of the system were in place: public welfare and church-based and non-profit welfare institutions. I will examine this aspect shortly.

Public welfare, which was now housed within the Federal Ministry of the Interior, thus retained its old legal foundations from 1924, changed and supplement them in 1953 by incorporating the postwar developments,[7] and in subsequent years, with aid to the disabled and those suffering from tuberculosis, it added two special areas in which the classic question about individual need was no longer asked but

[6] Jehle (1954, 1958). During the Nazi period, this writer had placed welfare "at the very center of the nation's struggle of selection" (O Jehle, Fürsorgerecht, 1937, p. 93f.). Reference in Schulte and Trenk-Hinterberger (1986, p. 45).

[7] "Gesetz über die Änderung und Ergänzung fürsorgerechtlicher Bestimmungen (FÄG) vom 20. August 1953," BGBl I, p. 967.

taken as a given.[8] Substantively this was a continuation of the "elevated welfare" in which the level of income determined ineligibility for assistance. No distinction was any longer drawn between groups, but the standardized characteristics were taken into consideration as part of the evaluation of individual cases.

b) Eligibility for Welfare

In one central regard, however, there was a change. The decisive step toward the modernization of welfare law was taken by case-law. Not only did the judicial system have to guarantee comprehensive legal protection (Article 19, Section 4, Basic Law), it also had to give shape to the constitutional promise of the "social state" (Article 28, Section 1, Basic Law). This changed the status of those seeking assistance. While there had previously been legal protection in cases of burdensome administrative actions (institutionalization, deportation), the consensus view was that the needy had no actionable legal right to support.[9] Instead, the associations providing welfare were to fight it out in court, who was responsible for the benefits. The first decisions by the higher courts also still hewed to this line.[10] The breakthrough came only with a decision by the Bavarian High Administrative Court of March 8, 1949, which declared that "it is, in any case, not consistent ... with the basic demands of the modern constitutional and social state to push those in need of help into a role of people whose entitlement to support arises only indirectly as a reflex effect of the fact that the welfare associations are obligated vis-à-vis the state to combat poverty."[11]

The practice of welfare followed this lead only slowly, probably mostly out of concern that this might open a Pandora's box and trigger a flood of legal actions by individuals suing for support. However, the administrative courts quickly embraced the new line (Gottschick 1963), and in so doing they based themselves partly on

---

[8] "Körperbehindertengesetz vom 27. Februar 1957," BGBl I, p. 147, and "Gesetz über Tuberkulosehilfe vom 23. Juli 1959," BGBl I, p. 513. This had been preceded by the "Verordnung über Tuberkulosehilfe vom 8. September 1942," RGBl I, p. 549.

[9] The old line was: "It follows from the historical development of public welfare measures, poor relief, the law on the residential right of relief, and, finally, the Reich Law on the Responsibility to Provide Social Welfare Assistance of February 13, 1924, that the person in need of support never has a legally actionable claim against those bearing the responsibility" ("Urteil des Preuß. Kompetenzkonflikts-Gerichtshofs vom 20.6.1931," in: ZfH 1934, 63).

[10] HessVGH, "Urteil vom 16. März 1949" (DÖV 1949, 377) and VGH Bremen, "Beschluss vom 29. Januar 1948", ND 1948, 120. See Gottschick (1963, pp. 435–442).

[11] "Urteil BayVHG vom 8. März 1949" (DÖV 1949, 375 = VGH 2, 11): "In Bavaria, persons in need of help have, in accordance with the principles of the Bavarian constitution, a legal claim to the granting of public welfare..." See Zacher (1972, pp. 95ff. [120]), with reference to Article 125 and Article 168, Section 3 of the Bavarian Constitution. The latter states: "Every resident of Bavaria who is unfit for work or who cannot be provided with work shall have a right to welfare provision."

regulations of the new state constitutions,[12] and partly on the federal Basic Law (Articles 1, 2, 19 IV).[13] As early as 1953, the State Administrative Court of Rhineland-Palatinate already spoke of an almost universally acknowledged case-law and state of the law.[14] This line of development was brought to completion by the decision of the Federal Administrative Court of June 24, 1954: invoking the Basic Law, it now accorded the needy a subjective-public right to the welfare benefits envisaged by the law (BVerwGE 1, p. 159). This decision once and for all solidified the status of the individual, who could now enforce his "claim" to public welfare in a court of law: directly in the case of legally defined benefits, and in the case of discretionary benefits at least through a legal review of the exercise of discretion. Given this quick emergence of a prevailing view, a response by the legislature was not really necessary. Nevertheless, a few years later it enshrined the principle with the following words: "There is an entitlement to social assistance to the extent that this law stipulates that the assistance must be granted. ...The form and extent of the social assistance must be decided according to due discretion, provided that this law does not rule out discretion" (§4 BSHG).

However, as the flipside of this entitlement to assistance one must also see the obligation to work, as well as the continued existence of workhouses, specifically for young people, the homeless, and persons without a fixed abode. It was not until 1967 that the Federal Constitutional Court prohibited this practice.[15] However, to this day—and now even more so in times of economic stagnation and empty public coffers—state "welfare" has retained its repressive side. As long as money is available, this side can remain hidden. At such times, the pressures toward taking on work (§§18, 25 BSHG) are concealed behind the façade. If money is lacking, pressure on recipients of social assistance also grows. This gives rise to conflicts, especially with regard to the support of single mothers, which probably enjoys overwhelming political support. In addition, the unemployed who have exhausted their benefits and to whom the labor market is closed, as well as all recipients of social assistance who are unfit for work, groups with little ability to speak out, come under disproportionate pressure.

[12] Article 51, Section 1 Constitution of Rhineland-Palatinate; Article 27, Section 1 Constitution of Bremen; Article 7, Section 1 Constitution of North Rhine-Westphalia.

[13] OVG Münster, "Urteil vom 13. April 1950," DVBl. 1951, p. 84; "Hamburg.OVG vom 22. Januar 1951," DVBl. 1951, p. 311; OVG Lüneburg, "Urteil vom 14. März 1951," DVBl. 1952, p. 772; OVG Berlin, "Urteil vom 29. Juni 1951," DVBl. 1953, p. 375; VGH Württemberg-Baden, "Urteil vom 15. Januar 1953," *Zeitschrift für das Fürsorgewesen* 1953, p. 170.

[14] LVG Rhineland-Palatinate, in NDV 1954, p. 351; Gottschick (1963, p. 437).

[15] BVerfGE 22, 181: "The compulsory commitment of an adult to an institution or a home which does not serve the protection of the public or the protection of the affected individual himself, but exclusively his 'betterment,' is unconstitutional."

c) Church-Based and Non-statutory Welfare

As previously indicated, in addition to "public" welfare, non-statutory welfare and the charitable-social activities of the large national churches moved to the fore in the postwar period. Alongside the rebuilt *Arbeiterwohlfahrt* (Workers' Welfare), the Red Cross, the *Zentralwohlfahrtsstelle der Juden* (Central Jewish Welfare Office), and the *Paritätischer Wohlfahrtsverband* (Joint Welfare Association), it was above all the (Protestant) *Innere Mission* (Inner Mission) and *Hilfswerk der EKD* (Relief Organization of the EKD; today combined into the *Diakonisches Werk*), as well as the (Catholic) *Caritasverband* (Caritas Association) that now came into their own (Flierl 1982). Suppressed by National Socialism, they took on heightened importance in the political vacuum after 1945. The Catholic Church and the Protestant state churches, the latter overarched by the EKD, were at the time the only larger institutions that possessed a guiding set of values, appeared to guarantee a moral reconstruction of the country, and which, not least, were able to draw upon international connections. Together with the "Christian" policy that was dominant after 1949, they shaped public life and expanded above all in the areas of hospitals, institutions for the handicapped, homes of every kind, aid for young people, pastoral care over the phone, drug counseling, but also with fluid crossover into adult and family education, Christian community centers and academies. This complex grew—parallel to the "economic miracle"—also through an intensive intertwining of tasks and financing with state-run social work. This growth seemed to confirm the coordination theory developed by the churches, according to which state and church were coequals and should delineate their spheres.

Within a mixture of liberal economic ideas and ecclesiastical social theory, there was now a principled—as well as legal—primacy of societal and ecclesiastical over state actors. This "subsidiarity principle," formulated in the social encyclical Quadragesimo anno in 1931, was on the way to being styled into a constitutional principle.[16] By contrast, the state actor, especially the federal states and municipalities, the real carriers of "welfare," always emphasized that the state bore the overall and final responsibility for the granting of subsidies financed by taxes.

d) The Federal Social Assistance Act

This was the starting situation in which it seemed increasingly urgent to modernize the obsolete "welfare." An important role in this process was played by the German Welfare Day held in Essen in 1957. At a time of rising prosperity, the belief was that poverty was in principle capable of being abolished by helping people help

[16] Isensee (1968), with extensive references, especially in a thoughtful appendix (333–381); Isensee (1988), Herzog (1987).

themselves. With that, the task at hand shifted from securing a livelihood to aid in certain standardized, special life situations. A citizen now possessed an actionable claim to support, for which a new form was also sought in the linguistic shift from "welfare" to "social assistance." This development was supported by the fact that rising prosperity made it possible to boost the standard welfare rates by 50 % between 1949 and 1955. This was no longer poor relief calculated as scantily as possible, but was already tending toward a subsistence minimum below the average working income. Under the preconditions of full employment and rising incomes, it appeared possible in principle to overcome poverty. This was the premise behind the reform of welfare law.

In 1960, the draft for a Federal Social Assistance Act [*Bundessozialhilfegesetz*, BSHG] was submitted to the *Bundestag* through close cooperation between the state, associations, and churches. It was passed by parliament on May 4, 1961, promulgated on June 30, 1961, and took effect on June 1, 1962.[17] It was no coincidence that 1961 also saw the creation of the European Social Charter, which contained an entitlement to government benefits to secure a livelihood (Article 13).

The new law now aggregated what had become a confusing subject matter and gave it the new name "social assistance" [*Sozialhilfe*]. There was a General Part (§§1–10), which placed front and center the task of making possible a life that was "compatible with the dignity of the human being," emphasized the personal responsibility of the individual and his family members, and wanted the aid to be understood as being individual. In spite of all the unavoidable schematization and equal treatment, the goal was to help the needy individual back on his feet, namely by means of preventive and follow-up aid, personal, monetary, and material support, depending on the assessment of the authorities in the exercise of their due discretion. Perhaps the actors were already aware at that time that an individualization that actually penetrates all the way to the individual is not possible within mass procedures taking place in the system of legal entitlement to aid. But the Act does show the effort to push the social administration to take on individual cases with a view toward "human dignity" (§1 BSHG, Article 1, Basic Law). Now that the basic misery had been banished, human dignity could also be interpreted as participation in the life of society, for example through a minimum of communication and the provision of basic cultural goods. This has led to extensive case law about the granting of radio and television hook-ups and about an entitlement to support for family celebrations and the like.

Newly conceived and expanded was the "support in special life situations" (§27 BSHG), in the hope that social assistance, once the general problem of poverty had been resolved through improvements in pension law and through the economic upswing and full employment, should turn more toward special areas, for example, the handicapped, the homeless, the blind, the old, and those "at risk" in other

[17] "Bundessozialhilfegesetz vom 30. Juni 1961", BGBl. I, p. 815. On the background see Giese (1986, pp. 249ff.).

ways.[18] The individual laws in favor of the physically handicapped and those suffering from tuberculosis were integrated into the Act. On the whole, the belief was that in this section of the Act—shaped by the guiding idea of prevention and rehabilitation—one could arrive at a higher degree of professionalization. The latter was in fact achieved, but not the fundamental shift to "support in special life situations." For in the last third of the twentieth century, poverty and chronic unemployment became permanent features of Western industrialized societies. In spite of rising productivity, it was not possible to overcome them. Mechanization and digitalization threw increasing numbers of people out of the labor force, more, at any rate, than were employed by the newly emerging technologies. By now there has been repeated confirmation that even the world's richest societies are constantly struggling to eliminate the basic problems of unemployment and inadequate training, and thereby remedy the most important structural causes of poverty. To that extent, over the long term the support for subsistence has proved the most permanent part of social assistance.

The program of the Social Assistance Act of 1961 was idealistic and—in retrospect—overly optimistic. It is explained against the background of what was at that time a still unbroken optimism of achieving "prosperity for all." At the same time, however, the older poor relief carried on with modern, more sophisticated means. It thus formed the transition to the deployment of the control techniques of the modern social state via positive aids to self-actualization, for example, through preventive and rehabilitative measures, which here, too, showed a repressive flipside (§§18–20, 25 BSHG). However, as long as the basic economic conditions were good, this kind of leverage was not used consistently and across the board.

One of the most important practical questions of the BSHG was how to draw the boundary between the state and society (Zacher 1964). Whether the churches and non-statutory welfare could be active only in a subsidiary function, where the state left fields to them, or whether, conversely, the state should withdraw where societal forces are active—this touched, back then as today, on fundamental questions not only of church law (Scheuner 1973, pp. 43–71; Stolleis 1973, pp. 376–404), but also of the distribution of power in the market of services and substantive orientations. The famous case over the constitutionality of the law (more precisely: of §§10, 93 I No. 2 BSHG) took place in the years 1962–1967, which can be seen as the incubation period of the domestic political crisis that burst into the open in 1968. The Federal Constitutional Court found a pacifying compromise (BVerfGE 22, pp. 180ff.) that allowed both sides to agree on pragmatic formulas for complementing each other and collaborating (Isensee 1968; Rinken 1971, pp. 33ff.). Since there were hardly any commercial providers of social services at that time, the issue

---

[18] As already noted, the compulsory commitment of "at-risk individuals" to closed institutions for the purpose of "improvement" (§ 73 Section 2, 3 BSHG) was repealed by the Federal Constitutional Court with the clear pronouncement that it was not the state's task to "improve" its citizens and therefore it did not have the right to deprive them of the freedom only to "improve them, if they posed no threat to themselves or others should they remain at liberty" (BVerfGE 22, pp. 218ff.).

revolved more around the independence of "non-statutory" welfare vis-à-vis a state animated by a planning euphoria than it did around what is today the more important question of state quality control over the products offered in the marketplace for services.

e) The Law in Practice

In the five decades since passage of the BSHG, the political and social environment of the law has undergone profound changes. Already from the early 1960s, it was becoming evident that the value system hitherto seen as binding and supported by the case law of the Federal Supreme Court and the Federal Constitutional Court would change. Whether this normative value system was in fact accepted and lived by the majority is an empirical question that cannot be answered here. Rather, the issue is whether the roles, behaviors, and ascriptions presupposed in political rhetoric, communications of the media, and in the law were treated as "indisputably" stable, as "obsolete," or as barely still discernible. What makes it so difficult to determine this is that the society of the early Federal Republic had been shaken to its very foundations by the Nazi regime, war, flight, and new beginnings. There was no such thing as a fixed starting point from which "changes" would have been measurable. Yet below the upheavals there were evidently persistent guiding patterns of bourgeois or peasant, proletarian or noble life from which one can extract clear prescriptions of what a "good life" had to look like. If one presupposes these, one can say this much: the exemplary family with its traditional distribution of roles between the genders, between "outside" and "inside," with the bread-winning function for the man and child-raising for the woman, and, further, a monogamous marriage that was in principle permanent, with divorce and children out of wedlock the exception—all this was functioning less and less in accordance with the rules. The number of divorces rose, as did that of single parents. The ratio of women in the workforce grew slowly but steadily, along with the level of women's vocational and professional qualifications. This led to a greater need for childcare in kindergartens, crèches, or all-day schools. Another factor that should not be underestimated in the change of family and work life was the extensive motorization of society, the acquisition of convenient household appliances, and—not least—the ubiquitous television, which expanded from evening entertainment to all-day programming. A society encouraged to consume around the clock with clever means developed new needs and thus also strategies of acquisitive behavior. In the 1990s came the revolution of electronic data processing, which not only favored working at home again, but also opened entirely new dimensions of communication with teleshopping, telebanking, research on the internet, and e-mail.

The "consumer society" that emerged in this way also has a different relationship than earlier societies to the old liminal markers of life, birth, and death. The decision in most cases to have fewer children is shaped also by the perfected possibilities of birth control, early diagnosis, and the liberalization of the abortion law. This has led to a change in society's age structure that was long foreseeable and is now shaping everyday life.

It therefore comes as no surprise that Germany, all pronouncements by politicians and legal decisions notwithstanding, has become a genuine immigration country. To that extent, the freedom of movement established within the European Union has brought about a robust intermixing of society with members of other European cultures and languages. An asylum law that was long applied very generously has allowed political refugees and also so-called economic refugees to make a home for themselves in Germany. In several large recruitment actions, non-European workers were brought into the country, above all from Turkey. By now, large West German cities have veritable Turkish streets and neighborhoods. Society is beginning to get used to the building of mosques and the wearing of headscarves, as well as the surely more important emergence of a Turkish middle class and a corresponding university-educated stratum in the second and third generation.

On the one hand, this complex society has an extraordinarily high national wealth. By global standards, it is among the very richest. On the other hand, it, too, has a growing number of people who are unable to keep up in the competition for work and income (Sell 2002). This includes the ever growing number of the elderly no longer able to pursue gainful employment. They need subsystems by their side, not only in financial terms (equity, pensions, social assistance), but also providers and caregivers who offer the kinds of services on which the elderly depend. Those disadvantaged in multiple respects, who need social assistance more so than anyone else, include also single parents. Full-time work is either not possible for them or cannot be expected of them. Society must help them out, for the simple reason to prevent harm to the most vulnerable, small children. Lastly, we are talking about the group of the unemployed, which has regularly counted around four million in recent years. Their situation rightfully dominates the political discussion, for others depend in turn on each unemployed person. Since unemployment insurance is not able to cushion the chronic unemployment of entire structurally weak areas, its benefits must be limited in size and duration. If they expire, the subsidiary system of social assistance must kick in. Over the long term this makes it into the primary system, in that it offers support for a livelihood for an indeterminate period.

The following can be said in conclusion: the BSHG of 1961, in the form in which it was confirmed by the Federal Constitutional Court in 1967, has proved itself for almost another five decades in a society that has undergone profound changes. Since 1976, social assistance is among the social rights of the Code of Social Law (§9 SGB I), even if it did not have a separate book devoted to it in the Code. Rather, the BSHG changed through more than 70 amendments, through the accompanying implementation decrees that have been enacted on the basis of the 12 authorizations contained in the Act, some from the federal government (7), some from the Federal Ministry for Labor and Social Affairs (5) that is in charge of these matters today. In addition, there were and are implementing laws from the states, though these are largely organizational in nature. Most of the changes to the BSHG can be ignored here, because they were prompted by changes to other laws and did not touch on essential points. However, important and revealing were the Amending Law of 1969, which brought above all an expansion of benefits,[19] and the Amending Law of 1974, which concerned disability law, home-based care, and the modernization of "aid for at-risk individuals" (§72 BSHG).[20] The Law of 1985 was then pulled into the orbit of savings measures: a new system for measuring the cost of living ("basket of goods") was established, but at the same time the rates for the elderly and single parents were raised.[21] What became particularly clear was the tendency to contain the costs of social assistance by "capping" benefits. At the same time, the penalties for turning down reasonable work were increased and the subordinate status of social assistance was emphasized.[22] On the whole, in the judgment of the experts, the legislature pushed to the limit of what is constitutionally acceptable by "capping" the rise in the standard rates, and may have already gone beyond it. Social assistance is thus in danger of reverting to poor relief, not least because other areas of social benefits have also come under pressure, with the result that newly entitled beneficiaries have streamed into social assistance. At the moment, the merging of social assistance and unemployment benefits on January 1, 2004, as well as the new distinctions between those capable of gainful employment, who remain with the labor administration, and those not capable, who are supposed to receive social assistance from the municipalities, is causing great difficulties.

Finally, a special kind of problem was and is social assistance for foreigners (§120 BSHG). When the issue arose in the 1980s and 1990s (for reason of finances and integration policy) of containing the influx of foreigners, in general, and of asylum-seekers, in particular, the legislature not only changed the law dealing with foreigners, but also took up §120 BSHG in an effort to keep the material benefits to foreigners so low that they would provide no incentive to come to West Germany. In addition, the basic right to asylum was drastically curtailed (Article 16a, Basic Law), the benefits to asylum-seekers were entirely removed from social assistance at the urging of the local authorities, and they were worked out in a separate law.[23] This created obvious tensions with the guiding principle of social assistance, which in §1 BSHG promises to preserve "human dignity" without making this dependent on the legal status under the foreigners' law or other additional criteria (Stolleis and Schlamelcher 1985, pp. 309–317).

[19] "ÄndG zum BSHG vom 14. August 1969," BGBL I, p. 1153.

[20] "ÄndG zum BSHG vom 25. März 1974," BGBL I, p. 777.

[21] "ÄndG zum BSHG vom 21. Juni 1985," BGBL I, p. 1081.

[22] "Gesetz zur Reform des Sozialhilferechts vom 23. Juli 1996," BGBl I, p. 1088.

[23] "Asylbewerber-Leistungsgesetz vom 30. Juni 1993," BGBl I, 1074.

f) Social Welfare in the SOZ and the GDR

The Soviet Occupation Zone (SOZ) that was created de facto with the capitulation on May 8, 1945, developed quickly into a political entity with its own dynamic and shrinking outside contacts. Stalin had spelled out his territorial demands already at the war conferences. In the declaration of June 5, 1945, which was confirmed by the Potsdam Agreement of August 2, 1945, the SOZ was established as an occupied territory with "supreme authority" exercised by the Soviet Union. It was initially set up on the basis of the law from the Weimar period and governed by orders from the Soviet Military Administration (Foitzik 1999; Weber 1993). It was in the spirit of these orders that the German central administrations were created from the middle of 1945 and after October 22, 1945, in the states of Thuringia, Saxony, Saxony-Anhalt, Brandenburg, and Mecklenburg.

Even though in the beginning there were certain reservations about a separate "social policy," out of fear that this amounted to carrying on a sector of policy with an identical counterpart in capitalism, the SED soon recognized the opportunity to demonstrate, through a "socialist social policy," what was special about the dictatorship of the proletariat in the areas of health care and worker protection, work-based social benefits, full employment, and the incorporation of women into the labor process. To that extent, labor policy, societal policy, and social policy constituted a unity (Schmidt 2001, pp. 705ff.). Social policy was intended to boost productivity, but not—as East Germany rulers believed they could see in the West—"repair" the strains and compensate the risks created by productivity (Schmidt 2001, pp. 685ff.).

As far as the basic security of the population was concerned, the traditional social welfare was initially continued. However, with the founding of the German Democratic Republic (GDR) on October 7, 1949, the decision was made that a larger welfare system would not exist in the future. Individual poverty and especially the "pauperization" of entire social strata would remain capitalism's mark of Cain (Wienand et al. 1997). For that reason, and because of the generally poor supply situation in the first years of the GDR, the level of benefits was kept rigidly low and pushed all those capable of working into the labor force. Housing policy and the comprehensive reach of the state, the party, and the businesses, also pushed the problems of the "homeless" and other forms of social deviance to the margin.[24]

From the outset, the GDR suffered from a shrinking population and a lack of workers. It was therefore one of the primary goals to exhaust all the potential of those fit to work. The "work-shy" and "asocials" were threatened with criminal prosecution and work education camps. The right and the duty to work formed the propagandistic and the repressive side of the same problem. Under these premises the basic security was to be resolved not individually, but collectively, for example through general price subsidies for food and rents, low prices for services and benefits for the basic provisions of life (electricity, gas, water, sewage, heating fuel,

[24] "VO über die Allgemeine Sozialfürsorge vom 23. Februar 1956," GBl I, No. 28/1956, p. 233.

transportation) and for indispensable consumer items. This basic security was considered the great achievement of the GDR, creating equality on a modest level for all those who did not belong to especially favored groups. Economically, however, these social subsidies devoured gigantic sums and blocked the necessary modernization of the housing stock and the infrastructure.

The workers who stood within the labor process were protected against poverty by a job guarantee and minimum wage regulations. And since nearly all women were part of the productive process thanks to the availability of child care for all children,[25] the poverty problem for single parents was eliminated. Truly disadvantaged in this system were only those groups that were unable to attract political attention or speak collectively—such as war victims no longer able to work, invalids and the handicapped (Rudloff 1998, p. 204), restitution cases and the displaced. Since poverty and unemployment officially did not exist, there was also no meaningful level of social assistance and no unemployment insurance (Rudloff 1998, pp. 191ff.; Schmidt 2001, pp. 711). But poverty did exist, also hidden and socially not accepted poverty. However, it was differently structured from poverty in the West.

It was only in the process of reunification that a short-lived East German Social Assistance Law was passed on June 21, 1990, but it was subsequently merged into the Western BSHG.[26] The adjustment processes after the collapse of the GDR have not been completed even after more than two decades, especially in the presence of persistent high unemployment and considerable differences in prosperity.[27]

3. The Long Road to the Children and Youth Services Act

The previously mentioned dispute before the Federal Constitutional Court (BVerfGE 22, pp. 180ff.) also revolved around the constitutionality of the newly regulated youth assistance. Here, too, the struggle was over where to draw the boundaries between the state and local communities, on the one hand, and non-statutory welfare and church institutions, on the other (§§5 and 8 JWG). In the process it became clear how close youth assistance was to social assistance, while at the same time being principally different by virtue of its pedagogical elements. The decision by the Federal Constitutional Court simultaneously marked

[25] In 1989, 82.3 % of all employable women between the ages of 15 and 60 were part of the workforce. See Schmidt (2001, p. 707).

[26] The basis was Article 24 of the "Vertrag über Schaffung einer Währungs-, Wirtschafts- und Sozialunion zwischen BRD und DDR vom 18. Mai 1990", (BGBl II, p. 537). With the "Einigungsvertrag vom 31.August 1990," (BGBl II, p. 889, Anlage I, Kap. X, Sachgebiet H Abschnitt III), the BSHG applies to the new states as of January 1, 1991, though with modifications (see Schellhorn and Schellhorn 2002, pp. 87–98).

[27] For 1992, the Deutsche Institut für Wirtschaftsordnung indicated that the average financial asset of West German households was 119,000 DM, that of East German households was 31,000 DM.

the tradition of a distinct legal field that reached back to the beginning of the twentieth century, with its origins in the age of *Jugendstil* and Youth Movement.

a) Youth Welfare After 1945

Like the welfare offices, the state youth offices confronted nearly insoluble tasks after 1945. Children and young people had suffered especially from the war: whether as orphans or in broken families, with unfinished or completely absent education and training, or as homeless, refugees, or expellees. The placement of homeless, roaming youths into families or homes, measures in favor of "neglected youths," job creation and work education were thus front and center (Hasenclever 1978, pp. 154ff.). The black market, smuggling, and prostitution were the most important problem areas, at least until the currency reform. Here, too, the reactivated charitable organizations of the church and the associations of non-statutory welfare took on important auxiliary functions, for example, by organizing care packages, brokering stays abroad, or setting up kindergartens. Under the control of the Allies, the organizations that had existed until 1933 were revived. In 1949, they merged into the *Deutscher Bundesjugendring* (German Federal Youth Council). At the same time, the relief organizations of youth social work, created especially in the refugee states (Schleswig-Holstein, Lower Saxony, Bavaria), combined into the *Bundesarbeitsgemeinschaft Jugendaufbauwerk* (Federal Working Committee Youth Buildup Work). The *Allgemeine Fürsorgeerziehungstag* (AFET, Conference on Correctional Education) was revived, and the official and private carriers of youth aid combined in 1949 into an *Arbeitsgemeinschaft für Jugendpflege und Jugendfürsorge* (AGJJ, Working Committee for Youth Welfare and Youth Work). Lastly, it was the American and British allies themselves who set in motion the "German Youth Activities," and who involved themselves primarily in political youth work. The chief motivation behind this was concern about Nazi and militaristic youth groups.

b) From the Reich Youth Welfare Act to the Child and Youth Welfare Act

The legal basis for the work of the youth welfare offices was initially still the Reich Youth Welfare Act (1922) in the reduced form it had been given in 1924, as well as the Juvenile Court Act (1923). Both were supplemented from 1946 through initial decrees and laws by the states. Thus, when the Basic Law was created, the old Youth Welfare and Youth Care could be considered at least more or less intact. Yet they did not carry enough political weight to be mentioned in the Basic Law in a way that was in keeping with their practical significance. The drafters were content with a combination of institutional guarantees and "defensive" basic rights in the areas of marriage, family, and school, and mentioned the field in the catalog of the legislature's powers, different from the Weimar Constitution, only indirectly with the words "public welfare" (Article 74, Section 1, No. 7, Basic Law). On the whole, in the wake of the experiences of the Nazi era, the Basic Law protected the rights of parents and privacy more strongly than it called upon and legitimated the state to become active in a supportive and constructive way.

Nevertheless, in the early years of the Federal Republic a variety of activities emerged aimed at improving the legal foundations, and at activating and invigorating the youth welfare offices. With the help of the new Federal Youth Plan, subsidies were periodically distributed, for example for placement in homes, training, vocational advancement, integration aid for young immigrants from the SOZ, and political youth work. The Bundestag cleaned up and modernized the adoption law, but chiefly it devoted itself to "warding off danger" by enacting new laws about the protection of youth in public and about the dissemination of writings dangerous to the youth.[28] Here, too, the first order of business was to shed the Nazi past, yet these laws were also documents of narrow, indeed anxious moral ideas. These were the years that witnessed demonstrations, police bans, and high court decisions against the film *Die Sünderin* ("The Female Sinner").[29] The legislature did not yet dare advocate a more emphatic strengthening of the pedagogical element in the area of juvenile delinquency. In a new Juvenile Court Law it merely expanded its area of application to adolescents over the age of 18 and introduced parole supervision. A complete decriminalization seemed entirely unrealistic, precisely because of the loosening of social bonds through the war.[30] The end of the first legislative period finally saw passage of an overdue amendment to the Reich Youth Welfare Act, which, first of all, eliminated the inflation-caused restrictions of 1924 which experts had long complained about.[31] Most of all, however, it imparted new contours to the Youth Welfare Office by organizing it as an independent agency of communal self-government, spelling out its obligatory tasks and improving its internal structure. At the same time, though, non-governmental youth aid was pushed to the fore; the work of the youth welfare offices was to remain "subsidiary."

In spite of these small steps by the legislature there were intense professional debates, memoranda, and above all advances in the practical work of the youth welfare offices (Hasenclever 1978, pp. 182ff.). The personnel situation improved along with the educational qualifications of the youth workers. In this way, beginning in 1957, new energies gathered for a legislative revision of the Youth Welfare

[28] "Jugendschutzgesetz vom 4. Dezember 1951," BGBl. I, p. 936; "Gesetz über die Verbreitung jugendgefährdender Schriften vom 9. Juni," BGBl. I, p. 377.

[29] See "OVG Rheinland-Pfalz vom 29. Mai 1952," OVGE 2 (1955), pp. 48–66.

[30] "Jugendgerichtsgesetz vom 4. August 1953," BGBl. I, p. 751.

[31] "Änderungsgesetz zum RJWG vom 28. August 1953," BGBl. I, p. 1035. See Muthesius (1950). A retrospective: Jordan and Münder (1987), Münder (1990, p. 43).

Act. From 1958 there were several drafts whose tendency was to strengthen parental responsibility and non-statutory welfare, while authorizing public youth welfare only in a subsidiary function. Ideological, financial, and constitutional problems blocked a broader consensus.

The new Youth Welfare Law (*Gesetz für Jugendwohlfahrt*, JWG) of August 11, 1961 (BGBl. I, p. 1193), which was voted in only by the government and took effect on July 1, 1962, was met with disappointment in practice and the political resistance of the opposition.[32] The positions of the legal challenges brought against the law (constitutional complaints, norm violations) were already prefigured in the unsatisfactory genesis of the law (NDV 1962, pp. 123ff., 331ff.). The court rendered a Solomonic decision by declaring the challenged regulations as constitutional, while at the same time recalling the decades of collaboration between public and non-statutory youth welfare and noting in passing that Youth Care (*Jugendpflege*) dominated by pedagogical elements was also part of "public welfare" (in the sense of Article 74, No. 7, Basic Law). With that, the repeatedly invoked "unity of youth aid" was preserved—an important precondition for the reform process that began with the political transformation of 1969.

Initially, the changes to the Youth Welfare Act emerged out of the gradual modernization of family law. The 1969 reform of the law dealing with non-married persons (BGBl. I, p. 1713), a clear developmental leap, led to changes in the JWG with respect to guardianship and foster children, and to the introduction of a duty for the youth welfare office to provide counseling and support. Small changes in the youth welfare office's sphere of competency came with the Adoption Law (BGBl. I, p. 1762). Further changes to the youth welfare act were triggered by the Act on the Reform of Marriage and Family Law of June 14, 1976, especially through the not uncontroversial introduction of the family court, then by the lowering of the age of maturity and marriageability to 18 (7.31.1974, BGBl. I, p. 1713), in line with the voting law and the military draft.

However, none of this could conceal the fact that the Youth Welfare Law of 1961 had lagged behind the possibilities of its time. As a result, from around 1970, under changed political circumstances, practitioners and scholars began to think about a revision. What also played a role in this was that by now the project of a Social Code (*Sozialgesetzbuch*)[33] had gotten under way and had brought forth once again the old differences of opinion as to whether youth welfare should be assigned to education law or social law. Added to this were rivalries between the Ministry of Labor and the Family Ministry, as well as financing concerns by the states and communities. In the end, though, the majority of politicians decided to include youth welfare law as Book Eight in the Social Code. Yet these differences did not play the decisive role in the broad debate that now began over the conception of a modern youth welfare law. Instead, for nearly two decades the well-known questions were back on the agenda: the role of the youth office and its overall

[32] Revealing is the assessment by the practitioner Hasenclever (1978, pp. 202ff.).

[33] Zacher (1973, 1988).

responsibility, the expansion of the pedagogical element on the basis of a weakly articulated federal competency,[34] the transformation of the laws into a genuine "benefits law," the further professionalization of youth welfare, the development of the problematic corrective education (e.g. Aich 1973), the state guarantee of a kindergarten place and how to set its value, and the delimitation of the entitlement criteria for the support of physically, mentally, and emotionally handicapped children in the Federal Social Welfare Act (BSHG) and the Youth Welfare Act (JWG).

The year 1973 saw publication of an interesting and far-reaching discussion draft for a new law. Assembled in this draft were the hopes of practitioners, but those hopes were evidently pitched too high. The subsequent draft bill from the ministry (1974) bogged down for political reasons, also in its updated version (Scherpner 1979). A third attempt undertaken by the Bundestag in 1980 (05.23.1980, BR-Drucks. 287/80) failed due to the opposition of the states on financial grounds. Undeterred, the ministry, and in it the responsible expert Wiesner, continued to push the issue. New drafts were presented in 1988/1989, which again made their way into parliament. Since concerns over how to finance the guarantee of a place in a kindergarten for all threatened to sink the law, the parties agreed to leave this issue to the states (§26 KJHG [Child and Youth Welfare Act]). As a result, the Child and Youth Welfare Act (*Kinder- und Jugendhilfegesetz*) was passed in the Bundestag with a large majority on March 28, 1990, and took effect on January 1, 1991 (BGBL. I, p. 1163). It is now part of the Social Code as Book Eight, which means that this question—long disputed among social workers and legal experts on social law—was also settled. Indirectly, this affirmed the line that wanted to take the law of youth aid out of the obsolete dichotomy between "youth welfare" intended to ward of dangers and "youth care" intended to provide pedagogical support, and to create a uniform, preventively oriented benefits law.

c) *Youth Welfare and Youth Aid in the SOZ and the GDR*

As soon as the Soviet Occupation Zone had evolved into the German Democratic Republic and the leadership of the SED had asserted itself, the socialist state's educational claim also took hold of East Germany's youth (Ramm 1990, pp. 96ff.). The youth organizations that are characteristic for this type of state were created and displaced the competing non-governmental and church-based organizations. Nationalization and centralization, a thorough-going politicization, and a broad

[34] For example, passage of the kindergarten laws of the states as implementing laws for the youth welfare act or in the exercise of the responsibility of the states for the educational system (e.g. Bavaria), the development of educational aid for adoptions or youthful delinquents, or the question of whether the promotion of parental and family education was still covered by the authority of Article 74, No. 7, Basic Law. On the latter see Stolleis (1978).

exclusion of the churches characterized youth work in the GDR.[35] And since genuine municipal government also ceased to exist after 1952, special local developments and private initiatives fell by the wayside. This was partly made up through measures put in place by enterprises (kindergartens, day nurseries, vacation planning) (Schmidt 2001, pp. 712ff., 757ff.).

Whereas unadjusted youths and juvenile delinquency could still be interpreted, during the first few decades, as phenomena of the transition period to socialism or as disruptive actions by the West ("rowdyism"), later the realization took hold that the "education to the socialist personality" often failed also under 'real socialism.' Although the authoritarian regime kept problems of unemployment and drug use under control, it was forced to concede that especially the destruction of the traditional image of the family was the source of neglect, alcohol consumption, and defiance of the system (Hoffmann 1974, 1981; Freiburg 1977). Still, the authoritarian structures were maintained, for example in institutional care. Youth welfare remained a marginal area within social policy with tight resources, little personnel, and a low level of professionalization—understandable in a state that did not wish to admit that behind the façade of propaganda the very problems that were officially a thing of the past kept reemerging. Only with the end East Germany did it become apparent that the collective education directed from the top had not only been ineffective, but had also produced considerable disorientation, aggression, and isolation.

4. Internal and External Burdens from the War

The twentieth century left more human victims and material destruction in its wake than any other century before. To an already horrific balance sheet, War II added millions of killed and missing soldiers, the murder of millions of Jews, and countless victims of hunger, exhaustion, and disease in all nations and national groups involved in the conflict. The civilian population was also affected on a scale previously unknown. Streams of refugees and expellees had to be cared for alongside the victims of the war in the narrower sense. Cities and landscapes, industrial plants and transportation systems lay in ruins. In a broader sense, the consequences of the human losses were also among the costs of the war—the unemployment of the post-war period and the investments that were never made. To that extent, nearly everything paid out to the "war victims" as social compensation and invested in reconstruction can be counted among the "burden from the war": that is, higher social charges, state subsidies for reconstruction, reparations (dismantling and removal of industrial plants, sale of products below market value), occupation costs, inflation and government debt, including the regulation of foreign debt (London Debt Agreement) (Albers 1959; Caesar 1987a). To keep all of this from

[35] Rudloff (1998, pp. 207ff.) for a comparison between the Nazi State, the Federal Republic, and East Germany. On family policy see Schmidt (2001, pp. 710ff., 754ff.).

proliferating beyond measure, legislation early on specified as burdens resulting from the war (Article 120, Basic Law) only those that had a direct causal connection to World War II (BVerfGE 9 [1959], p. 305).

The Western occupation zones and the Federal Republic had to respond as quickly as possible in all of the areas mentioned above in order to help widows and orphans, war victims and those placed into the same category. At the same time, war refugees and expellees, returning veterans, and refugees from the GDR had to be integrated and provided with the essential necessities. That was possible only through a comprehensive "equalization of burdens" in accord with the elementary demands of justice and thus also with political prudence. The victims of the Nazi regime, where survivors existed at all, were to receive material "compensation," a move that was to make clear, even if more as a gesture than anything else, that the Federal Republic, in asserting the continuity of the nation in terms of state law, had also accepted the terrible legacy of the Nazi regime both morally and materially. Only 50 years later was there a similar "gesture" for the forced laborers who had been brought to Germany during the war.

To resolve all of these problems, the state in part used old structures along with their personnel (providing for war victims), and in part set up entirely new bureaucracies (equalization of burdens, compensation for Nazi victims). The bulk of the transfer benefits were made between 1949 and 1958. But even today, the social security offices still have a larger number of war victims to look after. The Federal Office for the Equalization of Burdens (*Bundesausgleichsamt*) in Bad Homburg will also terminate its work only in about a decade: after the recovery of assets in the former GDR, the clawback of previous equalization of burdens payments is pending.[36]

a) Provision for War Victims, Provision for Soldiers

"War-disabled persons" (*Kriegsbeschädigte*), in the conventional definition of the Reich Provisioning Law, numbered 1.5 million on the territory of the Federal Republic after 1945. Initially the reestablished social security offices had no option but to continue applying the Reich Provisioning Law (RGBl. 1939 I, p. 663) previously in force. Out of the various state provisioning laws for war victims there subsequently arose as the first federal regulations—in accordance with the assignment of legislative competence to the federal government (Article 74, - Section 1, No. 10, Basic Law)—the Law for the Improvement of Benefits to War Victims of March 27, 1950 (BGBl. 1950 1, p. 77), the Law on Subsistence Allowance for Family Members of Prisoners of June 13, 1950 (BGBl. 1950 I, p. 204), and the Law on Returnees of June 19, 1950 (BGBl. 1950 1, p. 221).

[36] In the future, documenting the entire complex will be the responsibility of the Equalization of Burdens Archive (*Lastenausgleichsarchiv*) in Bayreuth, a branch of the Federal Archives (*Bundesarchiv*).

Passage of the Federal Law on War Pensions (*Bundesversorgungsgesetz*) of December 20, 1950 (BGBl. 1950 I, p. 791) concluded this first phase. The law took over large portions of the Reich Provisioning Law (curative treatment, sick pay, housing money, nursing allowance), but it limited the rules governing monetary compensation and sought new paths in the pension system by dividing benefits into the basic pension and the supplementary pension. The income-independent basic pension was to constitute a compensation for the sacrifices made (physical injury, loss of the breadwinner), while the partly income-dependent supplementary pension was granted under special conditions (§§32–34, 41, 47 BVG) as an aid to subsistence. To that extent, the supplementary pension constituted the existence of an element that served to limit the drawing of pensions within the middle classes. At the same time, however, the circle of beneficiaries had been expanded beyond soldiers. The modern war of extermination had affected the entire population, not only through bombings, but also punishments resulting from the war, the loss of freedoms, or harm to one's job or profession.

Concurrent with the Federal Provisioning Law, the structure of the relevant offices (Social Security Offices, State Social Security Offices, the Federal Pension Office) was standardized and an administrative procedure specific to the field was introduced.[37] However, following the creation of the 10th Social Security Statue Book, a separate regulation for the administrative procedures dealing with provisions for war victims has become unnecessary.

Naturally, the number of entitled beneficiaries has declined steadily during nearly six decades of peacetime. But in 1985 there were still 1.68 million war victims or their dependents entitled to benefits.

Alongside the war victims, which must be cared for in keeping with the idea of sacrifice, there are the active soldiers, who are not only entitled to "monetary benefits and benefits in kind, therapeutic care, and care as stipulated by special laws (§30 Soldiers' Law),[38] but who—along with their dependents—are included in health, pension and unemployment insurance. The pay of professional soldiers, as the pay in the public sector in general, is a salary entitlement. In the past, this was long obfuscated by the emphasis on the special character of public service (obligation of loyalty, obligation of providing subsistence, prohibition against striking, judicial character). Today, however, in view of a position that increasingly resembles that of employees, the wage character must be fundamentally recognized.

If one regards the professional soldier—and possibly also the draftee—as an employee, it would be consistent to assign a possible war-related disability to the

[37] "Gesetz über die Errichtung der Verwaltungsbehörden der Kriegsopferversorgung vom 12. März 1951", BGBl. I, p. 169; "Gesetz über das Verwaltungsverfahren der Kriegsopferversorgung (KOVwVerfG) vom 2. Mai 1955", BGBl. I, p. 202, revised May 6, 1976, BGBl. I, p. 1169. On this see Schönleiter and Hennig (1969).

[38] In the version of the announcement of April 22, 1969, BGBl. I; 314. Special laws are the Civil Service Remuneration Act, the Service Pay Act, and the Military Pensions Act.

accident insurance, to which the state as the employer would have to make contributions. To date this has not happened. The notion is raised here simply to point out that the classic concept of care is experiencing a partly factual, partly dogmatic narrowing of its field of application in the law relating to war victims and in the law governing the civil service. At the same time, however, beyond wars new sources of danger to the general public arise, especially in technologically highly advanced societies, which can be met only through the idea of the state assuming responsibility for the risks. Examples are oversized technological accidents that can no longer be dealt with through the tools of private law, including private insurances. Here the state, out of political considerations, helps with tax resources, because technologies are authorized and operated in the name of the collective. The same is true of natural disasters like "once-in-a-century floods," which are not caused by concrete human error, but for which a collective shared responsibility can be established (the sealing off of natural landscapes, the straightening and piping of rivers, climate change caused by human behavior).

Finally, one speaks of provisioning law in cases in which the state in principle should offer active protection, but has failed in concrete cases, that is, with victims of violent crime. In a consistent move, the legislature has not referred such victims to social assistance or to the entirely inappropriate accident insurance, but has created a factual state of care analogous to the care of war victims.[39] Applications for victim compensation from this law are processed by the social security offices.

b) Prisoner of War Compensation, Integration of Expellees and Evacuees

Since the care for war victims, following the notion of sacrifice, was focused at core on compensation for physical harm, there was a need for separate legal bases to compensate for the harm that prisoners of war had suffered through the loss of productive years, a loss that was assigned, like sacrifice, to the state as the sovereign over war and peace. The result was passage in 1950 of the so-called Returnee Law (BGBl. 1949/1950, p. 221), of the Prisoner of War Compensation Act (BGBl. I, p. 5 and BGBl. I, p. 1545) in 1954, and of the Prisoner Aid Act for those who had been incarcerated in the SOZ/GDR (BGBl. I, p. 498). The latter was a political law of the early Federal Republic. It was enacted after the uprising on June 17, 1953, but also in response to the "arrival of a larger group of Waldheim prisoners" (Schröcker 1963, p. 455). Its purpose was to help political victims of the GDR parallel to the refugees from the Soviet zone: that is, former internees in Soviet camps that had been handed over to the GDR, as well as other victims of "State Security" and GDR justice.

[39] "Gesetz über die Entschädigung für Opfer von Gewalttaten (OEG) vom 11. Mai 1976," BGBl. I, p. 1181; "Bundesversorgungsgesetz (BVG) i.d.F. der Bekanntmachung vom 22. Juni 1976," BGBl. I, p. 1633. On the motivation behind the law see Stolleis (1981).

Alongside the care for war victims, prisoners of war, and political prisoners, and compensation benefits, the dominant domestic political problem in the years of rebuilding after the war was the integration of refugees, evacuees, and expellees.[40] To deal with these problems, a series of continually revised and amended laws and ordinances was passed (overview in Ruland 2003). The Federal Expellee Law of May 19, 1953 (BGBl. I, p. 201), the Federal Evacuees Law (BGBl. I, p. 586, in the version of October 13, 1961, BGBl. I, p. 1865), the Foreign Pensions Law of August 7, 1953,[41] the Aid Law of July 15, 1965 (BGBl. I, p. 612, now the Refugee Aid Act of May 15, 1971, BGBl. I, p. 681), and the refugee laws of the states,[42] have—with the support especially from tax law—offered a variety of aid such as grants, cheap loans, exemptions, the approval of pension applications and the like, accelerated the integration of the nearly nine million expellees and the more than three million refugees from the GDR (by 1961), and thereby alleviated social tensions. It deserves to be mentioned that this process was initially set in motion by quick and effective engagement by the churches, which were in place after 1945 as the only intact major organization and were able to help through their ecumenical ties (Klapper 1987, vol. I, pp. 909–913). By now the entire apparatus has largely accomplished its task.

c) *Compensation of Burdens*

"Compensation of burdens" was first mentioned when it became clear, during the conversion of the currency, just how great the discrepancy was in the situation of the Germans in the West and the East. While the Germans in the Eastern territories had suffered a total loss, in the Western occupation zones they had largely been able to hang on to their real estate and other assets. A social balance between those who had suffered losses and those who had not was an urgent domestic political necessity. For that reason, a broadly based redistribution began already before the establishment of the Federal Republic. Its purpose was to compensate for damages and losses that had been caused by expulsions and destruction of the war and post-war period, and to alleviate hardships that had arisen in the wake of the

[40] The Economic Council of the Combined Economic Area passed the "Gesetz zur Förderung der Eingliederung von Heimatvertriebenen in die Landwirtschaft (Flüchtlingssiedlungsgesetz) vom 10. August 1949", WiGBl., p. 264.

[41] BGBl. I, p. 848. It recognized the claims acquired in other insurance schemes and passed these on to insurance carriers in the Federal Republic. This was thus a form of the principle, known from provisioning law, of state compensation for disadvantages the cause of which was attributed to the state.

[42] Wolff and Bachof (1978, pp. 257ff.). See also the summary: Eingliederung der Vertriebenen, Flüchtlinge und Kriegsgeschädigten in der Bundesrepublik Deutschland. Bonn, 1982 presented by the Federal Minister of the Interior (1982), and Prinz (2000).

reorganization of the monetary system (Homburg Plan).[43] Already the preamble to the first Currency Law that went into effect on June 20, 1948, spoke about the "regulation of the compensation of burdens" that was the responsibility of the German authorities. As a result, the Economic Council of the Combined Economic Area passed a Mortgage Protection Act on September 2, 1948, and designed an "immediate program," de facto a first compensation of burdens law, though it was not approved by the Allies (Bundesausgleichsamt 2002, pp. 12ff.). After the creation of the Federal Republic, it served as the revised basis for the Emergency Aid Law on August 8, 1949.[44] This in turn passed into the Equalization of Burdens Law of August 18, 1952,[45] which was followed by a few special laws.[46]

The basis was the idea of solidarity on the part of those who had suffered no harm with those who had suffered expulsion and "East damages" (earlier only beyond the Oder-Neiße line, later also within the territory of the GDR), and also with those in the West who had suffered war damages and loss of wealth from currency reform. The purpose was twofold: for one, without regard to social need, a balance between West and East was to be achieved by requiring Western fortunes to relinquish a certain share. In other words, this was a special levy among unequals in order to create "equality." For another, immediate assistance was to be offered from the perspective of social integration. A generalizing, quota-based equalization was thus combined with an individualizing social aspect.[47] Already these bifurcated purposes could arouse doubts, from a systematic perspective, whether one can speak of social law in this case. However, in a historical retrospective that can also do justice to the crucial domestic political implications, precisely this mixture of motivations seems sensible, for both issues were at stake: the correction of the economic imbalance between the two segments of the population, which was the shared political responsibility of all, and the alleviation of individual hardship.

The revenue needed for the equalization came from "equalization levies" (Article 106, Section 1, No. 5, Basic Law), capital levies, mortgage income taxes, and credit levies, which all collected into an Equalization Fund as a separate federal fund and supplemented with subsidies from the federal government and the states. It cannot be said that this reshifting hit contributors hard, for they paid these levies either out of investment income or burdened consumers via prices, which means that the recipients also helped again with the financing.

---

[43] Gallwas, article on "Equalization of Burdens" (1975) in EvStL. Revealingly enough, such an article was no longer included in the 3rd edn. of the EvStl.

[44] WiGBl. 1949, p. 205. The law did not apply to the French zone, but it was implemented there by relevant emergency aid laws by the states.

[45] BGBl. I, p. 445, in force as of September 1, 1952. See Bundesausgleichsamt (2002).

[46] "Gesetz über die Feststellung von Vertreibungsschäden und Kriegsschäden (Feststellungsgesetz) vom 21. April 1952," BGBl I, p. 237; "Gesetz über einen Währungsausgleich für Sparguthaben Vertriebener (Währungsausgleichsgesetz) vom 27. März 1952," BGBl I, p. 213; "Gesetz zur Milderung von Härten der Währungsreform (Altsparergesetz) vom 14. Juli 1953," BGBl I, p. 495. In retrospect Singbartl (1996).

[47] Gallwas (1975), Caesar (1987b), Nahm (1962/1967), Schillinger (1985, 1995).

Upon application, payment could be received from the Equalization Fund for expulsion damages, war-related property damage, so-called East damages and saver damages (Käss 1959). Provided the applicant met the requirements, there was a legal entitlement to these benefits. By contrast, the benefits determined by the social purposes were limited by the available funds and were also awarded at the discretion of the authorities. These were integration loans of every type, housing aid, benefits from the Hardship Fund for SOZ Refugees, subsidies for professional training and re-education, business start-up loans or subsidies. The administrative structure ran from the Equalization Offices to the State Equalization Offices to the Federal Equalization of Burdens Office, which administered the so-called Equalization Fund as an independent higher federal authority (Article 120a, Basic Law). These administrative bodies developed with a certain dynamic of their own, lawyers specialized, and a separate "Journal for the Equalization of Burdens" took account of what was happening. If one uses the large loose-leaf collections today, which collect the 21 amendments to the Equalization of Burdens Law enacted until 1986, the many accompanying laws (such as the Certification Law of April 21, 1952 [see note 46], the Currency Equalization Law of March 27, 1952 [see note 46], the Old Economy Law of July 14, 1953 [see note 46], or the Reparation Damages Law of February 12, 1969 [BGBl. I, p. 105]), and the countless legal ordinances and implementation regulations (Kühne et al. 1953; Bundesausgleichsamt 2002, pp. 19ff.), the question does arise whether this redistribution so important to the post-war period could not have been accomplished also with the help of tax law, on the one hand, and social law, on the other. Whatever one might think about it: the "equalization of burdens" disbursed a total of 145.3 billion DM in benefits between 1949 and 2001, a process that will be remembered as a great act of solidarity by the early Federal Republic. Its symbolic value was probably greater than the material effect of redistribution (Schaefer 1978).

d) So-Called **Wiedergutmachung** *("Restitution")*

Of great importance for diplomatic recognition was the decision by the Federal Republic, grounded in both political and ethical considerations, to declare itself the heir to the German Reich and to accept, alongside the debts of the Reich, above all the responsibility for the crimes of National Socialism.[48] Already before the founding of the Federal Republic, preliminary regulations had been enacted in the occupation zones and states that pertained above all to the return of property. In the US zone a larger solution was then envisaged: it recognized as persecuted persons those who had been persecuted and harmed for their political opposition to National Socialism, as well as for racial, religious, or ideological reasons. Moreover,

[48] Sagi (1981), Zweig (1987/2001), Goschler (1992, 2005), Herbst and Goschler (1989), Hockerts (2001).

compensation was to be paid to those who had actively opposed the regime or who had been disadvantaged because of their membership in an artistic or scholarly current rejected by the Nazi state. This regulation was later adopted by the Federal Republic.

Before it came to that, however, considerable obstacles had to be overcome. A political problem initially lay in finding the relevant partner to an agreement. The state of Israel, founded in 1948 and a subject of international law only after the Holocaust, was pushing for material aid. At the same time, after 1951 the Conference on Jewish Material Claims against Germany represented the victims scattered around the world; its spokesman was Dr. Nahum Goldmann. The question was further complicated by the fact that in 1953, when the talks entered into the decisive phase, the London Debt Conference took place with the participation of 23 states (Adenauer 1966, pp. 127–157; Goschler 2005). In the end, after negotiations in the Dutch town of Wassenaar, the two sides settled on specific sums and payment modalities in an agreement that was signed on September 10, 1952, in the Town Hall in Luxemburg.[49] It became the basis of the Federal Compensation Law (*Bundesentschädigungsgesetz*, BEG) of September 18, 1953.[50] The concentration on the Jewish victims of the Nazi regime, which unquestionably had to form the focal point, caused the smaller groups persecuted and murdered by the Nazis to recede into the background: Jehova's Witnesses, homosexuals, *Wehrmacht* deserters, but above all the Sinti and Roma and the handicapped people murdered under the terrible term "social hygiene," and, finally, the "forced laborers" brought in and exploited by the Nazi state. Those politically persecuted by the Nazi regime faced the special difficulty that they had to prove not only their opposition to National Socialism, but also the causality behind the persecution measures triggered by that opposition. Here a non-historical way of thinking about administration and the judicial system, trained toward legal restrictions, collided with elemental expectations of justice. And if the politically persecuted were also former communists—or even communists active in West Germany—the claims to restitution intersected in a truly paradox manner with the actions of the Cold War against the KPD (German Communist Party) outlawed in 1956 (von Brünneck 1978; Posser 1991).

At least with the BEG, which had been preceded by a special Restitution Law for the public sector in 1951,[51] the starting point for material restitution benefits had been created. The fact that these payments, while impressive in absolute numbers (by the end of 1998 they amounted to about 105 billion DM), remained rather

[49] On the German side, Hermann J. Abs was responsible for the London Debt Conference, Franz Böhm and Walter Hallstein for Restitution. That the negotiations, which had been watched with suspicion both in Israel and on the Arab side, came to a positive end can probably be attributed primarily to pragmatic reason and the personal authority of Nahum Goldmann and Konrad Adenauer.

[50] BGBl. I, p. 1387, later repeatedly amended. On the legislative materials: Bundesministerium für Finanzen and W. Schwarz (1974ff.).

[51] BGBl. I, p. 291. On the judicature see Maetzel (1963).

marginal compared to other expenditures has often come in for criticism, as has the hesitant, evasive administrative praxis and adjudication guided by dubious justifications (Arndt 1956).

5. Social Support and Promotion

a) Classification Issues

To this point the account of the development after 1945 has already shown that the young Federal Republic, in its economic upswing, on the one hand moved within the tracks of "tried-and-true" systems, and, on the other hand, became active in all social areas as part of its crisis management. Here more general goals often merged with specific socio-political ones. The jurisprudential classification of the various legislative strategies always remained uncertain.

For example, an attempt was made to subsume under the concept of (general) provisioning some measures of the benefits-providing state that seemed to be partial elements of a future "welfare" provisioning that was the same for all citizens, such as the legislation on the child allowance and housing allowance and support for the blind.[52] But this was not very convincing: after all, the aid to the blind regulated by state law could hardly be considered part of a not yet existing "general provisioning," while the aid to the blind governed by federal law remained folded into public assistance. Moreover, the motives of family and social policy underlying child and housing allowance legislation were fundamentally different from those behind the laws dealing with war damages, with the result that the common term "provisioning," which also encompassed the pay for civil servants, proved rather misleading. An effort was therefore made to create a relatively open area of "social promotion," in order to assemble there in an orderly fashion laws that belong together not through their legal forms, but rather through their social purpose and the fact of not being bound to an employment situation.

We are talking about those manifestations of the benefits-providing state through which the equalization of social deficits is pursued and controlling interventions carried out in social policy, without the ability to identify individual need, without co-payments by the recipient, or the equalization—as an expression of solidarity—of special sacrifices as typical criteria. However, here, too, a connection is made with existing social circumstances and distribution is based on a criterion of "equalizing justice." But the issue is not concrete hardship situations such as poverty, illness, accidents, occupational disability in old age, unemployment, or war damages, but circumstances described by the state as generally "worthy of promotion." The absence of measures of promotion would not directly deprive

[52] Representative Wolff and Bachof (1978). On this see now Demmel (2003).

anyone of his or her livelihood. It would merely indicate that the underlying public interest in the promotion, it whatever way it is constituted and legitimized, has changed. The benefits-providing state manifests itself in its purest form in measures of this kind. The historical roots in the warding off of dangers in the name of good public order that always still adhered to the efforts at social legislation discussed so far have been cast off. Here the state is not remedying acutely deficient situations or protecting preventively against dangers, but shaping society with positive planning and guidance. Social shortcomings in this sense are public shortcomings, not individual and private ones on a mass scale, on which social law had been historically premised.

"Social promotion" is therefore directly contiguous to the entire system of subsidies, to the law promoting education, science, and culture. For example, the socially motivated educational promotion of the needy (Richter 1996) and the promotion of the non-needy gifted lie very close together, in fact in some cases they merge one into the other. The social promotion of low-income families with many children carries over immediately into the promotion of the family as such, as provided primarily in tax law. The state can achieve an improvement in available housing either via social law through subsidies, loans, and incentives for individuals, or through the promotion of social housing with the help of earmarked funds for construction, tax write-offs, or loan subsidies.[53] At times the state follows both paths in order to pursue economic and socio-political goals in tandem. Housing assistance legislation, for example, and the granting of public contracts stands side by side. The road via social law may occasionally be preferred because social measures can be more favorably presented in political disputes than the promotion of a single sector of the economy that is usually remote from citizens or even disapproved of by them.

The area of "social care" is thus suited to a fundamental openness to the general administration of benefits. It becomes clear that the boundaries of traditional social policy, which was once intended as an answer to the "social question" of the nineteenth century, have been exploded once and for all. Social policy, originally deployed as remedy for a subsector of society defined as sick, that is, conceived of as a temporary measure and an exception from the principle of liberality, has become societal policy in a comprehensive sense. Its task is by no means limited, as has been claimed, "to adjusting the human conditions of life and social conditions to societal circumstances constantly changing thanks to technological processes and with rising expectations of prosperity," to be "more reactive than active" (Forsthoff 1971). Instead, the instruments in its toolkit are used to initiate long-term, profound social restructuring.

[53] The Bundesrat has come out against incorporating the housing allowance into the future Social Code, since it belongs substantively more to the complex of "public housing construction promotion" and the renovation of old buildings and should therefore be regulated in a code on housing law. Especially the fact that the housing allowance does not constitute a "social assistance benefit" ("Gesetz über Wohnbeihilfen," §1 Section 2: "Die Wohnbeihilfe . . . ist keine Leistung der Sozialhilfe"—("Housing assistance is . . . not a benefit of public assistance"), has benefited its application in praxis.

This applies, for one, to redistribution through social policy on society's horizontal level,[54] while, on the other hand, the simultaneous commitment of large portions of the GDP in the social budget enshrines precisely the status quo by making it difficult for the state to finance new kinds of social tasks for the community. But that applies also in a special way to the redistribution effect of education policy, which is becoming increasingly intertwined with social policy. The equalization of social deficits through an education policy that does not hide unequal starting opportunities, but compensates for them as best as possible, could in the long run change society more profoundly than all other redistribution measures that target only economic circumstances.

Since the boundaries of "social promotion" are open to the administration of general benefits, one can only indicate focal points of materials that relate to social policy. Here, too, one finds fairly old lines of development—that is to say, lines in social policy reaching back into the nineteenth or early twentieth century. The following sections only outline examples.

b) Disability Law

Characteristic for the development of social law in the Federal Republic since the 1970s has also been the progressive specialization and differentiation of aid measures. Societal problem areas, such as the growing number of disabled individuals, are targeted by various spheres of the law. The result is that entirely divergent approaches to a solution with divergent principles collide: for example, when it comes to the disabled, the kindergarten and school law, the law of public welfare (Article 74, Section 1, No. 7, Basic Law, §39 BSHG; §10 Section 2 KJHG), the social insurance law, labor law, the law on the care for war victims (Article 74, Section 1, No. 10, Basic Law), and the special area of law for the blind.[55] In the past the shared element was at best the goal of making possible for the disabled a life that was as close as possible to the standards of "normality." But that goal is doubly problematic: "normality" is defined by society, and whoever deviates from this definition initially bears the unilateral burden of adjusting to this "normality." As a result, in recent years the goal of a self-determined life in human dignity has asserted itself, in which the oppressive standard of normality is not to play a role.

After the long experiences with the specific problems of physical, mental, and emotional disabilities, the fact that a self-contained field of disability law does not exist[56] should be rather welcome: experience teaches us that a self-contained

[54] Zacher (1970). For a comparative view see now Degener (2005).

[55] BVerfGE 57, pp. 139, 166f. On help for the blind see §67 BSHG and the laws on the blind by the federal states. On this see Scholler and Krause (1978).

[56] Thust and Trenk-Hinterberger (1989, p. 21: "A uniform disability law does not exist.") See also von Maydell et al. (2003).

codification tends to erase the specific nature of aid and to create inclusion and exclusion effects. At least since 1974 there has been the Law on the Adjustment of Services for Rehabilitation (BGBl. I, p. 1881) in social insurance and in provisioning law. The Social Code guarantees the disabled a right to integration (§§10, 29 SGB I), and since 2001 it has contained a "codification" of disability law in Book IX of the Social Code. Beyond that, the labor and provisioning law continues the tradition of the 1920 Law on the Employment of the Severely Disabled.[57] The 1957 Law on the Disabled was incorporated into public assistance in 1961, which has since expanded the integration aid for the disabled (§§27 Section 1, Nos. 6, 39 BSGH) into one of its focal points, especially since an enlarging revision in 1974. That same year the Law on the Severely Disabled was also newly codified (BGBl. I, p. 1006). It sets employment quotas and alternative compensation expenditures, provides more vacation, and regulates representation within the workplace (Ebsen 1996).

In 1994, the statement "No person shall be disfavoured because of disability" was inserted into the Basic Law (Article 3, Section 2, Basic Law). While it does not in principle alter the state of the law, it sets a new accent with an explicit prohibition against discrimination, though it does not outlaw every kind of differentiation. In addition, it strengthens the duty of the state—already contained in the principle of the social state—to ensure the promotion and integration of the disabled. Moreover, the statement will fulfill its defensive and its positive function above all as a maxim of interpretation, and in this way exert influence also on private law.

Parallel to these legal expansions, refinements, and standardizations, a growing professionalization in the care of the disabled has been evident over the last few decades. Of course, the expertise imparted by education at universities and technical colleges, which leads to special qualifications, also has its downside. Like every professionalization, it raises costs and, more importantly, it also creates a sense that the care is "special," which occasionally impedes the heightened efforts to integrate the disabled, and which can actually create a ghettoization (Stolleis 1988). Finally, a change in social awareness can be detected: in modern societies, disabilities are losing—slowly enough, to be sure—their stigmatizing character. Thanks to patient educational work, much is being taken more for granted: for example, considerations during construction, the use of assistive devices in the workplace or in operating a vehicle. And the acceptance of all of this as a matter of course is a definite necessity: according to the latest statistics, 1 in every 12 citizens of the Federal Republic (6.7 million) is severely disabled, the majority of them elderly. This share will continue to grow. Disability will be perceived as something it should be, in any case, namely part of the "normality" that needs to be continuously redefined by society.

[57] This law of April 6, 1920 (RGBl. 1920, p. 458) concerned those disabled in the war and in occupational accidents.

c) Child Allowance

A telling example of the ideological strains on social benefits, of institutional disorder and uncertainty about the assignment of specific forms of aid, is the legislation dealing with the so-called *Kindergeld* ("child allowance"), which has stretched over more than 50 years. Its basic idea seems simple enough: parents are to receive financial compensation for the special burdens created by children. But what is the supporting justification? Is the goal to boost the birth rate, to create "justice" between those with many children and those with none or between the less well-off and the wealthy, or to balance out a "special sacrifice" on the basis of considerations pertaining to society as a whole?

After the end of National Socialism, it was not only an active population policy aimed at raising the birth rate that was tabooed. For decades the discipline of demography fell behind the developments taking place in other countries. It was no doubt the burden of this historical legacy that caused the discussion about allowances for families with many children to get off the ground only slowly in the 50s. At first no one wanted to contemplate a resumption of the child subsidies granted under the Nazi regime, let alone awards like the "Mother's Cross." As a result, the debate did not emphasize the population policy argument, but highlighted the inequality of the burdens on those with many children and those with none (Schubert 2003, pp. 512ff. on the German development in the twentieth century).

The first construction of the child allowance in the Federal Republic was still curious enough: initially, 25 DM was granted tax free for every third and subsequent child. The money was largely raised from contributions from employers,[58] even though there was no connection with an employment relationship. The Family Equalization Funds set up for this benefit were created under the Mutual Indemnity Associations that is under Accident Insurance (!).[59] When the child allowance was expanded to the second child in 1961, it was restricted to low-income families. The responsibility now passed to the Child Allowance Funds, which were annexed to the Employment Agency.

This construction, too, which led to four different child allowance laws, was less than satisfactory. As a result, as of January 1, 1975, the child allowance was structured as a benefit from the federal government independent of income.[60]

[58] The dispute this sparked was decided by the Federal Administrative Court (BVerfGE 11, p. 126). For a detailed discussion on the prehistory and subsequent development see Schubert (2003, pp. 525ff.).

[59] "Bundeskindergeldgesetz vom 13. November 1954," BGBl. I, p. 333; "Kindergeldergänzungsgesetz vom 23. Dezember 1955," BGBl. I, p. 841.

[60] BGBl. I, p. 413. Independent of income and occupation, all residents of the Federal Republic received child allowance (per month 50 DM for the first child, 70 DM for the second, 120 DM for the third and every subsequent child). The administration and payment of the allowances by the Federal Labor Office gave rise to a new branch of the benefit administration there beginning in 1974. On this see Hoppe (1975) and Schieckel (1975).

This implicitly defines children—beginning with the very first child—as a kind of "special sacrifice" that society should support with tax revenues. However, by force of tradition the employment agencies remained in charge. Finally, beginning on January 1, 1996, the legislature embarked on a path that led with logical consistence to tax law. What is now called "family equalization" is largely carried out in accordance with Section X of the Income Tax Law. In addition, there is still the Federal Child Allowance Law (revised version January 21, 1986, BGBl. I, p. 222), which is important only for marginal cases, and, since January 1986, the special Federal Parental Allowance Law (BGBl. I, p. 2154). Child subsidies from other insurance schemes are expiring, or have already done son. When it comes to the main issue under tax law, responsibility continues to lie with the Family Funds established at the Employment Agencies, that is to say, with the Federal Labor Office. Admittedly, an exclusive assignment to the Revenue Offices would not be satisfactory either, since the large number of those paying no tax are also supposed to receive the child allowance.

There is a deeper reason behind the difficulties of where to situate child allowance. Clearly, society's financial and non-material support for the child as the real guarantor of the future has no point of reference either in society or legal systematics. The system of social protection arose from the risks of the nineteenth century working world; in this system, children as objects of protection played a role that was only marginal and derived from the "bread-winner." Initially, child labor was considered harmful from the perspective of the next generation of military recruits (1839). Maternity protection asserted itself in the workplace (1878), subsequently made its way into the health insurance law (maternity allowance), and was then strengthened in various stages into the Maternity Protection Act of January 24, 1952 (Richardi 1987). Today, the matter is part of labor and civil service law and of the statutory health insurance, and it is flanked by law on the parental allowance with its stipulations about so-called parental leave (§§15, 16, Federal Child Rearing Allowance Law). Finally, of special importance is tax law, which takes children into account negatively in the form of an "exemption." Thus the social benefit of the child allowance is situated in the jurisdictional no man's land between social law, labor law, tax law, and general aims of social policy, for example that of boosting the birth rate.

d) Housing

Another piece of evidence for the differentiation of benefits provided by the social state is the support for adequate housing. Since the nineteenth century, specifically in the demobilization legislation following World War I, the "own home" or one's own "homestead" (*Siedlerstellen*) were among the important goals of social and family policy. Article 155 of the Weimar Constitution promised "to secure healthy housing to all German families, especially those with many children," a goal that the government tried to achieve with the Reich Settlement Law (1919) and the

Reich Homestead Act (1920). However, the difficulties afflicting housing construction in those years were trivial compared to the situation after the bombing raids of World War II. For nearly two decades, the housing market in the Federal Republic was controlled by the state because of its special relationship to social conditions and it was an area of the most varied legislative measures. Here one should mention the Housing Construction Bonus Law of 1952 in the version of September 18, 1969 (BGBl. I, p. 1677; BGBl. 1952 I, p. 139), the Housing Construction Amendment Law of August 24, 1965 (BGBl. I, p. 945), and the Housing Construction and Family Home Law in the version of September 1, 1965 (BGBl. I, p. 1617; correction, p. 1858).

With the transition from managed housing to the free market, compensation in social law had to be created for the negative consequences of liberalization. As early as 1955 the first possibilities existed to apply for subsidies for rent and public charges. In 1960 this turned into a Law on the Provision of Grants for Rent and Public Charges,[61] and eventually to the Law on Housing Subsidies of July 29, 1963 (BGBl. I, p. 508), and the so-called Housing Allowance Law.[62] However, there was controversy over whether its benefits should be considered "social benefits." They could have been interpreted also as instruments of housing construction policy, equalization of family burdens, or as an annex to the social rent law, especially since the law explicitly stated that the housing allowance was not a benefit of social assistance (§1, p. 2 WohnGG). Still, it was later incorporated into the Social Code (§§7, 26 SGB I) (Fuchs 1996). What likely also played a role in this was that the financially and bureaucratically freighted complex of social housing construction was not to be truly released into the market economy. Instead, authorities wrestled here with controls and "inappropriate occupancy charges" against abuses, confirming once again the experience that every intervention tends to bring further interventions in its wake, whether to contain or expand its benefits.

Another example of a close interlinkage of housing market controls, the promotion of home building, and the promotion of wealth formation in the hands of the socially weak is the Law on the Promotion of Wealth Formation of Employees of July 12, 1961 (BGBl. I, p. 909). Among the wealth-creating benefits it counts, along with savings measures favored by tax law, the expenses of home building savers according to the Home Construction Bonus Law and the Home Construction and Family Home Law. Single-family homes, saved "wealth" according to the Savings and Bonus Law of May 5, 1959 (later the so-called 624 DM Law), preferred shares from an employer, or "people's shares" (Veba, Volkswagen) were the options offered at the time by the legislature, options by which new paths of "social" wealth formation were sought out.

---

[61] "Gesetz über den Abbau der Wohnungszwangwirtschaft und über ein soziales Miet- und Wohnrecht vom 23. Juni 1960," BGBl. I, p. 389.

[62] "Zweites Wohngeldgesetz von 1970 i.d.F. vom 29. August 1977," BGBl. I, p. 1685.

e) Purpose-Orientation and Adversities of the System

The examples show the kind of convoluted paths that were pursued in social policy. Since the focus in the parliamentary process is always on the politically defined purpose of an intervention, but not on the creation or preservation of a systematic system of social protection, the result is hybrid theoretical constructs, mixtures, for example, of social insurance law, tax law, family law, and youth aid law. Frequently the corrections to an intervention are not made to the intervention itself, but in other legal spheres. The example of aid for the disabled also shows how initially all carriers of social insurance as well as social and youth assistance developed such aid, guided by the right ideas of prevention and integration, but that they managed to pull together for coordination and standardization only late and under cost pressures, because their own institutions had taken on a life of their own and resisted simplifying mergers. When it comes to the promotion of single-family homes or wealth formation, the social policy goal of equalizing differences in prosperity are served jointly by economic law, tax law, social law, and labor law. It is the purpose, not the systematic coherence of social law that defines the legal measures. The "jungle" of rules and regulations that is created in this way, and frequently complained about, is politically wanted or at least accepted. The still unfinished project of the Social Code reveals that the political energies are *not* focused on the task of simplifying and systematizing the material, a task that does not make for very good PR. Even the popular complaint about the regulatory "jungle," can still be politically instrumentalized—mostly in official speeches—as an appeal to common sense and the universal desire for "clarity."

6. Social Insurance After 1945

a) Setting the Course: Omnium Insurance (Einheitsversicherung) *or "Tried-and-True System"?*

With Germany's military, political, and economic collapse in 1945, the social insurance system, in particular, de facto hit absolute rock bottom.[63] The assets of the insurance carriers, which were largely tied to the state, had been destroyed, damaged, or diminished. In the beginning there would be no state subsidy, and the contribution revenues from the economic sector were naturally not adequate. The only thing that was intact was the normative framework of old-age and disability insurance for workers, employees, and miners. The administrative apparatus, too, still proved relatively functional, at least on the lower levels, which meant that a

[63] See for example, Heimerich (1946), Martzloff (1946). Comprehensive accounts in Tennstedt (1976), Hentschel (1983), Köhler (1990).

kind of normality was soon reestablished. Where Reich institutions were missing, as in the case of the Reich Insurance Office, State Insurance Offices stepped in. As for the benefits, as had happened in the crises of 1923 and 1929/1932, the insurances were kept afloat in part by the emerging states, in part by reducing or not increasing their benefits already devalued by inflation. By necessity, the rebuilding measures controlled by the occupying powers, and therefore territorially uncoordinated,[64] utilized the previous structures of insurance law. A standardizing top layer was absent, with respect to both formal and substantive law and adjudication. As a result, the legal foundations in the various occupation zones developed in divergent ways, but not dramatically so.[65]

In spite of the tense situation, which suggested narrowing one's focus to the immediate needs and what could be realized over the short term, a debate over a fundamental new orientation of social insurance soon arose. Old reformist hopes of overcoming the fragmentation of insurance carriers and the current need for uniform guidance both pointed toward a further reduction in the number of insurance carriers and to a leveling of the differences between blue collar and white collar workers. The overcoming of the organizational "fragmentation" propagated during National Socialism continued to reverberate, even if its ideological premises had disappeared.

The first regulations in this question still seemed clear. The guidelines of the Control Council in 1946,[66] continued in the Control Council's bills for a social insurance law in April and August of 1946,[67] envisaged a "uniform social insurance." With that, the realization of an earlier demand by the unions seemed to have moved within reach. The interzonal conference of the German unions therefore pushed for passage of the Control Council's bill (Behrendt 1959; Pirker 1960; Sörgel 1985, p. 201, 379f. with further references). Likewise the SPD, at its party conference in Hannover on May 11, 1946, demanded a "uniform social insurance," and the Bavarian Constitution spoke of a social insurance for "everyone," and the constitutions of Bremen, Hesse, and Rhineland-Palatinate of one that was "accessible to the entire nation" and of a "social insurance that binds together the entire nation."[68] As vague as these constitutional articles may have been, they did cling to the basic idea of social insurance and emphasized a tendency toward a reformist standardization of social insurance, specifically overcoming the old separation of blue and white collar workers. Connected to this were hopes for an integrative and

---

[64] For a detailed account see Wannagat (1965), Gräfin von Bethusy-Huc (1976, pp. 58ff., 139ff., 222ff.), Peters (1973/1978, pp. 123ff.).

[65] Schieckel (1946, 1947a, b). See the comprehensive account in Bartholomäi et al. (1977).

[66] "Richtlinien über eine einheitliche Neuordnung der deutschen Sozialversicherung (14 Punkte)." Reference in Schieckel (1947a, b).

[67] Drafts of April (1), August 30, 1946 (2), with another change on September 20, 1946 (3); see Schieckel (1947a, b).

[68] Article 171 Bavarian Constitution of December 2, 1946; Article 35, Section 1, p. 1 Constitution of Hesse of December 1, 1946; Article 53 IV Constitution of Rhineland-Palatinate of May 18, 1947; Article 57, Section 1 Constitution of Bremen of October 21, 1947.

stabilizing effect in domestic politics. Similarly, the bill that was presented in April 1946 by government representatives of Greater Hesse, first to the Social Policy Committee of the *Länderrat*, then to the *Länderrat* itself and to the military government, advocated a uniform insurance and a simplification of the process (Schieckel 1947a, b). To be sure, contrary currents favouring a return to the principle of voluntariness and cooperative self-help, and opposed to government provision certainly existed,[69] but they did not dominate the picture during the initial phase. Eventually, the complete reorganization of social insurance in Berlin (1945–1948)[70] and in the Soviet Occupation Zone[71] represented the most important challenge in the deliberations on how to restructure social insurance. In 1945, Berlin was given an Insurance Institute Berlin (*Versicherungsanstalt Berlin*, VAB), which encompassed all branches of social insurance. Financing came in equal parts from employers and workers. Contributions were 20 % of gross income, topping out at a maximum of 120 Reichsmark per month.

In the Soviet Occupation Zone, 11 central administrations had already been set up with Order No. 17 of July 27, 1945. Among them, the Central Administration for Labor and Social Welfare (*Zentralverwaltung für Arbeit und Sozialfürsorge*, ZVAS) was especially important.[72] Order No. 28 of January 28, 1947, introduced the public-law uniform insurance and a standard contribution of 20 %. The initially established five social insurance agencies were combined in 1951 (April 26, 1951, GBl., p. 325) and transferred to the Federation of Free German Trade Unions (*Freier Deutscher Gewerkschaftsbund*, FDGB). The practice in the Soviet Zone of using the labor courts as courts of appeal in disputes involving social insurance law (judgment proceedings for pension matters, otherwise decision-making procedures)[73] was in part seen as exemplary, but in part—and in the West overwhelmingly so—rejected as inappropriate.

The reorganization of social insurance in Berlin and in the Soviet Zone was inevitably pulled into the atmosphere of the emerging Cold War. The formula of the "uniform insurance on the Russian model," directed against the "leveling, monopolistic uniform insurance agencies,"[74] was a scare-mongering phrase that especially the Bavarian social administration liked to use to defend its own position within the "structured social insurance system." Very soon the merger of labor courts and social courts was also dismissed as a model, which, it was said, "hardly encourages

[69] The so-called Hamburg Plan (Schieckel 1947a, b).

[70] Menkens (1951); fundamental was the "Anordnung des Magistrats Berlin über Wiederaufbau und Ingangsetzung der Sozialversicherung vom 14. Juli 1945," VOBl. 1945, p. 64.

[71] Early accounts in Fischer (1946), Riedel (1946), Bohlmann and Fischer (1945/1947), Krieger (1947). For an overview as of 1965 see Wannagat (1965, pp. 135–148); see now also Schmidt (2001, pp. 708ff., 749ff.).

[72] A comprehensive account is given by Hoffmann (1996).

[73] Kaiser (1949); "Mitteilung Nr. 1287," in BB 1949, p. 394.

[74] Stoldt (1949), against Schieckel, at the time considered "one of the most active champions of the uniform insurance (*Einheitsversicherung*)" (Heyn 1950). See also the hints in the Festschrift für Schieckel (Müller 1978).

emulation" (Lohmüller 1949, p. 110). Reservations were still expressed against the first Federal Minister for Labor, Anton Storch (Hockerts 1980a, b), because he had spoken out in favour of a uniform insurance before 1949.

In this way, all theoretical deliberations on the future shape of social insurance were harnessed to the various material conditions and balances of political power of reconstruction, as well as to the growing division of Germany into an eastern and a western sphere, a division that was becoming increasingly apparent following the last joint session of the Control Council on March 20, 1948. Accordingly, the restart of social insurance in the Western zones was initially above all a "starting up" while foregoing any fundamental changes. The economic stabilization of the insurance carriers, the reestablishment of self-administration (BGBl. I, p. 124), the processing of currency reform, the "adjustment of social insurance benefits to the changed wage and price structure,"[75] the management of the streams of Nazi victims (WiGBl. 1949, p. 263) and refugees through insurance law, the regulation of the time periods interrupted by the war (BGBl. 1952 I, p. 737), and much more absorbed the energies. Since there was neither a uniform ideological concept in the West nor a uniform coercive military authority as in the Soviet Zone, "reconstruction" was superimposed upon the reform intentions. The more time went by, the more a uniform insurance became an unreachable goal of reform.[76] West Berlin, too, with its political orientation toward the Federal Republic, returned to a structured system. At the end of this process stood the declaration of the Hamburg Party Platform of the CDU on April 22, 1953: "We will maintain the tried-and-true form of a structured social insurance" (Mommsen 1964, p. 591).

b) *Social Court and Labor Court Jurisdiction*

The lively debate about the reorientation of social insurance after 1945,[77] the central question of which revolved around the question "structured system" or "uniform insurance," entailed corresponding frontlines also on the question of legal protection (Stolleis 1979). Opting for the legal policy option of "uniform insurance" usually also meant opting for the merger of labor court and social court jurisdiction. By contrast, those who came out in favour of the structured system also wanted a structured judiciary. That the latter—under the banner of a constitutional

[75] "Gesetz über die Anpassung von Leistungen der Sozialversicherung an das veränderte Lohn- und Preisgefüge und über ihre finanzielle Sicherstellung vom 17. Juni 1949," WiGBl. 1949, p. 99; "Knappschaftsversicherungs-Anpassungsgesetz vom 30. Juli 1949," WiGBl. 1949, p. 202; "Gesetz über Verbesserungen der gesetzlichen Unfallversicherung vom 10. August 1949," WiGBl. 1949, p. 251.

[76] The best account of this in Hockerts (1980a, b, Chapter 1).

[77] Sitzler, Curschmann, Heimerich, Polligkeit, Sauerborn (1946, No. 18, 14ff.), Eckert (1947), Schieckel (1947a, b, 1949).

state and a separation of powers—would now have to be "real," independent jurisdiction seemed self-evident.

As a result, in the Western occupation zones the previous adjudication in matters of social insurance was initially continued. The Reich Insurance Office, which had once served as the final court of appeal, no longer existed. The Insurance and Higher Insurance Offices decided on complaints, appeals, and reviews, and there soon emerged troubling discrepancies in this adjudication. In addition, ambiguities emerged in the demarcation against the newly reestablished administrative jurisdiction in the British and American zones, because it was not clear whether the Insurance Offices could still be considered "special administrative courts." Matters pertaining to unemployment insurance were decided in the British zone by the Higher Insurance Offices, in the US zone by the State Employment Offices. Finally, the old Reich Provisioning Court was also gone as the highest court on matters of care for war victims. In this area different solutions were devised in all three Western zones, and further difficulties arose in the demarcation against the administrative jurisdiction. The labor court jurisdiction that had been set up again since 1946 separately from the regular judicial system functioned at the state level, but it did not yet have an appeal instance, as the Reich Labor Court had been at the Reich level.

The organizational and substantive fragmentation of adjudication in social insurance, unemployment insurance, and care for war victims, on the one hand, and fundamental doubts about judicial independence and a separation of powers, on the other, were pushing for a solution. That solution emerged between 1948 and 1953 within a sphere circumscribed by the forces of the previous tradition of adjudication and social administration, of the desires for reform on the part of the unions and social democracy.

During deliberations over the Basic Law, the simplest idea—reestablishing the Reich Insurance Office along with its judiciary functions—proved incompatible with the postulates of the separation of powers and judicial independence. Likewise, in the end the hope for a merger of labor court and social court jurisdiction failed for political reasons, because employers feared an excessive accumulation of power by unions, and because many jurists had doubts as to whether it really made sense to bring the disputes of labor law, which were at their core issues of private law, under the same roof with the disputes of social law, which involved issues of public law. The original trend in this direction reversed between 1949 and 1951. The initial plan to combine the two highest federal courts was abandoned. In the end, it came down to the interpretation of the formula "labor and social jurisdiction" (*Arbeits- und Sozialgerichtsbarkeit*) (Article 96 in the original 1949 version of the Basic Law): were these two separate jurisdictions or a single one? The decision was made in favor of separate jurisdictions, and supervision was also distinguished,[78] but both courts were housed on two floors of a single building in Kassel.

[78] Supervision over the Federal Labor Court lay with the Federal Labor Ministry in agreement with the Federal Minister of Justice that of the Federal Social Court lay with the Federal Minister for Labor.

After that, a "social court law" still had to be debated and passed. Here the enlistment of laymen as professional judges was discussed. For some, this went too far, for others, not far enough. Expanding the jurisdiction to cases involving the care for war victims and the law for the severely disabled was also controversial. But there was real urgency, and the unresolved cases were multiplying. The Social Court Act was passed on September 3, 1953, and took effect on January 1, 1954 (BGBl. 1953 I, p. 1239). The Federal Social Court was inaugurated on September 11, 1954. There was now a new branch of adjudication with three instances and lay participation. The higher and state insurance offices now ceased to render legal decisions.

The first 28 judges who sat on the Federal Social Court came largely from the previous Reich Insurance Office, the Reich Provisioning Court, or the insurance carriers on the Reich level (Stolleis 1979, p. 47). Along with substantive continuity, this guaranteed the continuity of personnel, which was necessary to manage the enormous backlog of procedures dealing with care of war victims (in the beginning about two thirds of all disputes) as well as the pension cases that began to grow rapidly (Arndt 1964, p. 2147). Subsequent expansions of the court's competence to include cases of "restitution", aid for detainees, foreign pension law, compensation for victims of violence, and the general broadening of social insurance to new groups also expanded the court, but they did not alter its character as the decisive institution for the development and standardization of social law (von Maydell 1985; Kummer 1996).

c) *Institutional Rebuilding of Social Insurance*

As we have seen, the rebuilding of social insurance and its institutions in the Western occupation zones took place initially on the old normative foundations of the Reich Insurance Act and using the personnel of the existing administrations on the state level. After the decision had been made in favor of the "tried-and-true system" in the interplay between the allied and German decision-makers and within the context of the Cold War, the transition to a new state to be formed out of the Western zones was already beginning to emerge. As a result, the SPD and the KPD also held back with new proposals and focused on the needs of the day.

As in nearly all areas of the new state that was about to be created, the ministerial bureaucrats of the Reich assumed once again the relevant positions in the Federal ministries. This had already become evident in the establishment of the state administrations, in the central bureaucratic agencies of the British zone, as well as in the authorities of the Bizone and the Trizone. At all levels of administration and the judiciary, in the sciences, in the system of associations, and in the churches, there were signals of a readiness to leave the past behind and to provide reciprocal assistance. At times "waiting periods" were expected, but once they were over the reintegration took place. The domestic political calculus was "integration" (Garner 1993; Frei 1996, pp. esp. 69ff.). The goal was to integrate all the countless former functionaries who had been classified as "*Mitläufer*" (fellow travelers) by the de-Nazification process. Those who bore heavy guilt went underground, changing their names or leaving the country; former emigrants were slow to return, especially since their reception was by no means friendly. When it came to the electoral calculus, both groups were of virtually no interest. It is therefore no coincidence that the word "integration" also launched the triumphal march of Rudolf Smend's "theory of integration," at its core less a legal theory than a politological-psychological theory about the preconditions and workings of a state. It could be used to establish that a state formed and preserved itself as spiritual values through the interaction and vital assent of its citizens (Günther 2004).

The repercussions of this general political line after about 1948 were far-reaching and deeply influenced not only the collective retrospective view of the era of National Socialism, that is "*Vergangenheitspolitik*" (policies for dealing with the past) (Frei 1996; Reichel 2001), but simultaneously also the future of the country. Below the ministerial level, the new ministerial bureaucracy was made up largely of civil servants from the old Reich bureaucracy. The new Federal Ministry of Labor, led by the Christian union official Anton Storch, had emerged out of the Central Office for Labor in the British zone and, following the creation of Bizone, out of the Frankfurt Agency for Labor (*Verwaltung für Arbeit*) (Hockerts 1980a, b, pp. 107ff.). Storch continued a tradition that went back to the Reich Economic Office (1917) and the Reich Economic Ministry (1919) that emerged out of it. The Reich Labor Ministry had in turn arisen out of the latter's division of labor and social policy, and between 1920 and 1928 it was headed by the Christian union official Heinrich Brauns (Zentrum) in 13 cabinets. A similar continuity developed also in the Federal Republic in this department: over a span of 53 years there were only eight ministers of labor, four from the CDU (35 years) and four from the SPD (18 years). The department, operating since 1957 under the name "Federal Ministry for Labor and Social Affairs," formed the platform for the now impending reforms of social insurance, while public assistance and youth welfare remained with the Ministry of the Interior, and the equalization of burdens with the Ministry of Finance. The latter was of course involved in all undertakings relevant to finances. It was only in 2002 that the Ministry of Labor and the Ministry of Economics were combined again into a single ministry (Wolfgang Clement, SPD), in an effort to take more effective measures against both the endemic unemployment and economic stagnation.

The "Führer principle" that was introduced in social insurance in 1934 was, of course, no longer acceptable. Social insurance was to return as quickly as possible to self-administration. But how this was to be accomplished was in dispute. The share of power for a large bureaucracy that was to develop again in the future was decided upon within the triangle of unions, employers' associations, and the state. At issue were not so much "principles," but key functions in the distribution of a lot of money and influence. The self-administration without state involvement initially pursued by the unions and the employers went too far for the Allies. On accident insurance the employers wanted to continue to have the only say, on unemployment insurance the state—involved through the employment agencies—did not relinquish its influence, on health insurance the previous model of a division into threes was to be given up in favor of parity. In the end, the parties—in the self-administration law passed on February 22, 1951—arrived at a model of social partnership between capital and labor (BGBl. I, p. 124). To be sure, it was a hastily deliberated law with considerable deficiencies, and it had to be amended already in the following year. But the main question was settled, and the law did serve as the basis for the social elections that took place in 1953 for the first time since 1928. Looking back, the most important innovation in this area was the transition to the "*Verbändestaat*" (state of associations) (Kaiser 1956/1978; Steinberg 1985): from that time on, the associations of employers inserted themselves between the insured and the employers and determined the selection of representatives.[79]

On the question of whether to separate or merge the insurances for blue collar and white collar workers, the "tried-and-true" line of separation—consolidated by social sensitivities and tangible material interests—asserted itself again (Hockerts 1980a, b, pp. 150–155). Over the opposition of the DGB unions and the SPD, the German Union of Employees achieved the creation of a Federal Insurance Fund for Salaried Employees (BGBl. 1953 I, p. 857). This was nothing other than the reestablishment of the old Reich Insurance Agency for Salaried Employees, which had been forced to shut down in 1945. Now, after the social elections of 1953 had noticeably weakened the DGB unions, the resistance to a return to the old institutional state of affairs disappeared. Subsequently, the political energies shifted to the—in the final analysis more consequential—standardization of the benefits law, which was achieved in 1957.

Things unfolded somewhat differently in the establishment of the Federal Office for Employment and Unemployment Insurance. Here, employers and unions sought to keep out the state in an effort to push through a genuine self-administration. But for the government that was out of the question because tax revenues flowed into this insurance (unemployment assistance) and because the employment agencies exercised their tasks of job counseling and job placement in a sovereign manner. The government therefore opted for one-third parity, excluding unemployment insurance. After the first draft had failed in the *Bundesrat*, because the federal states were unable to push through the wholesale takeover of their personnel into the federal bureaucracy, the law was passed largely unchanged in 1952 (BGBl. I, p. 123). As Hentschel (1983, p. 159) put it: "This was not less but more state influence than in Weimar. And the social partners (*Tarifpartner*) had to resign themselves to it." However, since the participation of employers, employees, and the state proved its worth against all misgivings, unemployment insurance was also included in 1969. This also reflected the heightened state responsibility for a "high level of employment" that had already been enshrined in the Law for Promoting Stability and Growth in the Economy of June 8, 1967.

[79] Overview of the state of affairs today in Hendler (1996). A position determination worth reading is Standfest (1989).

The completion of the organizational rebuilding meant the establishment of a Federal Insurance Office that corresponded to the former Reich Insurance Office; it came into being as an independent federal agency only in 1956.[80] It is in charge of the social insurance carriers under direct federal oversight, with the exception of the Federal Office for Labor and the federal agencies responsible for accident insurance. This oversight is legal oversight, that is, it respects the right of the supervised to self-governance, comparable to the control through the jurisdiction of the social court which is limited to legal questions.

d) Pension Insurance

The Situation of Pensioners in the Wake of Currency Reform

From the currency reform of 1948, to the pension reform of 1957, all the way to today, the question of what recipients of pensions (old-age and disability pensions, pensions for widows and orphans) can expect at the end of their working life or at the death of the "breadwinner" is among the highly charged domestic political issues. The question of pensions touches on structural problems of society. It contains a long-term promise by the political establishment to the working generation, something like this: the state takes part of the remuneration earned today, either to collect it as capital stock for use a generation later as a fund to pay out pensions, or to pay it out immediately to the pensioners in the hope that those still unborn will later be willing to do the same. In both cases, pension payments should represent a ratio of the level of earnings achieved while working that is regarded as just. This commits either current or future funds, and does so within a timeframe that exceeds several times over the usual political thinking in terms of legislative sessions. Pensioners are supposed to receive an "equivalent" to the contributions they made that was not only nominal but value-related, and they were to share in society's growing prosperity. This guarantee was to be "secure," because the state guaranteed to fill any potential shortfalls with state subsidies (Article 120, Basic Law). After the currency reform, about 80 % of the population was affected by these existential questions.

A pension system that is based on the nominal value of the currency ("Mark=Mark") and pays the pensions out of an accumulated capital stock has to run into trouble if money is devalued or war destroys the de facto value of the capital stock. Germany experienced both of these devastating scenarios in the twentieth century. As a result, one of the most important packages of measures of the postwar period was to "adjust" the essentially unchanged pension system. In the transition to a new currency, pensioners—who were already disadvantaged—were

[80] "Bundesversicherungsamtsgesetz (BVAG) vom 9. Mai 1956," BGBl. I, p. 415. On this see Bogs (1977).

to be brought along, of course only on a scale that the reviving economy could absorb. While the social pensions were converted at a ratio of 1:1 in the currency reform of June 1948, because of the interim devaluation of money, the conversion led to a de facto devaluation of pensions by 20–25 %. In this situation, those on the Frankfurt Economic Council already recognized the need to quickly enact a "law on the adjustment of the benefits of social insurance to the changed wage and price structure and to make it financially secure." However, opposition from the private sector, the finance ministers of the federal states, and from the Allies, who did not believe that a clear improvement in the condition of pensioners was affordable, delayed the law. It did not come into force until June 1, 1949, after the establishment of the Federal Republic (WiGBl. 1949, p. 99). It provided, along with higher contribution payments, an increase in pensions and the introduction of a minimum pension, as well as a future, unconditional widow's pension in the Workers' Pension Insurance, and an improvement in the disability threshold for workers—on the whole, then, adjustments to the status of the white-collar worker. In health insurance, the contributions were now divided between employers and employees. This law was complemented by laws for miners' and accident insurance. Those "persecuted by National Socialism" also received compensation for withheld benefits, lost insurance periods, and other reductions. As Detlev Zöllner summed up: "The social insurance adjustment law was substantively the conclusion of zonal legislation, but at the same time also the prelude to the federal government's expansive legislation that now began" (Zöllner 1981).

But while wages and prices rose in the emerging economic miracle (between 1948 and 1953 by 80 %), pensions initially fell behind. Pensioners were in danger of becoming impoverished (details in Hockerts 1980a, b, pp. 201ff.), even though the 25 % increase deemed necessary in 1951 was realized—with some qualifications—through a pension supplement law (BGBl. 1951 I, p. 505) and a complementary inflation adjustment law (BGBl. I, p. 507). The government continued to operate with short-term remedies through "supplements," which were in turn financed by eliminating subsidies in the federal budget that had become expendable. The result had been a de facto indexing of pensions already between 1949 and 1953, parallel to the rising wages (Hockerts 1980a, b, p. 193). With that, the social expenditure ratio rose to about 20 %. The reserves of the pension insurance increased in lockstep (1953: 3.6 billion DM; 1957: 17.2 billion DM).

The early Federal Republic thus continued to be a social intervention state, whose free market sectors did strengthen, but did not seem able to get by without state guidance—for example in housing construction and the housing market, in agriculture and through the gradually dismantled subsidies for basic foodstuffs, in municipal services of general interest, through countless direct and indirect forms of assistance of tax and aid law, as well as in all of social policy with its traditionally strong status within the federal government.

But there was also resistance to this basic "statist" line, for one from representatives of the private sector, who already back then considered the adjective "social" a corruption of the principles, for another from church circles, who feared from the development of the so-called "welfare state" a "tendency toward the extermination of all recognized effectiveness of the church's social welfare work," indeed a tendency toward omnipotent totalitarianism (Stolleis 1973, p. 382). As late as 1958, prominent theologians could still look upon state social policy as the "decomposition product" of Christian brotherly love (Thielicke 1958, p. 348). Even if the primary concern behind this defensive posture was the church's concern over the unimpeded development of church-based charity and youth work, it did have an effect also on the "welfare state" reorganization of the entire system of social protection. Ever since, the further expansion of social benefits has always been accompanied by charges that too much state assistance paralyzes individual initiative and hands people over to state maintenance.

Adenauer's Pension Reform

After the first problems had been overcome, a kind of "reflection pause" took place in social insurance law between 1951 and 1956.[81] It was obvious, however, that the entire system of social benefits had become increasingly confusing and complex, and that in the area of pension insurance the discrepancy between the "economic miracle," on the one side, and those dependent on a structurally outdated insurance system, on the other, had intensified. As a result, beginning in the early 1905s forces emerged within the SPD and the Ministry of Labor that sought a more modern conception. In the process, the SPD was still under the influence of the English model of an egalitarian basic insurance for all, and therefore tended more toward tax financing than individual justice through linkage to the different wage levels. Within the CDU there appeared side by side elements of a Catholic social doctrine friendly to unions, small business and corporate interests, concerns about a "leveling" welfare state, and anxieties about the stability of the currency.

Only when the condition of previously neglected pensioners living in poverty or forced to rely on foreign help assumed political dimensions, did the government and the opposition react. The initial plans called for a comprehensive social reform, indeed a social code,[82] but subsequently the perspective was gradually narrowed to the most urgent problem, pension insurance. Memoranda and reports were written, among which the Rothenfels Memorandum by the professors Hans Achinger, Joseph Höffner, Hans Muthesius, and Ludwig Neundörfer stood out.[83] It became ever more clear to all those involved just how specific to its time the model of Bismarck's social insurance had been. Neither the value of money nor the economic and demographic preconditions were stable. Now the Germans had the experience of war and inflation, they realized that society was aging, and that this also led to

[81] Comprehensive account of the postwar development in Gräfin von Bethusy-Huc (1976, pp. 139ff.); Peters (1973/1978, pp. 123ff.).

[82] For example, in 1954 the cabinet decided "to codify the entire social law still in this legislative session" (Hockerts 1980a, b, p. 263).

[83] Bogs (1955); *Neuordnung der sozialen Leistungen. Denkschrift, auf Anregung des Herrn Bundeskanzlers erstattet von den Professoren Hans Achinger, Joseph Höffner, Hans Muthesius, Ludwig Neundörfer* (Cologne, 1955).

rising costs in the health care system. Pensioner poverty below the level of "welfare" seemed politically intolerable also in relationship to East Germany (Wannagat 1965, pp. 106ff.). The GDR was struggling with the exodus of its population to the West and therefore painted the nightmare of Western pensioners facing the threat of impoverishment.[84] The Federal Republic made do with a "special supplement law" to deal with the problem (BGBl. 1955 I, p. 733), but this could not be a permanent solution.

Instead, a way had to be found that could relieve everyday politics from the constant readjustment of pensions, and at the same time still lead to the desired big reform of the entire system of social benefits. To a very considerable degree it was the achievement of Konrad Adenauer to have chosen this path with unswerving political instinct. Scholarship has now confirmed this verdict.[85] Adenauer certainly thought in political-strategic terms, but he was also sustained—in this regard not unlike Bismarck—by a religiously based notion of the state's overall responsibility as a guarantor. That is why he initially strengthened the rather unwilling Ministry of Labor, rebuffed the concerns of the Ministry of Finance, set up a "social cabinet" headed by him, and introduced into the debate above all Wilfried Schreiber and his basic ideas (Schreiber 1955). Schreiber, the managing director of the Association of Catholic Entrepreneurs (*Bund Katholischer Unternehmer*), accentuated the two key points: pensions should be paid out of the payroll taxes of the generation active today, not out of the saved assets of social insurance (pay-as-you go). In addition, pensions should be linked to the general wage level through a pension formula and in this way take on the function of a substitute for wages. Schreiber believed that it was superfluous for pension insurance to accumulate reserves; for periods of crisis he thought about state subsidies (Oeter 1971, pp. 359ff.).

Contained therein were countless unresolved details, for example the issue of "idle time," specially among women, the guarantee of a minimum base for pensions, the inclusion of the self-employed, the question about the bases for the indexing of pensions, and much more. The basic issue of the equalization of family burdens also remained unresolved (Oeter 1971). But Schreiber's basic ideas did assert themselves step by step, even though banks and insurance companies, employers, and economists warned about taking this road into unchartered territory. The pragmatists of the large popular parties and the unions came to an understanding, with the result that an issue-based "grand coalition" took shape. To that end ballast had been cast overboard: organizational questions remained untouched, and the self-employed were also not incorporated,[86] blue collar and white collar

[84] On old age security in the GDR see Schmidt (2001, pp. 708ff., 749ff.).

[85] Fundamental Hockerts (1980a, b) following on this Zöllner (1981, pp. 141ff.).

[86] With that, the right of the self-employed to voluntarily join the statutory pension insurance introduced with the law of December 21, 1937, was abolished again. For tradespeople this exclusion was reversed again as early as 1960. The insurances for farmers and eventually also for artists and journalists stood under the goal of "inclusion," though in varying forms. But all other self-employed and liberal professions were compelled in this way to establish their own pensions schemes.

workers were—following the trend toward a "classless society"—equalized, but not combined under a single roof.

The three pension reform laws of 1957[87] thus created the "generational contract" through the introduction of the pay-as-you-go system that was so consequential for the following decades.[88] They took into account the principle of individual justice, because the contributions and the pensions were based on earnings. At the same time, in their totality they should be guided by the productivity of the general economy, that is, accord with a just balance. The pension was now to be a wage replacement (better: old-age wage), not merely a supplement to subsistence. Pragmatic limitations to the systems arose through the contribution assessment limit, which in turn limits the future pension on the upside. In calculating the pension, earnings and contributions were related to one another in that the basis was the income that the insured person would have had—should an insurance claim kick in—if he had earned the average of his income through his entire working life, raised to the wage level at the time the insurance came into effect (the so-called pension formula).

An immediate consequence of these innovations was a strong increase in the pension income (by 65–71 %), thus bringing pensioners in line with the still uninterrupted economic miracle. Not only did this bring Adenauer an absolute majority of votes, it also had an "importance that is hard to overestimate" for the internal integration of the Federal Republic (Hockerts 1980a, b, p. 425). Perhaps even more important for the long term was the indexing of the entire system of social insurance that had become unavoidable. One could no longer proceed from the assumption that it could be limited to pension insurance. This also made it clearer than before what kind of political importance the basic economic precept that one can distribute only what is generated has for the relationship between the generations, especially in a western industrial society fixated on growth and accordingly vulnerable.

In the decades that followed, the principles of 1957 were repeatedly modified, but were not fundamentally abandoned. There was a consistent annual increase in the amounts in the contribution and benefit law of the blue collar and white collar insurances, as well as in miners' pension insurance. In addition, the circle of the insured expanded, benefits extraneous to insurance multiplied, and the pension formula was changed just as the role of state subsidies was transformed. At its core, though, the introduction of the pay-as-you-go system and of indexing was an epochal decision. Whether these fundamental principles can be maintained when society's old-age burden peaks in 2030 is an open question at this time. This question will be addressed later.

---

[87] "Gesetz zur Neuregelung des Rechts der Rentenversicherung der Arbeiter vom 23. Februar 1957," BGBl. I; 45; "Gesetz zur Neuregelung des Rechts der Rentenversicherung der Angestellten vom 23. Februar 1957," BGBl. I, p. 88; "Gesetz zur Neuregelung der knappschaftlichen Rentenversicherung vom 21. Mai 1957," BGBl. I, p. 533.

[88] Detailed appraisal in Wannagat (1965, pp. 115ff.).

The Self-Employed

Looking back, the just mentioned expansion of the circle of those insured turns out to be the development that accompanied social insurance from its beginnings—unfazed by wars and inflation. After old-age pension had originally been intended as a supplement to the livings costs of workers and their families, it gradually became a wage substitute. After industrial workers, agricultural workers were added, then white collar workers, then tradespeople (1938/1960: BGBl. 1960 I, p. 737), then farmers (July 27, 1957, in the version of September 14, 1965, BGBl. I, p. 1449), finally other self-employed workers and members of the liberal professions (1937, given up again in 1957). In part this was based on laws, that is, on the forced recurrent broadening of pension insurance, in part this was achieved through clauses with favorable conditions for voluntary participation.

A clear example for this long term movement was the creation, in the end, of an obligatory insurance against illness, old age, and disability for the approximately 100,000 artists and journalists working today.[89] In terms of health insurance they are members of a General Health Insurance Scheme (*Allgemeine Ortskrankenkasse*) or a Supplementary Insurance (*Ersatzkasse*),[90] for pension insurance they are considered white collar workers. Since there is no employer in the strict sense, a social insurance contribution for artists was introduced for the employer's share of the contributions and strengthened through a federal supplement. In institutional terms, the insurance has been placed into the hands of the Artists' Social Insurance in Wilhelmshaven, a division of the State Insurance Office Oldenburg-Bremen. It remained this way also after the inclusion of artists and journalists from the new federal states.

If one focuses on the compulsory character of the insurance schemes, the so-called Occupation Pension Schemes are also part of this long-term expansion movement, even if they arose in the pension reform of 1957 through the exclusion of the self-employed and the liberal professions from the statutory pension insurance (Scheuner 1954; Boecken 1996). They are based on the idea that only a compulsory mandate can achieve an actuarially adequate number of insured to provide protection against the typical risks within a group. Thus, in a more or less deliberate extension of the notion of Guild Funds, special systems were created in which "occupational" groups were compulsorily insured. Those were consistently professions with academic training (doctors, dentists, veterinarians, pharmacists, architects, civil engineers, lawyers, notaries, certified auditors, and sworn accountants), but also district master chimney sweepers, independent of whether they were self-employed or employees. Although their pension schemes had existed

[89] "Künstlerversicherungsgesetz vom 27. Juli 1981," BGBl. I, p. 705, by now amended repeatedly and supplemented by ordinances on the configuration of the institution and the output of the social insurance contribution. In 1987 the Federal Constitutional Court declared the law constitutional, BVerfGE 75, pp. 108ff.

[90] The result is that they are now also included in the compulsory insurance.

since the 1920s,[91] for the most part they were created only in the 1960s and 1970s on the basis of state laws,[92] largely in response to the pension reform of 1957, which had left out the liberal professions. Today, nearly 600,000 individuals are insured under that scheme, primarily doctors and lawyers. The pension schemes are based on the system of capital cover, out of which they pay their benefits; they are thus close to the idea of private life insurance. As a rule they are attached to the chambers of the liberal professions. With that, they continue the public law corporate structure that is so pronounced in Germany also in the area of social insurance (Kannengießer 1998, pp. 11ff.). The century-long trend toward the expansion of compulsory insurances to the entire population in the direction of a "national insurance" is thus countered by a movement toward the creation of special professional schemes with a homogenous internal structure. Favorable conditions are granted in these schemes (in line with the income level of the insured), for these special schemes do not carry any benefits extraneous to the insurance and they do not have to carry out vertical social equalization. Where much equality exists, inequality is thus sought out, and it comes as no surprise that it is sought by those who were initially excluded from the pension insurance, but who were and are interested—for "professional" reasons—in avoiding the general pension level and no doubt also the dangers that threaten the statutory system.

Further Development of the Pension System

Today, nearly a third of all the direct social benefits in the Federal Republic are provided by the statutory pension scheme. We are talking about the enormous sum of around €200 billion, which tracks both inflation and economic growth through continual adjustment of contributions and benefits. All told, over the last four decades, pensions have grown nearly 2.3 times (adjusted for inflation). Pensioners have benefited from economic growth at a disproportionate level (details in Leopold 1999, pp. 138ff., 254ff. for the years 1977–1999). This rise is evident also for pension income on the territory of the former East Germany. If one takes into account that the number of pensioners has also grown substantially, the scale at which the "pension," originally intended merely as a supplement to the livelihood, has grown becomes evident.

This system, which works with reserves of only a few months, has to run into trouble when contributions decline and expenditures rise (with the additional burden of extraneous benefits). The total sum of contributions declines because the number of gainfully employed is shrinking. The age structure of society has

[91] The Bavarian doctors' pension scheme was set up on October 1, 1923. See Kannengießer (1998, pp. 114–128).

[92] Organizationally, the 79 occupational pension schemes (as of 3.1.2002) have been aggregated since 1978 in a "Arbeitsgemeinschaft Berufsständischer Versorgungseinrichtungen e.V." (Consortium of Professional Association Pension Schemes), based in Cologne.

changed in an unfavorable way: the so-called net reproduction rate, which refers to the number of children per couple, declined strongly between 1965 and 1975 and has now settled at around 0.6, which is significantly lower than the replacement rate of 2.4. At the same time, life expectancy has risen: for men who are 60 today it stands at around 80 years, for women of that age at around 84. The pension payment periods have increased by around 6 years since 1960. Estimates are that in 2030 there will be 88 pensioners for every 100 workers.

This being the case, the pension reform of 1972 (BGBl. I, p. 1965) initially appears to have been a social policy error. It brought in new contribution payers (opening), it allowed for an early departure from working life (flexible retirement age), and it improved the pension conditions for those with lower incomes (pension based on minimum income) if they had merely 25 insurance years to show for themselves (Peters 1973/1978, pp. 185ff.). This placed such a strain on pension finances that a number of savings measures had to be taken between 1978 and 1985. Still, the problems grew worse because there were simultaneous expansions, for example "the inclusion of the disabled (1975) and of artists (1981) into pension insurance" (Ruland 1996, p. 890f.), the equalization of widowers with widows, and the crediting—so important for many women—of the time spend on child rearing as a fictive contribution period. In the end, though, expansions and consolidations remained more or less balanced.

However, a bare decade later the financing problems became so obvious that a new solution had to be looked for. In the so-called Pension Reform 1992 enacted in 1989, the attempt was made—alongside important standardizations and simplifications—above all to break the cycle of constant increases in contributions.[93] Revenues, indexed expenditures, and the always necessary federal subsidy (Article 120, Basic Law) were now placed into relationship to one another in such a way that one could think this was a self-regulating system of communicating channels. Its architects also believed that the built-in automatism had achieved a certain de-politicization of the decision-making process and that the increase in contributions had been cut in half. But that proved an illusion only 4 years later. An economic slump and high unemployment forced the pension insurance to fall back on the statutory fluctuation reserve. The missing contribution income because of unemployment was joined by early pensions, far more than the system was able to absorb. The economy unburdened itself in this way from older workers and hired no replacements or cheaper and younger ones. Society as a whole bore this burden of a deliberate increase in the number of pensioners through taxes and higher contributions. The latter, as "incidental wage costs," in turn burdened the international competitiveness of the strongly export-oriented German economy. The legislature therefore attempted in 1996 to contain the disastrous consequences of the practice of early retirement through a new model of old age part-time work.

[93] BGBl. 1989 I, p. 2261. On the dual character of this law as a savings law and a codification see Ruland (1996, p. 891f.).

The departure from working life of one worker was to be linked with the entry—promoted by the Employment Office—of another worker (BGBl. 1996 I, p. 1078).

However, since unemployment persisted, the legislature was already forced in the following year to incorporate a demographic factor into the pension adjustment formula and to agree on new cuts (BGBl. 1997 I, p. 2998, effective January 1, 1999). Like its predecessors, this law, which took effect on January 1, 1999, remained merely another stage. Long term, except for the demographic propositions, there are hardly reliable forecasts about the development of the economy. Still, on the basis of experience, one can eliminate two radical models of future pension reform laws as unfeasible. For one, a return to capital cover seems blocked. It has been calculated that the capital sum needed for pension entitlements and rights would amount to €5 trillion. The question of how such a sum could be raised and invested remains unanswered. More serious is the shrinking of the subsequent generation, which is supposed to achieve the conversion of this return on equity into productive labor, tangible goods, and services.

For another, the conversion to a purely egalitarian basic pension from tax revenues is not a feasible path, since such a basic pension would raise serious problems of equality. It would be difficult to distinguish it from social welfare and would violate the merit principle. If one leaves aside also the complete abolition of the statutory pension insurance as utopian, one can realistically contemplate only a combination of a tax-funded basic pension and a supplementary merit pension based on contributions paid in. This would have to be joined by a broad unburdening of this system from extraneous benefits, that is, the giving up of social benefits built up over decades for individuals unable or not required to pay contributions.[94]

At the same time, the two other pillars of old-age provision need to be strengthened: company pension schemes and self-funded retirement.

Company pension schemes are widespread in Germany and have achieved a considerable volume. A solid one quarter of the companies finances such a scheme. In addition, there are special social security benefit funds for the building industry and an additional old-age provision for blue collar and white collar workers in the public sector. One could also—if this thought experiment is permitted—see the old-age provision for civil servants as a kind of collective insurance by the totality of tax payers for a specific stratum of functionaries, usually employed for a lifetime.

However, what is understood by company pension schemes in the narrower sense are only those institutions that—on the basis of a promise by the employer—provide the employee benefits when they come due: benefits paid either directly by the employer, an independent relief fund, a pension fund (mutual insurance association), or a life insurance taken out for the employee by the company. In the final analysis, all of these forms are based on the labor contract or on supplemental agreements, which can also be regulated via a collective bargaining agreement or company agreements. Since 1974 a special law has existed to support these forms of

[94] Overview in Ruland (1996, pp. 877ff.).

old-age provision (BGBl. 1974 I, p. 3610): it regulates some of the major issues, but leaves a good deal open and thus entrusts it to contract law and adjudication. The issues dealt with by the law often concern problems by economically weak or insolvent businesses to keep the promises they had once made, the questions of indexing benefits, the cancellation of promises, and the extent of co-determination in this area. It is obvious that young enterprises in their start-up phase, trade businesses, or smaller businesses, that is, the very businesses on which the expectations of the national economy rest and which also contribute to spreading the risk of recession broadly, tend to hold back on these schemes. But larger enterprises also reach their limits quite readily if they cut their workforce substantially and at the same time are committed to direct pension guarantees. Still, the most recent data on manufacturing enterprises and commerce convey a positive impression of this important branch of social security (Leopold 1999, p. 321; Rungaldier and Steindl 1987; on the present: Bruno-Latocha and Tippelmann 2003).

For some time now—more precisely: ever since the danger of the burden posed by old-age provisions has entered public awareness—personal provision has become an urgent recommendation. The younger generation, whose confidence in the security of pension entitlements is vanishing with the experiences of regularly recurring "pension reforms," began to reorient itself beginning in the 70s—of course that applies only to that segment of the generation with good earnings. The providers of life insurance policies and pension models based on private savings know that a lucrative and growing market segment is taking shape. Even institutions like the *Bausparkassen*, which are intended for the public service, are participating in this competition.

e) Health Insurance

New Beginning

Just like pension insurance, the nearly 2,000 health insurance funds that existed in West Germany around 1950 also had to cope with a difficult new beginning (Schlencker 1994). Health insurance had been affected in a special way by the political and racist measures of the National Socialists. That is why the initial concern was focused on "starting up," combined with the restoration of self-administration, where parity between employers and employees now existed. The first legal measures also included the expansion of insurance protection to individuals who, as refugees or expellees, returnees from the war or for other reasons, did not belong to the health insurance funds that still existed in West Germany. The health insurance for pensioners introduced in 1941 was restricted in 1956: only those who had health insurance as employees would continue to be covered. All others would receive an insurance contribution supplement. In this way, in spite of these restrictions, important expansions in the number of those insured took place already during the first two legislative sessions.

As far as the relationship to *Kassenärzte* (doctors treating patients in public health insurance funds) was concerned, the model in practice since the emergency decrees of 1931/1932 was essentially retained. The health insurance funds affiliated in state associations and in a federal association (BGBl. 1955 I, p. 524) negotiated overall compensation with the comparably organized associations of *Kassenärzte* and their federal organization. Distributing that compensation to the authorized doctors was the task of the association of *Kassenärzte* (Alber 1992, pp. 41ff.). This area of the law had to be newly regulated now.

The *Kassenarzt* Law of August 17, 1955 (BGBl. 1955 I, p. 513) initially eliminated the organizational differences that had emerged after 1945, as well as the differences between the *Kassenarzt* law and the law governing public fund dentists (*Kassenzahnärzte*) in order to subsequently integrate both into the Reich insurance system. Finally, the rules governing accreditation dating from the Nazi period were also replaced by a new regulation.[95]

Structural Problems

However, it was not long before a structural conflict emerged in the following years that has characterized the health care system to this day. Within the polygon of differing interests (contribution payers on the side of employers and the side of employees, patients, doctors along with their associations, pharmacies, hospitals run by various carriers, the pharmaceutical industry, health insurance funds[96] along with their associations), the federal government with Minister of Labor Blank attempted cost containment already in 1959 by shifting from the all-inclusive and necessarily anonymous benefit to fees for individual services, by introducing deductibles for patients, and by lifting the restrictions on accreditations for *Kassenärzte*. This was initially thwarted by opposition from the unions and the SPD, but also—as expected—from accredited doctors. However, the issue reemerged with the first recession in West Germany in 1966/1967 and became more urgent.

What the *Kassenärzte* had still tried to prevent in 1959 was implemented a short time later by the Federal Constitutional Court. Following the famous "Apothecary Judgment" of 1958 (BVerfGE 7, p. 377), there was reason to expect that the accreditation restrictions on *Kassenärzte*, which had fixed the ratio of doctors to patients at 1:500, would also have to fall. In fact, the dirigiste "accreditation" as a *Kassenarzt* by the Associations of *Kassenärzte* was indeed questionable from a constitutional point of view. It was now abolished by a decision by the Federal Constitutional Court on March 23, 1960 (BVerfGE 11, p. 30). However, this

[95] "Zulassungsordnung vom 17. Mai 1934," RGBl. I, p. 399; "Zulassungsordnung für Kassenärzte und Zahnärzte vom 28. Mai 1957," BGBl. I, p. 572/608, 582.

[96] The funds (*Kassen*) references here include the *Ersatzkassen* (alternative funds). On the special history of the latter see Rehkopf (1994).

interpretation of Article 12, Section 1 of the Basic Law, focused entirely on the individual's self-actualization, trigged a societal and economic chain reaction—namely a rise in the number of medical students (the response to which in turn was restrictions on admission to the study of medicine), which resulted in an increase in the density of doctors (and pharmacists), the consequences of which was in turn cost increases, an intensification of competition, and significant changes in medical behavior. The elimination of legal barriers thus worked in the same direction as the rising scientific and technical standards of the health care system. In this way, the density of care and the economic importance of the entire complex increased continuously over the decades. In 1996, the statutory health insurance spent around 273 billion DM.

Expansion

What contributed significantly to the intensification and rising costs of the system were the consistent expansion of the circle of insured person and the improvement in benefits. In the process, very effective socio-political progress and humanitarian intentions intertwined with electoral calculus. For example, the Law for the Improvement of the Economic Security of Workers in Case of Illness of June 26, 1957 (amended on July 12, 1961 [BGBl. 1957 I, p. 659; BGBl. 1961 I, p. 913]), raised sick pay from 50 to 65 % of wages. Employers were obligated to pay a subsidy to boost sick pay up to 90 % (after 1961 up to 100 %) of income. Thus, for blue collar workers an equalization to the status of white collar employees was achieved only in 1961—leaving aside the other problematic aspects of this solution in terms of both insurance and labor law. Shortly before the election date that ended the so-called Grand Coalition, a new regulation of this issue came about through the Law on the Continued Payment of Wages Remuneration in Case of Illness of July 27, 1969 (BGBl. I, p. 946). The augmentation of sick pay through a subsidy was replaced by the continued payment of the wage for 6 weeks by the employer. Since this in turn took the pressure off the health insurance funds, the health insurance contribution of 2 % by retirees, introduced in 1968 and in fact necessary to financing the health insurance, was abolished again after federal parliamentary elections in 1969. In 1978, the circle of beneficiaries had to be restricted again for cost reasons (affirmed by BVerfGE 69, pp. 272ff.). To this day, health insurance for pensioners has been the target of reforms in health insurance (Ruland 1996).

A new commission on the further development of the social health insurance all in all banked on expansion. With the initial reformist optimism of the social-liberal government, increasing and indexing the compulsory insurance threshold and the contribution assessment ceiling brought new members into the funds, especially white collar workers, only about 60 % of whom had joined the statutory health insurance. Other white collar workers, whose employers had to pay a subsidy for this purpose, could join voluntarily. Beginning in 1975, compulsory insurance was extended also to the disabled in workshops, institutions, and homes, who, if they were not already insured as workers in institutions, were able to join voluntarily. Incidentally, the latter led to a shifting of these cases from the social assistance previously burdened (§39 BSHG) to the health insurance funds. Included in 1975 were also all students and interns. Anyone who was in the process of vocational training could join voluntarily. Likewise, independent farmers, family members working with them, and the retired elderly living with them were subject to compulsory insurance in 1972. Since there was no desire to bring them into the insurance for blue collar or white collar workers, separate professional agricultural insurance funds were created, which were linked with the agricultural accident insurance (Hagedorn 1982; Breuer and Lehle 1996; Zöllner 1989). Finally, in 1981 artists and journalists were also covered by health insurance within the framework of a social insurance law created specifically for them (BGBl. I, p. 705; Finke 1996). On the whole then, the legislature pursued—as in pension insurance—the tendency to spread the insurance risks among the largest number of carriers and to gain as many new contribution payers as possible, also in order to approach in this way a national insurance.[97]

External motivations supplemented this trend. The World Health Organization's 1946 target of "the attainment by all peoples of the highest possible level of health" was vigorously used in German social jurisdiction, as was the open-ended concept of illness proclaimed by the WHO. The sick were to be given everything they needed as early and as comprehensively as possible (BSGE 35: 10; 37: 130 [134]; 39: 167; Ecker 1984, pp. 299ff.). This was also in keeping with the spirit of the Social Code, which was set in motion in 1969/1970 and the General Part of which took effect in 1975. The regulations laid down in the opening section thereof were aimed at optimizing social rights through the interpretation and exercise of discretion (§2 Section 2 SBG I) and at the broadest possible education and counseling for citizens (§§13, 14 SGB I). As supportive as these normative guidelines are, within the context of a widespread and deeply rooted attitude of always granting or preserving the maximum benefit, they have had the effect of raising costs.

Benefits

This trend toward expansion was also seen on the benefits side, at least until 1975 (Zöllner 1981, pp. 157ff.). It is evident not only in the measures for early detection (ultimately cost-reducing), for example in cancer care (1971), but also in the obligation of the health insurance funds to provide rehabilitation services beyond medical treatment (1974). As a measure flanking the resolution of the controversy over §218 of the Criminal Code, the financing of abortions and sterilizations was

[97] The number of those in the health insurance rose continuously in the twentieth century (1911–1938 from 10 to 23.2 million; in West Germany 1951–1990 from 20 to 37.8 million; through reunification and since to 50.8 million). During the same period, the number of health insurance funds dropped from 22,000 to 482.

added in 1975. A much more far-reaching example is the decision taken at the time to boost the insurance benefits for hospital care—parallel to the simultaneous expansion of hospitals. The problems that were afflicting hospital financing urged new regulations. The Basic Law was amended in 1969 to provide the federal government with the authority to ensure "the economic viability of hospitals and the regulation of hospital charges" (Article 74, Section 1, No. 19a, Basic Law). Subsequently the legislature passed the Hospital Financing Law of June 29, 1972,[98] followed by relevant state hospital laws and the Federal Nursing Care Ordinance of April 25, 1973.[99] Out of this complex there arose in turn a series of demarcation issues, quarrels over personnel structure, co-determination, and billing modalities (Metz 1977). However these questions were resolved, the network of care was more closely knit in this way—and became more expensive. The rise in expenses for the insurance funds that was triggered by the reform of hospital financing is estimated at 25 % annually. All in all, the broadening of the circle of those entitled to benefits and of benefits themselves led to substantial increases in costs and premiums, even if the latter could be postponed temporarily.

Since then, the financing problems in the health care system have grown exponentially. A battle began to contain benefits on the cost side and to stabilize premium rates on the income side. "Cost control" became a permanent issue.[100] The cost control laws of 1977, 1979, 1981, the 1984 Law to Reform Hospital Financing, the Health Care Reform Act that took effect on January 1, 1989, the Health Care Structure Act that took effect on January 1, 1993, and other measures employed the most varied array of techniques. Reformers not only sought to bring the various actors to the table and persuade them to arrive at agreements ("concerted action in the health care system"), but they also mobilized scientific and social policy expertise in diverse commissions to exert outside pressure on the decision makers. In the laws themselves all variants of restrictive, prohibitive, and controlling measures were combined—in part to reach the service providers, in part to reach service recipients or their beneficiaries. We are talking about the introduction of maximum limits, the drawing up of positive and negative lists on pharmaceuticals, the introduction of elements of planning in the hospital system (need plans, formation of focal points, reduction of capacities), the budgeting of expenses, and other interventionist instruments, but most of all the tightening of eligibility rules and the control of abuses. An important tool of intervention—though one that is still employed with restraint—is copayments. At the same time, though, politicians are trying to appeal to individual responsibility, create transparency, introduce elements of competition, and create positive incentives, such as

[98] BGBl. 1972 I, p. 1009, amended by the "Haushaltsstrukturgesetz vom 18. Dezember 1975", BGBl. I, p. 3091, and the law of December 14, 1976, BGBl. I, pp. 3341, 3365.

[99] BGBl. 1973 I, p. 333, with several later changes, see Tuschen and Quaas (2001).

[100] From the discussion see, for example, the "Tagung des Deutschen Sozialrechtsverbandes 1987: Die Strukturreform der Krankenersicherung" (Wiesbaden, 1988), with references to the demographic, medical, legal, and political framework conditions.

premium reductions for healthier individuals or premium increases for higher risks through conduct that is harmful to health. The dilemma of regulatory policy is obvious. All major parties want to preserve the traditional system, which is already a compromise between personal responsibility and care steered by the sovereign authority. At the same time, though, they are all aware that the relentless demographic shift, the equally inexorable cost increase in the areas of wages and salaries, as well as medical technology that is pushing into new areas (improvement in diagnosis through tomography and nanotechnology, microinvasive and prenatal surgery, gene technology, reproductive technologies, and so on) will make it impossible to continue along the old path.[101]

As a result, the interaction of expansion in personnel and increases in benefits on the side of the health insurance funds, of available medical technology and of the system of education and training on the side of the market, gave rise to a serious problem. The cost control laws have had profound economic effects, for example on spas, massage therapists, dentists, apothecaries, opticians and audiologists, the taxi industry and funeral businesses. On the other hand, the cost control laws have in part merely revealed that the market was overcrowded thanks to the favorable conditions that had prevailed until then, and not only with respect to the self-employed, but also in the health care segment of the non-statutory and church-based welfare system, the growth of which had rested on the expansion of the health insurance funds (Knieps 1996).

The "health care reforms" that have periodically recurred for about three decades wrestle not only with the external causes of rising costs, but also with problems that are produced by detailed interventions themselves. Restrictions of every sort invariably generate forces that seek—in defiance of the restrictions—to preserve the existing level of revenue and benefits, even if only to maintain the profitability of establishments (e.g. doctor's practice, apothecary, hospitals, rehabilitation facilities, pharmaceutical companies). The underlying dilemma is that an insurance conceived as "social" must be able to stand up to the laws of the market. Health insurance has not yet cast off its origins in the social question of the nineteenth century, even though it has become a national insurance. The equal payment of premiums by employers and employees is a relic of that age. Moreover, in actuarial terms the free insurance of family members should be converted into a contribution payment. And that contribution should be calculated on the basis of risk, not income. That is the current recommendation of economists. There is no denying that the logic inherent in their arguments is persuasive. However, whether the system can be overturned in this way is a political question with a lot of unknowns. The major national parties shy away from drawing the necessary consequences. And while the smaller parties are encouraging the legislators to do

[101] In 2002, the statutory health insurance distributed its total expenditures as follows: 32 % for hospital treatment, 16 % for medical treatment, 16 % for pharmacies, 8 % for dental treatment, 6 % for net administrative costs, 5 % for sick pay, 17 % for other items. Source: Bundesministerium für Gesundheit und soziale Sicherheit.

it, they know full well that they are unable to bring about the transformation because they lack the political power.

The Health Care System in the German Democratic Republic

The health care system in the German Democratic Republic as it emerged after the war through the overlay of the old legal foundations with the model of the Soviet Union (Kirchberger 1986) was fundamentally different from its Western counterpart. "Buried alternatives" from the workers' movement re-emerged and were now implemented.[102] At its center stood the intention, in the face of the extensive permeation of work and life in "real socialism," to anchor the health care system within the enterprises. The prime goal was to preserve and restore the population's labor power (Peschke 1962, pp. 479ff.). This also meant that preventive care and after care—through education, admonishment, and the requisite facilities—were to be given clear precedence over therapy. If a working person fell ill, he was to be cared for with all material benefits and services from the hand of the state, in principle free of charge. Finally, outpatient and inpatient care was to be combined through polyclinics and outpatient facilities.

The health care system created in this way in principle no longer envisaged any self-employed doctors. Their offices—especially in the countryside—were converted into state-run ones. The same was true of apothecaries, hospitals, and rehabilitation facilities, though the latter always had a small private and church-based sector. The health care system functioned at the level of enterprises as well as the territorial district level with a network of institutions for preventive, diagnostic, and therapeutic measures. Occupational medicine and occupational hygiene were expanded, as were preventive and surveillance measures; large enterprises set up their own outpatient facilities and polyclinics.[103] During the Honecker era the initially non-existent free choice of doctors was introduced to improve the continuity of treatment.

The accomplishments of the system were considerable (intensive care within the enterprise, material benefits and services free of charge, sick pay, pregnancy leave, maternity leave, child birth bonus, and maternity grant). The density of doctors was satisfactory, at least statistically. Reality often looked differently. The standard compensation with its demotivating consequences, the high burden on doctors from ancillary bureaucratic tasks, the physical decay of the facilities, the lack of modern equipment, medical research retarded by a lack of international exchange and financial reasons, stagnation in the import of western pharmaceuticals—all of this detracted considerably from the picture painted by propaganda (Labisch 1983;

[102] Hansen et al. (1981), especially 97ff. on the outpatient clinics of the Weimar period.

[103] In 1988 there existed "in the GDR 623 polyclinics, of which 151 were enterprise polyclinics. Involved in care were also 1932 outpatient clinics, of which 354 were enterprise outpatient clinics." Knieps and Tophoven (1990).

Kiewel 1990; Weber 1990 with further references). After the dissolution of East Germany's health care system with the introduction of western health insurance on January 1, 1991, different participants in that system preserved different memories. The divergent perspectives of patients, doctors, and economists were reinforced further by the east-west dichotomy. Certain hopes that one could take over the "good sides" of the socialist health care system were not fulfilled. By now the new federal states are participating fully in the advantages and weaknesses of the western system.

f) Accident Insurance

The rebuilding of commercial accident insurance after 1945 took place largely by way of analogy to the pension and health insurance as far as the material starting points, the initial lack of a top organizational level,[104] and the differing policies of the occupation zones were concerned.[105] The Professional Associations organized themselves on the state level in part new, in part they continued to operate under the oversight of the occupying powers. In Berlin, accident insurance was transferred into the omnium insurance that was set up there; its specific features were eliminated. In 1948, the western sectors and the eastern sectors split apart, with the result that in the following years the western sectors had to be coordinated with the Federal Republic. In the Bizone and Trizone in West Germany, accident insurance and its self-governance were reestablished on the old model. Various plans and draft bills were swept away in part by the course of events, in part by the generally growing distance to the model of the "omnium insurance." By contrasts, in the Soviet Occupation Zone and the later GDR, accident insurance passed into the omnium insurance overseen by the Free German Trade Union Federation (FDGB). The task of accident prevention was taken up by the municipal Occupational Safety Boards (Aulmann 1979). The self-administration of accident insurance carried by entrepreneurs no longer existed.

In the West, then, the issue was the new beginning within the traditional structures. Initially this meant palpable cutbacks in services so the costs could be borne in the first place. At the same time, refugees (Wickenhagen 1980, vol. I, pp. 309–311), returning prisoners of war, surviving dependents of war dead, and displaced persons had to be included in the accident insurance. This was regulated on the level of the states and within the Economic Council. However, within the legislation of the Economic Council of the Bizone, which focused largely on pension insurance, accident insurance played a role in so far as adjustments to the

[104] The "Reichsverband der gewerblichen Berufsgenossenschaften" (Reich Association of Professional Associations) was shut down in June of 1945. It reconstituted itself beginning in 1948 as the "Hauptverband." For a detailed discussion of this see Wickenhagen (1980, vol. I, pp. 314–317).

[105] Wickenhagen (1980, vol. I, pp. 293ff.); an apt summary in Breuer (1996).

currency reform had to be carried out (Wickenhagen 1980, vol. I, p. 311f.). This was done through the Law on Improvements to the Statutory Accident Insurance of August 10, 1949, though it also consolidated existing legislation and brought small improvements in substance, for example the fixing of minimum pensions. A few days later the accident insurance protection for those persecuted by the Nazi regime was also put in order.

The development of accident insurance during the first two legislative sessions in West Germany was characterized by extensive legislative stagnation. The essential things were done—for example, the annual increase in the pension level to the changed wage level,[106] the incorporation of expellees and refugees into accident insurance (BGBl. 1960 I, p. 93), or the continuously lengthening list of occupational diseases.[107] Needless to say, the technical regulations also continued to operate, for example those on how to handle explosives, dusts, toxic or radioactive materials, about work under higher air pressure, and much more. It would be inappropriate to dismiss these regulations as "merely technical," for they shaped everyday working life, developed a potent steering effect on the economy, and their specifications are political in nature.

Only the third legislative session witnessed the reorganization of the field postponed until then. The Accident Insurance Revision Act of April 30, 1963 (BGBl. I, p. 241) rewrote nearly the entire third book of the Reich Insurance Code, including maritime accident insurance and agricultural accident insurance. The benefits improved through indexing, a lowering of the age limits, the lifting of the threshold on annual earnings, and the strengthening of rehabilitation possibilities. Special emphasis was now placed on accident prevention, ahead of rehabilitation and pension payments.

Alongside these necessary but not spectacular changes, expansions occurred also in accident insurance, for example through the inclusion of prisoners, individuals working in an honorary capacity, as well as pupils, students, and children in kindergartens. As in the case of pension and health insurance, here too there was, following the phase of reconstruction (1945–1955), an expansion that was economically driven until 1966 and after 1969 also politically desired. However, it is characteristic for accident insurance that it was spared existential difficulties, thanks to its financing by employers and its practical successes in accident prevention. Of all branches of insurance, accident insurance (in existence since 1884) is

[106] The Twenty-First Adjustment Law was issued on July 25, 1978, BGBl. I, p. 1089.

[107] "3. Verordnung über Ausdehnung der Unfallversicherung auf Berufskrankheiten vom 16. Dezember 1936," RGBl. I, p. 1117. The "4. VO vom 29. Januar 1943" (RGBl. I, p. 85) then listed 27 diseases. The "5. VO vom 26. Juli 1952" (BGBl. I, p. 395) listed 40 illnesses; the "6. VO vom 28. April 1961" (BGBl. I, p. 505) listed 47 illnesses. The decree in 1970 (BGBl. I, p. 3329) knew 55 occupational illnesses. Since 1992 (BGBl. I, p. 2343), the number has been above 60. Overall see § 551 Section 2 RVO. Flanking: "Verordnung über gefährliche Arbeitsstoffe vom 17. September 1971", BGBl. I, p. 1609, and "Gesetz über Betriebsärzte, Sicherheitsingenieure und andere Fachkräfte für Arbeitssicherheit vom 12. Dezember 1973," BGBl. I, p. 1885.

the one that has caused the fewest political problems to this day and whose finances rest on the most solid footing.[108]

g) Job Placement and Unemployment Insurance

The Job Placement and Unemployment Insurance created in 1927 under Minister of Labor Heinrich Braun, and the public law Reich Office for Job Placement and Unemployment Insurance created for this purpose, had entered a seemingly hopeless crisis during the death throes of the Weimar Republic. Mass unemployment had drained the reserves that had been barely built up. The last parliamentary government had fallen over the effort to restructure this insurance. When the reserves had been built up again under the National Socialists with the help of deficit spending and armaments contracts, the government did not lower the contribution rate (1930: 6.5 %), but collected the surpluses in the Reich Fund for Labor Deployment and used them to finance the war. The Reich Office had been integrated into the Ministry of Labor already in 1938; from this time on, at the latest, there was thus no such thing as a self-administrating branch of social security.

For the year 1945 this meant, quite apart from the loss of assets, that one had to begin all over again. The requisite substructure of Labor Offices and State Labor Offices was now created in the occupation zones and in the states. In 1952, as we have seen, the Federal Office for Job Placement and Unemployment Insurance was set up in Nuremberg. Payments to the unemployed rose rapidly, parallel to the upsurge in the economy.

Across four legislative periods, the Labor Offices continued to use the largely unchanged law of 1927, the Job Placement and Unemployment Insurance Act. But at least job placement had been made into a monopoly of the federal government, and there now existed individual entitlements to a professional or vocational education.[109] Impulses for reforms were absent as unemployment initially declined steadily and then disappeared de facto in the phase of full employment. It was possible to boost benefits, for example in 1959 in the construction industry through the introduction of bad weather compensation and measures to promote winter construction, while simultaneously lowering contributions from the above-mentioned 6.5 % to below 2 %.[110] Job placement was taken over by the free market; at times, unemployment insurance seemed almost expendable.

---

108 "Gesetz zur Neuregelung des Rechts der gesetzlichen Unfallversicherung vom 30. April 1963", BGBl. I, p. 241.

109 "Gesetz zur Änderung und Ergänzung des Gesetzes über Arbeitsvermittlung und Arbeitslosenversicherung vom 16. April 1956", BGBl. I, p. 243, amended again on December 23, 1956, BGBl. I, p. 1018.

110 Contributions subsequently rose to 4.3 % between 1987 and 1991, and then back up to 6.5 %.

However, during the first disruption of the market in the recession of 1966/1967, people remembered the state's responsibility for creating jobs. Paragraph 1 of the Stability Act of 1967 described a "high level of employment" as one of the four goals, along with price stability, a balance in foreign trade, and an appropriate level of economic growth. That is also why the simultaneously drafted Employment Promotion Act (*Arbeitsförderungsgesetz* [AFG] passed on June 25, 1969: BGBl. I, p. 582) placed active intervention front and center, while insurance proper was moved to the back. The basic belief that the problem of unemployment was essentially a problem of qualifications and that the training and labor sector should be shaped in an interventionist way was also evident from the flanking laws on professional and vocational education (BGBl. 1969 I, p. 1112) and the promotion of training.[111] Today, as well, after the AFG was integrated into Book III of the Social Code, the core of the insurance benefits is surrounded by a dense circle of measures that promote employment (Wagner 1996).

These interventionist measures are aimed at both job seekers themselves and at employers, in fact, support is even possible for relevant facilities for vocational training or further training or the vocational integration of the disabled. The Labor Offices are supposed to provide counseling and job placement, to facilitate the step into independence, but also to offer incentives for employers to create new jobs. Looking at the structure of the laws, the so-called wage replacement benefits (unemployment allowance, subsistence allowance, short-time allowance, unemployment aid tied to means-testing, and winter compensation allowance) appear only as secondary aids. When the second period of recession began in 1973 and a large number of bankruptcies occurred, the legislature added insolvency payments as another benefit (BGBl. 1974 I, p. 1481; on this see Matthes 1974). This benefit was to secure employees and workers the still outstanding net earnings (inclusive of contributions to health insurance, nursing care insurance, pension insurance, and labor promotion) for the last 3 months prior to the opening of bankruptcy proceedings (§§183ff. SGB III).

In recent years it has become evident that the tool kit available to the Federal Agency for Labor to remedy sustained "structural" unemployment is not adequate. Wages and incidental wage costs that are high by international standards have prompted the private sector to shift production abroad and to cut jobs at home. The rapidly advancing automation is working in the same direction. The base of three to four million unemployed that has been evident in the Federal Republic for some years is partly due to global trends, and partly to a lack of professional qualification or unfavorable business conditions. Added to this is that more highly qualified workers and those with better income are using the system to fill "orientation phases" and gaps between various kinds of work. In the process it is clear that the conventional labor administration cannot maintain its monopoly over job

[111] "Bundesgesetz über individuelle Förderung der Ausbildung (BAföG) vom 26. August 1971 i.d. F. vom 6. Juni 1983", BGBl. I, pp. 645, 1680; most recently amended by the "Ausbildungsförderungsreformgesetz vom 19. März 2001", BGBl. I, p. 390.

placement, because there are numerous specific, unofficial markets. The traditional processes of job placement no longer seem sufficient, and evidently there are also attempts to use statistics to make services look better. All that suggests that the tool kit should be tightened, that services that are not effective enough should be given up, and that the effects of promotion measures should be very carefully observed.

h) Nursing Care Insurance: The Fifth Pillar

Between health insurance and welfare (social assistance) there have stood, ever since the introduction of social insurance, those people who, while not sick in the medical sense, are directly dependent on the support of others. They are "in need of care" or "helpless" (§68 Section 1 BSHG; §44 SGB VII; §35 Section I, p. 1 BVG), they need help communicating with others or managing their own household. This circle of individuals is growing in direct relation to changes in the demographic structure. Once it reaches a certain size, the risk also changes its appearance. The more often it manifests itself, the more readily it can be grasped by the mechanisms of social insurance, which are laid out for mass phenomena (Igl 1996).

In the past, those in need of care were looked after largely in families, and to a large extent that applies also to the present. Today only about one fifth of these individuals live in homes and similar institutions. What has changed, however, are the personal contribution and the financing of external services. In the past, the extended family assumed the nursing care, in terms of both personnel and costs, in a sense as a self-supporting system. Support was then provided by charitable or non-profit aid. In the meantime, however, the structure of the (agriculturally constituted) extended family has been replaced by that of the nuclear family and the growing number of one-person households (Heinemann-Knoch and von Kardorff 1989). This new structure makes possible gains in freedom, but in cases of crisis it is no longer self-supporting. Working people can no longer manage round-the-clock care on their own. But the more a society trains caregivers as a special profession, the more problems over the financing of care services arise. The ratio of elderly within the population as a whole is rising along with their individual life expectancy. As a result, the number of nursing cases has also been rising for a long time, and it will continue to do so.[112]

In view of this development, social assistance, which was obligated to support nursing services via §27 Section 1 No. 9 BSHG, found itself increasingly overburdened. The nursing cases could not be situated within health insurance, because for the most part there was no gainful employment and because these were

[112] Of the 1.6 million people in need of care (1998), 1.25 million were over 60 years of age, 100,000 were between 40 and 60, 300,000 were younger than 40. By 2010, the nursing cases of 60-year olds was expected to have risen to 3.8 million. As an overview see Irmak (2002, pp. 1924–1961).

not cases of illness. And most were and are not cases of accident insurance. For retirees whose pension was inadequate to finance the care there was the added humiliation of being forced to accept welfare services after a life of work. Social assistance, in turn, had to have recourse to the children. Whatever other entitlements to nursing services existed, for example in the support for victims of war, did not cover the normal case.

Thus the problem grew, and finding a solution was only a matter of time and political decision. Conceivable would have been an expansion of health insurance or pension insurance, but also the creation of a fifth pillar of social insurance by dissolving the link to the employment relationship.

The result, after lengthy debates, was the creation of a national insurance for nursing care on May 26, 1994, though in association with the health insurance, in which 92 % of the population is already insured (BGBl. I, p. 1014). For the remaining 7 % (including civil servants entitled to support), private nursing care insurance is available. Although this is an insurance for all, it is not the citizens "as such" who are enlisted in the financing; instead, half is paid for by individuals, half by employers. The latter in return receive compensation in the form of giving up one "state recognized holiday"—an instructive example for the amalgamation of questions of social policy and financing with those relating to the law on church-state relations (Article 140, Basic Law/Article 139 WRV). Organizationally, nursing care insurance is under the roof of the statutory health insurance or—with equal conditions—under the private obligatory insurances.

Those defined as in need of care are individuals who, because of a physical, mental, or psychological illness or disability, require permanent help for the normal and regularly recurring activities of daily life, namely in the areas of personal hygiene, alimentation, mobility, and household work. Heretofore, most of these persons were and are cared for at home by their families or through community outpatient services.[113] This, too, will change to the extent that traditional family structures will continue to erode and it is likely to become increasingly difficult to combine gainful employment with the in-home care for an elderly person.

Depending on the severity of the case, the benefits of nursing care insurance comprise in-home care, non-cash services, a care allowance, and in-patient care.[114] The social protection of care-providers can also be covered. Responsibility for the kind and extent of benefits and services lies with the nursing care insurance funds, which in turn cooperate with the care givers and the institutions providing care. With that, the basic constellations and interests are similar to those in health insurance. The nursing care insurance funds will have to absorb or pass on growing cost pressure. Since July 1, 1996, the insurance premium has been 1.7 %, but it is foreseeable that it will continue to rise. Here, too, cost control laws and the creation

[113] Of the 1.6 million individuals in need of care, only 400,000 are cared for as residents in nursing homes.

[114] The law (§ 15 Section 1 Nos. 1–3 PflegeVG) distinguishes three levels of care: considerable need for care (I), serious need for care (II), grave need for care (III).

of stronger controls can be expected. Should costs rise again, additional compensations or a complete conversion to self-financing on the part of insured persons will have to follow.

Now that more than a decade has passed since the introduction of nursing care insurance, one can say this looking back: anyone who expected that the Siamese twins of industrial society and social state could separate, and that the pressure of the problems would lead to a reprivatization of risks, greater individual responsibility, and neighborly solidarity, must be disappointed. But anyone who considered the unstoppable further growth of collective, bureaucratized protective institutions a natural process, can feel vindicated. Presumably the occasionally entertained hopes for a simple life without a net of collective security is an illusion, in any case, because the return to a self-supporting society could be achieved only by passing through the purgatory of a catastrophe and a drastic reduction in the level of society. On the other hand, the creation of further "pillars" of social insurance in the belief that the financing can be arranged somehow seems equally illusionary. Over the long term that path leads to the paralysis of the economic dynamism, which has to generate the contributions from both the insured and the employers. It therefore came as no surprise that in the reform debate of 2003, suggestions about reprivatizations and cost control reemerged, aimed at abolishing the deficit-running nursing care insurance, and replacing it with a tax-financed Federal Nursing Care Services Law with benefits indexed to income.[115] The attempts to date to cover the deficit by leaning more heavily on those without children were not really successful. The conversion to a capital basis was also not carried out. For demographic reasons the number of benefit recipients will continue to rise. Thus, a large market is opening up for private insurance, with arrangements for either nursing pension or the financing of nursing aids. As of yet, though, the ageing society has not come up with a clear decision whether it wants to see the new risk solved through either the collective-statist approach or by way of reprivatization.

References

Abelshauser W (1981) Wiederaufbau vor dem Marshallplan. Westeuropas Wachstumschancen und die Wirtschaftsordnungspolitik in der zweiten Hälfte der vierziger Jahre. Vierteljahrshefte für Zeitgeschichte 29:545ff

Adenauer K (1966) Erinnerungen 1953–1955. Stuttgart, pp 127–157

Aich P (ed) (1973) Da weitere Verwahrlosung droht…Fürsorgeerziehung und Verwaltung: Zehn Sozialbiographien aus Behördenakten. Reinbek

Alber J (1992) Das Gesundheitswesen der Bundesrepublik Deutschland. Frankfurt am Main

Albers W (1959) Kriegsfolgelasten. HWSW 6:365ff

Arndt A (1956) Warum und wozu Wiedergutmachung? Juristen Zeitung 211–213

[115] Proposal by the Working Group Nursing Care of the so-called Rürup Commission. Report in the FAZ of March 1, 2003.

Arndt A (1964) 10 Jahre Bundesarbeitsgericht und Bundessozialgericht. Neue Juristische Wochenschrift 2147

Aulmann H (1979) Die Neuordnung der Sozialversicherung und des Arbeitsschutzes in der DDR unter besonderer Berücksichtigung der Unfallversicherung und der Unfallverhütung. In: Berufgenossenschaft, pp 153ff.

Bartholomäi R et al (ed) (1977) Sozialpolitik nach 1945. Festschr.f. Ernst Schellenberg. Bonn Bad Godesberg

Behrendt A (1959) Die Interzonenkonferenzen der deutschen Gewerkschaften. Berlin

Benz W (1981) Versuche zur Reform des öffentlichen Dienstes in Deutschland 1945–1952. Deutsche Opposition gegen alliierte Initiativen. Vierteljahrshefte für Zeitgeschichte 29:216ff

Beveridge W (1942) Social insurance and allied services. Her Majesty's Stationery Office. London (German: Der Beveridgeplan. Sozialversicherung und verwandte Leistungen, 1943. Zürich New York)

Boecken W (1996) Berufsständische Versorgungswerke. In: von Maydell B, Ruland F (eds) Sozialrechtshandbuch, 2nd edn. Neuwied, pp 1043ff

Bogs W (1955) Grundfragen des Rechts der sozialen Sicherheit und seiner Reform. Berlin

Bogs W (1977) Das Bundesversicherungsamt im Rückblick. In: Schewe D (ed) Die Praxis des Bundesversicherungsamtes. Bonn-Bad Godesberg, pp 195ff

Bohlmann F, Fischer E (1945/1947) Entwicklung und Stand der Sozialversicherung in der Sowjetischen Besatzungszone. Jahrb. f. Arbeit und Sozialfürsorge 1:206

Breuer J (1996) Geschichtliche Entwicklung. In: Schulin B (ed) Handbuch des Sozialversicherungsrechts, vol II. Unfallversicherungsrecht. Munich, pp 1–46

Breuer J, Lehle K (1996) Sondersysteme der Sozialversicherung – Landwirte. Die agrarsoziale Sicherung. In: von Maydell B, Ruland F (eds) Sozialrechtshandbuch, 2nd edn. Neuwied, pp 1079ff

Bruno-Latocha G, Tippelmann O (2003) Betriebliche Altersversorgung im Umbruch – aktuelle Entwicklungen durch das AvmG (Altersvermögensaufbaugesetz). Deutsche Rentenversicherung (1–2):13–29

Buchheim C (1988) Die Währungsreform 1948 in Westdeutschland. Vierteljahrshefte für Zeitgeschichte 36:189ff

Bundesausgleichsamt (ed) (2002) Fünfzig Jahre Lastenausgleichsgesetz. Bilanz einer einmaligen Solidarleistung des deutschen Volkes. Bad Homburg

Caesar R (1987a) Kriegsfolgelasten. In: Staatslexikon, vol 3, 7th edn. Freiburg

Caesar R (1987b) Lastenausgleich. In: Staatslexikon, vol 3, 7th edn. Freiburg

Davis FDR (1986) The new deal years, 1933–1937. New York

Degener T (2005) Disability discrimination law: a global comparative approach. In: Lawson A, Gooding C (eds) Disability rights in Europe: from theory to practice. Oxford, pp 87–106

Demmel H (2003) Die Entwicklung und Bedeutung der öffentlich-rechtlichen Blindengeldleistung als Sozialleistung. Berlin

Ebsen I (1996) Schwerbehindertenrecht. In: von Maydell B, Ruland F (eds) Sozialrechtshandbuch, 2nd edn. Neuwied, pp 1353ff

Ecker W (1984) Sozialgerichtliche Rechtsfortbildung. In: Entwicklung des Sozialrechts. Aufgabe der Rechtsprechung. Cologne, pp 299ff

Eckert J (1947) Zur Neugestaltung der deutschen Sozialversicherung, 2nd edn. Munich

Eichenhofer E (1990) Recht der sozialen Sicherheit in den USA. Baden-Baden, pp 13ff

Federau F (1962) Der Zweite Weltkrieg — Seine Finanzierung in Deutschland. Tübingen

Finke H (1996) Sondersysteme der Sozialversicherung – Künstlersozialversicherung. In: von Maydell B, Ruland F (eds) Sozialrechtshandbuch, 2nd edn. Neuwied, pp 1109ff

Fischer E (1946) Die Neuordnung der Sozialversicherung. In: Arb.u. Sozialfürsorge, pp 232–235

Flierl H (1982) Freie und öffentliche Wohlfahrtspflege. Aufbau, Finanzierung, Geschichte, Verbände. Munich

Foitzik J (1999) Sowjetische Militäradministration in Deutschland (SMAD) 1945–1949. Struktur und Funktion, Berlin

Forsthoff E (1971) Der Staat der Industriegesellschaft. Munich, p 109
Frei N (1996) Vergangenheitspolitik. Die Anfänge der Bundesrepublik und die NS-Vergangenheit. Munich, in particular pp 69ff
Freiburg A (1977) Aufgaben, Organisation und personelle Probleme der Jugenhilfe in der DDR. Theorie und Praxis der sozialen Arbeit 3ff
Fuchs M (1996) Wohngeldrecht. In: von Maydell B, Ruland F (eds) Sozialrechtshandbuch, 2nd edn. Neuwied, pp 1421ff
Gallwas H-U (1975) Lastenausgleich. EvStL, 2nd edn. Stuttgart, p 1457
Garner C (1993) Der öffentliche Dienst in den 50er Jahren: Politische Weichenstellungen und ihre sozialgeschichtlichen Folgen. In: Schildt A, Sywottek A (eds) Modernisierung im Wiederaufbau. Die westdeutsche Gesellschaft der 50er Jahre. Bonn, pp 759–790 (769–775)
Giese D (1986) 25 Jahre Bundessozialhilfegesetz. Entstehung – Ziele – Entwicklung. ZfSH/SGB 249ff
Goschler C (1992) Wiedergutmachung. Westdeutschland und die Verfolgten des Nationalsozialismus 1945–1954. Munich
Goschler C (2005) Schuld und Schulden. Die Politik der Wiedergutmachung für NS-Verfolgte seit 1945. Göttingen
Gottschick H (1963) Öffentliche Fürsorge und Verwaltungsgerichtsbarkeit. Die Öffentliche Verwaltung 435–442
Gräfin von Bethusy-Huc V (1976) Das Sozialleistungssystem der Bundesrepublik Deutschland, 2nd edn. Tübingen
Günther F (2004) Denken vom Staat her. Die bundesdeutsche Staatsrechtslehre zwischen Dezision und Integration 1949–1970, phil. Diss. Munich
Hagedorn K (1982) Agrarsozialpolitik in der Bundesrepublik Deustchland. Kritik und Alternativmodelle zur Alterssicherung in der Landwirtschaft. Bonn
Hansen E, Heisig M, Leibfried S, Tennstedt F (1981) Seit über einem Jahrhundert.... Verschüttete Alternativen in der Sozialpolitik. Cologne
Hasenclever C (1978) Jugendhilfe und Jugendgesetzgebung seit 1900. Göttingen
Heimerich H (1946) Die Krise der deutschen Sozialversicherung. BB I/II:23
Heinemann-Knoch M, von Kardorff E (1989) Sozialpolitische Aspekte der Pflegebedürftigkeit. In: Riedmüller B, Rodenstein M (eds) Wie sicher ist die soziale Sicherung? Frankfurt, pp 182–209
Hendler R (1996) Organisation und Selbstverwaltung der Sozialversicherung. In: von Maydell B, Ruland F (eds) Sozialrechtshandbuch, 2nd edn. Neuwied, pp 207ff
Hentschel V (1983) Geschichte der deutschen Sozialpolitik 1880–1980. Soziale Sicherung und kollektives Arbeitsrecht, Frankfurt am Main
Herbst L, Goschler C (eds) (1989) Wiedergutmachung in der Bundesrepublik Deutschland. Munich
Herzog R (1987) Subsidiaritätsprinzip. EvStl., vol 2, 3rd edn. Stuttgart, column 3564–3571
Heyn W (1950) Die Grenzen der Sozialversicherung. RdA 417
Hockerts HG (1980a) Anton Storch (1892–1975). In: Aretz J, Morsey R, Rauschner A (eds) Zeitgeschichte in Lebensbildern, vol 4. Mainz, pp 250ff
Hockerts HG (1980b) Sozialpolitische Entscheidungen im Nachkriegsdeutschland. Alliierte und deutsche Sozialversicherungspolitik 1945 bis 1957. Stuttgart
Hockerts HG (2001) Wiedergutmachung in Deutschland. Eine historische Bilanz 1945–2000. In: Jahrhundertschuld – Jahrhundertsühne. Munich, pp 91–142
Hoffmann J (1974) Zur Geschichte des Jugenhilferechts in der DDR. RdJB 241ff
Hoffmann J (1981) Jugenhilfe in der DDR. Grundlagen, Funktionen und Strukturen. Munich
Hoffmann D (1996) Sozialpolitische Neuordnung in der SBZ/DDR. Der Umbau der Sozialversicherung 1945–1956. Munich
Hoppe W (1975) Neues Bundeskindergeldgesetz in Kraft getreten. BB 97
Igl G (1996) Pflegeversicherung. In: von Maydell B, Ruland F (eds) Sozialrechtshandbuch, 2nd edn. Neuwied, pp 1003ff

Irmak KH (2002) Der Sieche. Alte Menschen und die stationäre Altenhilfe in Deutschland, 1924–1961. Essen
Isensee J (1968) Subsidiaritätsprinzip und Verfassungsrecht. Eine Studie über das Regulativ des Verhältnisses von Staat und Gesellschaft, 2nd edn. Berlin (2001)
Isensee J (1988) Gemeinwohl und Staatsaufgaben im Verfassungsrecht. In: Handbuch des Staatsrechts, vol III, §57. Heidelberg
Jehle O (1954/1958) Fürsorgerecht, 2nd edn (1954), 3rd edn (1958). Munich
Jordan E, Münder J (eds) (1987) 65 Jahre Reichsjugendwohlfahrtsgesetz. Münster
Kaim-Caudle P (1979) Moving on from Beveridge. In: Zacher HF (ed) Bedingungen für die Entstehung und Entwicklung von Sozialversicherung. Berlin, pp 223–248
Kaiser H (1949) Das Verfahrensrecht in der Sozialversicherung der sowjetischen Besatzungszone Deutschlands. ZBl f. Sozialvers 141
Kaiser JH (1956/1978) Die Repräsentation organisierter Interessen. 2nd edn (1978). Berlin
Kannengießer W (1998) In eigener Verantwortung. Die berufsständischen Versorgungswerke und ihre Arbeitsgemeinschaft. St. Augustin, pp 114–128
Käss F (1959) HWSW VI. Tübingen, pp 528–532
Keese H (1950) Die öffentliche Fürsorge, 2nd edn. Stuttgart
Kiewel A (1990) Das System in der Gesundheitssicherung in der DDR. In: Die Krankenversicherung, pp 109–111
Kirchberger S (1986) Public-health policy in Germany, 1945–1949: continuity and new beginning. In: Light D, Schuller A (eds) The German experience. Cambridge
Klapper G (1987) Flüchtlinge und Vertriebene. EvStL, vol 1, 3rd edn. Stuttgart, pp 909–913
Knapp M (1981) Reconstruction and west-integration: the impact of the Marshall-plan on Germany. ZgStW 137:415ff
Knieps F (1996) Krankenversicherungsrecht. In: von Maydell B, Ruland F (eds) Sozialrechtshandbuch, 2nd edn. Neuwied, pp 703ff
Knieps F, Tophoven C (1990) Grundzüge des DDR-Gesundheitswesens. Zur Struktur der Leistungserbringung. Die Ortskrankenkasse 13:406–410
Köhler PA (1990) Entwicklungslinien der 100jährigen Geschichte der gesetzlichen Rentenversicherung. Die Zeit von 1891–1957. In: Ruland F (ed) Handbuch der gesetzlichen Rentenversicherung. Frankfurt am Main
Krieger E (1947) Die Sozialversicherungsgrundsätze in der Sowjetischen Besatzungszone Deutschlands. ZBl. f. Sozialvers 25–27
Kühne W, Wolff B et al (1953) Kommentar über die Gesetzgebung über den Lastenausgleich. Cologne
Kummer P (1996) Das sozialgerichtliche Verfahren. In: von Maydell B, Ruland F (eds) Sozialrechtshandbuch, 2nd edn. Neuwied, pp 603ff
Labisch A (1983) Die medizinsiche Grundversorgung der Deutschen Demokratischen Republik. Zeitschrift für Sozialreform 74–96 and 146–164
Leopold D (1999) Die Geschichte der sozialen Versicherung. Sankt Augustin
Lohmüller W (1949) Die volkspolitische Funktion der Rechtsprechung auf dem Gebiet der Sozialversicherung. ZBl f. Sozialvers 108 (110)
Maetzel WB (1963) Schwerpunkte des Wiedergutmachungsrechts. Die Öffentliche Verwaltung 449–454
Martzloff P (1946) Um die deutsche Sozialversicherung. Die Gegenwart No 10/11, p 37
Matthes H-C (1974) Einige Bemerkungen zum Gesetz über Konkursausfallgeld. BB 1351
Menkens H (1951) Die Berliner Sozialversicherung seit 1945. RdA 351ff
Metz H (1977) Reform des Gesundheitssystems. In: von Münch I (ed) Aktuelle Dokumente. Berlin
Mommsen W (1964) Deutsche Parteiprogramme der Gegenwart. Dt. Handbuch der Politik, vol 1, 2nd edn. Munich, p 591
Müller K (ed) (1978) Sozialrecht in Wissenschaft und Praxis : Festschrift für Horst Schieckel. Percha, p 5f
Münder J (1990) Das Jugendwohlfahrtsgesetz von 1922 "in Kraft getreten" 1953. RdJB 43

Muthesius H (1950) Reichsjugendwohlfahrtsgesetz. Stuttgart
Nahm P (1962/1967) Der Lastenausgleich. 2nd edn (1967). Stuttgart
Oeter F (1971) Der Ausgleich der Familienlasten. In: Külp B, Schreiber W (eds) Soziale Sicherheit. Cologne, pp 359ff
Ogus A (1979) Conditions in the formation and the development of social insurance: legal development and legal history. In: Zacher HF (ed) Bedingungen für die Entstehung und Entwicklung von Sozialversicherung. Berlin, pp 337–348
Ogus A (1981) Landesbericht Großbritannien. In: Köhler P, Zacher HF (eds) Ein Jahrhundert Sozialversicherung. Berlin
Orthbandt E (1980) Der Deutsche Verein in der Geschichte der deutschen Fürsorge 1880–1980. Frankfurt am Main
Peschke P (1962) Geschichte der deutschen Sozialversicherung. Der Kampf der unterdrückten Klassen um soziale Sicherung. Berlin-Treptow
Peters H (1973/1978) Die Geschichte der sozialen Versicherung, 3rd edn (1978). Bonn Bad Godesberg
Pirker T (1960) Die blinde Macht, vol 1. Munich
Posser D (1991) Anwalt im Kalten Krieg. Ein Stück deutscher Geschichte in politischen Prozessen 1951–1968. Munich
Prinz F (2000) Die Integration der Vertriebenen und Flüchtlinge in Bayern. Versuch einer Bilanz nach 55 Jahren (Haus der Bayer. Geschichte). Augsburg
Ramm T (1990) Jugendrecht. Munich
Rehkopf H (1994) Geschichte und Reformperspektiven der Ersatzkassen. In: Schulin B (ed) Handbuch des Sozialversicherungsrechts, vol 1. Krankenversicherungsrecht. Munich, pp 48ff (§2)
Reichel P (2001) Vergangenheitsbewältigung in Deutschland. Die Auseinandersetzung mit der NS-Diktatur von 1945 bis heute. Munich
Richardi R (1987) Mutterschutz. EvStl. vol I, 3rd edn. Stuttgart, pp 2188–2192
Richter I (1996) Ausbildungsförderung. In: von Maydell B, Ruland F (eds) Sozialrechtshandbuch, 2nd edn. Neuwied, pp 1469ff
Riedel C (1946) Die Struktur der neuen Sozialversicherung. In: Arb.u. Sozialfürsorge, pp 136f
Rinken A (1971) Das Öffentliche als verfassungstheoretisches Problem. Berlin
Rudloff W (1998) Öffentliche Fürsorge. In: Hockerts HG (ed) Drei Wege deutscher Sozialstaatlichkeit. Munich
Ruland F (1996) Rentenversicherung. In: von Maydell B, Ruland F (eds) Sozialrechtshandbuch, 2nd edn. Neuwied, pp 983–986
Ruland F (2003) Sozialrecht. In: Schmidt-Aßmann E (ed) Besonderes Verwaltungsrecht, 12th edn. Berlin, pp 779–882
Rungaldier U, Steindl H (eds) (1987) Handbuch zur betrieblichen Altersversorgung. Vienna
Sagi N (1981) Wiedergutmachung für Israel. Die deutschen Zahlungen und Leistungen. Stuttgart
Saint-Jours Y (1981) Landesbericht Frankreich. In: Köhler P, Zacher HF (eds) Ein Jahrhundert Sozialversicherung. Berlin
Schaefer KH (1978) Lastenausgleich – eine Bewährungsprobe des sozialen Rechtsstaats. In: Bachof O et al (eds) Verwaltungsrecht zwischen Freiheit, Teilhabe und Bindung. Festgabe aus Anlaß des 25jährigen Bestehens des Bundesverwaltungsgerichts. Munich, pp 551–568
Schellhorn W, Schellhorn H (2002) Das Bundessozialhilfegesetz, 16th edn. Neuwied
Scherpner H (1979) Geschichte der Jugendfürsorge, 2nd edn. Göttingen
Scheuner U (1954) Berufsständische Versorgungseinrichtungen und Grundgesetz. In: Rohrbeck W (ed) Aktuelle Probleme der Versicherungswirtschaft vom Standpunkt der Versicherungswissenschaft betrachtet. Berlin, pp 71–108
Scheuner U (1973) Die karitative Tätigkeiten der Kirchen im heutigen Sozialstaat. Verfassungsrechtliche und staatskirchenrechtliche Fragen. In: Essener Gespräche, vol 8, pp 43–71
Schieckel H (1946) Der derzeitige Stand der deutschen Sozialversicherung. DRZ 142
Schieckel H (1947a) Die Neuordnung der Sozialversicherung. DRZ 218f

Schieckel H (1947b) Gegenwartsprobleme der Sozialversicherung. Munich
Schieckel H (1949) Der gegenwärtige Stand der Reform der deutschen Sozialversicherung und ihre Aufgabe. RdA 129
Schieckel H (1975) Kindergeldgesetze. Percha
Schillinger R (1985) Der Entscheidungsprozeß beim Lastenausgleich 1945–1952. St. Katherinen
Schillinger R (1995) Der Lastenausgleich. In: Benz W (ed) Die Vertreibung der Deutschen aus dem Osten. Frankfurt, pp 231–243
Schlencker R-U (1994) Geschichte und Reformperspektiven der gesetzlichen Krankenkassen. In: Schulin B (ed) Handbuch des Sozialversicherungsrechts, vol 1. Krankenversicherungsrecht. Munich, pp 15ff
Schmidt MG (2001) Grundlagen der Deutschen Demokratischen Republik. In: Bundesministerium für Arbeit und Sozialordnung und Bundesarchiv (ed), Geschichte der Sozialpolitik in Deutschland seit 1945, vol 1, Grundlagen der Sozialpolitik. Baden-Baden
Schmidt MG (2012) Der deutsche Sozialstaat. Munich
Scholler H, Krause P (1978) Die Neukonzeption des Sozialhilferechts und die Situation blinder Menschen. Munich
Schönleiter W, Hennig W (1969) Kommentar. Berlin
Schreiber W (1955) Existenzsicherheit in der industriellen Gesellschaft. Cologne
Schröcker S (1963) Verfolgung und Widerstand. Grundgedanken der Rechtsprechung des Bundesverwaltungsgerichts zum Häftlingshilfegesetz. DÖV 455
Schubert W (2003) Familienlohn, Kinderbeihilfen und Familienstimmrecht (salaire familiale, allocations familiales et suffrage familiale) in Deutschland bis zur Zeit der frühen Bundesrepublik und in Frankreich seit dem 19. Jahrhundert. In: Eckert J (ed) Der praktische Nutzen der Rechtsgeschichte. Heidelberg, pp 497–535 (see pp 512ff about the German development in the 20th century)
Schulte B, Trenk-Hinterberger P (1986) Sozialhilfe. Eine Einführung, 2nd edn. Heidelberg
Schwarz W (1974–1986) Die Wiedergutmachung nationalsozialistischen Unrechts durch die Bundesrepublik. Munich
Sell S (ed) (2002) Armut als Herausforderung. Bestandsaufnhame und Perspektiven der Armutsforschung und Armutsberichterstattung (Schr. D. Gesellschaft für Sozialen Fortschritt, vol 23). Berlin
Singbartl H (1996) Das Erfolgsrezept der Eingliederungspolitik. Staatsbürger (Beilage der Bayer. Staatszeitung) No 12. Munich, pp 1–6
Sitzler, Curschmann, Heimerich, Polligkeit, Sauerborn (1946) Zur Neuordnung der Sozialversicherung, 47 Leitsätze. BB No 18:14ff
Sörgel W (1985) Konsensus und Interessen, 2nd edn. Opladen, p 201, pp 379f
Standfest E (1989) Selbstverwaltung in der Sozialversicherung: Mittel demokratischer Sozialpolitik? In: Riedmüller B, Rodenstein M (eds) Wie sicher ist die soziale Sicherung? Frankfurt, pp 165–181
Steinberg R (ed) (1985) Staat und Verbände. Zur Theorie der Interessenverbände in der Industriegesellschaft. Darmstadt
Stoldt E (1949) Selbstverantwortung und Selbstverwaltung in der Sozialversicherung. RdA 407ff
Stolleis M (1973) Sozialstaat und karitative Tätigkeit der Kirchen. ZevKR 18:376–404
Stolleis M (1978) Eltern- und Familienbildung als Aufgabe der Jugendhilfe. Stuttgart
Stolleis M (1979) Entstehung und Entwicklung des Bundessozialgerichts. In: Deutscher Sozialgerichtsverband (ed) 1979: Sozialrechtssprechung. Verantwortung für den sozialen Rechtsstaat. Festschrift zum 25-jährigen Bestehen des Bundessozialgerichts. Cologne Berlin
Stolleis M (1981) Entschädigung für Opfer von Gewalttaten – erste Konkretisierungen durch die Rechtsprechung. In: Winter G, Thieme W, Zacher HF (eds) Im Dienst des Sozialrechts, Festschrift für Georg Wannagat. Cologne, pp 579–598
Stolleis M (1988) Behinderte und nichtbehinderte Kinder im Kindergarten. Rechtsfragen zur gemeinsamen Erziehung. Stuttgart

Stolleis M (2003a) Besatzungsherrschaft und Wiederaufbau deutscher Staatlichkeit 1945–1949. In: Isensee J, Kirchhof P (eds) Handbuch des Staatsrechts, vol 1, §5, 3rd edn. Heidelberg, pp 269–313
Stolleis M (2003b) Geschichte des Sozialrechts in Deutschland. Stuttgart
Stolleis M, Schlamelcher G (1985) Zur Verfassungsmäßigkeit des §120 BSHG. NDV 65:309–317
Tennstedt F (1976) Sozialgeschichte der Sozialversicherung. In: Blohmke M, von Ferber C et al (eds) Handbuch der Sozialmedizin, vol 3. Stuttgart, pp 385–492
Thielicke H (1958) Theologische Ethik, vol II/2. Tübingen, p 358
Thust W, Trenk-Hinterberger P (1989) Recht der Behinderten. Eine systematische Darstellung für Praxis und Studium, 2nd edn. Weinheim
Tuschen KH, Quaas M (2001) Bundespflegesatzverordnung. 5th edn, Stuttgart
von Brünneck A (1978) Politische Justiz gegen Kommunisten in der Bundesrepublik Deutschland 1949–1968. Frankfurt
von Maydell B (1985) Hundert Jahre sozialgerichtliche Rechtsprechung. In: Verhandlungen des Deutschen Sozialrechtsverbandes, Dritter Sozialgerichtstag 1984. Wiesbaden, pp 29–52
von Maydell B, Pitschas R, Schulte B (eds) (2003) Behinderung in Asien und Europa inm Politik- und Rechtsvergleich. Mit einem Beitrag zu den USA. Baden-Baden
Wagner K-P (1996) Arbeitslosenversicherung/Arbeitsförderung. In: von Maydell B, Ruland F (eds) Sozialrechtshandbuch, 2nd edn. Neuwied, pp 119ff
Wannagat G (1965) Lehrbuch des Sozialversicherungsrechts, vol 1. Tübingen
Weber A (1990) Das Gesundheitswesen in der Deutschen Demokratischen Republik. In: Die Sozialversicherung, pp 97–101
Weber H (1993) Die DDR 1945–1990, 2nd edn. Munich
Wengst U (1988) Beamtentum zwischen Reform und Tradition. Beamtengesetzgebung in der Gründungsphase der Bundesrepublik Deutschland 1948–1953. Düsseldorf
Wickenhagen E (1980) Geschichte der gewerblichen Unfallversicherung. Wesen und Wirken der gewerblichen Berufsgenossenschaften. Munich
Wienand M, Neumann V, Brockmann I (1997) Fürsorge, Opladen
Wolff HJ, Bachof O (1978) Verwaltungsrecht III, 4th edn. Munich
Zacher H (1964) Freiheit und Gleichheit in der Wohlfahrtspflege. Cologne
Zacher HF (1970) Entschädigungssysteme. Die Öffentliche Verwaltung 6
Zacher HF (1972) Zur sozialen Programmatik der Bayerischen Verfassung. Festschrift zum 25jährigen Bestehen des BayVerfGH. Munich, pp 95ff
Zacher HF (1973) Das Vorhaben des Sozialgesetzbuchs. Percha
Zacher HF (1988) Sozialgesetzbuch. In: Staatslexikon, vol 8, 7th edn. Freiburg, pp 1296–1299
Zacher HF (2013) Social policy in the Federal Republic of Germany. Berlin
Zöllner D (1981) Ein Jahrhundert Sozialversicherung. Landesbericht Deutschland. In: Köhler P, Zacher HF (eds) Ein Jahrhundert Sozialversicherung. Berlin, pp 57ff
Zöllner D (1989) Agrarsozialpolitik. In: Blüm N, Zacher HF (eds) 40 Jahre Sozialstaat Bundesrepublik Deutschland. Baden-Baden, pp 413–422
Zweig RW (1987/2001) German Reperations and the Jewish World. 2nd edn (2001). London

VIII. Social Law as a Scientific Discipline

The history of social law and social policy in Germany, shaped by constant interaction between politics and legislation, administrative praxis and jurisprudence, is—if one uses the terminology in the strictest sense—barely older than a few decades. It was only in the second half of the twentieth century that what is today called "social law" amalgamated into a field that was perceived and labeled as a unified whole. As in most cases like this, it is hardly possible to say precisely when that happened. It is characteristic of scientific and intellectual history that the signals for changes in the collective perspective cluster in certain phases. A situation is perceived as unsatisfactory: a new word is sought, several coinages are tried out, and one prevails in a kind of semantic evolution. We are talking about the gradual creation of consensus in the "scientific community," when a collective term for diverse legal fields is found and makes it seem promising to offer relevant courses and textbooks. In Germany, this process took place between 1960 and 1980, evident from the titles of textbooks, the establishment of *Habilitation* for social law, and the creation of institutes and professional associations. In the Federal Republic, two men who were especially active in this development were Georg Wannagat, the former president of the Federal Social Court, and Hans F. Zacher, a public law jurist from Munich. The latter, in particular, provided crucial impulses for social law as the founding director of a Max Planck Institute for Foreign and International Social Law.[1] His 1961 *Habilitation* thesis of 1,200 pages for the first time grasped what had happened in the early Federal Republic in social policy and social law as a process of historical layering. The thesis established periods of social policy and placed the "formal constitutional right of social intervention" front and center. When it was published (Zacher 1980), its author reflected on when "social law" had emerged out of the various subfields (welfare/social assistance, youth welfare/youth aid, social insurance, labour promotion, care for war victims, housing

[1] Summary in Zacher (1993a, b). An impression of his influence is also provided by the Festschrift for his 70th birthday, *Verfassung, Theorie und Praxis des Sozialstaats* (Heidelberg, 1998), especially the appreciation by Ruland (1998), pp. XVII ff.

DOI 10.1007/978-3-642-38454-7_8,

allowance, child allowance and so on). A conceivable starting point for "social law" in the Federal Republic could have been the creation of a social judiciary (1953/1954),[2] but according to Zacher, the impetus was not enough to knit together the disparate elements. The essential impulses then came from schloarship, for example through the introduction of the overarching formula "social protection" (*soziale Sicherheit*) (Bogs 1989) and corresponding notion of a "right to social protection" (Wannagat 1989), and then from the new division of the matter into systems of preventive care, social compensation, and social equity (Zacher 1993a, b). But social policy itself pushed early on for a unifying terminology (Hockerts 1980a, b, pp. 223ff.). From the 1950s on, it had begun to learn to see the social benefits systems as a unity and to calculate its expenditures as a whole. Out of the antagonistic interests of the ministries of labour and finance, a "social budget" was created whose elements were increasingly understood as communicating channels. In 1960, the 43rd Conference of German Jurists in Munich for the first time dealt in a working committee on social law with the topic "The impact of constitutional norms on the law of social protection." After all, the codified summation of all materials already planned in the run-up to Adenauer's pension reform, the so-called "Social Code" (Rothenfels Memorandum, 1955), which was then programmatically mentioned in the SPD's Godesberg Program (1959) and in Willy Brandt's 1969 government declaration and was also officially put in motion, had already provided the most important impetus. Here, too, Hans F. Zacher played the decisive role (Zacher 1974–1979, 1999). Especially the formulation of the General Part gave a push toward conceptual thinking (Hauck 1973, 1975; Wannagat 1978). Since that time, textbooks and lecture courses converted to the title "social law" (von Maydell 1987). In the process, a tradition that deviated from that in other countries emerged in the sense that labour law in Germany (which tends to be shaped by private law) is no longer seen as part of (public law) social law (von Maydell 1994). In the present account for the period after 1945 this aspect has been left out,[3] of course more out of pragmatic considerations: after all, the functional connection between both areas of the law is obvious, and cannot be invalidated by pointing to the supposedly principled differences between private law and public law.

Nevertheless, what appears today as a uniform "social law" still bears the traces of historical layers. The General Part of the Social Code by no means bridges the differences between the subfields. The tax-financed systems and the insurance systems stand side by side, and the provision, compensation, and equalization systems have very divergent traditions. The stroll through history has shown that solidarity-driven aid by family units, neighborly help, and charitable institutions were part of the oldest layer. To this day, the non-profit and church-based social work bears traits that are reminiscent of the beginnings. Social assistance still possesses elements of early modern "*Policey*" (good public order). Classic social insurance was a product of the struggle against the "social question" of the late

[2] For the effect of judicature on social law see the essay in Wannagat (1984).

[3] Well worth reading is the overview by Kissel (1989).

nineteenth century. Youth welfare and youth care point to their origins around 1900. The insurance against unemployment was part of the crisis management of the late Weimar Republic. Nursing care insurance is a response of the late twentieth century to the aging process of society, namely a response with by now traditional means.

For the longest time, no one in Germany spoke of "social law" in the sense of a uniform sphere of the law shaped by its "social purpose." Rather, the term "social law" emerged initially in the natural law textbooks of the seventeenth and eighteenth centuries, where it described the law that emerged, following the conclusion of the (fictive) social contract, as the law of human socialization as such ("socialitas"), that is, positive law endorsed (again, fictively) by all. In the nineteenth century, beginning in 1850, a new variant emerged. From the perspective of an antagonism between the state and the individual, an effort was made to overcome the political tensions through the concept of autonomous, organic entities of society. This notion underlay Robert von Mohl's sketch of a "law of society," with the goal of creating an intermediate realm through self-regulating "interest crystallizations." Since the old order of hierarchical classes and its social subdivisions was broken, Liberals who recognized the danger of this vacuum were searching for something to take its place. The lifting of the ban on associations that was evident throughout Europe (England 1824, France 1864, Saxony 1861, North German Federation 1869, Austria 1870) pursued the political goal of making the "cooperative" self-organization of the workers' movement possible and in this way also be able to bind it. Franz Mehring's proposal that "comrade" (*Genosse*) be the form of address within the workers' movement is in line with this. The co-operative system arose and was regulated by law.[4] Jurisprudence responded to this by forming a "social law" in the sense of a "co-operative association theory." The legal historians (G. v. Beseler, O. v. Gierke) supplied the national-historical explanation that a special characteristic of the development of German law had always been its "social" character (Pfeiffer-Munz 1979). In 1864, Otto Bähr conceived of his "social law" as a law of human associations that overcame the dichotomy of public and private (Bähr 1864/1961). Hermann Roesler sought a "social law" and a corresponding "social administrative law" as the right of free societal associations (Roesler 1870, pp. 9ff.; Roesler 1871–1873). Otto von Gierke created not only a monumental legal history of associational thinking and acting, but also a theory of human associations that mediated between individualism and collectivism.[5] No doubt it was shaped by a romanticizing nostalgia, but it proved especially suitable for the post-liberal interventionist state of industrial society. The left-liberal reception of Gierke's work (H. Preuss, H. Sinzheimer) pointed directly to the political conceptions of a social labour, municipal, and state law of the

[4] "Gesetz betr. Die Erwerbs- und Wirtschaftsgenossenschaften vom 1. Mai 1889," RGBl. 1889, p. 55, "i.d.F. vom 20. Mai 1898," RGBl. 1898, p. 810.

[5] Gierke (I: 1868, II: 1873, III: 1881, IV: 1913; 1902). On this see Dilcher (1974/1975, pp. 319–365).

twentieth century. Both the path toward communal "*Daseinsvorsorge*" (services of general interest) as well as the proclamation of the social state on the constitutional level in the Federal Republic have their intellectual origins here.[6]

Below these theoretical currents, which responded with the concept of a "social law" to the challenges of the modern industrialized estate, the disparate subfields of modern social law continued to develop in their separate spheres. The divergences of scientific treatment, if not the complete absence of scientific efforts, still impeded a unitary perception. Typically, the spheres within administrative praxis grew and were initially ordered and described by practitioners as needed. With few exceptions, this holds true to this day for social aid, child and youth aid, even if an unmistakable professionalization of praxis is evident in certain subareas (disability law, youth aid). By contrast, the law of worker insurance (today social insurance) early on attracted the attention of the jurisprudence of public law and the simultaneously emerging labour law. The scientific treatment began in the late nineteenth century (Heinrich Rosin) and continued in the Weimar period (Fritz Stier-Somlo, Walter Kaskel, Erwin Jacobi, Lutz Richter) (Mikešić 2002). In the Federal Republic, as we have seen, it was then Walter Bogs, Georg Wannagat, Wilhelm Wertenbruch, and above all Hans F. Zacher who helped to win recognition for the "right of social protection" or "social law," which was increasingly conceived as a unity. The subsequent and today still active generation of social law jurists consists essentially of the students of these pioneers.

Paradoxically, the crisis of the "welfare state," which has taken on dramatic features in Germany, in recent years stimulated the scientific treatment of social law, and at the same time affected it in a negative way. While in the 1980s there was still a great readiness to support social law in legal education and to accept it into the canon of indispensable basic knowledge, by now it has dropped to the status of an "elective subject" again. The call for a reduction of "social" incidental wage costs that is heard in all industrialized states and the turn from a "social free market economy" to a neo-liberal global "market" are evidently also weakening the energy for a scientific penetration of social law, even though this energy is urgently needed precisely in this phase of structural change.

References

Adickes F, Beutler G (1903) Die sozialen Aufgaben der deutschen Städte. Leipzig

Bähr O (1864) Der Rechtsstaat. Eine publicistische Skizze (reprint 1961)

Bogs W (1989) Miterlebte Phasen bei der Planung und Verwirklichung des sozialen Rechtsstaats Bundesrepublik Deutschland. In: Blüm N, Zacher HF (eds) 40 Jahre Sozialstaat Bundesrepublik Deutschland. Baden-Baden, pp 305–314

[6] Isele (1963); on "municipal socialism" see Adickes and Beutler (1903), Lindemann (1906), Genzmer (1909).

Dilcher G (1974/1975) Genossenschaftstheorie und Sozialrecht: Ein "Juristensozialismus" Otto von Gierkes? Quaderni Fiorentini I:319–365
Genzmer S (1909) Der Gemeindesozialismus und seine gesetzlichen Schranken im preußischen Kommunalrecht. Archiv für Öffentliches Recht 25:161
Hauck K (1973) Der Allgemeine Teil und die Gesamtkodifikation des Sozialgesetzbuches. VSSR 330ff
Hauck K (1975) Die Kodifikation des Sozialrechts als Beitrag der sozialen Sicherung. In: Zacher HF (ed) Soziale Sicherung durch soziales Recht. Festschrift für Horst Peters zum 65. Geburtstag. Suttgart, pp 83ff
Hockerts HG (1980a) Anton Storch (1892–1975). In: Aretz J, Morsey R, Rauschner A (eds) Zeitgeschichte in Lebensbildern, vol 4. Mainz, pp 250ff
Hockerts HG (1980b) Sozialpolitische Entscheidungen im Nachkriegsdeutschland. Alliierte und deutsche Sozialversicherungspolitik 1945 bis 1957. Stuttgart
Isele HG (1963) Otto von Gierkes Bedeutung für das moderne Arbeitsrecht. Festschrift Maridakis II
Kissel OR (1989) Die Entwicklung des Arbeitsrecht als Teilstück des Sozialen Rechtsstaats. In: Blüm N, Zacher HF (eds) 40 Jahre Sozialstaat Bundesrepublik Deutschland. Baden-Baden, pp 459–477
Lindemann H (1906) Die deutsche Städteverwaltung, 2nd edn. Stuttgart
Mikešić I (2002) Sozialrecht als wissenschaftliche Disziplin. Die Anfänge 1918–1933. Tübingen
Pfeiffer-Munz S (1979) Soziales Recht ist deutsches Recht. Otto von Gierkes Theorie des sozialen Rechts. Zürich
Roesler H (1870) Sociales Recht und Privatrecht. Berliner Revue 9ff
Roesler H (1871–1873) Lehrbuch des deutschen Verwaltungsrechts, I: Das sociale Verwaltungsrecht, 2. Abt. Erlangen
Ruland F (ed) (1998) Verfassung, Theorie und Praxis des Sozialstaats, Festschrift für Hans Friedrich Zacher zum 70.Geburtstag. Heidelberg, (in particular pp XVII ff)
von Maydell B (1987) Untersuchung über die sozialrechtliche Ausbildung der Juristen an den Universitäten in der Bundesrepublik, insbesondere im Wahlfachstudium. Schriftenreihe des Deutschen Sozialgerichtsverbandes, vol XVI. pp 110ff
von Maydell B (1994) Zum Verhältnis von Arbeitsrecht und Sozialrecht. In: Heinze M, Söllner A (eds) Arbeitsrecht in der Bewährung. Festschrift für Otto Rudolf Kissel. Munich, pp 761–772
Wannagat G (1978) Die Bedeutung des Allgemeinen Teils des Sozialgesetzbuches für die Entwicklung des Sozialrechts. In: Müller K (ed) Sozialrecht in Wissenschaft und Praxis : Festschrift für Horst Schieckel. Percha, pp 347ff
Wannagat G (1984) (ed) Entwicklung des Sozialrechts - Aufgabe der Rechtsprechung. Cologne
Wannagat G (1989) Erinnerungen. In: Blüm N, Zacher HF (eds) 40 Jahre Sozialstaat Bundesrepublik Deutschland. Baden-Baden, pp 399–409
Zacher HF (1974–1979) Materialien zum Sozialgesetzbuch (Loseblatt). Percha
Zacher HF (1980) Sozialpolitik und Verfassung im ersten Jahrzehnt der Bundesrepublik Deutschland. Berlin
Zacher HF (1993a) Alterssicherung – Spiegel der gesellschaftlichen Entwicklung (1987). In: Zacher HF (ed) Abhandlungen zum Sozialrecht. Heidelberg, pp 498ff
Zacher HF (1993b) Grundfragen des internationalen Sozialrechts. In: Zacher HF (ed) Abhandlungen zum Sozialrecht. Heidelberg, p 433
Zacher HF (1999) Sozialgesetzbuch (Loseblatt). Starnberg

IX. Europeanization of Social Law

1. National Social Systems and International Cooperation

If one looks at social law as a historically evolved stock of norms, which arose along with industrial society and permanently stabilized the Western industrial societies in their present form, it makes sense to look for the shared European features where historically comparable problems had emerged. For that reason we should remind ourselves of the beginnings.

What the European states substantially shared was their experience of the Industrial Revolution between the middle of the eighteenth century and the middle of the twentieth century, at the latest—that is to say, the rupture with the agrarian way of life and the hierarchical society of groups that reshaped all conditions of life. The phase shifts were considerable, if one draws the arc from the most advanced industrialized countries of the nineteenth century to the remaining agrarian landscapes in southern and southeastern Europe. In the end, though, nobody could escape the revolutionary process. Everywhere the "social question" was emerging, everywhere the proletariat took shape. Political pressure from below and reformist answers from above led to a twofold reaction: there was communication across national borders and internally specific "welfare state arrangements" were created that were shaped by the respective national culture, including the legal culture (Kaufmann 1997). In the process types of social states emerged whose contours are today becoming increasingly blurred by the growing European integration.

Continental Central Europe places pronounced emphasis on the state's responsibility for social protection and offers broadly conceived social insurances for the core risks of life. The more liberally structured "civil societies" of England and Ireland tend to opt for a basic security and leave more to private provision. The Scandinavian model of a perfect welfare state with a strongly elaborated service sector—the standard for many years—still exists, but it has run up against its economic limits. In southern Europe, finally, a mixed model of elaborated old age security and weak basic provision has emerged. In the wake of the collapse of the

M. Stolleis, *History of Social Law in Germany*,
DOI 10.1007/978-3-642-38454-7_9, © Springer-Verlag Berlin Heidelberg 2014

"Eastern bloc," the countries of east-central and eastern Europe are busy restructuring their previous systems and are being intensively advised during this process.[1]

To begin with, however, a look back at international communication: since the early nineteenth century, thoughts had been given to how one could implement the necessary protective measures for workers while at the same time avoiding competitive disadvantages. Restrictions were to be in place especially for working women and children, but in addition also limits on working hours, bans on materials hazardous to health, protective equipment on machinery, and much more. Since every measure incurred costs, international agreements were soon propagated to remove the competitive pressure to that extent. The British industrialist Robert Owen was the first, in 1818, who sketched out an international social policy in memoranda to the European governments. Similarly, Adolphe Jérome Blanqui spoke out for international conventions in 1838.[2] In the last third of the nineteenth century, it was German *Kathedersozialisten* ("socialists in the academic chair," Georg Adler, Lujo Brentano), as well as social democracy and the unions who worked in the same direction.

The transition to praxis was carried out by international professional associations, such as the 1884 Glass Workers, followed by others, who then merged in the Amsterdam International. Beginning in 1881, the Swiss Federal Council tried to encourage international conferences, in addition to which there were French and German efforts. In 1881, Switzerland made another attempt, but then stepped back when the German emperor, Wilhelm II, took the initiative and summoned the Berlin International Workers' Protection Conference in March of 1890. An International Congress for Social Policy followed in 1897 in Zurich. At the same time, preparations were under way in Brussels for an International Association for Statutory Worker's Protection, which came into being in Paris in 1900. It maintained an International Labour Office in Basel. Its commissions dealt with child labour, commercial toxins, night work by young people, the maximum work day, outwork, and the insurance system (Lass 1910). To that extent one can speak of an Europeanization of labour and social law already around 1900.

The successes of these efforts were reflected in the Berne International Conventions of 1905/1906. They concerned the prohibition against night work by women in industry and the ban on white phosphorus for matches. Another Convention was being prepared when the World War broke out. Since by now a number of bilateral agreements on workers' protection existed,[3] which, incidentally, were continued by the Allies (conferences in Leeds 1916, Berne 1917), there were

[1] Gesellschaft für Versicherungswissenschaft und -gestaltung e.V. (GVG), ed., *Sozialpolitische Beratung in Osteuropa* (Berlin, 2003).

[2] Blanqui (1838, 2 vols.). Not to be confused with his brother, the radical socialist Louis A. Blanqui (1805–1881).

[3] For example, the agreement between France and Italy of 1904, concerning the reciprocity on savings accounts, workers' protection, and insurance contributions.

enough points of connection to mark a new prelude for international labour and social policy in the Treaty of Versailles of 1919. A position paper,[4] prepared by an assembly of unionists in Berne, entered into the peace negotiations and eventually became Part XIII of the Versailles Treaty (Articles 387–426). Article 427 then gave rise to the International Labour Organisation (ILO), which was constituted in Washington in November 1919.[5] Its activities during the Weimar Republic and under National Socialism following Germany's withdrawal from the League of Nations (1935) can be left aside here. In any case, when the creation of European institutions were contemplated after World War II, there had already been about 50 years of joint efforts to improve conditions in the workplace and the social protection of those in the workforce.

2. European Law and the Emerging European Constitution

Today's European Union arose over decades in a tentative political process pursued by the nations of Western Europe. This process reflects the gradual overcoming of nationalisms, made possible by the traumatic experiences of two World Wars, as well as the realization that only a united Europe would still have a voice within the dualism of the Cold War.[6] Countless groups and initiatives, whose roots for the most part reach into the period after 1919, propagated this task. Most urgent, but also politically the easiest to communicate, was economic cooperation. In response, the Organization for Economic Cooperation and Development (OECD) was created in 1948, the Council of Europe in 1949, the European Convention on Human Rights (ECHR) in 1950, the European Coal and Steel Community (*Montanunion*) in 1951, the planned but failed European Defense Community in 1952, the European Atomic Energy Community in 1957, and likewise in 1957 the European Economic Community, which in a sense completed the first push toward integration.[7] The latter was gradually expanded (1973, 1981, 1986, 1995, 2002) through the addition of numerous states and rebuilt, also gradually, into a political entity all its own. At its core, though, it was set up to create a free flow of goods and capital, freedom of movement for workers, the freedom of the self-employed to establish themselves, and the freedom to provide services.

---

[4] Concerning vocational education, limitations on working hours for young people and women, maternity protection, wage equality for men and women doing the same work, the eight-hour day, job placement, insurance for all.

[5] See for example Fehlinger (1924), Ritzmann (1925). On the term "social policy" that emerged at the time see von Wiese (1921), Günther (1922).

[6] Winston Churchill's Zurich speech of September 19, 1949, in which he spoke about the need to "re-create the European family," is seen as an essential trigger.

[7] "Vertrag zur Gründung der Europäischen Wirtschaftsgemeinschaft vom 25. März 1957", BGBl. II, p. 766.

So far no comparable integration process has taken place in social policy. To be sure, from a European Social Charter (1961), to a Council Decision about an Action Program in Social Policy (1974), a Community Charter on the Fundamental Social Rights of Workers (1989), to the political milestones of the treaties of Maastricht (1992) and Amsterdam (1997), a remarkable direct and indirect alignment processes of the national systems of social law did take place,[8] but in the end the systems remained under national control.

As far as the alignment processes are concerned, which have been effective all the same, today the principle of equal pay for men and women for equal work is not only codified (Art. 141 European Community Treaty [ECT]), but is also enforced by the European Court of Justice (ECJ). Likewise, parallel to the fundamental principle of the free movement of workers, the transferability of entitlements to benefits under social law has been settled (Art. 42 ECT). Worker protection law has also been largely harmonized (Art. 138 ECT). What is more, the principles of the Social Charter (1961) and the Community Charter of the Basic Social Rights of Workers (1989) have been integrated into today's treaty law of the European Union and in this way can serve as the target for future work and an interpretive aid for the ECJ.[9] Through the permanent law-making activity of the European institutions, and specifically through the adjudication of the ECJ, the "basic social rights" of freedom of movement, equal treatment, and the prohibition against discrimination (also with respect to social and tax law), rights of access to education and vocation, and the social protection of migrant workers have been secured in multifarious ways. For example, it was decided that glasses purchased abroad or orthodontic treatment performed in another country had to be reimbursed by the national health insurance fund. Monetary benefits from the German nursing care insurance must also be paid to entitled individuals living outside the country.[10] Without a doubt, problems will arise in this area in the future, since benefit standards vary in the member countries and will diverge even more following the expansion of the European Union (Schulte 2001, pp. 74ff.). This could give rise to individuals flocking to the better services and material benefits, the better hospitals and nursing care facilities. The benefits systems would have to protect themselves anew through regulations that limit access, but those would clash with the principle of freedom of movement (Schulte and Barwig 1999).

Notwithstanding these difficulties, the political and economic dynamic of an enlarged Europe will tend to push for a dismantling of the differences between the "national welfare state arrangements." The chosen path to achieving this is not the sovereign establishment of European law; instead, efforts are made to reduce,

---

[8] Best overview in Berié (1993).

[9] A comprehensive account in Schulte (1998, 2001); Bundesministerium für Arbeit und Sozialordnung, Max-Planck-Institut für ausländisches und internationales Sozialrecht, Akademie der Diözese Rottenburg Stuttgart, ed., Soziale Grundrechte in der Europäischen Union (Baden-Baden 2000/2001).

[10] Details in Schulte (1998, pp. 48ff.). Further discussion in Fuchs (2002).

through "open cooperation," at least the disadvantages for migrant workers and to ease the tensions between the national systems, since the existence of excessively large differences cannot be in anyone's interest (Haverkate and Huster 1999; Eichenhofer 2003). A uniform economic zone with an ever broader intra-European mobility of workers will entail, with a certain inevitability, also the harmonization of social protection, because the social and political costs of inequality are too high on both sides. Economic and social security are today inextricably intertwined. Freedom of movement and competition cannot be narrowed down to an economic perspective. Economic prosperity without a base of social protection leads to fissures in society. The modern European social state, however much it may raise the costs of labour by international standards, is not an impediment to a successful economy, but in a political and economic sense its indispensable basis and precondition. The discussion over the "costs of the social state" often obscure the fundamental realization that social transfers have a redistributive effect, secure the basic livelihood of the population, and spare the political system crises that could become dangerous to the democratic principle.

It is likely that in the future this process of alignment will be supported by European constitutional law more strongly than hitherto. The planned European constitution will contain a separate section about basic social rights. Its elements have been ready ever since the European Convention on Human Rights in 1950 (Articles 2–13 EConvHR; 136–145 ECT). The Commission Report of 1999, drafted under the leadership of Spiros Simitis, enumerates these rights.[11] In opposition to this trend and the activities connected with it, it has always been argued that a European constitution without a corresponding "people," without a common political public, and without a transnational party system is like a house without a roof. But this metaphor is misleading, especially from a historical perspective. After all, constitutions are often texts that are legally and political ahead of their time and pave the way for a consciousness that is tentatively emerging. This makes it possible for norm and reality to approximate and pervade each other. In this case, a politics that exerts a genuine shaping effect instead of merely following opinion polls has the task of spelling out the clear long-term advantages of harmonization over against short-term difficulties.

References

Berié H (1993) Europäische Sozialpolitik. Von Messina bis Maastricht. In: Kleinhenz G (ed) Soziale integration in Europa I. Berlin, 31 ss

Blanqui AJ (1838) Histoire de l'économie politique en Europe, 2 vols. Paris

Eichenhofer E (2003) Sozialrecht der Europäischen Union, 2nd edn. Berlin

Fehlinger H (1924) Die internationale Arbeitsorganisation und ihre Ergebnisse. Berlin

[11] "'Affirming Fundamental Rights in the European Union: Time to Act', Report of the Expert Group on Fundamental Rights, President: Spiros Simitis," Brussels, February 1999.

Fuchs M (2002) Free movement of services and social security – Quo Vadis? European Law Journal 8:536–555
Günther A (1922) Theorie der Sozialpolitik. Berlin und Leipzig
Haverkate G, Huster S (1999) Europäisches Sozialrecht. Baden-Baden
Kaufmann FX (1997) Herausforderungen des Sozialstaates. Frankfurt am Main
Lass L (1910) Die Staatsverträge auf dem Gebiete der sozialen Versicherung. Jahrbuch des Öffentlichen Rechts IV:268–293
Ritzmann F (1925) Internationale Sozialpolitik, ihre geschichtliche Entwicklung und ihr gegenwärtiger Stand. Mannheim
Schulte B (1998) Europäische Sozialpolitik und die Zukunft des Sozialstaats in Europa. Bonn
Schulte B (2001) EG-rechtliche Rahmenbedingungen für nationale Sozialpolitik. In: Schmähl W (ed) Möglichkeiten und Grenzen einer nationalen Sozialpolitik in der Europäischen Union. Berlin, pp 9–92
Schulte B, Barwig K (eds) (1999) Freizügigkeit und Soziale Sicherheit. Die Durchführung der Verordnung (EWG) No 1408/71 über die soziale Sicherheit der Wanderarbeitnehmer in Deutschland. Baden-Baden
von Wiese L (1921) Einführung in die Sozialpolitik, 2nd edn. Leipzig

X. Long Term Perspectives for Social Protection

The frequently asked question of what we can learn from history in general, and from the history of social protection, in particular, leads to two contradictory answers: (1) there is nothing to be learned, because history never repeats itself and because no normative statements can be extracted from descriptive statements. (2) All that is ever learned, and that includes what is wrong, is learned from "history," namely from individual and collective experiences: for we know only what is behind us, but not what is ahead of us. In this sense, typical constellations and experiences can surely be bundled into some kinds of theses. What can be inferred from them bears all the uncertainties that are characteristic of forecasts. Moreover, experiences must be assessed—that is, in the final analysis societies decide, on the basis of the normative objectives dominant within them, which forms and benefits of social protection they want and which they reject.

1. Changing Societies and Social Protection

A study of the historical processes to protect humans against the typical social risks attests to a direct dependency of this protection on the particular forms in which societies are constituted. Certain social forms give rise to specific protections, to care—sometimes good, sometimes not so good—for children and the elderly, the sick and disabled, the poor, and the victims of accidents, each group in its own particular way, or occasionally even to exclusions of these groups. At all times a de facto balance emerges between way of life, resources, and the specific needs of a society's conditions of life, a balance that must be achieved if a society wants to attain a certain measure of stability and staying power.

In this way, a vast array of forms of protection arose, from the family and clan to life communities and communities of risk bearers, from there to the formation of special "social" professions and protective institutions. In the process, the simplicity or complexity of these forms of protection corresponds necessarily to that of the underlying social structure. Nomads protect themselves against risks differently

M. Stolleis, *History of Social Law in Germany*,
DOI 10.1007/978-3-642-38454-7_10, © Springer-Verlag Berlin Heidelberg 2014

from farmers, agrarian societies differently from technological industrial worlds with a division of labour. Poor and affluent societies likewise differ in their social problems and solution strategies. The crucial factors are climate and other geographical conditions, the size of the national product, socio-political structures, level of education, gender relations, the degree to which processes of exchange are monetized, and much more.

Within this tableau, the social protection systems of the European-American industrial states of the twentieth century assume a singular historical position. They are atypical, not only compared to other countries of the world today, but even more so across historical time. Never before have there been such large institutional apparatuses for redistribution, never before was so much redistributed. Unparalleled is the concentration of professionals working within the social sector. Nowhere else are as many social benefits offered and consumed as in the wealthy countries of the northern hemisphere, while about one third of humanity currently lives on less than a dollar a day.

2. Slowness in Responding to Economic Crisis

If one derives from the historical development of human societies the "law" that simpler formations are replaced by more complex one, because greater complexity offers greater evolutionary advantages,[1] by necessity this would also have consequences for the ancillary systems of social protection. One would then have to assume that a consistently pursued division of labour and accumulation of added value could also create more maneuvering room for the distribution of surpluses. Greater redistribution would then mean a higher degree of social pacification and internal stability.

At first glance, this perspective draws its persuasive force from the experiences of four to five generations in highly industrialized European societies. The temporal and regional field of observation is thus fairly narrow, which by itself weakens the validity of the thesis. Moreover, the success of the way of life that has been attained in industrial societies is by no means permanently secured. It is a historical experiment, just as other cultures of world history were experiments. The underlying political, economic, and ecological conditions of the model are subject to their own inherent dynamic and are not programmed for an optimum. In other words, breakdowns are also possible, already because questions of resources and the ecological framework remain open. In addition, the suspicion persists that an overly optimistic successful model of social protection in industrial societies may have absorbed elements of an idealistic developmental model, similar to the evolutionistic theories of the nineteenth century, which posited necessary "stages" from the bottom to the top (wildness–barbarity–civilization). Applied to social

[1] On the unspoken preconditions of this presumed upward movement see Kößler (1998).

protection, a parallel, graduated model could be developed: from the self-sufficiency of small units to mutually supportive solutions among those joined by a common profession or shared fate, to the solidarity of all within a national or even European framework; from smaller to ever larger institutions, because the participation of potentially "all" shrinks the financial risks; from the performance of all functions by one authority to the gradual development of specialized knowledge, and toward ever growing specialization and professionalization.

Yet the history of science and scholarship teaches us that one should keep one's critical faculties especially alert when constructing such models. The belief in a fundamentally upward moving development of human socialization has become brittle, to say the least. More skeptical spirits dismiss it altogether. The arrogance of a Eurocentric world view was profoundly shaken not least by two World Wars. And the classification of a "First, Second, and Third World"—which attests to a certain condescension because it implies stages of civilization—is losing its meaning. By now, all of these worlds are so closely intertwined that they should be seen instead as reciprocally interacting subsystems of one unified world. It is apparent that the wealthy countries are still able to hang on to their wealth and social protections at this time, but that they are also being threatened by ageing societies and the economic competition from more active and demographically younger regions. At the same time, it is becoming clear that the wealth of the northern hemisphere is accompanied by growing poverty, rising illiteracy, and rapidly increasing population density in the southern hemisphere. A secure way that might lead to a more equal distribution of wealth, energy reserves, the utilization of common good, and social protection is not in sight at the moment. After all, there are crucial questions that pertain to immanent structural problems of the safety systems: is it not possible that reducing the financial risks by shifting it onto potentially everyone's shoulders might at the same time increase the political risks, because even the smallest shocks to social protections could affect the people as a whole? Might not the shifting of life's risks onto external institutions, which has been practiced for generations, cause the capacity for solidarity in the smallest units to atrophy? What are the repercussions on the employment behavior of entire societies from the fact that the comprehensive safety systems permanently claim a high percentage of the national product?

These two questions also indicate where the primary problem of social protection seems to lie at this time, namely the slowness in responding to economic crisis. The institutional arrangements and the jobs that go with them, the capital that has been committed, and above all the expectations of the recipients of benefits resists quick changes. As a result, if the balance of political power between the government and opposition is fairly even, stalemates occur easily. To be sure, this "path dependency" is, on the one hand, an advantage: precisely because the safety system does not mirror every economic slump in size and timing, it is able to fulfill a bridge function and support the majority of the population until the next economic upswing. On the other hand, however, in this very cumbersomeness lies the problem that the system, conceived in good times, devours the last reserves in extended bad times and stands in the way of the upswing, because it perpetuates an excessively high level of entitlement. The latter is not a phenomenon that is necessarily linked with social insurance. It is the general weakness of wealthy democratic societies that they are evidently able to find their way back to a lower standard of living through voluntary self-regulation only with great difficulty.

3. The German Model

In spite of all the skepticism about teasing out long-term trends from the historical material, the concentration on smaller and more concretely defined fields of observation seems the path with the greatest promise of success. Although this increases the falsifiability within a global framework, it also boosts the certainty about the observed terrain itself. Statements can be verified against the historical material and national statistics. In this sense one can say the following about the German development:

a) The forms of social protection typical of the present come from various historical layers. Today, the oldest and the most modern forms still exist side by side. The oldest include familial and neighborly aid and municipal poor relief, which already presupposes structures of a smaller community and a certain specialization of tasks. Beginning in the Middle Ages, we then see special institutional forms of the church, such as the nursing orders with their hospitals and a wealth of other charitable establishments. These, too, have existed down to the present. Also in the Middle Ages, mutual-aid arrangements specific to certain professions became visible, in part for situations of special risk (sailors, miners), in part on the basis of shared interests in manifold co-operative, guild-like organizations. Those did not vanish, but they were merged into the institutions of social protection that emerged out of them. In addition, "social" equalization mechanisms developed for cases where the state committed an injustice, failed, or inflicted harm, the more state and society became visible as separate, distinguishable entities, and it was possible to hold the state (or at least the treasury) accountable for the material consequences of its actions. These institutes and institutions, too, have continued to exist into the present since the early modern period in the form of welfare law (*Versorgungsrecht*). Finally, the social question of the industrial age gradually gave rise to social insurances, some of which were created independently, some under the incorporation of older institutions.[2]

   Over the course of the twentieth century, all of these safety systems were woven together into a dense social network of the welfare state, both through inherent growth—parallel to the rise in the national product and population growth—and through external pressures in the wake of wars and inflation. By now there are countless internal interactions of this historically evolved and

[2] Under the aspect of modernization, see the study of Alber (1987).

overall "unsystematic system," if one may formulate this paradox in this way. Accordingly, what is lost is the understanding that the basic ideas behind the various elements come from entirely disparate historical stages and that their underlying principles are different. The longer the interweaving that has long since begun persists and intensifies, the more difficult it becomes to legitimize separate institutions with their own specific traditions, financing, and clientele. The all-embracing social state, which is also politically guided in a unitary way, tends toward the elimination of peculiarities, no matter how much those who profit from them may protest. Since civil service pensions, the care for war victims, contribution-financed benefits, material aids and services are all financed out of the gross domestic product, the desire keeps asserting itself to eliminate the organizational differentiation on the income side, at least as long as it is still possible to make sufficient differentiations on the spending side according to principles of justice. Politics, too, which shifts funds—"contrary to the system"—from flourishing subsystems to ailing subsystems, contributes in its way to a leveling of the various sources of income.

b) A second long-term observation concerns the growing externalization of the protections. What was originally handled in the spatially and physically tangible proximity of the social unit of the "house," is gradually shifting outside. The more the way of life becomes concentrated in urban centers, and the more the individual moves within varied social roles, the more the risks of life can be managed in specialized institutions and with the help of specialists. Cases of serious illness are moved to the "hospital" or to houses outside the city gates. All manner of healthcare and auxiliary professions emerge. At the same time, the externality of the economic protection develops through the shift of the risk of the individual or his family to larger communities of solidarity. And those in turn continue to grow, the more the experience is made that larger communities of solidarity are also financially more resilient.

At the end of this development we then find the modern phenomenon that hardly a single existential life risk is truly experienced and suffered within the sphere of one's own life. In most cases, birth and death have been banished from the domestic sphere and are experienced in specialized clinics. Death itself is mostly hidden from the family. But all other more difficult problems are also "outsourced" by the nuclear family arranged around two earners. Neither the size of the average apartment nor the modern rhythm of work allows for sustained attention to "problem cases." The disabled are cared for in specialized pedagogical institutions and homes, those in need of care in nursing homes, and the elderly in retirement homes. The same holds for drug addicts, problem children, and other individuals and groups who do not conform to the average pattern of readiness to work and orientation toward social norms. Society unburdens itself in this way by raising the financial means and assigning the social problems to changing groups of specialists. It unburdens itself organizationally, because in this way the "normal" processes remain intact. But it also unburdens itself psychologically: for quite some time now, psychologists and sociologists have observed that human suffering, agonizing dying, and death itself are seen as disturbances of a happy life, to which humans believe they are entitled. In the face of the hopes, fed by modern medicine, that in principle all diseases are curable, death no longer appears as the natural end to life, but an aggravating failure of medical care not yet perfected. Advertising, too, which tends to work with positively tinted, up-beat images, contributes to the notion that humans are usually beautiful, healthy, and prosperous. That is why poverty and its attendant symptoms are also not only semantically concealed, but are even driven out of the elegant shopping centers of cities (Terwiesche 1997), very much in the spirit of early modern "*Policey*" (good public policy).

c) The material risks of illness, accident, disability, old age, and unemployment were transferred to external social insurances between 1883 and 1927; in 1994, nursing care insurance was added as a latecomer. These social insurances have moved a long way from the old institutions of solidarity among those sharing dangers or a profession; the sheer size and complexity, the compulsory character, the state guidance of burdens and benefits, the subsidies from tax revenue, the social "self-governance" largely emptied of real participation of the insured confirm all the theorems of modern organizational sociology: distancing and bureaucratization, the inherent dynamic of apparatuses, and feelings of outside control among those affected.

Of course, the widely attestable manifestations of the externalization of risks through the shift to teams of specialists and institutions should not be accompanied to quickly with obvious tones of cultural criticism. Externalization also means a boost in professionalism and a gain in freedom for the individual. The system of social protection, which has become so complex and efficient in the course of history, allows for top-level medical care and a density of care that would have seemed entirely unthinkable to earlier periods. The direct connection between the construction of the large protection systems, on the one hand, and the densification of medical and social professions and relevant institutions, on the other hand, is obvious. The more productive these systems became, the more they tie up material resources and human energies. Anyone who had to submit to them, voluntarily or because of compulsory insurance, relinquished freedoms, but in return he or she also gained "freedom from fear."

This meant simultaneously an unburdening of the family, which developed from the extended family—which was also a social network—to a nuclear family, and currently seems to be dissolving into even smaller units (temporary partnerships, single parents, one-person households). The individual was released into freedom, "set free" within an ambivalent system. Thanks to the externalized and monetized aid systems, the individual could free himself from the helping assistance of one's closer surroundings and exist in self-chosen independence. For many elderly, who do not wish to be a "burden" on their children, today's social protections means real freedom. In the same way, today the younger generation can decide much more freely than before whether to stay within the family unit or leave it. The same holds true for women, who have gradually freed themselves from dependence on a "breadwinner," especially through their own professional training and employment, and through the attendant transformation of an accessory into an independent social protection.

Thus, gains and losses stand side by side. As a gain—notwithstanding all conceivable divergences on questions of valuation—one can regard the growth in personal freedom and the qualitative and quantitative growth in the network that has been spun against the typical risks of life. For countless people, today's social protection means freedom from fear of hunger and cold, illness, the struggle against daily survival, but especially also freedom from personal dependencies. The average life expectancy has grown by more than a generation over the last 100 years (1891: men 37.1, women 40.2; 1996: men 73.7, women 80.0), and it continues to rise. For this kind of dignified life into old age, people are evidently willing to contribute a substantial portion of their income. However, as a loss they simultaneously experience the feeling of being at the mercy of anonymous bureaucracies, the phenomena of alienation in external institutions, and the monetization of human contact.

4. Social Protection and the Legitimation of Democracy

Finally, the creation of the large social protection systems over the course of the last century has had repercussions on politics. This phenomenon must be distinguished from the always present external motivation from social policy itself. It goes without saying that the first state initiatives to improve worker protection, the insurance fund system, or liability in cases of workplace accidents were "politically" motivated. And that is even more true for the targeted establishment of social insurances. However, repercussions of this now large complex on the other areas of politics have been evident only when social budgets and the bureaucracies administering them took on a certain weightiness. This is obvious when it comes to the commitment of formerly inconceivable sums in the area of social benefits. It becomes equally clear in the personnel expansion of the sector of public social services, in the interweaving of state and non-state institutions, and in the now established collective—if sometime diffuse—conviction of all citizens that the state is in principle "responsible" for the areas of health care and old-age provision, the labour market, basic provision, and concern for specific risk groups. The expectations connected with this guide politics.

Externally, this is evident not only in the multifarious institutions of the "structured system," in their budgetary funding and the number of personnel employed there, but also in the creation of the modern association system. It has found one of its essential areas of action in the "social," especially if one includes the shaping of labour and economic conditions by associations of employers and workers. The mass society of the twentieth century emerged out of the society of the nineteenth century, which still bore traces of the division into estates in the eighteenth century. Relevant groups that can afford not to work at all, no longer exist. The initially still existing differences between blue collar and white collar workers are been ground away by the pressure of the maxim of equality, much like the freedom of the self-employed. In the end the latter were incorporated—voluntarily or by legal compulsion—into the systems that were gradually expanding into a "national insurance," or at least into the more comfortable professional provisioning systems. This means that the vast majority of all citizens, who confer the foundation of legitimacy on politics with their vote, are simultaneously also bearers and beneficiaries of social protections. In turn the latter, in keeping with their basic construction, depend on the existence of "work," or, as far as the supplemental state subsidies are concerned, on a tax system that siphons of societal productivity.

In other words: the citizen, the contribution payer, and the benefit recipient are three sides of the same person. The citizen and the contribution payer respond to the political signals with the ballot, the contribution payer can, if the burdens become too oppressive, give a nod to the citizen as worker, and also seek to evade the burdens more of less illegally, for example in the shadow economy. Finally, the benefit recipient, as we know from experience, does not exactly show solidarity in his actions; instead, as a "homo oeconomicus" he strives to obtain as many benefits as possible or the largest possible benefits. For all three, the organization of shared interests—whether in parties or associations—offers itself as a way of enhancing one's ability to push through one's interest. This kind of organization succeeds the better, the more socially recognized the interests are. It fails in the end when only pure poverty constitutes the only shared element. Experience has taught us that associations of social aid recipients, for example, have little capacity for "engaging in conflict." That is why organizations of representative advocacy, citizens' initiatives, or clearing offices of interest mediation—like the "German Association for Public and Private Welfare"—have emerged in that area (Münsterberg 1896; Orthbandt 1980).

However the question over the representation of the various interests and the organization in the struggle over fixing and distributing the social expenditure ratio may be decided, the "big politics" of the western industrialized states must take this into account. Over the course of the historical development, it has become dependent on the existence of work and the social protection accompanying and supporting it. Parliamentary decisions and corrective court decisions are interlocking this sensitive complex most closely with all other spheres of politics. Since the loyalty of the masses depends crucially on the functioning of social protection, disturbances there have an immediate effect on the other areas. All western parliamentary systems operate in this way and use the balancing pole of legislation not only to bring "equality" and "justice" into harmony, but also to convey the sense that they are doing so to the trinity that is the citizen, contribution payer, and benefit recipient.

However, this is not yet a full accounting of the historically demonstrable repercussions of the social protection systems on politics. They are found not only in the ambivalence of greater personal freedom, an extended life expectancy, and high-quality professional care, on the one hand, and a narrowing of political maneuvering room, on the other. In fact, social protection has reshaped the entire material transfer of the western industrialized states. By way of transfer benefits, society today finances the health care system and the old-age provision of pensioners for a full generation longer. This transfer, generated by the higher productivity of labour multiplied many times over by machines and the productivity growths in other countries, forms an important factor in the consolidation of purchasing power. Under democratic premises, this factor is nearly immobile: its rise can probably be gently slowed, but it cannot be truly reduced, especially in Germany, which continues to remember the political consequence of the austerity pursued by Brüning and Papen in the early 1930s. In economic terms, alongside the well-known complaint about the excessive incidental wage costs, one must therefore also bear in mind that social benefits have an economic and internal political stabilizing effect. Historical experience tells us that free-market systems do well by redistributing a relatively large share of the wealth that is generated. They preserve purchasing power, moderate domestic political tensions, and dampen economic fluctuations (Huf 1998). That is true not only within a given nation, but also in the relationship between rich and poor states within a federation of states and globally. If the French Revolution proclaimed that "[a]ny society in which the guarantee of the rights is not secured or the separation of powers not determined has no constitution at all,"[3] for the twentieth and twenty-first centuries one can say that a state under the conditions of industrial society cannot exist without social protections—a statement that, incidentally, seems to apply also to the dictatorships of the twentieth century.

To the stable social protections corresponds the equally stable expectations of their beneficiaries. To be sure, there are various forms and benefit levels in these protections.[4] However, adjusting the protection systems downward if national income drops is extraordinarily risky politically and hard to implement. Nothing is less popular. But in looking back over the development since the Industrial Revolution, one cannot close one's eyes to the fact that a secondary system coupled ineluctably to productivity will run into difficulties if the most important parameters shift. It is therefore by no means a given that the social insurance that has "proved" itself for more than a 100 years will be able survive the demographic cliff of the next generation intact.[5] If it cannot, for example because the factor of dependent labor undergoes a fundamental transformation, it would have to be replaced—in the most gentle manner possible—by a system that redistributes in a similar manner and meets the fundamental standard of equality and justice.

The effects of these efforts are uncertain, however, since the maneuvering room is tightly constrained, primarily for economic reasons. We have grown accustomed to drawing the developmental prospects of the social state against the backdrop of

[3] Article 16 of the French Constitution of September 3, 1791. See Mohnhaupt and Grimm (1995, p. 106).

[4] Hauser (1999); Verband Deutscher Rentenversicherungsträger, ed., *Rentenversicherung im internationalen Vergleich* (Frankfurt, 1999).

[5] Zacher (1987, in 1993, pp. 498ff.), Stolleis (1999).

continual economic growth. Since the mechanisms of redistribution have so far encompassed only the growth rates, both the constitutional state of "vested rights" and the redistributive social state have persisted in their law. The theoretically often formulated tension between both spheres could be reconciled in practical social policy. However, as soon as the fundamental premise of continuous economic growth proves false, and the growing economy becomes a "stationary" one, the frame of reference for social policy changes.

In this way, the political system, which derives its legitimacy to a significant degree from the functioning of services of general interest and the area of social benefits, comes under pressure. It must legitimize itself primarily among those who are affected at the very basis of their private existence by the stagnation or even reduction in social benefits, and who will therefore be willing to extend only a qualified trust to a socially restrictive policy. In the lead up to this process of legitimation, it is especially the parties whose policies were traditionally focused on the reformist improvement of the social state that will come under pressure. In the shrinking of the growth rate to zero they will recognize a perilous constraint on their previous policy and feel a compulsion to shift their orientation. More so than conservative parties, to whom the social state has always remained nothing more than a necessary evil, they must cushion the disappointment of their voters. It is uncertain which direction the invariable re-orientation this entails will take. Both an accommodation with the political enemy (to achieve a distribution of responsibility for the reduction in and restructuring of social benefits) and a class-warfare turn from the distribution of growth rates to the distribution of existing wealth are possible alternatives. It is obvious that these alternatives could also mean division and fragmentation.

In Germany in 2013, these considerations do not seem to be up to date.

In the midst of the European financial crisis, Germany has held its own well with a high export rate and low unemployment. But this picture is deceptive. The critical stage of European economic policy is not over for a long time. Even slight changes in external conditions may put the social system under pressure again, as since the economic recession of 1973/1974. This system is comparatively very expensive and due to the high protection of fundamental rights, which is constituted by the jurisprudence of the Federal Constitutional, also motionless. Because of the progressive aging of the population, which cannot be compensated by immigration, the costs will continue to rise.

Especially the progressive technologization of the health care system and the economically unfavorable demographic trend (declining birth rate, rising life expectancy) provide clues to this trend. The result will be that the area of fundamental political decisions will be deformed in some way by the tensions between the stagnation of economic growth and the rise in social expenditures (positing both as a hypothesis). It cannot be ruled out that this deformation will affect the most sensitive point in the triangle "economic growth – social state – democracy," namely the goals—developed under the tacit premise of prosperity—of the "democratization of all areas of life," the "actualization of all basic rights aimed at self-development," "emancipation," and the "open society."

This asserted link between the economic performance of the system as a whole and the opportunities for self-development and co-determination granted by it exists in two directions. The formation of egalitarian-democratic principles, on the one hand, and of material equality, on the other, have challenged each other in the historical process. Just as an economically rising middle class began to demand political equality in the early nineteenth century, the formal equality of all voting citizens fully established after 1919 demanded a corresponding material equalization through the social state. The emancipation of the productive forces from the pre-industrial constraints proved a motor of political emancipation, and sharpened the perception of material inequalities. The mutual interlocking of democracy and social state achieved today is stable only as long as both elements are themselves stable and that economic growth posited by both is not substantially threatened.

The power relationship between "state" and "social state" has now been inverted. During the formative phase of the social state, the social benefits provided by the state and society were hardly more than reluctantly granted sedatives for the lower classes. Their purpose was to "heal social harms," to defuse an ominous internal conflict. But the more the once formal guarantees of the constitutional state and formal equality of the citizen-voter was turned into something material and was undergirded by the redistributive provisions of the social state, the clearer the dependence on the economic foundation of these provisions became. By now, the social state has occupied the terrain in such a way that the sphere for political decisions outside of economic and social policy has become ever narrower. The subservient character of those decisions has come to the fore to the degree that guidance of the global economy and social redistribution have grown into the primary purposes of the system as a whole. The unpleasant consequence of this development is that the elaboration of democratic participatory rights, individual and collective emancipation, in short—political freedom, can be increasingly understood merely as functions of economic and social policy.

It was therefore understandable why an economic historian and theorists, as part of his reflections on the "limits to growth," made the worried prediction 30 years ago that the West, with growth at a standstill and unchanged social demands,[6] would be "more likely to move toward times of dictatorial control ... than a continuously progressing emancipation" (Borchardt 1974, p. 26). That would have meant that the social state, casting off its civic-constitutional garb, would have continued to exist in a non-democratic form. Happily that prediction did not come true, on the contrary: countries in southern and eastern Europe have returned into the circle of democracies. Moreover, there is the hope that the ever stronger communicative and economic interconnectedness of the European sphere will also give rise to a lived constitutional order that will make it increasingly difficult for one member to withdraw from the democratic consensus if economic troubles damage the social state.

[6] It is doubtful, however, that the social demands will remain the same. Habermas (1973, p. 104) has rightly pointed out that the demands, too, can be steered by the system.

And yet: in the past, emphatic warnings have been issued about the anti-liberal and anti-democratic tendencies of the "welfare state." What often resonated in these warnings were also notes of concern by the middle classes that the wage-dependent population would lose the capacity for hard work through a perfected system of social benefits. There were also tones of a general cultural criticism that pointed to the dangers of a prevention and surveillance state acting under democratic premises; in this state, the social benefits played the role of a sedative with which the masses were to be pacified and distracted. Finally, practical politicians asked what should happen if the level of the social state was no longer sustainable for economic reasons, but the democratic institutions proved incapable of making the necessary cuts in the consensus of the parties. The memory of the transition to a presidential dictatorship at the end of the Weimar Republic, when democracy broke apart over a marginal issue of social policy, remains ever present as a German warning sign of the twentieth century: it was, we can recall, the beginning of the end.

That is why the precise way in which the interlacing of democracy and social state works, beyond pleasant-sounding formulas of mediation, is of considerable interest to research policy. At this time the most important thing is to devise solutions that resemble a squaring of the circle. The juxtaposition of the state that provides benefits and the state that provides guidance should be preserved, as should their democratic organization. But the issue is not only "organization," but the preservation of the democratic-republican spirit of a civil society under economic and demographic conditions that are becoming more and more difficult. That freedom and democratic processes must rank above prosperity is an experience and demand deeply burned into Germany history of the twentieth century. No material hardship, however, grave, must be allowed to justify infringing upon the substance of civil rights and liberties and of democracy.[7] In that sense, the weighting made by the Basic Law, to give strong weight to democracy and civil liberties, but weaker weight to the social state, must still be considered correct after more than 50 years of developing the social state. An argument from historical experience can be added. A nondemocratic social state would quickly change its character from the loss of the democratic force that has driven it so far. Where the citizens concerned no longer share in power even as voters, social benefits will soon be regarded as superfluous expenses and maintained at the lower range of what the population is barely able to tolerate.

The prosperity of a society, the redistributive social state, and the republican structure that sustains the entire polity (Frankenberg 1994, 1996, 2003) are thus interdependent. Just as the substance distributed by the social state stems from the sphere of production, the social state, conversely, guarantees a broadly disbursed prosperity among the consumers of that production. Just as the constitutionally secured "free self-realization" of the citizen forms the basic principle of free market production and the democratic principle serves to mobilize the social state,

[7] One of the most important fundamental texts in this regard is that of Denninger (1994).

economic productivity and the social state, in turn, are the guarantors of political stability and thus of democracy itself. The realization of this dependence and the susceptibility to breakdown should prompt a differentiated approach in all three areas, and, above all, help to avoid the illusion that in the democratic constitution of the polity one has gained a possession that can never be lost again.

References

Alber J (1987) Vom Armenhaus zum Wohlfahrtsstaat. Analysen zur Entwicklung der Sozialversicherung in Westeuropa, 2nd edn. Frankfurt am Main

Borchardt K (1974) Dreht sich die Geschichte um? Modelle für Wachstumsschranken. Ebenhausen

Denninger E (1994) Vielfalt, Sicherheit und Solidarität: Ein neues Paradigma für Verfassungsgebung und Menschenrechtsentwicklung? In: Denninger E (ed) Menschenrechte und Grundgesetz. Weinheim, pp 13ff

Frankenberg G (1994) Solidarität in einer "Gesellschaft der Individuen"? Stichworte zur Zivilisierung des Sozialstaats. In: Frankenberg E (ed) Auf der Suche nach der gerechten Gesellschaft. Frankfurt am Main

Frankenberg G (1996) Die Verfassung der Republik. Autorität und Solidarität in der Zivilgesellschaft. Baden-Baden

Frankenberg G (2003) Autorität und Integration. Zur Grammatik von Recht und Verfassung. Frankfurt am Main (here in particular see: Der Staat – Szenen eines Rückzugs oder: Von der Staatslehre zur Verfassungstheorie, pp 171ff)

Habermas J (1973) Legitimationsprobleme im Spätkapitalismus. Frankfurt am Main

Hauser R (ed) (1999) Alternative Konzeptionen der sozialen Sicherung. Schriften des Vereins für Socialpolitik (new series), vol 265. Berlin

Huf S (1998) Sozialstaat und Moderne. Modernisierungseffekte staatlicher Sozialpolitik. Berlin

Küßler R (1998) Entwicklung. Münster

Mohnhaupt H, Grimm D (1995) Verfassung. Zur Geschichte des Begriffs von der Antike bis zur Gegenwart. Berlin

Münsterberg E (1896) Generalbericht über die Tätigkeit des deutschen Vereins für Armenpflege und Wohltätigkeit. Leipzig

Orthbandt E (1980) Der Deutsche Verein in der Geschichte der deutschen Fürsorge 1880–1980. Frankfurt am Main

Stolleis M (1999) Die große Aufgabe der Sozialpolitik. Neue Juristische Wochenschrift 52:699f

Terwiesche M (1997) Innenstädte – eine obdachlosenfreie Zone? Verwaltungsrundschau 410–415

Zacher HF (1987) Alterssicherung - Spiegel der gesellschaftlichen Entwicklung. In: Zacher HF (ed) Abhandlungen zum Sozialrecht. Heidelberg, pp 498ff (1993)

Zacher HF (ed) (1993) Abhandlungen zum Sozialrecht. Heidelberg

XI. Index

M. Stolleis, *History of Social Law in Germany*,
DOI 10.1007/978-3-642-38454-7, © Springer-Verlag Berlin Heidelberg 2014

U

V

W

Y

Z

MIX
Papier aus verantwortungsvollen Quellen
Paper from responsible sources
FSC® C105338
FSC
www.fsc.org

If you have any concerns about our products,
you can contact us on
ProductSafety@springernature.com

In case Publisher is established outside the EU,
the EU authorized representative is:
Springer Nature Customer Service Center GmbH
Europaplatz 3, 69115 Heidelberg, Germany

Printed by Libri Plureos GmbH
in Hamburg, Germany